THE RAPTURE
AND
END TIME
PROPHECIES
FOR BEGINNERS

Hugh Wesley Wilson

Copyright © 2014 Hugh Wesley Wilson

ISBN: 978-1-60383-492-6

Published by:
Holy Fire Publishing
www.ChristianPublish.com

Cover Design: Jay Cookingham

Printed in the United States of America and the United Kingdom

THE RAPTURE
AND
END TIME PROPHECIES
FOR BEGINNERS

Explaining the Catching Up of followers of Jesus
And
What takes place in the World Afterwards
Bible Prophecy In Today's News

By Hugh Wesley Wilson

Preface

If you know very little or you don't know anything at all about the Rapture or End Time Prophecies, then you will want to read this.

When you hear someone refer to Jesus coming back again just what are they referring to? Do you know that there will actually be two returns of Jesus, one only in the air where he does not come back down to the earth but only returns to remove those that are truly his, that are part of his Church to take them back to heaven with him. Then an actual 2nd coming where he comes back down to the earth and will establish his earthly kingdom which will last for a thousand years. After the 1000 years there will be eternity.

The bible gives a promise of hope to those that have accepted Jesus into their lives. The bible says those that are in Jesus are not appointed onto wrath, that they will not experience the wrath of God, that Jesus will return to remove them before he pours out his judgment and wrath on a Christ rejecting world. It's come to be called the rapture. With the first part of this book we will look at the scriptures that deal with the rapture, the catching up of his Church. With the second half of this book we will look at the prophecies of the bible that deal with the future.

We can see predictions in the bible that were foretold thousands of years ago unveiling right in our on time. We can see world events lining up and coming into place exactly like the prophecies of the Old Testament and the book of Revelation foretell. No other book or writers have been accurate up to 100% like the prophecies of the bible. There has been no other person that has been able to predict the future like the prophets of the Bible.

One of the prophecies you can read or hear in the news today is the constant talk about Globalization, about a one world government with one man to be the head. Daniel and Revelation tell us that there will indeed be a one world government and a man the bible calls the anti-Christ to be in charge. The bible also tells us that there will be a worldwide nuclear war, this will be World War III. This will occur during the time the bible describes as the judgment and wrath of God just before Jesus returns back down to the earth.

After reading this book, when you look at the world today, you will be amazed at what you see unfolding before your very eyes. You will have a good understanding about the rapture and about bible prophecy. You will see that the bible has accurately predicted history thousands of years in advance. We can now look back on history and see how the Bible foretold events that were made hundreds to thousands of years before the events occurred, and that they came true exactly as the prophets of the bible foretold. With these fulfilled prophecies of the past coming true literally, we can be assured that the prophecies for the future will come true just as literally as those of the past. The Bible should be read like you would read any other book. Unless it's clear that symbolism is being used to make a point or explain what is trying to be conveyed by the author you should take the Bible literally even when reading about what is referred to as end time prophecies. There are those that want to interpret the end time prophecies especially those concerning Jesus' second coming and the 1000 year reign of Christ here on earth allegorically, having just a spiritual meaning or symbolic meaning. To me it makes sense that if all the prophecies in the old testament came true literally, with all the prophecies about Jesus' first coming being fulfilled literally then we should expect prophecies about the end times and his second coming to come true literally also. Why would God change?

Hebrews 13: 8Jesus Christ is the same yesterday and today and forever.

With seeing how accurately the bible has predicted past events, and with seeing prophecies being fulfilled and falling in place in our time just as the bible has foretold, with seeing how the prophecies of the bible are true, we can be assured that the rest of the bible is just as true. You should be able to see that the bible is indeed the word of God.

Opening Remarks

This is a result from what I have learned from over 30 years of studying. And yet after more than 30 years of studying I'm still learning and finding out more about the Rapture and End-time prophecies. This is made up from many sources that I have studied over the years.

I've put here in this book what I thought would be enough to educate someone about the Rapture and End Time Prophecies that concern the time just before Jesus' return down to the Earth.

While I'm calling this a study of the Rapture and End Time Prophecies this is in no way everything that could be taught on the subjects. There's just so much. It all just couldn't be put into one book. There are just too many prophecies to cover in one book.

There are differences of opinion concerning the timing of the Rapture, will the catching up of the Church be before, in the middle or at the end of the tribulation. The reason for these differing viewpoints on the timing of the rapture in relation to the tribulation is that the Bible nowhere tells us explicitly when the rapture will occur, but there is scriptural evidence in relation to the tribulation and the rapture, so we must search the scriptures putting them together to determine when Jesus will return for the Church. Here in this book I will explain why I feel Jesus catches us up before the tribulation, before the destruction that will come upon the earth which will be the last 7 years before Jesus returns back down to the earth. There is just too much in the bible that has lead me to believe that Jesus will remove the Church before the tribulation. I believe from the scriptures that I will address you will see that the bible does teach a pre-tribulation rapture.

With the second half of this book I will address not only prophecies that have been fulfilled, but also the prophecies that deal with our future.

Prophecy is a blessing.

Revelation 1: 3Blessed is the one who reads the words of this prophecy, and blessed are those who hear it and take to heart what is written in it, because the time is near.

One reason for studying Revelation and end time prophecies especially for us today is that we can see things that were foretold more than 2000 years ago being fulfilled right before our very eyes.

We can see Prophecies from the Old and New Testaments that have already been fulfilled and we can see others unfolding. What should that do for our faith and trust in the Lord. We can see that His word is true. That he is in control. That's the main theme you see throughout the book of Revelation, for it is the revelation of Jesus Christ. Rev. 1: 1The revelation of Jesus Christ, which God gave him to show his servants what must soon take place.

Seeing all these things coming into place does indeed bless the one who reads the words of these prophecies and also blesses those who hear it, that is those who take to heart what is written in it, because the time is near.

I'm not one to try to put dates on his return. Those that do I think miss the point. But it is amazing to see all that is happening and falling into place today. Jesus' return for the Church could be in the next 2 or 3 years or sooner or it could be in the next 20, 30 or 100 years we just don't know. But all this is amazing. With so much happening, I don't really see how it could be that much longer.

If you would like to study further, some of the authors I have read or watched on TV or video are, Hal Lindsey, Grant R. Jeffrey, Perry Stone, Jack Van Impy, Thomas Ice, Tim LaHaye, David Reagan, Ed Hindson, John Hagee. All of these men have web sites and have a weekly TV program that's on TBN, DayStar, SkyAngel as well as local channels. Hal's TV program is The Hal Lindsey Report, Perry's is Mana-fest with Perry Stone, Jack's is Jack Van Impe Presents, David's is Christ In Prophecy, John Hagee's is John Hagee Today and Ed's is The King is Coming. Of course you've probably heard of Tim LaHaye from the Left Behind books. He co-wrote them along with Jerry Jenkins.

Hal Lindsey's books, The Rapture, The Late Great Planet Earth and There's A New World Coming are the first books I read on the subjects.

RaptureReady.com, I like and recommend this site, it has a lot. While the authors may not agree with each other on every single thing they all do agree on the pre-tribulation rapture, that the rapture will happen before the beginning of the tribulation. I've learned a lot from RaptureReady.com. It has links to many other Rapture websites that I've read. It also has many other topics on this site. From this site you can find so many other topics and sites on bible prophecy that you couldn't begin to read through them all. At least it will take you a good while.

Sadly, Grant Jeffery died from cardiac arrest in May 2012. You can still get his books through book stores or from the internet.

Table of Contents

Chapter Six

Chapter Seven

Chapter Eight

Chapter One

A Quick Overview

1. An Overview of the End Times.

The Rapture or the catching up of the Church as Paul describes it in 1 Thessalonians and Jesus' second coming are two separate events. The Rapture is when Jesus will come in the air, catch up the Church from the earth, and then return to heaven with the Church. Jesus does not come down to the earth. (1 Thes, 4:16-18) (1 Cor. 15:51-52). Jesus' second coming, the Second Advent is Christ returning with His saints, descending from heaven and coming down to the earth to establish His earthly kingdom (Zech. 14:4-5; Mat. 24:27-31). We will address this in the first half of this book.

You have the 7 years of the Tribulation taken from Daniel chapter 9, Daniels 70th week. There were 490 years allotted to Israel which stopped 7 years short. This last 7 years will be a time that God will judge Israel and the nations. I will also address this later.

At the end of the 7 years you will have the last battle of Armageddon. Actually most of the tribulation will be World War III, WWIII. It just will culminate in one last battle.

Then you will have Jesus coming back to stop man from completely destroying himself and the earth. He will then set up his earthly kingdom for 1000 years of which time Satan will be bound and locked up. At the end of the 1000 years Satan will be loosed one more time and he will deceive some that were born during the 1000 years into rebelling against Jesus. They will be defeated; Satan will be thrown into the lake of fire. Then there's the Great white throne judgment where God judges all who have lived on the earth from the beginning, that is all whose names are not written in the Lambs book of Life. Then God creates a new heavens and new earth and we will have the blessed eternity with God. See Revelation chapters 19 thru 22.

Armageddon, WWIII will happen during the 7 years of the tribulation. It will first start with Russia, along with Iran and the northern African Muslim nations along with other Muslim nations attacking Israel. This is described in the book of Ezekiel and Daniel. Iran will have a major role in this. Russia and her allies, and all the Muslim nations will attack Israel. The bible in Ezekiel chapters 38 and 39 foretells all this and names the nations involved. Isn't it amazing that Russia has already allied itself with Iran and the Muslim (Islamic) nations. Russia is their means of arms support. I will address this later in our look at Ezekiel 38 and 39.

Well the leader of the new world government whom the bible calls the Anti-Christ will have signed a seven year treaty with Israel and the Islamic nations seemingly bringing peace to the Middle East. We see this in Daniel chapter 9. He will have to come to Israel's aid. He will defeat Russia, their allies and the Islamic nations. Then in the middle of the 7-year agreement with Israel the anti-Christ will break the contract and turn on Israel by entering and defiling the newly built Temple and will proclaim himself to be God. The Jews will have to flee Jerusalem to escape. He will have a partner, like a vice president called the False Prophet that will head up all the world religions bringing them under one umbrella. He will cause everyone on the Earth to worship the beast, the anti-Christ. He will cause everyone in order to be able to buy or sell, that they must take his mark or be killed or imprisoned. I'm sure you have heard about the mark of the beast. 666. We see this can be done now with microchips. Most likely you won't be able to work, have a bank account or anything without this mark. The bible also talks about the kings from the east, China and those with her. It looks like China will see its opportunity and will come against the Anti-Christ and his army. China and Russia have already become allies; it could be that China will come against the anti-Christ because of China's ties with Russia. Revelation says that the Euphrates River will be dried up to make way for the kings of the east. They will meet outside of Jerusalem in the valley of Megiddo in what is called the battle of Armageddon. Now this is what just gets me, I just can't understand the hardness of man's heart. After this battle, after WWIII and after just about totally destroying everything, what's left of all the nations will now unite with the Anti-Christ, come together to battle against the Rider on the White horse and his armies we see in Rev. 19. That is Jesus and those with him coming from heaven. That's just amazing.

Well that was a quick overview. We will go over much of this later.

There are some specific events that had to take place for the 'end time' prophecies of the bible to come true literally. One being that Israel would have to be a nation again and the Jews would have to have control of Jerusalem. This happened in May of 1948 and in June of 1967. Before the reestablishment of Israel as a nation again many didn't see how the prophecies that are called end time prophecies could be taken literally. Well, now with these two major events we can see that just as all the other prophecies that have been fulfilled came true literally that the end time prophecies concerning Israel and the world will come true just as literally. With what is happening in the world today we can see that they are indeed coming true literally.

Another condition for the end times that we can see falling into place and the whole world calling for now including the United States is a one world government, the globalization of all the worlds' nations, the new world order. I'm sure you've seen this on the news and read about it. It's being talked about more now since 2009 than any time in history. A one world government is not a bad thing in itself; Jesus' government will be a one world government after he returns. It's just this world government will be one without the one true God; it will be a government and world without Jesus.

The bible reveals that there will be a global government. During the 7 years of the tribulation, the world will have been divided up into 10 regions. Some believe that the European Union, which will become the revived Roman Empire that Daniel speaks of, would be made up of 10 prominent nations with controlling power that already exist. Well this is truly amazing. When I first heard this I just was amazed. The EU already has the plans in place to divide up the whole world into 10 regions with North America as one of them. And this is foretold in the bible. This is the globalization you here so much talk about. Europe has been talking about it, now the U.S. is. It looks like the economic collapse all over the world will help bring this about. Amazing.

18

The bible also says that there will emerge one man who will be liked by the entire world to become the leader of this new one world government. This man will not be a Christian even if he claims to believe in God. He will actually turn out not to believe in any God. He will not hold to the teachings and principles of the bible. He will do things politically that will be opposite of what the bible teaches.

The bible reveals that the conflict between the Muslims and the Jews will continue to get worse; it all will be over Jerusalem and the existence of Israel as a nation. The leader that gets the peace agreement signed between Israel, the Palestinians and the Islamic nations will turn out to be the one the bible calls the anti-Christ.

The bible also says there will be a one world currency, a one world economy which with modern technology will move to everyone having to take a mark, possibly be micro chipped with all their personal and financial information on it doing away with physical money, bank cards and credit cards. Again, we see this in the news now.

The bible also says there will be a one world religion which includes all the worlds' religions. This global religion will say there are many ways to God.

We will address the prophecies of the end times first with Matthew then in the second part of this book starting with Ezekiel, then Daniel and finally the book of Revelation.

2. The Tribulation

Let's take a quick look at Daniel chapter 9 verses 24 thru 27 so you can see where the 7 years of the Tribulation come from. It will help with understanding the purpose of the rapture and it's timing in relation to the tribulation. We will look at Daniel in more detail later.

The Tribulation Period is the last 7 years allotted to Israel. It is the last 7 years before Jesus returns at His Second Coming. Daniel gives us a "prophetic time clock" which predicts both the first and second comings of the Messiah (Dan. 9:24-27).

> Dan. 9:24a "Seventy 'sevens' are decreed for your people and your holy city

With each 'seven' being 7 years, this would mean there are 490 years, 70 x 7 decreed for Israel.

The Jews not only had a week of days, but also a week of years. (See Gen. 29:27-30, Lev. 25:4, 8). It's just like we now refer to a period of 10 years as a decade. You can see the use of 7 for many things throughout the Old Testament. This prophecy clearly refers to the week of years. The clock ticked for 483 years, the first 69 weeks (of years), then the Messiah was revealed when Jesus rode into Jerusalem on a donkey. This is when Jesus was first proclaimed to be the Messiah. That same week Jesus was crucified. Then the clock stopped, creating a gap in time that has lasted 2000 years. We are currently living in this time gap, waiting for the clock to start ticking again. This time gap is what we now know as the Church age. The clock will start ticking again sometime in the future when the Antichrist confirms a covenant with Israel for 7 years, the last week (of years), 7 years. This is referred to as the tribulation. At the end of these 7 years, Jesus will return a second time to establish his earthly kingdom.

The first 69 weeks or 483 years were fulfilled when Jesus rode into Jerusalem as the Messiah on Palm Sunday (Luke 19: 37-44).

A Quick Overview

Zechariah chapter 9 prophesied this.

> 9 Rejoice greatly, O Daughter of Zion!
>   Shout, Daughter of Jerusalem!
>   See, your king comes to you,
>   righteous and having salvation,
>   gentle and riding on a donkey,
>   on a colt, the foal of a donkey.

God's prophetic time clock stopped ticking on that day.

After the clock stopped, two things were to happen before the clock could start ticking again: The Messiah was to be "cut off" (Jesus' crucifixion) and Jerusalem was to be destroyed, which happened in 70 A.D. (Dan. 9:26). The next thing that Daniel reveals is the Ruler that will make the 7 year covenant with Israel. Daniel does not record what happens in the time between the stopping and starting back up of God's prophetic time clock. We will look at why later.

The clock will start ticking again for the last week of years when the Antichrist confirms a covenant with Israel for 7 years (Dan. 9:27). In the middle of the 7 years, he will enter the temple and stop the sacrifices, thus splitting the Tribulation Period into two halves of 3 ½ years. We see the last half referred to as 1260 days, forty-two months and time, times and half a time.

1,260 days (Rev. 11:3), (Rev. 12:6),

42 months (Rev. 11:2, 13:5),

Time, times, and a ½ a time (Rev. 12:14, Dan 7:25, 12:7) A time was one year, times was two years and of course, a half time was half a year, 3 ½ years.

This period of time of 1260 days, 42 months and Time, times, and a ½ a time are based on a prophetical year of 360 days with 30 days each month. The Jews as well as other nations of the Middle East used a calendar of 360 days instead of a calendar of 365 days as we do now.

It would be 1260 days / 30 days equaling 42 months, 3 ½ years.

Daniel informs us that the Antichrist will stop the sacrifices in the Jewish temple "in the middle of the week". This act is referred to as the "abomination of desolation" (Dan. 9:27). Paul also speaks of the abomination when he informs us the Antichrist will take his seat in the Jewish Temple and declare himself to be God (2 Thess. 2:3-4). Jesus also said, "So when you see standing in the holy place [the rebuilt Jewish temple] 'the abomination that causes desolation,' spoken of through the prophet Daniel—let the reader understand, then let those who are in Judea flee to the mountains" (Matt. 24:15-16).

Isn't it interesting Jesus said, "let the reader understand." Who is the reader? (Someone reading his or her Bible). What is the reader supposed to understand? Those alive during the tribulation are to understand that when they see the Antichrist go into the temple, there are only 3 ½ years left until the Second Coming! The Antichrist will be destroyed on the same day Jesus returns to earth and Satan will be bound for a 1000 years. (2 Thess. 2:8, Rev. 19:20, Rev. 21:1).

From reading Daniel and the book of Revelation it's clear that the books are talking about the same things, Daniel gives us generalities, the book of Revelation gives us the details. Most of the book of Revelation is dealing with the last 3 ½ years on earth before Jesus returns.

Chapter Two

The Rapture of the Church

1. Some Basic's

The Apostle Paul gave a clear description of the rapture in his letters to the Thessalonians and Corinthians.

(1 Thes, 4:16-18) (1 Cor. 15:51-52).

> 1TH 4:16 For the Lord himself will come down from heaven, with a loud command, with the voice of the archangel and with the trumpet call of God, and the dead in Christ will rise first. 17 After that, we who are still alive and are left will be caught up together with them in the clouds to meet the Lord in the air. And so we will be with the Lord forever. 18 Therefore encourage each other with these words.

> 1 Cor. 15:51 Listen, I tell you a mystery: We will not all sleep, but we will all be changed— 52in a flash, in the twinkling of an eye, at the last trumpet. For the trumpet will sound, the dead will be raised imperishable, and we will be changed.

Many argue they don't believe in the rapture because the word "rapture" is not in the bible. The word "rapture" comes from Paul's "caught up" in verse 17 of 1 Thessalonians. The words "caught up" are translated from the Greek word harpazo, which means "to carry off," "snatch up," "to seize upon with force", or "grasp hastily." Harpazo became the Latin word raptus; out of the Latin Vulgate translation of the Bible. Raptus is where we get the English word "rapture." So this event that the Church now calls the rapture could be called "the catching up of the Church". The word Rapture just became the word to describe this event. Just like the word Deity has become the word used to refer to the Father, Son and Holy Spirit and the word tribulation to describe the last 7 years before Jesus returns.

The Rapture of the Church

The rapture of the church is often paralleled to the "raptures" of Enoch (Genesis 5:24) and Elijah (2 Kings 2: 12). In each case, the individual was caught up into-heaven.

As far as we know from the bible, Enoch is the first to be raptured and taken to be with the Lord. Genesis 5: 24 Enoch walked with God; then he was no more, because God took him away. Enoch was translated, or caught up, without dying, and went directly to be with the Lord, Enoch was raptured. We know this by the fact that the bible does not say that he died like it does for the others mentioned in Gen. Chapter 5. We also know this from the writer of Hebrews, chapter 11 verse 5.

> Heb. 5: 5By faith Enoch was taken from this life, so that he did not experience death; he could not be found, because God had taken him away. For before he was taken, he was commended as one who pleased God.

Like Enoch, Elijah was translated to heaven without dying.
See 2 Kings Chapter 2.

> 2 Kings 2: 1When the LORD was about to take Elijah up to heaven in a whirlwind, Elijah and Elisha were on their way from Gilgal.

> 11 As they were walking along and talking together, suddenly a chariot of fire and horses of fire appeared and separated the two of them, and Elijah went up to heaven in a whirlwind.

He was taken up by the angels.

> Hebrews 1:7In speaking of the angels he says, "He makes his angels winds, his servants flames of fire."

So we can see that Enoch and Elijah were raptured, taken up to heaven like the Church will be. They are foreshadows of what is to come.

At His ascension, our Lord Himself was "taken up" into heaven (Acts 1:9). We also see in Revelation chapter 11 that the two wittiness's are caught up to heaven.

Concerning Jesus returning for the Church, the catching up, the Rapture, The Lord Jesus Christ said, "I will come back and take you to be with me that you also may be where I am." John 14:3

When he appears,   we shall be like him, for we shall see him as he is. 1 John 3:2

The Apostle Paul,

> 1COR 15:51 Listen, I tell you a mystery: <u>We will not all sleep, but we will all be changed</u>-- 52 in a flash, in the twinkling of an eye, at the last trumpet. For the trumpet will sound, the dead will be raised imperishable, and we will be changed.

> 1TH 4:13 Brothers, we do not want you to be ignorant about those who fall asleep, or to grieve like the rest of men, who have no hope. 14 We believe that Jesus died and rose again and so we believe that God will bring with Jesus those who have fallen asleep in him. 15 According to the Lord's own word, we tell you that we who are still alive, who are left till the coming of the Lord, will certainly not precede those who have fallen asleep. 16 For the Lord himself will come down from heaven, with a loud command, with the voice of the archangel and with the trumpet call of God, and the dead in Christ will rise first. 17 After that, we who are still alive and are left will **be caught up together** with them <u>in the clouds to meet the Lord in the air</u>. And so we will be with the Lord forever.

So from these and other scriptures we can see that there will be a time when Jesus will return and raise those that have died in him and rapture, catch up those that are still alive with those that were dead. Notice in these scriptures there is no mention of coming down onto the earth. Look at John 14:3 and 1 Thessalonians 4:17 again. The rapture will be a time when Jesus will recreate the bodies of those that have died in him and reunite their bodies and spirits and then transform those that are still alive and are in him and take the believers to heaven. Jesus' second coming, the Second Advent is Christ returning with His saints, descending from heaven and coming down to the earth to establish His earthly kingdom (Zech. 14:4-5; Mat. 24:27-31).

The different views on the rapture come from how one views the time of the rapture in relation to the 7 years of the tribulation. Remember, the Tribulation is the final 7 years before Jesus returns down to earth at the Second Coming. The most controversial aspect of the Rapture is its timing. Some place it at the end of the Tribulation, making it one and the same event as the Second Coming. Others place it in the middle of the Tribulation. Still others believe that it will occur at the beginning of the Tribulation.

There are 4 main views on the Rapture.

A **pre-tribulation (pre-trib)** view has the catching up of the Church before the 7 years of the tribulation that the book of Daniel and Revelation speaks of. This view sees the whole 7 years as judgment from God, and as the wrath of God, starting with the release of the anti-Christ, when he signs an agreement with Israel. This view sees the Day of the Lord as the whole 7 years.

A **mid-tribulation (mid-trib)** view has the Rapture occurring in the middle of the tribulation, after the first 3 ½ years. This view sees the first 3 ½ years as the wrath of satan or the wrath of man and the last 3 ½ years as the wrath of God. This view sees the Day of the Lord as only the last 3 ½ years.

A **post-tribulation (post-trib)** view has the rapture occurring after the 7 years of the tribulation, with the Church going through the 7 years of tribulation. This view sees the rapture with Jesus' 2nd coming. It has Jesus taking the Church up to meet him in the air and then immediately coming back down to the earth. This view sees the Day of the Lord, the wrath of God as only the 7 bowls occurring in a single day, the actual day Jesus returns to the earth.

A **pre-wrath** view is the newest. It has the Rapture sometime after the middle of the tribulation but before Jesus' 2nd coming. Pre-wrath believers believe that Christ will Rapture the Church just before the Battle of Armageddon. This view sees only the last 7 bowls as the wrath of God and the 7 seals and trumpets as the wrath of Satan. This view sees the Day of the Lord as only the 7 bowl judgments.

Important Terms Used in Prophecy

Rapture: When Jesus returns in the air to receive the church and returns to heaven (John 14:1-3, 1 Thess. 4:13-17). All Christians who have died will be resurrected and those who are alive will be instantly translated into glorified bodies (1 Cor. 15:51-54). This is not the same event as the Second Coming.

Second Coming: When Jesus physically returns from heaven to come back down to the earth. (Rev. 19:11-21) He returns with the saints.

Millennium - 1000 years of history during which Christ will reign on earth as the King of Kings, which follows the Second Coming (Rev. 20:2-7). This will be the ultimate one world government with Jesus as King, President of the whole world.

Abomination of Desolation: A future incident when the Antichrist enters into the rebuilt Jewish temple and declares himself to be God. (Dan. 9:27, Matt. 24:15, 2 Thess. 2:3-4). This occurs in the middle of the 7-year tribulation period.

28

Eschatology: The study of end-time events.

New Earth: At the end of the Millennium, God will create a new heaven and a new earth which will last for eternity (Rev.21:1, Isa. 65:17, 66:22, 2 Pet. 3:10-13).

New Jerusalem: The heavenly city, at the end of the Millennium, after God has created a new heaven and a new earth will come down out of heaven to the New Earth, (Rev. 21:1-2, 10-27).

Premillennialism - That Christ will return to Earth before the Millennium, before the 1000-year reign of Christ here on earth. All those that believe in a Rapture, whether pre, mid, post or pre-wrath and a 7 year tribulation period are Premillennialist.

Postmillennialism - That Christ will return after reigning from Heaven during this present age, after the 1000 years. There's no rapture.

Amillennialism - That Christ is already reigning now spiritually, there won't be a literal 1000-year reign of Christ on earth. This view sees Revelation and other prophetic scriptures as only symbolic, allegorical. When it comes to prophecy, it doesn't believe you should take the bible literally. There's no rapture or 7 years of tribulation. Believes Satan is already bound.

Preterits - Believe all end time prophetic scripture were fulfilled in 70 a.d. when Rome destroyed the Temple and Jerusalem. There's no rapture or 7 years of tribulation. They believe Jesus returned in 70 a.d in the form of the Roman army, that Jesus didn't or won't return visibly. They also believe Jesus is ruling only spiritually. Also looks at Revelation and other prophetic scriptures as only symbolic, allegorical. When it comes to prophecy, don't believe you take the bible literally.

Mystery - An event not previously revealed in the Old Testament Scriptures, but now made known in the New Testament.

The day of Pentecost – the birth of the Church. This was the day the Church officially began. See Acts 2.

Jacobs trouble. Jacob was one of the sons of Isaac who was the son of Abraham, it was Abraham, Isaac and then Jacob. God changed Jacobs name to Israel. The 12 tribes of Israel came from each of the 12 sons of Jacob. The time of Jacobs's trouble comes from the 2nd seven years that Jacob had to work for his father-in-law to get his younger daughter Rachel as his wife. These seven years were troublesome years for Jacob. See Genesis chapter 29. These seven years is another example for the seven years of the tribulation. They are a type of the last seven years allotted to Israel.

The Tribulation; is the final 7 years before Jesus returns to earth at the Second Coming. It begins when the Antichrist confirms a 7-year covenant with Israel, also known as Daniels 70th week or the time of Jacobs Trouble. The tribulation is split into two halves of 3 ½ years each, divided in the middle when the Antichrist stops the sacrifices in the temple (Dan. 9:24 - 27), the Abomination of Desolation. The last 3 ½ years are also referred to as 1,260 days (Rev. 11:3, 12:6), 42 months (Rev. 11:2, 13:5), and time, times, and a 1/2 time (Rev. 12:14, Dan 7:25, 12:7).

The Antichrist: A future dictator who attempts to control the world just prior to the Second Coming of Christ. (2 Thess. 2:3-9).

Although in the bible this man is never actually called "the antichrist", he is referred to by many different names in the Bible, though John in 1 John chapter 2 refers to there being a particular man who will be the anti-Christ.

18Dear children, this is the last hour; and as you have heard that the antichrist is coming, even now many antichrists have come. This is how we know it is the last hour.

22Who is the liar? It is the man who denies that Jesus is the Christ. Such a man is the antichrist—he denies the Father and the Son.

Bible scholars have begun to use the term "the Antichrist" as a collective term to cover all the names.

Different Names for the Antichrist

- "the little horn"--Dan. 7:8
- "the prince that shall come"--Dan. 9:26
- "the willful king"--Dan. 11:36
- "the man of sin"--2 Thess. 2:3
- "the son of perdition"--2 Thess. 2:3
- "the lawless one"--2 Thess. 2:8
- "the beast"--Dan. 7:11, Rev. 11:7, 19:19-20, 20:10
- "the beast out of the sea"--Rev. 13:1-8 also referring to the one world government, the revived roman empire.

The False Prophet:

The Antichrist (beast out of the sea) Rev. 13:1, will have a helper, (beast out of the earth), Rev. 13:11, like a vice president, a man called "the false prophet" (Rev. 19:20). This false prophet will cause people all over the world to worship the beast, the Antichrist and will perform great signs, even making fire come down out of heaven to the earth (Rev. 13:12-13). He will cause everyone to receive a mark on his or her right hand or forehead so that no one will be able to buy or sell without the mark, the name of the beast or the number of his name (Rev. 13:16-18). Those who take the mark of the beast will eventually be cast into the lake of fire (Rev. 14:9-11). The Antichrist and the false prophet will be thrown into the lake of fire at Jesus' 2nd coming (2 Thess. 2:8, Rev. 19:20).

2. Differences between the Rapture and the 2nd Coming

The Rapture and the 2nd Coming of Christ are not the same events. The Rapture is not another name for the Second Coming. The Rapture is when Jesus comes in the air for His Church, but He does not come down to the earth, He meets the Church in the air and takes the Church, his bride back to heaven, to the Father's house. The 2nd Coming is when Jesus comes back to earth to rule and reign for 1000 years.

The difference between the rapture and the 2nd coming becomes clear when you notice the distinction between the coming of Christ in the air to remove His church and the coming of Christ to the earth to rescue Israel and set up His kingdom. With the Rapture Jesus does not come down to the earth, at his 2nd coming he does.

In the Old Testament, there were 2 different pictures painted of the Messiah. One of Christ's first coming when He came in humiliation to suffer (Isa. 53:2-10, Ps. 22:6-8, 11-18) and the second of Christ's coming as a conquering king when He will reign on earth in power and glory. (Ps. 2:6-12, Zech. 14:9, 16).

As we look back on these scriptures, we see they predicted two separate comings of the Messiah, the 1st coming as a suffering Messiah and the 2nd coming (still future) as a reigning King. Failure to distinguish these two phases was a key factor in Israel's rejection of Jesus as the Messiah at His first coming. In the same way, failure to see clear distinctions between the rapture and Second Advent (coming) has led many to a misinterpretation of scriptures concerning God's future plan.

In the New Testament there's two future comings of Christ presented. The first coming is the catching up of the church into the clouds before the seven-year tribulation and the second coming occurs at the end of the tribulation when Christ returns to the earth to begin His 1,000 year kingdom. We see two phases of Jesus' return.

The Rapture of the Church

As we see in **1 Thes. 4:15-17** and **John 14:1-3**, the Rapture is a secret event where Jesus does not come down to Earth, but meets His Church in the air and takes us to be with Him where He is, which is heaven. Its specific timing will remain unknown until it actually happens.

At the Rapture Jesus comes as a thief. No one will see him.

> Mt. 24: 42"Therefore keep watch, because you do not know on what day your Lord will come. 43But understand this: If the owner of the house had known at what time of night the thief was coming, he would have kept watch and would not have let his house be broken into. 44So you also must be ready, because the Son of Man will come at an hour when you do not expect him.

On the other hand, The Second Coming is an event where Jesus comes all the way down to Earth with His Church to establish his Kingdom here. It will not be a secret because the general time of His coming will be known on Earth over 3 ½ years in advance, everyone on Earth will witness His arrival. **Matt. 24:29-30** says it will happen immediately after the Great Tribulation and all the nations will see the Son of Man coming on the clouds in the sky.

> Mt. 24: 27For as lightning that comes from the east is visible even in the west, so will be the coming of the Son of Man. 29"Immediately after the distress of those days " 'the sun will be darkened, and the moon will not give its light; the stars will fall from the sky, and the heavenly bodies will be shaken.' 30"At that time the sign of the Son of Man will appear in the sky, and all the nations of the earth will mourn. They will see the Son of Man coming on the clouds of the sky, with power and great glory.

You see with the Rapture there is a resurrection, but in Revelation 19 which tells of Jesus' 2nd coming there is no mention of a resurrection taking place with his return. In Revelation 20 after Jesus has returned you see only those believers that were killed during the tribulation being resurrected. Furthermore, with the Rapture you see that those that are still alive and remain will be changed, transformed, but with Revelation 19 and 20 there is no such statement. Another important point, if the rapture occurred with the 2nd coming, resurrecting the dead in Christ and changing those that are still alive in Christ, then this would cause there to be no one to enter the kingdom of God as mortals. Everyone that have been raised and those raptured are immortal, like Jesus is now. The bible clearly teaches that although people will live a lot longer they still will be mortal as we are now.

According to 1 Corinthians 15:51, all the righteous will be changed, and Matthew 25:41-46 says that all the unrighteous will be sent into everlasting punishment. Only those found righteous will enter into the kingdom of God. If the rapture were to occur at the second coming and the wicked are cast into hell at that time, who would be left to populate the millennium? There has to be mortals who are righteous, you could say saved, that have accepted Jesus to enter the kingdom of God after Jesus has returned. Children will be born during the millennium (Isa. 11:6-8). Only people in their natural (non-resurrected) bodies will be able to have children (Matt. 22:30). With a Pre-Tribulation rapture, the people saved after the rapture who are alive at the second coming will populate the earth during the Millennium.

If there were no distinction between the two phases of Christ's coming, if the rapture was at the same time as his second coming, then there would be no mortals to enter the kingdom. The righteous would have been transformed with the rapture thus not leaving anyone on earth to go into the kingdom of God as mortals. Those alive during the 1000 years, although a person's life span is said to be as a tree, they could possibly live through the whole 1000 years, if they sin they will die, considered to be cursed. If the rapture is at the same time as the second coming then all that go into the 1000 years would be immortal, incapable of sinning or dying. There has to be mortals that enter into the 1000 years.

More important, who does Satan lead in worldwide rebellion against Christ at the end of the millennium if not those unbelievers born during the 1,000 years? Initially, only believers will inhabit the kingdom (Ezek. 20:33-44; Mt. 25:31-46).

> Rev. 20:7 When the thousand years are over, Satan will be released from his prison 8 and will go out to deceive the nations in the four corners of the earth--Gog and Magog--to gather them for battle. In number they are like the sand on the seashore.

There has to be mortals to enter into the 1000-year kingdom of Christ. The Church believers are changed into glorified immortals at the rapture. We have been changed, glorified, made perfect at the rapture so we cannot be lead into rebellion.

The Bible clearly teaches that Christ could return for the Church at any time without any certain event taking place first. This is referred to as Imminency. But it also teaches that certain catastrophic events will take place before his 2nd coming during the tribulation, the 7 years prior to His return down to the earth -- putting the Lord's people in a state of readiness and expectation. This problem can be resolved if the coming of Christ is seen in two phases. His coming in the air will be sudden and without warning, but His coming to the earth will be expected by those who are alive during the tribulation and who know the scriptures of the bible.

The Bible presents a day we can't know (the Rapture) and a day that will be known (the 2nd coming). Matthew 24:42 and 25:13 says to watch for you will not know the day or the hour of Jesus' return, while Matthew 24:30 says all the nations will see him return. We see in Revelation chapter 19 that the armies of the world are waiting for his return, so they know when he is returning. The known and unknown days must happen at different times, meaning they are two separate events.

First Thessalonians 4:13-17 says the righteous will be taken and the wicked are left behind. Matthew 13:24 - 30, 47 - 50 says the wicked are taken first and the righteous are left behind. This is describing two separate events, the rapture and the second coming.

Paul speaks of the rapture as a "mystery" (1 Cor. 15:51-54), that is a truth not revealed to the Old Testament saints. It was not revealed until its disclosure by the apostles (Col. 1:26), making it a separate event, while the second coming was predicted in the Old Testament (Dan. 12:1-3; Zech. 12:10; 14:4).

In the New Testament, we have 2 descriptions of Jesus returning. These 2 different descriptions of Jesus' coming point to two separate events we call "The Rapture" and "The Second Coming."

Some Differences between the Rapture and the 2nd Coming.

The Rapture	The 2nd Coming
1 Translation of all believers	No translation at all
2 Imminent, any-moment	Follows definite predicted signs
3 Before the day of wrath	Concluding the day of wrath
4 He comes in the air only	He comes down to the earth
5 With a trumpet sound	No trumpet mentioned
6 Tribulation begins	Millennial Kingdom begins
7 Comes for His Bride	Comes with His Bride
8 Believers taken to heaven	Believers come from heaven
9 Happens in a moment	Everyone will see him returning
10 Occurs at an unknown time	Will be known 1260 days before
11 A Mystery	Foretold in Old Testament
12 A message of hope and comfort	A message of Judgment
13 Resurrection of those in Christ	No resurrection
14 No angels involved	Angels gather for judgment
15 No reference to Satan	Satan bound after he returns

All these will be addressed in detail later.

3. A Promise to the Church

The Rapture is a promise made only to the Church. This promise is that Jesus will return in the sky and take up His Church, both the living and dead, to Heaven, in glorified bodies.

The Rapture was not revealed to the Old Testament prophets because it is a promise to the New Testament Church and not to the Old Testament saints of God who lived before the establishment of the Church. In 1ˢᵗ Cor. 15 verse 51 Paul said the rapture was a mystery.

> 1 Corinthians 15 51Listen, I tell you a mystery: We will not all sleep, but we will all be changed— 52in a flash, in the twinkling of an eye, at the last trumpet. For the trumpet will sound, the dead will be raised imperishable, and we will be changed.

Paul's reference here to being changed is a description that the saints will receive glorified bodies that will be perfect, imperishable and immortal (1 Cor. 15:42-44, and 50-55). As we will see later, the Church was kept hidden from the Old Testament Saints.

The Old Testament saints will be resurrected at the end of the Tribulation and not at the time of the Rapture of the Church. Daniel reveals this in Daniel 12:1-2 where he says that the saints of that age will be resurrected at the end of the "time of distress."

The first mention of the Rapture in Scripture is found in John 14:1-4. Jesus said, "I will come back and take you to be with me that you also may be where I am". We will look at this later.

The most detailed description of the actual events related to the Rapture is given by Paul in 1 Thessalonians 4:13-18. He says that when Jesus appears, the dead in Christ (Church age saints) will be resurrected and caught up first. Then, those who are alive in Christ will be caught up "to meet the Lord in the air." Paul then exhorts us to "comfort one another with these words."

Scriptures that show a Pre-Trib Rapture of the Church.

From the Old and New Testament you see that God is going to judge the people of the Earth for their sins in a terrible time called the Day of the Lord when He'll pour out His wrath on mankind. Reading **Matt. 24** you see that this time of judgment is going to be so bad that if the Lord didn't put a stop to it no one would survive. But the Lord will put a stop to it by returning in power and glory.

In **1 Thes. 1:9-10** you have a pretty clear statement. Jesus rescues us from the coming wrath and takes us to heaven because we are not appointed to wrath. We also get a clear indication in the timing of the rapture in relation to the wrath of God in **1 Thes. 1:10, and to wait for his Son from heaven, whom he raised from the dead—Jesus, who rescues us from the coming wrath.** The Greek word translated "from" in this passage is "apo." Literally, means we're to be rescued from the time, the place, or anything that has to do with God's wrath. It denotes both departure and separation. It shows that the Church will be removed from the time of God's wrath altogether, taken completely away from it, not just protected while going thru the time of God's wrath. This is supported by **1 Thes. 5:9** that declares, **"God did not appoint us to suffer wrath but to receive salvation through our Lord Jesus Christ."** In the "who, what, where, when, and why" methodology, you have the Who, (Jesus) the what, (rescues us) and the when (the time of the coming wrath). Reading on you come to **1 Thes. 4:15-17** and get the where (from Earth to the clouds, then back to heaven with him, John 14) and in **1 Thes. 5:9** the why (because we're not appointed to wrath).

Some argue that this is referring to being rescued from Hell. Does Jesus' return in the air to take his Church back to the Fathers house rescue us from Hell? The answer is no. Those that have already accepted Jesus into their lives are already rescued from Hell, that's why you're able to be taken back to the Heaven with Jesus in the first place. No, this is referring to being rescued from the wrath of the tribulation.

The Rapture of the Church

The Church is not destined For God's Wrath. Revelation 3:10 also
indicates that the church is not destined for "the hour of trial which
shall come upon the whole world."

> Revelation 3: 10Since you have kept my command to endure
> patiently, I will also keep you from the hour of trial that is
> going to come upon the whole world to test those who live on
> the earth.

Scripture speaks of "the time of Jacob's trouble" (Jer. 30:7) as that
future time when Israel will be brought to repentance in preparation
for the coming of her Messiah. Israel will suffer before her restoration,
but as we just saw, 1 Thessalonians 1:10 and 5:9 indicates that the
church will escape that time of God's wrath. Since we know that the
Lord hasn't returned to the earth yet, we know that God's wrath on the
earth is still in the future. From there you can logically conclude that
since we're not appointed to wrath, our rescue has to precede it. From
I Thessalonians chapter 4 we see The Lord himself will come down
from Heaven into the air and suddenly snatch us away from Earth,
catching us up to join Him there. In chapter 5 you see that we won't
know the exact timing of this event but only that it will precede the
coming wrath.

Paul described believers as ambassadors for Christ.

> 2 Corinthians 5: 20We are therefore Christ's ambassadors, as
> though God were making his appeal through us.

An ambassador is one who represents a dignitary, often in a foreign
land. The Church has been given its Great Commission by Jesus

> Matthew 28: 16Then the eleven disciples went to Galilee, to the
> mountain where Jesus had told them to go. 17When they saw
> him, they worshiped him; but some doubted. 18Then Jesus
> came to them and said, "All authority in heaven and on earth
> has been given to me. 19Therefore go and make disciples of all
> nations, baptizing them in the name of the Father and of the

Son and of the Holy Spirit, 20and teaching them to obey everything I have commanded you. And surely I am with you always, to the very end of the age."

Notice Jesus said the Church is commissioned until the end of the age. That would be this present age, the Church age that began on the day of Pentecost, see Acts 2.

Mark 16: 15He said to them, "Go into all the world and preach the good news to all creation. 16Whoever believes and is baptized will be saved, but whoever does not believe will be condemned.

Ephesians 6: 19Pray also for me, that whenever I open my mouth, words may be given me so that I will fearlessly make known the mystery of the gospel, 20for which I am an ambassador in chains. Pray that I may declare it fearlessly, as I should.

When God the Father decides that the world has reached the point of global rejection of his Son Jesus, then He will recall His ambassadors, the Church before the judgment of the tribulation.

The church is described as heavenly citizens.

Philippians 3: 20But our citizenship is in heaven. And we eagerly await a Savior from there, the Lord Jesus Christ, 21who, by the power that enables him to bring everything under his control, will transform our lowly bodies so that they will be like his glorious body.

It makes perfect sense that the Church, God's ambassador is to be raptured before God's judgment comes against those who have rejected his Son. This is one of many purposes for a pre-tribulation rapture of the church.

4. Any-moment expectation (Imminence)

A key point of a pre-tribulation Rapture view, Keep Watch.

What Is Imminence?

Imminence, as it relates to Bible prophecy, simply means that the return of Jesus Christ for the Church can happen at any moment. There will be no warning signs. We as Christians remain on alert 24 hours a day, 7 days a week.

The only way for the rapture to be truly imminent from the early Church days until now is to have it transpire before the tribulation. If the Church were required to wait until after the tribulation, after the manifestation of certain events, then there would be no doctrine of Imminence. There would be no need for anyone from the day Jesus left until now to be waiting for and watching for his return for the Church. All the scriptures that tells us and commands us to keep watch wouldn't apply to us.

The pre-tribulation rapture is the only view that allows for the rapture to be imminent in its timing. All the other views require a number of prophetic occurrences to take place before the rapture can be declared imminent. For anyone from the beginning of the Church up to now to be looking for the imminent return of Christ, as we see in the gospels and the epistles, you have to believe in a pre-trib rapture.

Jesus repeatedly said that His return for the Church would be at a time unknown. The Lord even said his return for the Church would be "as a thief" when most people generally won't be expecting Him to come.

Because an imminent or any moment rapture is one of the major teachings of pre-tribulationists, opponents of this view attempt to dismantle the imminency of the rapture although Jesus said,

MT 24:42 "Therefore keep watch, because you do not know on what day your Lord will come.

You just cannot escape Jesus' restriction against knowing the timing of the rapture. In fact, Jesus was so restrictive about the rapture, He said its occurrence would come as a total surprise. MT 24:44 So you also must be ready, because the Son of Man will come at an hour when you do not expect him.

The Apostle Paul in 1 Thessalonians 4: 13 – 18.

1TH 4: 13Brothers, we do not want you to be ignorant about those who fall asleep, or to grieve like the rest of men, who have no hope. 14We believe that Jesus died and rose again and so we believe that God will bring with Jesus those who have fallen asleep in him. 15According to the Lord's own word, we tell you that we who are still alive, who are left till the coming of the Lord, will certainly not precede those who have fallen asleep. 16For the Lord himself will come down from heaven, with a loud command, with the voice of the archangel and with the trumpet call of God, and the dead in Christ will rise first. 17After that, we who are still alive and are left will be caught up together with them in the clouds to meet the Lord in the air. And so we will be with the Lord forever. 18Therefore encourage each other with these words.

1Thessalonians 5:1-6

1Thes. 5: 1Now, brothers, about times and dates we do not need to write to you, 2for you know very well that the day of the Lord will come like a thief in the night. 3While people are saying, "Peace and safety," destruction will come on them suddenly, as labor pains on a pregnant woman, and they will not escape.

4But you, brothers, are not in darkness so that this day should surprise you like a thief. 5You are all sons of the light and sons of the day. We do not belong to the night or to the darkness. 6So then, let us not be like others, who are asleep, but let us be alert and self-controlled.

With these verses you can see the flow, the order in which these events will occur. In chapter 4 Paul is talking about the Rapture. Verse 1 of chapter 5 he says about the times and dates he doesn't need to write them for he had already told them that no one will know the time or dates and then flows into referring to the tribulation. You see the destruction of the tribulation comes after the rapture.

Notice the link of the Rapture with the Day of the Lord. The day of the Lord is the tribulation, the destruction. He said that no one will know the times or the dates of the Day of the Lord, but he just finished talking about the Rapture linking the two together. So it appears that the day of the Lord will start with the Rapture. This doesn't mean that this is when the anti-Christ signs the covenant with Israel starting the 7-year countdown to the return of Jesus. We don't know how long it will be after the rapture and when the anti-Christ signs the agreement with Israel. You can be assured that with millions of people suddenly missing from the earth, there will be confusion and destruction all over the world. This most likely will help the political leader that will become the anti-Christ get the power to get control over the nations of the world.

The Rapture is called our blessed hope.

Titus 2:13 - The blessed hope
    13 while we wait for the blessed hope--the glorious appearing of our great God and Savior, Jesus Christ,

The Rapture could occur at any time, it will be at an unknown time, making it imminent.

    MT 24: 36"No one knows about that day or hour, not even the angels in heaven, nor the Son, but only the Father.

MT 24: 42"Therefore keep watch, because you do not know on what day your Lord will come. 43But understand this: If the owner of the house had known at what time of night the thief was coming, he would have kept watch and would not have let his house be broken into. 44So you also must be ready, because the Son of Man will come at an hour when you do not expect him.

MT 25:13"Therefore keep watch, because you do not know the day or the hour.

MK 13:35 "Therefore keep watch because you do not know when the owner of the house will come back--whether in the evening, or at midnight, or when the rooster crows, or at dawn. 36 If he comes suddenly, do not let him find you sleeping. 37 What I say to you, I say to everyone: `Watch!' "

LK 12:35 "Be dressed ready for service and keep your lamps burning, 36 like men waiting for their master to return from a wedding banquet, so that when he comes and knocks they can immediately open the door for him. 37 It will be good for those servants whose master finds them watching when he comes. I tell you the truth, he will dress himself to serve, will have them recline at the table and will come and wait on them. 38 It will be good for those servants whose master finds them ready, even if he comes in the second or third watch of the night. 39 But understand this: If the owner of the house had known at what hour the thief was coming, he would not have let his house be broken into. 40 You also must be ready, because the Son of Man will come at an hour when you do not expect him."

LK 21:36 Be always on the watch, and pray that you may be able to escape all that is about to happen, and that you may be able to stand before the Son of Man."

The only way to be counted worthy and to escape all that is about to happen, to escape the tribulation is to be born again thus being taken in the Rapture.

Because it is clear from the scriptures that we will have no way of knowing when Jesus will return for the Church, the tribulation is a problem for the rapture. From Matthew 24 and the book of Revelation we see there will be many signs before Jesus' return down to the earth. The revealing of the anti-Christ is the first sign. Actually the Rapture will be the first sign. From the revealing of the anti-Christ at the signing of the treaty between him, Israel and the Palestinians there is one sign after another. The any moment expectation we see taught in the scriptures doesn't fit with any other rapture view. All the other views have signs before the rapture. By signs I mean specific events that are mentioned by Jesus in the gospels and in the book of Revelation. If the rapture were to occur any time after the beginning of the tribulation then there would be no need to be watching for him now. This would cause all the commands in the gospels and the epistles to wait for and keep watch not apply to anyone before the tribulation.

There are no signs that need to be fulfilled before the Rapture, unlike the second coming. Jesus gave many signs, as does John in the book of Revelation to let the readers during the tribulation know that his second coming is close. There are no such signs for the Rapture. Although we now can see with the re-gathering of the Jews back to their land and then the rebirth of Israel as a nation in 1948, and in June of 1967 Israel regaining control of Jerusalem that these are signs of the end times, and now with all the talk about globalization we can see we are indeed in the last days. We can see that things are beginning to fall into place for the tribulation, but the rapture isn't dependent on any signs being fulfilled. But these and numerous other signs must be fulfilled before the second coming.

If the Church were required to go through part or all of the seven-year tribulation, you would expect the New Testament writers to have warned us to be prepared for perilous times. On the contrary, the New

Testament writers repeatedly tell the Church to be comforted by the "coming of the Lord".

If a person should make it through the tribulation until the point when the mid-trib, pre-wrath, and post-trib folks expect the rapture to occur, it would then become possible for the rapture to be classified as "imminent." However, once you solve the problem of imminency, you create another one regarding the restrictions against knowing the timing of the rapture, because the duration of the tribulation is already known. Again, this would cause all the scriptures commanding one to watch, not to apply to us now or to all those that came before us.

WATCHING AND WAITING IN THE EPISTLES

The rapture of the church could happen at any-moment, without signs or warnings. Thus a church age believer should be constantly watching and waiting for our Lord. The posture of watching and waiting for the Lord clearly implies that the rapture is what Bible teachers have called "imminent." Again, Imminence means that Christ could come for His church at any-moment; that there are no signs relating to the rapture; that no prophecy has to be fulfilled before Christ could call us to meet Him in the air.

Note some of the many passages in the Epistles that teach this:

1 Corinthians 1:7

> Therefore you do not lack any spiritual gift as you eagerly wait for our Lord Jesus Christ to be revealed.

We see from this that Christ's coming for His church is seen as imminent.

The Rapture of the Church

Philippians 3:20

> But our citizenship is in heaven. And we eagerly await a Savior from there, the Lord Jesus Christ,

Paul tells us to be in a constant expectation of the Rapture.

Notice Paul said that the believer's "citizenship is in heaven, and we eagerly wait for a Savior, the Lord Jesus Christ." This verse strongly emphasizes that our focus is upon waiting for Christ now, which would exclude knowing the time of His arrival. For if the time of His coming could be known, then we would be waiting for a certain day or hour as would be the case after the anti-Christ is revealed. Instead, eagerly waiting for Jesus to catch us up to meet him in the air implies that the timing is not known.

1 Thessalonians 1:10

> and to wait for his Son from heaven, whom he raised from the dead—Jesus, who rescues us from the coming wrath.

Titus 2: 13

> 11For the grace of God that brings salvation has appeared to all men. 12It teaches us to say "No" to ungodliness and worldly passions, and to live self-controlled, upright and godly lives in this present age, 13while we wait for the blessed hope—the glorious appearing of our great God and Savior, Jesus Christ,

Our Blessed Hope is the imminent return of Jesus—at the rapture. We are to look for Jesus, not signs relating to His coming.

1 Peter 1:13

> Therefore, prepare your minds for action; be self-controlled; set your hope fully on the grace to be given you when Jesus Christ is revealed.

Our focus should be on Jesus and His coming for his Church, not on signs or conditions that we may think indicates His return. Jesus will be revealed to the Church when he catches us up, at the rapture. (While we can see things lining up in the world as the bible has predicted we still cannot predict just when the Rapture will occur).

His return to catch up the Church has no signs, but there are numerous signs that point to his second coming to the earth.

The rapture calls for watchfulness because "it will be sudden and unknown before-hand."

I'm not going to take up a lot here on this since we should look to the bible as our source but here's a couple of the earliest Church fathers that taught the imminent return of Jesus for the Church, a 7 year tribulation before the 2nd coming of Jesus and that there will be a 1000 year reign of Christ here on earth.

The book of Revelation was written in 95 a.d. So you can see how close these two early Church fathers were to the time of John.

Irenaeus (A.D. 120-202), died as a martyr for his faith, wrote Against Heresies, one of the most important prophetic writings of the primitive Church. Irenaeus was a disciple of **Polycarp** (A.D. 69-155), who was personally taught by the apostle John who received and wrote Revelation. The writings of Polycarp have been lost to history. I've read that his writings were burned in a fire. But there are many early commentaries that quote him as well as Irenaeus. We do have many writings from Irenaeus. Irenaeus taught a pre-millennial view, that Jesus would literally return and set up his earthly kingdom here on earth for a literal 1000 years, a 7-year tribulation and the rapture of the Church.

Hippolytus, the bishop of Portus (160-236), was a Greek but was associated with the Latin Church. He was a disciple of Irenaeus and wrote extensively about the prophecies.

Well I could go on and on up through history. For me, with Irenaeus being the closest to the source of the book of Revelation, with Irenaeus being taught by Polycarb who was personally taught by the Apostle John, with Irenaeus teaching a pre-trib Rapture of the Church, a 7 year tribulation and a 1000 year reign of Christ on Earth out of Jerusalem, all of which would happen in the future, this should be enough to prove what the apostle John taught.

He also said that John received the Revelation on the Isle of Patmos in 95 A.D. as do many commentaries on the book of Revelation from the early Church. We can't get any closer to the source (John) than this.

If you would like to read more on the teachings of the early Church get Grant R. Jeffrey's book 'Triumphant Return". He's answering arguments against the Preterist view. He goes down through all the century's listing who taught a literal view of prophecy and an imminent return of Christ.

Virtually all-serious scholars of Church history, regardless of their personal views regarding the Millennium, acknowledge that the early apostolic Church believed in an imminent Coming for the Church.

> 1Cor. 16:22 If anyone does not love the Lord--a curse be on him. Come, O Lord! NIV

> 1 Cor.16:22 If any man love not the Lord Jesus Christ, let him be Anathema **Maranatha**. 23 The grace of our Lord Jesus Christ be with you. KJV

The word Maranatha was a very popular greeting used by the Christians of the early Church when meeting fellow believers. It demonstrated their ever-present hope for the imminent return of Jesus Christ to catch up His faithful followers.

Maranatha is formed from three Aramaic words: Mar means "Lord" ana means "our", and tha means "come". In Aramaic, Maranatha literally means "our Lord comes". In English, it translates "The Lord

Comes". The wide spread use of the Maranatha greeting demonstrates the universal expectation of the early Church that Jesus could return at any point in time to catch up the saints.

Now as far as the second coming goes, the Bible couldn't be plainer. It clearly states that Jesus' return will be known and seen by all on the earth.

> MT 24:27 For as lightning that comes from the east is visible even in the west, so will be the coming of the Son of Man.

> MT 24:30 "At that time the sign of the Son of Man will appear in the sky, and all the nations of the earth will mourn. They will see the Son of Man coming on the clouds of the sky, with power and great glory.

As we've just seen, no one knows of the time of the rapture.

> MT 24:36 "No one knows about that day or hour, not even the angels in heaven, nor the Son, but only the Father.

> MT 24:42 "Therefore keep watch, because you do not know on what day your Lord will come.

Because there exists both a known and an unknown day, this is how many scholars have logically concluded that there must be two different events occurring--the rapture and the second coming.

The Bible warns us to live in holiness because Jesus could return for the Church at any moment, without warning. Jesus, in Luke 12:37 and 40, admonished, "It will be good for those servants whose master finds them watching when he comes ....You also must be ready, because the Son of Man will come at an hour when you do not expect him." We must live in a dynamic spiritual balance. While we are commanded to live in holiness and urgently witness as though He will return before the dawn, we are called to plan and work to fulfill the Great Commission as if He will tarry for another hundred years.

If you haven't already, it is your choice. Ultimately, you must choose heaven or hell as your eternal destination.

If you choose to commit your life to Jesus Christ, if you are still alive, you will be assured that you will meet Him at the Rapture as your Savior. If you reject His claims to be the Lord of your life, you will have chosen to meet Him as your final judge at the end of your life. The apostle Paul quoted Isaiah when he said, "Every knee shall bow before me, every tongue shall confess to God" (Rom. 14:11; Isa. 45:23).

Revelation 22:7, 12, 20

"Yes, I am coming soon."

Amen. Come, Lord Jesus.

Chapter Three

The Rapture in the Gospel of John

1. A Study of John 14

A study of John 14:3 provides further evidence that Jesus' coming for His Church will be a pre-tribulation one.

This is one of the strongest parallels and evidence that Jesus was describing a pre-trib rapture.

First let's look at John 14 and see just what Jesus was telling them.

John 14

> 1"Do not let your hearts be troubled. Trust in God; trust also in me. 2In my Father's house are many rooms; if it were not so, I would have told you. I am going there to prepare a place for you. 3And if I go and prepare a place for you, I will come back and take you to be with me that you also may be where I am.

Notice he said he is going to his Father's house to prepare a place for them, which now is also addressing the Church. In his Father's house are many rooms. His Father's house is in heaven. And he said that he would come back and take them, the Church there to be with him, that we would be where he is. He's coming from heaven to the earth. Here He describes "a coming for" His saints to take them to the Father's house. This is a description of the Rapture in contrast to the Second Coming. "This passage indicates that the believer is going to go to heaven, to the Father's house at the time of Jesus' coming for Him." This will not occur at the Second Coming because that will be a time in which Jesus comes *with* His saints, who are already in heaven, not *for* His saints as John 14:1-3 requires. Furthermore at Jesus' 2nd coming he is not going back to heaven, he is coming down to the earth. Jesus is unveiling a new revelation about the Rapture of the Church.

Here in John 14 Jesus is giving a new and unique revelation; He speaks of something that no prophet had promised. Nowhere in the Old Testament is it written that the Messiah would come and instead of gathering His saints into an earthly Jerusalem, He would come and take them to the Father's house, take them to heaven. All the Old Testament prophets spoke of the Messiah coming to earth and establishing the Kingdom of God. This coming and taking them to be with him is something totally new, not revealed in the Old Testament times. Why, because the Church was not revealed to the Old Testament prophets and saints. Paul said the Church was a mystery.

> Ephesians 3:2Surely you have heard about the administration of God's grace that was given to me for you, 3that is, the mystery made known to me by revelation, as I have already written briefly. 4In reading this, then, you will be able to understand my insight into the mystery of Christ, 5which was not made known to men in other generations as it has now been revealed by the Spirit to God's holy apostles and prophets. 6This mystery is that through the gospel the Gentiles are heirs together with Israel, members together of one body, and sharers together in the promise in Christ Jesus.

> 9and to make plain to everyone the administration of this mystery, which for ages past was kept hidden in God, who created all things. 10His intent was that now, through the church, the manifold wisdom of God should be made known to the rulers and authorities in the heavenly realms,

> Colossians 1: 24Now I rejoice in what was suffered for you, and I fill up in my flesh what is still lacking in regard to Christ's afflictions, for the sake of his body, which is the church. 25I have become its servant by the commission God gave me to present to you the word of God in its fullness— 26the mystery that has been kept hidden for ages and generations, but is now disclosed to the saints. 27To them God has chosen to make known among the Gentiles the glorious riches of this mystery, which is Christ in you, the hope of glory.

Also notice in promising to come back and take them to be with him, where he is, He speaks of a coming which is not for the deliverance of the Jewish remnant, not of a coming to establish His kingdom on the earth, not a coming to judge the nations, all of which were taught by the prophets and will occur at his second coming when he comes down to the earth, but he speaks of a coming which concerns only His own and removing them from the earth.

It should be clear now Jesus was referring to the Rapture of the Church.

Jesus was actually using the Jewish wedding custom as a parallel to his coming for the Church. A good clue is in the statement 'In my Father's house are many rooms, and I am going there to prepare a place for you'. We will look at this further. This place he is preparing could be the New Jerusalem, the city of God we see in Revelation chapter 21. But just how long would it take him to prepare a place for us. It's been 2000 years now. It's not like he has to physically build it like we would here on earth. All he would do is just speak it into existence. As I will show you in the next subject, this is from the Jewish wedding custom; the groom would go and prepare a room for himself and his bride at his Father's house.

There are interesting parallels between the Jewish wedding and the Rapture.

Only a Pre-Tribulation Rapture will fit into this scenario.

First there were three groups of people present at every Jewish wedding: the groom, the bride, and the invited guests.

There will also be three groups of people involved in the marriage of the Lamb.

1. The Groom. This is Jesus (2 Cor. 11:2, Eph. 5:23-27)
2. The Bride. This is the Church (2 Cor. 11:2, Eph. 5:22-32, Rev.19:7)
3. The Guests. Those saved after the Rapture (Matt. 25:1-10).

There are also 3 parallels with the Jewish wedding and the marriage of the Lamb.

1. The Wedding Contract (Betrothal). This is when a person is saved (2 Cor. 11:2).
2. The Wedding Ceremony (Groom receives his Bride). This is the Rapture (John 14:2-3).
3. The Wedding Feast (Guests are invited to the celebration).This is after the Second coming. (Mat. 25:1-10)
   (Rev. 19:9) "Blessed are those who are invited to the marriage supper of the Lamb" --A bride is not invited to her own wedding! The Church was married to Christ at the Rapture and the wedding feast will occur on earth after the Second Coming. Those people saved after the Rapture will be invited to participate in the wedding feast.

Here in John 14 Jesus was using the illustration from the Jewish wedding to describe the process in how it will be for those who are in him, that are part of his Church, his bride. Next I will explain the Jewish wedding custom and why only a pre-trib rapture of the Church can work as a parallel with the Jewish wedding.

Before I explain in more detail the Jewish wedding custom, here's a statement made by Jesus when he was about to raise Lazarus from the dead. It sounds like a hint to the rapture.

John 11: [25] Jesus said to her, "I am the resurrection and the life. The one who believes in me will live, even though they die; [26] and whoever lives by believing in me will never die.

Jesus saying the one who believes in him will live; even though he dies, they would have understood this as to referring to the resurrection. But whoever believes in him would never die, that there would be some that would never die, this wasn't taught in the Old Testament. Put this together with what we have read here in John and in I and II Thessalonians and 1 Cor. 15:51-52. This is a reference to the rapture.

2. Understanding John 14:1-3.

John 14: 1"Do not let your hearts be troubled. Trust in God; trust also in me. 2In my Father's house are many rooms; if it were not so, I would have told you. I am going there to prepare a place for you. 3And if I go and prepare a place for you, I will come back and take you to be with me that you also may be where I am.

How the Jewish Wedding custom was at the time of Jesus.

Jesus was using the wedding custom as a parallel to his coming back for the Church.

The custom was first the Wedding Contract (Betrothal). The groom and/or his Father would pick a bride. In John 4:19 it says of Jesus, we love him, because he first loved us. The bride and groom would agree on getting married. We agree to be married to Christ at salvation, when we accept him as Lord and Savior. The groom and his Father would go and pay the Father of the bride to be the price for her. You were legally married at this time. They would be legally married before any ceremony, before going to the Father's house, before living together. Remember Mary and Joseph. How Joseph thought to divorce her quietly yet they hadn't been together or had a wedding ceremony or banquet. Like our engagement but legally binding. They were considered husband and wife at betrothal. You have the Father and Jesus paying the price for the church (bride) on the cross. Paul describes us as married to Christ.

The groom would return to his father's house where, if there was not already one he would build a room onto his father's house. If there was a room he would prepare it for his bride. This room was also known as the bridle chamber. When the room was completed and the allotted amount of time had gone by the Groom's Father would tell his Son to go and get his bride. No one except the Father would know when this would be not even the Groom. This could be up to 12 months. The bride would be making herself ready during this time. When the Father would tell his Son it was time to go get his bride he would leave his father's house and return to the brides house to get her at a time unknown to her, at least the exact time wasn't known. The bride and her attendants, bridesmaids would watch and wait. When they heard the announcement that the bridegroom was returning the bride would make final preparations and then the bride and her bridesmaids would go out to meet the Groom. The streets would be lit. There would be a procession back to the Fathers house. We see in 1 Thes. 4: 16 of the rapture Paul says, For the Lord himself will come down from heaven, with a loud command, with the voice of the archangel and with the trumpet call of God.

The Wedding Ceremony (Groom receives his Bride). They would then enter the room he had prepared for her, the bridle chamber which they would stay in for 7 days. This was also known as the bridle week. They wouldn't come out. Their meals would even be brought to them. (The honey moon). There would be a friend of the Groom who would wait outside the bridle chamber to be told that the marriage had been consummated. The friend of the Groom would then announce it to those there and then there would be a banquet that would last the whole 7 days. You see a reference to this in John 3: 29. John the Baptist speaking to his disciples. "The bride belongs to the bridegroom. The friend who attends the bridegroom waits and listens for him, and is full of joy when he hears the bridegroom's voice. That joy is mine, and it is now complete." It was at a Wedding banquet that Jesus performed his first miracle of turning water into wine. Now this friend of Jesus is the Holy Spirit.

On the 7th day they would come out and have The Wedding Feast or supper (Guests are invited to the celebration). You see all this mentioned in Genesis chapter 29 with the story of Jacob, Leah and Rachel.

Well you can see this parallel in Jesus coming to the earth, The Church's (brides) home. Paying the price for us (His bride), dying on the cross. Going back to his Father's house (heaven) and preparing a room (rooms) for us.

The rapture you have him returning to receive his bride. The Wedding Ceremony (Groom receives Bride).

You see Christ's Bride is in Heaven with him before his 2nd coming, before He returns to the earth! "Let us rejoice and be glad and give him glory! For the wedding of the Lamb has come, and his bride has made herself ready. Fine linen, bright and clean, was given her to wear." (Fine linen stands for the righteous acts of the saints.) Then the angel said to me, "Write: <u>Blessed are those who are invited to the wedding supper of the Lamb!</u>" And he added, "These are the true words of God." Revelation 19:7-9. Those that live through the tribulation and are saved, found righteous will be the guest's invited to the wedding feast that will occur here on earth after Jesus and the Church, his bride has returned.

At the end of the 7 years of the tribulation period you see Jesus returning with his bride to the earth and then you have the Wedding Supper (feast) Rev. 19. Well, you see the parallel, how they would stay in the room for 7 days. The tribulation period is 7 years. The Church (bride) will be in her room (heaven) with Jesus for 7 years. Only the pre-tribulation rapture will work with the Jewish wedding custom.

We read in the Old Testament how God has gone out of his way to establish a pattern with the number 7. 7 days of creation. On the 7th day he rested. There were 7 steps leading into the tabernacle. Every 7th year was a sabbatical year for the land. Study the different Feasts in the Old Testament and see how often 7 is used for days or weeks etc. You see the number 7 used all throughout the Old Testament. In the book of Revelation you have 7 lamp stands, 7 spirits, 7 Church's, 7 seals, 7 trumpets, 7 bowls. I could go on and on.

It is obvious that verses 2 and 3 are referring to the Rapture and not his 2nd coming. None of the Rapture views dispute this, but for the Jewish wedding custom to be a reference to the Rapture, the Church, the bride of Christ has to be in heaven, the bridal chamber for the 7 years of the Tribulation. This requires the rapture to be before the tribulation. With the bride and groom being 7 days in the bridal chamber and the Church being in heaven with Jesus 7 years of the Tribulation we have the same pattern.

The number 7 has been seen as God's number or the number of God. The number 6 is referred to as man's number. Man was created on the 6th day. 7 is also a number for completeness.

So when Jesus was telling them that he would go to his Father's house and prepare a place for them and then return to get them and take them to his Father's house they, being Jewish understood the parallel to the wedding ceremony and feast. It's obvious they didn't comprehend everything fully until after the day of Pentecost when they received the Holy Spirit. The Holy Spirit then would bring all things back to their remembrance. The pieces then started coming together.

Let me point out one more fact from the Jewish wedding custom and how it relates to the Church

Baptism. Did you know that John the Baptist didn't introduce baptism? It was already part of Judaism. It was also part of the Jewish wedding custom. The bride to be would submerge herself in the ceremonial water to cleanse herself making herself ready for her husband. It is called Mikvah. Part of the custom was that the bride would experience a Mikvah prior to her wedding. She would do this before the bridegroom came for her. The word Mikvah means a pool of living water used for ritual purification. Jewish brides today continue to go to the Mikvah or Tevilah, the ritual immersion in water as part of their physical and spiritual preparation for the wedding ceremony. This ancient Jewish custom represents a separation from an old life to a new life, from life as a single woman to life as a married woman. It also symbolizes a change in status and authority, of her coming out from under the authority of her father to under the authority of her husband. Does this Sound familiar. This is what takes place for us now when we are baptized. And we are baptized into Christ before he has returned for us, before we are taken to the Father's house. So here is another example of a parallel with the Jewish wedding custom.

So, the betrothal, the paying of the price for the bride, the leaving for his Father's house, returning from the Father's house to get his bride, then being in the bridal chamber for 7 days, after the 7 days coming out of the bridle chamber and having the wedding supper, you can see the parallel of what Jesus has done and will do for us with what he said in John 14 and the Jewish wedding custom.

So, from all this, you can see the parallel of the Jewish wedding custom and the pre-trib rapture of the Church. With the bride and groom being in the bridal chamber for 7 days, only the pre-trib rapture can match up with the 7 years being a parallel with the 7 days. The post-trib view having Jesus coming for his bride after the 7 years does not parallel with the Jewish wedding custom of the groom coming for his bride and then taking her to his Father's house for 7 days. Neither can the pre-wrath or the mid-trib views. The mid-trib view would only have 3 ½ days, years.

Putting all this together it is clear evidence for a pre-trib rapture.

Look at 1 Thes. 4:

> 16 For the Lord himself will come down from heaven, with a loud command, with the voice of the archangel and with the trumpet call of God, and the dead in Christ will rise first. 17 After that, we who are still alive and are left will be caught up together with them in the clouds to meet the Lord in the air. And so we will be with the Lord forever.

This also seems to be a parallel with the Jewish wedding custom. Jesus himself will come down from heaven, from the Father's house for his bride, with a loud command. With the wedding custom there would be the guests of the groom announcing his coming and trumpets sounding. There was a big precession through the streets.

God has used types and patterns throughout history. We see in the Old Testament of many Jewish customs and rituals that were a parallel or foreshadow of Jesus.

The Rapture in the Gospel of John

And as we have seen, there are also parallels in the New Testament.

The Passover, the sacrifices, the lambs, the scapegoat, the Manna the Israelites ate during the 40 years in the desert and the feasts all were foreshadows of Jesus and what he did for us on the cross. Enoch and Elijah being caught up, being raptured, Noah and his family going into the ark before the judgment of the flood was poured out, Lot and his family told to get out, actually were lead out of Sodom and Gomorrah before God destroyed them. All of these are types and patterns that we can now look back on. With Noah and Lot you can see a pattern of God removing the righteous before he pours out judgment on an unrighteous world.

Numbers often have a special meaning, like 3, 7, 40, on the 3rd day, on the 7th day, for 40 days etc. In the book of Revelation we see there are 7 seals, 7 trumpets and 7 bowls. And there are 3 series of judgments. You can see in both the Old and New Testaments that numbers are often used as patterns with a special meaning.

For example, Jesus said in the second chapter of John:

> JN 2:19 Jesus answered them, "Destroy this temple, and I will raise it again in three days."

> JN 2:20 The Jews replied, "It has taken forty-six years to build this temple, and you are going to raise it in three days?" 21 But the temple he had spoken of was his body. 22 After he was raised from the dead, his disciples recalled what he had said. Then they believed the Scripture and the words that Jesus had spoken.

This happened literally, on the 3rd day. But something that is interesting is how this is an example of how what Jesus said can have 2 meanings. The actual temple was destroyed. It will be raised (rebuilt) in the 3rd day. We are in or coming up onto it starting the 3rd thousand year since Jesus was crucified.

Look at what was said by Hosea.

> HOS 6:2 After two days he will revive us; on the third day he will restore us, that we may live in his presence.

Now look at what Peter said:

> 2PE 3:8 But do not forget this one thing, dear friends: With the Lord a day is like a thousand years, and a thousand years are like a day.

Jesus was literally raised from the dead after 2 days, on the 3rd day and the temple will literally be rebuilt after 2 days, on the 3rd day. This is an example of how patterns in the bible work.

Here's another example of a type or pattern.

The 7th Day and the 3rd Day.

In using a day like a thousand years and a thousand years are like a day means we are in or about to be in mans' 7th thousand year since Adam and Eve's fall. Christ's reign on earth will be for a 1000 years. The 7th day. On the 7th day God rested. The 1000 years of the kingdom of God will be a time of rest for the earth (sabbatical year). At the end of the 1000 years we see the new heaven and new earth. This would be the 8th day. 8 is a number for new beginnings.

Hosea said, after two days he will revive us; on the third day he will restore us, that we may live in his presence. This promise was to Israel. Using II Peter 3:8 a day is like a thousand years we have 2 days, 2 thousand years since Jesus died on the cross and the vale in the temple was ripped into. The Romans destroyed Jerusalem in 70 AD. So we're in or close to starting the 3 thousandth year since Jesus was here, the 3rd day. After two days he will revive us, in other words, on the 3rd day. Jesus rose on the 3rd day.

Luke 24: 46He told them, "This is what is written: The Christ will suffer and rise from the dead on the third day,

The gospels are full of references to Jesus rising on the 3rd day. Look at this parallel,

Matthew 12: 39He answered, "A wicked and adulterous generation asks for a miraculous sign! But none will be given it except the sign of the prophet Jonah. 40For as Jonah was three days and three nights in the belly of a huge fish, so the Son of Man will be three days and three nights in the heart of the earth.

We are approaching the 3rd and 7th day, so we could be close to Jesus' return for the Church. The scriptures tell us to be waiting and looking for his return. Jesus said we wouldn't know the day or the hour but we could know the season, the general time. Matthew 24:36. It's just like it was when he was here on earth. He was constantly getting on to the Pharisees for not knowing the time, the season in which they were living. Most people, even in the Church do not recognize the season in which we are in now. They don't recognize the signs of the times. Jesus died and rose around 33 a.d.

It's interesting that the 3rd day and the 7th day fall in together. If Jesus had come a thousand years before we would be in the 4th day. If he came a thousand years later we would be in the 2nd day. This shows that God has everything happening on his timetable and he is in control. 3 has always had a pattern like 7. You see this with Father, Son and Holy Spirit and Body, Soul and Spirit.

So from what we have just seen with Jesus' use of the Jewish wedding custom it is strong evidence that the Church will be taken up to the Father's house before the tribulation, before the 7 years start. The 7 years compared with the 7 days just fit the pattern that God has used throughout history right from the beginning of creation.

Chapter Four

A Look at First and Second Thessalonians

1. I Thessalonians Chapters 4 & 5

> 1TH 4:13 Brothers, we do not want you to be ignorant about those who fall asleep, or to grieve like the rest of men, who have no hope. 14 We believe that Jesus died and rose again and so we believe that God will bring with Jesus those who have fallen asleep in him. 15 According to the Lord's own word, we tell you that we who are still alive, who are left till the coming of the Lord, will certainly not precede those who have fallen asleep. 16 For the Lord himself will come down from heaven, with a loud command, with the voice of the archangel and with the trumpet call of God, **and the dead in Christ will rise first**. 17 <u>After that, we who are still alive and are left will</u> be **caught up <u>together</u> with them in the clouds to meet the Lord in the air**. And so we will be with the Lord forever. 18 Therefore encourage each other with these words.

The main subject here is concerning the rapture. As we've seen earlier, this here is one of the clearest scriptures that reveal the Lord's coming only in the air to take those that belong to him back to heaven. Remember, the Greek word for 'caught up' being translated into Latin then into English is where we get the word 'Rapture'.

Paul is explaining to them about their loved ones and friends that have already died that were in Christ. The Thessalonians were troubled by false teachings that their loved ones that had already died would not be part of the rapture, thinking they would not see their loved ones again. He is assuring them that they will see their love ones again, that they will take part in the rapture, and that they will meet them in the air when Jesus returns. So he tells them not to grieve like those that have no hope.

Notice there's no mention of Jesus coming down to the earth, but only of the Church meeting him in the air. Remember, we just saw from our look at the 14th chapter of John that Jesus is going to take us to the Fathers house, to heaven.

Now Paul said that the dead in Christ would rise first, THEN we which are still alive will be caught up <u>together</u> with them in the air. First the dead are raised then those left alive. Here in lies a clear distinction between Jesus coming only in the air and coming back down to the earth. Verses 13 thru 18 are clearly referring to the Rapture, to the Church being caught up in the air and returning to heaven to be with the Lord. There's no mention of coming down to earth.

In Revelation 19 which is of Jesus returning to the earth we don't see any mention of a resurrection and the saints being transformed, being caught up, why, because the rapture occurs before Jesus' 2nd coming back down to the earth. In Rev. Chapter 20 after he has returned down to earth we see a mention of only those that have died in the Lord <u>during</u> the tribulation being raised to life. Again, notice this is after he has returned not when he returns.

> REV. 20: 4I saw thrones on which were seated those who had been given authority to judge. And I saw the souls of those who had been beheaded because of their testimony for Jesus and because of the word of God. They had not worshiped the beast or his image and had not received his mark on their foreheads or their hands. They came to life and reigned with Christ a thousand years.

If the rapture just happened, if the rapture occurred on the day Jesus returns or even just before, then these we see in Rev. Chapter 20 would have been raptured before Jesus returned down to the earth, as a result, there would not be anyone to go into the kingdom of God as mortals, all the righteous would have been raptured and changed into immortals. We see in Rev. 19 that the unrighteous that are gathered against him are slain by the word of his mouth and then the rest of the unrighteous are weeded out after he has returned, the separation of the sheep and the goats, Matthew 25.

> Mt. 25: 31"When the Son of Man comes in his glory, and all the angels with him, he will sit on his throne in heavenly glory,

32All the nations will be gathered before him, and he will separate the people one from another as a shepherd separates the sheep from the goats.

We see after Jesus has returned that he will sit on his throne to judge. We will look at this later in our look at Matthew.

The kingdom of God starts out with only those that are found righteous, those that have accepted Jesus as the Son of God. It is clear that these in Revelation chapter 20 are only those that died during the tribulation. John seems to make a point of distinguishing them. If the rapture takes place at the same day when Jesus is coming down to earth, or just before the day Jesus returns then these, which have died in Jesus, would have already been raised, they all would have been raptured. So the rapture has to occur well before Jesus returns back down to the earth. I will show later how by the time of the bowl judgments that everyone that will be saved have already been saved. No one else will be saved after the 7th trumpet, after the bowl judgments have started.

For those that don't know the book of Revelation, there are 3 series of judgments, the Seals, Trumpets and the Bowls with the 7 bowls completing God's wrath and judgment.

One of the first things that has puzzled me concerning the post-trib view is why would there even be a need for a rapture of the living saints if we were only going to meet in the air and come right back down, if Jesus wasn't taking us back to heaven as John 14 and 1 Thessalonians teach. It seems that he could just change us into immortals. With the post-trib view there couldn't be a changing of the living saints at all since there has to be people saved to go into the kingdom as mortals. As you have seen, the scriptures teach there will be a changing of those that are alive in Christ at the rapture. We see this also in Paul's letter to the Corinthians.

1 Cor. 15: 50I declare to you, brothers, that flesh and blood cannot inherit the kingdom of God, nor does the perishable

inherit the imperishable. 51Listen, I tell you a mystery: We will not all sleep, but we will all be changed— 52in a flash, in the twinkling of an eye, at the last trumpet. For the trumpet will sound, the dead will be raised imperishable, and we will be changed. 53For the perishable must clothe itself with the imperishable, and the mortal with immortality. 54When the perishable has been clothed with the imperishable, and the mortal with immortality, then the saying that is written will come true: "Death has been swallowed up in victory."

All those that are raised to life or changed at the rapture will receive an immortal physical body; those that live through the tribulation and are found righteous will take part in the earthly kingdom of God but don't receive an immortal physical body until after the 1000 years when God creates the new heaven and new earth.

Remember, Jesus left and went back to heaven. He said he is coming back, from heaven, to take us back to where he came from. At the rapture he is taking us back to heaven, to the Father's house.

> John 14: 2In my Father's house are many rooms; if it were not so, I would have told you. I am going there to prepare a place for you. 3And if I go and prepare a place for you, I will come back and take you to be with me that you also may be where I am.

Let's continue reading 1 Thessalonians chapter 5.

> 1TH 5:1 Now, brothers, about times and dates we do not need to write to you, 2 for you know very well that **the day of the Lord will come like a thief in the night**. 3 While people are saying, "Peace and safety," **destruction will come on them suddenly**, as labor pains on a pregnant woman, and they will not escape.

This is not referring to the second coming, notice he said the **day of the Lord** will come like a thief in the night in contrast with Jesus saying in the gospels that his second coming will be as lighting flashing from east to west and that every eye will see his second coming. Also by the end of the tribulation there has been no peace and safety, WWIII is coming to a climax. When Jesus returns to come back down to the earth, all the armies of the world are gathered together to fight against him. Rev. 19: 19Then I saw the beast and the kings of the earth and their armies gathered together to make war against the rider on the horse and his army.

So the day of the Lord here cannot be referring to the day of his 2nd coming, his second coming will not be like a thief.

Jesus said of his second coming,

> Mt. 24: 27For as lightning that comes from the east is visible even in the west, so will be the coming of the Son of Man...30"At that time the sign of the Son of Man will appear in the sky, and all the nations of the earth will mourn. They will see the Son of Man coming on the clouds of the sky, with power and great glory.

Concerning the rapture and the day of the Lord Jesus said,

> Mt. 24: 36"No one knows about that day or hour, not even the angels in heaven, nor the Son, but only the Father 42"Therefore keep watch, because you do not know on what day your Lord will come. 43But understand this: If the owner of the house had known at what time of night the thief was coming, he would have kept watch and would not have let his house be broken into. 44So you also must be ready, because the Son of Man will come at an hour when you do not expect him.

There is a clear distinction between verse 36 and verse 30. One event cannot be both as a thief at an unknown time and also be known and seen by everyone on the face of the earth.

A Look at First and Second Thessalonians

In 1 Thes. 4:13-17 Paul is describing the rapture. Notice in 1 Thes. 5:1-3 he said destruction will come on them suddenly, describing the tribulation. He goes from talking about the rapture right into the day of the Lord, linking them together. In verse 1 he said about times and dates we do not need to write you, saying the day of the Lord will come like a thief. But he started off in 1 Thessalonians 4 by describing the rapture. If the rapture is before the tribulation as the pre-trib view says then this makes perfect since. Jesus said the rapture and the events he was describing in Matthew 24, the events occurring during the tribulation would come at an unknown time. Matthew 24: 36 No one knows about that day or hour, not even the angels in heaven, nor the Son, but only the Father. In verse 42 he said, "Therefore keep watch, because you do not know on what day your Lord will come" referring to the Rapture. It would seem that the rapture and the tribulation are linked together. I will address this in more detail in are look at Matthew chapter 24.

We can see that Paul had previously taught them on this for he said in 1 Thes.5:2 that they already knew that the day of the Lord would come like a thief in the night. We can see that this cannot be referring to any time during the tribulation for peace is taken from the earth with the 2nd seal in Revelation chapter 6. Rev. 6: 3When the Lamb opened the second seal, I heard the second living creature say, "Come!" 4Then another horse came out, a fiery red one. Its rider was given power to take peace from the earth and to make men slay each other. To him was given a large sword.

This really doesn't work out for the pre-wrath or post-trib views for by the end of the Tribulation there has been war; WWIII comes to its climax at the battle of Armageddon at the end of the 7 years of the Tribulation. By this time the whole world has just about been totally destroyed by all the nuclear and other weapons of mass destruction. If Jesus doesn't return then all would be lost.

So, this cannot be a reference to his second coming for his second coming will not be as a thief. We see in Matthew 24 that every eye will see his return. We see in Revelation chapter 19 that the armies of the world are gathered together to fight against him.

So from the scriptures we have just looked at it is obvious that there's a coming as a thief, at a time unknown to anyone, that will not be visible and there's a coming that is known and which is visible. These two cannot happen at the same time.

Paul here puts the rapture before the day of the Lord, the tribulation. The day of the Lord will not start until after the rapture.

Take a look at this scripture that is about The Day of the Lord.

> AMOS 5:18 Woe to you who long
> for the day of the LORD!
> Why do you long for the day of the LORD?
> That day will be darkness, not light.

If the day of the Lord that Amos is referring to is the day that Jesus returns, his second coming, then why would He say why do you long for the day of the Lord. Why would he say woe to you unless the day of the Lord is referring to the tribulation? The day Jesus returns to the earth will be a glorious day that all Israel has been waiting for. The tribulation will be a day of darkness, a day of destruction. Just read the book of Revelation and you will see all the destruction that will be taking place during those 7 years. The book of Revelation is not about a single day but of the whole 7 years of the tribulation.

To help us with understanding what is being said, let us use the term we are used to today, let us exchange saying 'the day of the Lord' with 'the tribulation'.

> 1TH 5:1Now, brothers, about times and dates we do not need to write to you, 2for you know very well that the (the tribulation) will come like a thief in the night. 3While people are saying, "Peace and safety," destruction will come on them

suddenly, as labor pains on a pregnant woman, and they will not escape.

It could be, because of the peace agreement people are saying peace and safety, they could be saying, now there is, will be peace; there will be peace and safety at last because of this agreement with Israel and the Islamic nations.

Right after the rapture there will be mass confusion and probably destruction, but the 7 years of the tribulation won't officially start until the anti-Christ and Israel sign the covenant agreement together with the Islamic nations. The destruction of the tribulation doesn't start immediately with the signing of the peace agreement; it starts with the 2nd seal, and apparently suddenly, not that long after the signing of the peace agreement. The day of the Lord will start with the rapture but not the 7 years of the tribulation. We don't know how long it will be after the rapture and the signing of the peace agreement. The rapture will actually be the first sign that the day of the Lord has arrived.

It appears from the book of revelation that there will be war during the first 3 ½ years. The rider on the 2nd horse takes peace from the Earth. And we see with the 6th seal it appears that nuclear weapons have finally been used. The pre-trib view sees the whole 7 years as the day of the Lord (the time of the tribulation), which starts with the 1st seal, the revealing of the anti-Christ, while the mid-trib view sees only the last 3 ½ years as the day of the Lord, (the great tribulation). With what the seals describe it sure doesn't sound like there is peace and safety during the first half of the tribulation, which would be the time before the mid-trib rapture view. The pre-wrath and the post-view really have trouble with how they will be saying there's peace and safety when there has already been war and destruction by the time the rapture would occur according to their views. There have been massive nuclear exchanges and radiation fallout by the time of their rapture views.

1TH 5:4 But you, brothers, are not in darkness so that this day should surprise you like a thief.

All Christians are called to keep watch so that day will not take them by surprise. The pre-trib view watches for the signs of the times, the season in which we live, but not for any specific signs since the rapture can occur at any time. With all the other views there are signs during the tribulation that will occur before their rapture. But Jesus said in Matthew that he will come for the Church at a time unknown to us and that the tribulation would start at a time unknown. The mid-trib view will be able to calculate when the mid-point of the tribulation will be from the signing of the covenant between Israel and the anti-Christ. Daniel says that the anti-Christ will break the covenant with Israel in the middle of the 7 years. That will not allow the rapture to occur at an unknown time, a time known only by the Father or the tribulation to start at an unknown time (Matt. 24). If the last half of the tribulation is the day of the Lord and if it's only when the anti-Christ enters the temple and defiles it that he is revealed as is with the mid-trib view, if this is when the day of the Lord starts, then the day of the Lord couldn't come as a thief as Paul said. Everyone alive during the tribulation that knows the scriptures will be watching for this event. Anyone alive at the signing of the treaty between Israel and the anti-Christ that know the scriptures will know what is happening. They will know who the anti-Christ is then.

As I've mentioned already, if the rapture was to occur with the second coming at the end of the tribulation that wouldn't be a time unknown either for we see in the book of Revelation that the anti-Christ has what is left of the nations gathered together to make war against Jesus and those returning with him. They obviously know when he is coming. So his second coming or the day of the Lord as the post-trib view claims wouldn't be like a thief. Also Revelation says that from the time the anti-Christ sets himself up in the temple, after the first half of the tribulation there will be 1260 days. Daniel 12 verse 7 says "It will be for a time, times and half a time when the power of the holy people has been finally broken, all these things will be completed." And in verse 11 "From the time that the daily sacrifice is abolished and the abomination that cause desolation is set up, there will be 1290 days." So Jesus' second coming can be calculated from the time the anti-Christ enters into the Temple causing the 'abomination that causes desolation'.

76

It could be that it will be after 1260 days when the last battle of Armageddon will take place, when all the nations of the earth gather in the valley of Megiddo to fight against each other and then 30 days later when Satan (the anti-Christ) has the armies of the nations gathered together to fight Jesus at his return. See Rev. 19. Either way, they will be able to calculate the time of his second coming. We will look at this in our study of Daniel and Revelation.

> 1 TH 5: 4 But you, brothers, are not in darkness so that this day should surprise you like a thief. 5 You are all sons of the light and sons of the day. We do not belong to the night or to the darkness. 6 So then, let us not be like others, who are asleep, but let us be alert and self-controlled. 7 For those who sleep, sleep at night, and those who get drunk, get drunk at night. 8 But since we belong to the day, let us be self-controlled, putting on faith and love as a breastplate, and the hope of salvation as a helmet.

Although the mid, pre-wrath and post view folks like to say that this is proof that the Church will know when the rapture will occur, they still can't get past the fact that Jesus and Paul said that Jesus' coming for the Church will be a surprise, like a thief, at an unknown time. Read verse one again, Paul didn't say we would know when the rapture would occur, he said that it just wouldn't take us by surprise, that is if we are watching and are aware of what is happening in the world.

Paul was only saying here that because we are not in darkness, because we are watching that the rapture won't take us by surprise like it will those that are not watching and looking for the Lords return to take the Church back to heaven with him.

Notice with verses 5 thru 8 there is a contrast between the believer and unbeliever. Unlike at Jesus' second coming down to the earth where the unbeliever knows he is returning; here, no one knows when he is returning, only the believer will be watching for him. It's only the believer that is awake, alert. The believer is commanded to know the signs of the times, the season, just like when Jesus was here the first

77

time. I think Paul referring to us belonging to the day and being sons of the light goes back to Genesis chapter one.

> Gen. 1: 3 And God said, "Let there be light," and there was light. 4 God saw that the light was good, and He separated the light from the darkness. 5 God called the light "day," and the darkness he called "night." And there was evening, and there was morning—the first day.

The Sun wasn't created until the fourth day. Jesus also said "I am the light of the world. Whoever follows me will never walk in darkness, but will have the light of life." John 8:12. Jesus also said referring to believers in Matthew 5 verse 14, "You are the light of the world. Unbelievers are of the night, of the darkness. This light is life, truth, knowledge and understanding. Darkness is death, deceit and all that is false. (2 Cor. 6:14, 1 Jn. 1:5-7, Jn. 3:19-21, Jn. 8:12, Eph. 5:8, Col. 1:9-13, Acts 26:18, 2 Jn. 7-11).

Again, Paul wasn't saying the believer would know when Jesus was coming for the Church, but we just will not be caught by surprise; we will know the time is getting close. Also notice what Paul said to the believer, the one awake, watching, "But since we belong to the day, let us be self-controlled, putting on faith and love as a breastplate, and the hope of salvation as a helmet."

Here in verses 1 thru 8 Paul is referring to the day of the Lord, to the tribulation being started after the Rapture linking the Rapture with the day of the Lord. Just like when Jesus was here the first time they had all the signs of the time they were in. Jesus even acknowledged this. It is the same now and will be even more so the closer we get to the Rapture. We are told to keep watch and recognize the time, the season in which we are living. With all that is happening in the world and especially concerning Israel it's rather obvious we are living in the 'end' of the last days and that we could be close to Jesus returning for the Church, therefore close to the beginning of 'the day of the Lord'.

The re-gathering of the Jews and the rebirth of Israel in 1948 was one major prophesied event that had to occur before the tribulation. Up until 1948 the Jews had no country yet the book of Revelation refers to the Jews, Israel and Jerusalem. There have been many other things lining up with what must be in place for the tribulation like the birth of the European Union, all the talk about globalization, the coming one world government which will become the Revived Roman Empire that Daniel and Revelation mentions. Another one is the fact that the Palestinians and the Islamic nations want to divide up Jerusalem and Israel. Look at what Joel said.

> Joel 3: 2 I will gather all nations
> and bring them down to the Valley of Jehoshaphat.
> There I will enter into judgment against them
> concerning my inheritance, my people Israel,
> for they scattered my people among the nations
> and **divided up my land**.

Those who are 'sons of the light and sons of the day', those who are aware of what's happening in the world, not asleep know the season. It will not take those that are watching like a thief. We can see that the Rapture could happen at any time. But unfortunately there are those, even Christians that are asleep, not aware of the fact that world events are now fulfilling and aligning up with bible prophecy.

Jesus commanded us to keep watch.

> MT 24:42 "Therefore keep watch, because you do not know on what day your Lord will come.

> MT 25:13 "Therefore keep watch, because you do not know the day or the hour.

> MK 13: 35 "Therefore keep watch because you do not know when the owner of the house will come back--whether in the evening, or at midnight, or when the rooster crows, or at dawn.

36 If he comes suddenly, do not let him find you sleeping. 37 What I say to you, I say to everyone: `Watch!' "

Why would we be told so much to keep watch if it wasn't so important? This has applied to every Christian since the day of Pentecost.

We are commanded to watch for his coming for us, the Church. There are no signs that must occur before the rapture but in Matthew 24 Jesus gives numerous signs to watch for that point to his 2nd coming. If the rapture is to occur at any time during the tribulation then there would be no need for anyone to be or to have been watching for Jesus since he left. We wouldn't need to be watching until we see the signs that he described in the Gospels. All the scriptures that tell us to wait for Jesus' return for us would have no meaning to us now.

1 Thessalonians 5:9

> For God did not appoint us to suffer wrath but to receive salvation through our Lord Jesus Christ.

Compare with what John said in Rev. 3:10

Message to the Church of Philadelphia

Revelation 3:10

> Since you have kept my command to endure patiently, I will also keep you from the hour of trial that is going to come upon the whole world to test those who live on the earth.

Here Jesus said that he would keep the Church from the time of the hour of trial, remove the Church from it altogether. The Strong's Greek Lexicon translation G1537 is (out of, from, by, away from). It is not keep 'through' as the post-trib view says.

Although this is usually used by the pre-tribulation view it could still be used by the other views for each view sees us being delivered from the hour of trial, the wrath of God. It then hinges on how long the hour, the day of the Lord is. I believe I have shown already that the day of the Lord, the tribulation starts with the revealing of the anti-Christ at the first seal and that this starts the 7 years of the tribulation. I believe we've just seen that the tribulation does not start until after the rapture. We will see in our look at II Thessalonians chapter 2, the day of the Lord, the tribulation cannot start until the anti-Christ is revealed first.

II Thes. 2:3 Don't let anyone deceive you in any way, for (that day will not come) until the rebellion occurs and the man of lawlessness is revealed, the man doomed to destruction. Paul also mentions that there is someone holding back the revealing of the anti-Christ.

> LK 21:34 "Be careful, or your hearts will be weighed down with dissipation, drunkenness and the anxieties of life, and that **day** (the tribulation) will close on you unexpectedly like a trap. 35 For it will come upon all those who live on the face of the whole earth. 36 Be always on the watch, and pray that you may be able to **escape all** that is about to happen, and that you may be able to stand before the Son of Man."

> 2PE 2:4 For if God did not spare angels when they sinned, but sent them to hell, putting them into gloomy dungeons to be held for judgment; 5 if he did not spare the ancient world when he brought the flood on its ungodly people, but protected Noah, a preacher of righteousness, and seven others; 6 if he condemned the cities of Sodom and Gomorrah by burning them to ashes, and made them an example of what is going to happen to the ungodly; 7 and if he rescued Lot, a righteous man, who was distressed by the filthy lives of lawless men 8 (for that righteous man, living among them day after day, was tormented in his righteous soul by the lawless deeds he saw and heard)-- 9 if this is so, then the Lord knows how to rescue godly men from trials and to hold the unrighteous for the day of judgment, while continuing their punishment.

We can see that we are not appointed to suffer wrath and that God has a pattern of removing his own from the time of his wrath, but all the views can still use this statement for their views. Each view has a different opinion for the time of the wrath of God. Each view sees the day of the Lord and the wrath of God being one and the same they just differ on their interpretation for when and how long the day of the Lord is. But notice and consider this, in Luke 21:36 Jesus said "pray you will be able to escape ALL that is about to happen". Doesn't it sound like he means all the tribulation, all 7 years? He said that day (the tribulation) would close on you unexpectedly like a trap. Jesus' second coming will not close on them unexpectedly for they will know when he's coming back for you see they will be gathered together to make war against him and his army. Rev. 19. That day couldn't close on anyone unexpectedly after the anti-Christ signs the treaty with Israel for this will be the first sign that the tribulation has started and to who the anti-Christ is. This then is strong evidence that the day of the Lord, the tribulation referred to here is the whole 7 years. The second half of the tribulation, the great tribulation, the mid-trib view, couldn't be what Jesus or Paul are referring to either, for you would know who the anti-Christ is when he signs the covenant agreement with Israel and you will be able to determine the day, (1260 days from the signing of the covenant agreement) when the mid-point would occur when the anti-Christ enters the temple and defiles it. The same is true with a post-trib view; there will be 1260 days from the time the anti-Christ sets himself up in the temple to the battle of Armageddon and if Jesus doesn't return at the 1260 days then there will be 30 more days to Jesus' 2nd coming. Either way they will be able to calculate the timing of his return. So it appears that the wrath of God, the day of the Lord encompasses the whole 7 years. Plus the last 7 years are the last 7 years allotted to Israel. There's 7 years allotted, not 3 ½.

The tribulation is a unique and special time in God's plan. It's called the time of Jacob's trouble. Jacob is a reference to Israel.

> Jeremiah 30:7 Alas! for that day is great, so that none is like it: it is even the time of Jacob's trouble, but he shall be saved out of it. KJV.

It's a time God will judge Israel and the nations. It's a time to prepare the world for the kingdom of God. The judgments are actually God trying to do everything he can to get people to accept him, to accept Jesus before he returns to establish his kingdom. For you see twice in the book of Revelation, in chapter 9 and 16 that John records that they still refused to repent.

There are some that don't believe in a Rapture at all because the early Church Christians suffered and were persecuted so much, many even died for the faith. But none of that could be called a judgment from God or the wrath of God. If anything that was the wrath of Satan. Nowhere in the book of Revelation is there the statement the wrath of Satan but just the opposite; it's the wrath of God. It is Jesus that is opening the seals of the scroll that was handed to him by God the Father.

We are plainly told that we who trust in Christ are not under condemnation (Romans 8:1). Whenever God judges the unrighteous, He delivers those who trust in Him. This is seen in the Biblical stories of the Flood in the days of Noah, the judgment of Sodom and Gomorrah (Lot and his family saved).The events of the Tribulation are judgments from God, to judge Israel and the nations, to judge all that have rejected Christ. As we have seen from the scriptures of the past, it would be consistent for Him to deliver the Church before it begins.

> 1 Thessalonians 5: 10He died for us so that, whether we are awake or asleep, we may live together with him. 11Therefore encourage one another and build each other up, just as in fact you are doing.

Paul restates the fact that whether someone has died in Christ or is still alive at the rapture, we all will receive our resurrected bodies and meet together in the air to return with Jesus. Knowing this, we are to encourage and build each other up.

Next we will take a look at 2 Thessalonians to see if we can get more insight and a clearer picture of what Paul meant as to the length of the day of the Lord and the Rapture. As we will see, even the Thessalonians had been confused by some false teaching, that's why Paul wrote this second letter.

2. II Thessalonians 2

2TH 2:1 <u>Concerning the coming of our Lord Jesus Christ and our being gathered to him,</u>

Remember what we've already read in I Thessalonians. This being gather to Jesus is referring to the rapture.

1TH 4: 15 According to the Lord's own word, we tell you that we who are still alive, who are left till the coming of the Lord, will certainly not precede those who have fallen asleep. 16 For the Lord himself will come down from heaven, with a loud command, with the voice of the archangel and with the trumpet call of God, **and the dead in Christ will rise first.** 17 <u>After that, we who are still alive and are left will</u> be **caught up together with them in the clouds to meet the Lord in the air.** And so we will be with the Lord forever.

Remember also what Jesus said.

John 14: 2In my Father's house are many rooms; if it were not so, I would have told you. I am going there to prepare a place for you. 3And if I go and prepare a place for you, **I will come back and take you to be with me that you also may be where I am.**

So their first concern here was over the rapture. With the rapture being connected to the day of the Lord, the tribulation, then their concern had to be over the timing of the rapture. Let's read verses 1 thru 12 together first then I will address them.

2TH 2:1 Concerning the coming of our Lord Jesus Christ and our being gathered to him, we ask you, brothers, 2 not to become easily unsettled or alarmed by some prophecy, report or letter supposed to have come from us, saying that (the tribulation has already come) <u>the day of the Lord has already come.</u> 3 Don't let anyone deceive you in any way, <u>for that day</u>

(the tribulation) will not come until the rebellion (falling away) occurs and the man of lawlessness is revealed, the man doomed to destruction. 4 He will oppose and will exalt himself over everything that is called God or is worshiped, so that he sets himself up in God's temple, proclaiming himself to be God. 5 Don't you remember that when I was with you I used to tell you these things? 6 And now you know what is holding him back, so that he may be revealed at the proper time. 7 For the secret power of lawlessness is already at work; but the one who now holds it back will continue to do so till **he** is taken out of the way. 8 And <u>then</u> the lawless one will be revealed, whom the Lord Jesus will overthrow with the breath of his mouth and destroy by the splendor of his coming. 9 The coming of the lawless one will be in accordance with the work of Satan displayed in all kinds of counterfeit miracles, signs and wonders, 10 and in every sort of evil that deceives those who are perishing. They perish because they refused to love the truth and so be saved. 11 For this reason God sends them a powerful delusion so that they will believe the lie 12 and so that all will be condemned who have not believed the truth but have delighted in wickedness.

First, notice that with verse 1 Paul starts off with referring to the rapture and said in verse 5 that when he was with them he taught them on these things. So they had been taught about the Rapture and the day of the Lord, the tribulation. Second notice in verse 1 and 2 they were concerned, unsettled or alarmed by some prophecy, report or letter supposed to have come from Paul saying that the rapture and (the tribulation) "<u>the day of the Lord had already come</u>". You can see how this would confuse them if Paul taught a pre-trib rapture for we see in Paul's first letter that he taught on the rapture and offered them great hope of escaping God's wrath. With verse 3 he tells them not to let anyone deceive them in any way. You see again that he connected the day of the Lord with the Rapture, the Rapture first then the day of the Lord, the tribulation.

Let's take a look at a statement in chapter 1 of 1 Thessalonians where Paul refers to the 2nd coming.

> 1 Thes. 1: 6God is just: He will pay back trouble to those who trouble you 7and give relief to you who are troubled, and to us as well. This will happen when the Lord Jesus is revealed from heaven in blazing fire with his powerful angels. 8He will punish those who do not know God and do not obey the gospel of our Lord Jesus. 9They will be punished with everlasting destruction and shut out from the presence of the Lord and from the majesty of his power 10on the day he comes to be glorified in his holy people and to be marveled at among all those who have believed. This includes you, because you believed our testimony to you.

This is clearly referring to the day of Jesus' second coming when he returns back down to the earth. You see he is revealed with blazing fire and his powerful angels. So he is seen returning. There's no mention of our being gathered together to him or the day of the Lord. Also we see no mention of angels with the rapture. Look again at how he starts 2 Thessalonians chapter 2.

> 2TH 2:1 Concerning the coming of our Lord Jesus Christ and our being gathered to him, we ask you, brothers, 2 not to become easily unsettled or alarmed by some prophecy, report or letter supposed to have come from us, saying that (the tribulation has already come) the day of the Lord has already come.

You can see the subject of the 2nd coming stopped in chapter 1 and now he starts this subject of the rapture and the day of the Lord. You can see here that Paul has the rapture, our being gathered to Jesus in verse 1 before the tribulation, the day of the Lord in verse 2. So what were they concerned about? With Jesus saying in Matthew that his second coming would be like lighting that flashes and lights up the whole sky, that everyone will see him return down to the earth, the only thing they could have been concerned about is missing the rapture or there not being a rapture and that they were in the tribulation. **If Paul taught a post-trib rapture they wouldn't have been concerned, they would have expected to go through the tribulation.** So what could they have been concerned about if it wasn't missing the rapture and being in the tribulation.

Their concern was that the day of the Lord, the tribulation had already started and that the rapture had already occurred. All this started with a false report or letter. With seeing that Paul placed the rapture before the tribulation and they were concerned that they were in the tribulation, this shows that Paul could not have taught that the rapture occurs with the 2nd coming. Now, with verse 3 Paul explains how the tribulation will begin.

> 3 Don't let anyone deceive you in any way, <u>for that day</u> (the tribulation) will not come until the rebellion (falling away) occurs and the man of lawlessness is revealed, the man doomed to destruction.

We see that what Paul is referring to cannot come until a falling away occurs and the man of lawlessness is revealed first. Notice again how he started with referencing the rapture first, (the coming of our Lord Jesus Christ and our being gathered to him) then goes into the day of the Lord, the tribulation. Again, if Paul had taught them a post-trib or mid-trip rapture then they wouldn't have been concerned that they were in the tribulation, they would have expected it, but if Paul taught a pre-trib rapture then they would have been concerned if they were in the tribulation, for that would mean that they missed it, they were not raptured. We see that Paul has the rapture before the revealing of the anti-Chirst and that the tribulation, the day of the Lord cannot start until after the anti-Christ is revealed. I believe the anti-Christ is revealed with the first seal in Revelation, with the signing of the peace agreement with Israel and the Islamic nations, but we know for sure he is revealed to the Jews in the middle of the tribulation when he (Satan) enters into the Temple and claims to be God, the abomination of desolation, Matthew 24, Daniel 9 and Revelation 12. So a post-trib view would require the revealing of the anti-Christ to have to take place before the rapture, but Paul said the day of the Lord cannot occur until the anti-Christ is revealed first and the rapture must take place before the wrath of God. This is true for the pre-wrath view also, for the anti-Christ would be revealed before the rapture.

Paul said the rapture must occur before the day of the Lord, before the revealing of the anti-Christ, before the wrath of God begins.

Read verse 1 thru 3 again,

> 1 Concerning the coming of our Lord Jesus Christ and our being gathered to him, we ask you, brothers, 2 not to become easily unsettled or alarmed by some prophecy, report or letter supposed to have come from us, saying that (the tribulation has already come) the day of the Lord has already come. 3 don't let anyone deceive you in any way, for that day (the tribulation) will not come until the rebellion (falling away) occurs and the man of lawlessness is revealed, the man doomed to destruction.

The anti-Christ will be revealed before the tribulation. This actually starts the 7 years of the tribulation. Again, we see that Paul has the rapture before the tribulation.

Look again at what we read in 1 Thessalonians chapters 4 and 5.

> 1 Thes. 4:13Brothers, we do not want you to be ignorant about those who fall asleep, or to grieve like the rest of men, who have no hope. 14We believe that Jesus died and rose again and so we believe that God will bring with Jesus those who have fallen asleep in him. 15According to the Lord's own word, we tell you that we who are still alive, who are left till the coming of the Lord, will certainly not precede those who have fallen asleep. 16For the Lord himself will come down from heaven, with a loud command, with the voice of the archangel and with the trumpet call of God, and the dead in Christ will rise first. 17After that, we who are still alive and are left will be caught up together with them in the clouds to meet the Lord in the air.

And so we will be with the Lord forever. 18Therefore encourage each other with these words.

1 Thes. 5: 1Now, brothers, about times and dates we do not need to write to you, 2for you know very well that the day of the Lord will come like a thief in the night. 3While people are saying, "Peace and safety," destruction will come on them suddenly, as labor pains on a pregnant woman, and they will not escape. 9For God did not appoint us to suffer wrath but to receive salvation through our Lord Jesus Christ.

Furthermore, if Jesus was taking us up only to make a big U turn back, why would he have to take us up in the first place.

You couldn't say that he takes us up to protect us from his coming. We won't need to be protected from Jesus' return. We see in Rev. 19 that those that are gathered there against him are destroyed by the word of his mouth. There is no battle. I think that Jesus would be perfectly capable of not allowing his word to destroy the righteous. And remember, we've already read that Jesus said in John chapter 14 when he returns for his Church, his bride he was going to take us back to the Father's house. When he returns at his second coming he is not going back to heaven but coming down to the earth.

The order in which Paul has these statements will not fit with the rapture occurring at the 2nd coming. To say that the 'day of the Lord' is referring to the day of his second coming just doesn't work.

Paul said that the tribulation would not come until after the rebellion (falling away) and the man of lawlessness is revealed, the anti-Christ. The anti-Christ is revealed with the first seal of the scroll in Revelation chapter 6. So even with the mid-trib view the anti-Christ is revealed 3 ½ years before their rapture would occur. You just can't get away from the fact that the tribulation cannot start until after the anti-Christ is revealed which starts the wrath of God and the rapture must take place before the wrath of God.

The anti-Christ will be revealed after the Rapture has taken place, the beginning of the tribulation starts with the signing of the covenant with Israel. This starts the 7-year count down. Daniel said this period of time will be 7 years, not 3 ½ years.

So again, why would they have been so concerned if they were taught any view other than a pre-trib view?

The only explanation that makes since is that Paul taught Jesus' coming for the Church, the rapture, would occur before the tribulation, before the day of the Lord. And as we have seen, the day of the Lord is the whole 7 years.

The mid-trib view says he will be revealed at the middle of the tribulation when he sets himself up in the temple, so with that they use this verse also for their rapture view. But those that are saved after the opening of the first seal, after the signing of the covenant between the anti-Christ and Israel, those that have studied the scriptures, or those studying them after a pre-trib rapture will know who he is. Just think, if any of us were here when this treaty is signed, we would know that this man who is head of the new one world government which will be the Revived Roman Empire, especially if the world has already been divided up into 10 regions as we see from Daniel and the book of Revelation, we would know he is the one the bible calls the man of sin, the anti-Christ. And I'm sure there will be other things that he does that will lead people who know the scriptures to suspect him before he brings about the peace agreement between Israel and the Islamic nations. Remember, we don't know how long it will be between the rapture and the signing of this agreement. President Clinton tried to get a 7 year peace treaty signed between Israel and the Palestinians but it did not take place. God will allow only the man who will be the anti-Christ to bring about this 7 year agreement.

Paul also said before the man of sin is revealed there would be a "rebellion" (apostasy, a falling away). The tribulation, the day of the Lord will not start until both the apostasy and the man of sin is revealed.

So this falling away from the faith cannot be referring to the first half of the tribulation. Paul said the tribulation would not begin until FIRST there is a falling away and then the revealing of the anti-Christ. So we see there will be a falling away before the start of the tribulation. The word apostasy is from the Greek word apostisia, which means a falling away, forsaking, a defection from the truth. We can see this occurring now in the world and in many denominations. Not only can we see the world forsaking God and the truth we can even see a forsaking of the truth in some Churches. Not only in the world but there are those that claim to be Christians that don't believe that Jesus is the only begotten Son of God, that he is God in the flesh, that he was born of a virgin or that he literally rose from the dead, or that the bible is the infallible word of God. There are some that don't believe there's a hell or that Satan still exists when there is so much even in the New Testament. There are many other truths of the bible that are being forsaken; there is a clear defection from the truth, NOW. I'm sure there will be a greater falling away from the truth of the bible and Jesus in the world after the rapture. Thankfully there will be those that come to believe the truth about Jesus after the rapture. We also see a growing tolerance of sin in the world and among many denominations and it's only going to get worse. Jesus said that before the tribulation started that it would be like it was during the days of Noah. Matthew 24. Paul said this would happen before the anti-Christ is revealed and before the tribulation begins. We see the Apostate Church in Revelation chapter 3 occurs before the opening of the seals of the scroll, we see the Apostate Church exists before the revealing of the anti-Christ.

So there has to be a rebellion, a defection from the faith and truth AND the man of lawlessness, the anti-Christ must be revealed first before the tribulation can start. The anti-Christ will be revealed when he signs the 7-year covenant agreement with Israel and the Islamic nations. We see the revealing of the anti-Christ with the first seal in Revelation Chapter 6. With this starting the tribulation, the wrath of God, the rapture must take place sometime before the revealing of the anti-Christ.

Notice again the order in which he said all this. He first started with the Rapture, verse 1 'Concerning the coming of our Lord Jesus Christ and our being gathered to him'. With verse 3 he told them not to be deceived, that the day of the Lord, the tribulation will not come until the rebellion occurs and the man of lawlessness is revealed, the man doomed to destruction'. **That day in verse 3 is referring back to verse 2,** the tribulation (saying that the day of the Lord has already come), not to verse one, the rapture (the coming of our Lord Jesus Christ and our being gathered to him). If Paul had the rapture in mind in verse 2 and 3 it would have been clearer to say our being gathered to him again, but he uses two different statements.

Let's exchange the words Rapture and the Tribulation in the verse's.

1Concerning the Rapture, we ask you, brothers, 2not to become easily unsettled or alarmed by some prophecy, report or letter supposed to have come from us, saying that the tribulation has already come. 3Don't let anyone deceive you in any way, for (the tribulation will not come) until the rebellion occurs and the man of lawlessness is revealed, the man doomed to destruction.

Paul used two separate statements, (the coming of our Lord Jesus Christ and our being gathered to him) and (the day of the Lord) showing he had two separate events in mind.

The anti-Christ will not be revealed until after the rapture. Paul will make this clearer starting with verse 6. Paul mentions one more thing that must happen before the revealing of the anti-Christ, the man of sin that clears it all up.

6 And now you know what is holding him back, so that he may be revealed at the proper time.7 For the secret power of lawlessness is already at work; but the one who now holds it back will continue to do so till he is taken out of the way. 8 And then the lawless one will be revealed, whom the Lord Jesus will overthrow with the breath of his mouth and destroy by the splendor of his coming.

The anti-Christ cannot be revealed until this 'he' the restrainer is removed.

Notice Paul said that the secret power of lawlessness is already at work. John in one of his letters said this also.

> 1 John 4: 2This is how you can recognize the Spirit of God: Every spirit that acknowledges that Jesus Christ has come in the flesh is from God, 3but every spirit that does not acknowledge Jesus is not from God. This is the spirit of the antichrist, which you have heard is coming and even now is already in the world.

So someone has to be removed, taken out of the way before the anti-Christ can be revealed. Remember in verse 3 Paul said that the day of the Lord, the tribulation would not come until the revealing of the anti-Christ.

> 2 Thes 2: 3Don't let anyone deceive you in any way, for (that day will not come) until the rebellion (apostasy) occurs <u>and the man of lawlessness is revealed,</u>

The Removal of the one who is holding him (the anti-Christ) back.

In verse 7 we are told that there is someone that is now preventing the revealing of the man of sin, the anti-Christ, that the man of sin will not be revealed until this (He) someone is taken away. It seems very probable that this "someone" is the Holy Spirit as He indwells individual members of the Church.

So it would appear to me that the one who is holding the revealing of the anti-Christ back is actually the Church. The "he" in 2 Thessalonians 2 verse 7. This would clear the way for a worldwide deception thus the acceptance of the anti-Christ.

The 'He' cannot be the Holy Spirit as a whole for He is still present during the tribulation for no one can be saved apart from the Holy Spirit. The Holy Spirit was present during the Old Covenant. It's the Holy Spirit of the New Covenant that is removed with the Church.

The 'He', this someone cannot be referring to any government as some believe or to Satan for Satan certainly wouldn't hold himself back. It doesn't make since but there are some that say it is government that is holding him back. Just which government is now or will be holding back sin or Satan. Even our own government is allowing more and more sin and falling for Satan's deceptions.

Notice that Paul says 'the one who' holds him back will do so till 'He' is taken out of the way. This could not be referring to a government or any natural earthly power. His reference is in a form of a person, in the singular, who and He. The anti-Christ will actually control the new one-world government of the finial years before Jesus returns.

This one holding the anti-Christ back could not be any one man for even the angel Gabriel could not stand up against the power of Satan alone. But the power of the Holy Spirit in the Church is greater than anything Satan could come up with. Jesus said concerning the Church,

> Matthew 16:18 And I say also unto thee, That thou art Peter, and upon this rock I will build my church; and the gates of hell shall not prevail against it. (King James).

> 1 John 4: 4 You are of God, little children, and have overcome them, because **He** who is in you is greater than he who is in the world.

Here's another point that the Church cannot be present during the tribulation, in the book of Revelation you see that the gates of hell are prevailing against the saints. Rev. 13: 7He was given power to make war against the saints and to conquer them. These saints then cannot be a part of the Church. These saints in the book of Revelation are just like saints during the Old Testament times.

The word saint is found in the Old Testament but the Church was not born until the day of Pentecost. These saints of the Old Testament were not part of the Church. The saints of the tribulation are not part of the Church. The tribulation is Daniels last week that was allotted to Israel, Daniel's people, the Jews, see Daniel 9.

Since the Holy Spirit is still present during the tribulation the one that is holding back the revealing of the anti-Christ has to be the Church, all the true Christians in the Church. It's only Christians that speak out against sin in the world. The world already looks at Christians that speak out against such things as a bunch of radicals and troublemakers that should just keep their mouths shut.

1Cor. 3:16 Don't you know that you yourselves are God's temple and that **God's Spirit lives in you?**

1Cor. 6:19 Do you not know that your body is a temple of the **Holy Spirit, who is in you**, whom you have received from God? You are not your own;

This is the Holy Spirit of the New Covenant, of the Church age. The Holy Spirit was present during the Old Testament but not in the fullness he is now. He did not indwell them then like he does us now. You see in Acts one and two that the Holy Spirit was given on the day of Pentecost. This was the start of the Church. In the Gospels Jesus told the disciples that they were to receive the Holy Spirit later.

John 14: 25"All this I have spoken while still with you. 26But the Counselor, the Holy Spirit, whom the Father will send in my name, will teach you all things and will remind you of everything I have said to you.

But the Holy Spirit was already present. Jesus was referring to the new ministry of the new covenant of the Holy Spirit, the indwelling of believers by the Holy Spirit. Now we have the fullness of the Father and <u>Son</u> in the Holy Spirit.

It's now the Church, Jesus in the Church that is holding back the revealing of the anti-Christ. The Church is probably holding back more right now than we realize.

The Church is the body of Christ, Christ to the world.

2Cor. 5:17 Therefore, if anyone is in Christ, he is a new creation; the old has gone, the new has come! 18 All this is from God, who reconciled us to himself through Christ and gave us the ministry of reconciliation: 19 that God was reconciling the world to himself in Christ, not counting men's sins against them. And he has committed to us the message of reconciliation. 20 **We are therefore Christ's ambassadors, as though God were making his appeal through us**. We implore you on Christ's behalf: Be reconciled to God. 21 God made him who had no sin to be sin for us, so that in him we might become the righteousness of God.

Gal. 2:20 I have been crucified with Christ and I no longer live, **but Christ lives in me**. The life I live in the body, I live by faith in the Son of God, who loved me and gave himself for me.

1 John 4:17 In this way, love is made complete among us so that we will have confidence on the day of judgment, **because in this world we are like him**.

Eph. 2:22 And God placed all things under his feet and appointed him to be head over everything for the church, 23 **which is his body**, the fullness of him who fills everything in every way.

1Cor. 12:27 Now you are the **body of Christ**, and each one of you is a part of it.

1Cor. 2:16 "For who has known the mind of the Lord that he may instruct him?" But we have the **mind of Christ**.

Col. 1:18 And he is the head of the body, **the church**;

Col. 1:24 Now I rejoice in what was suffered for you, and I fill up in my flesh what is still lacking in regard to Christ's afflictions, for the sake of his body, **which is the church**.

We, the Church are the body of Christ.

Eph.1:19 and his incomparably great power for us who believe. That power is like the working of his mighty strength, 20 which he exerted in Christ when he raised him from the dead and seated him at his right hand in the heavenly realms, 21 far above all rule and authority, power and dominion, and every title that can be given, not only in the present age but also in the one to come. 22 And God placed all things under his feet and appointed him to be head over everything for the church, 23 **which is his body**, the fullness of him who fills everything in every way.

Eph.3:10 His intent was that now, **through the church**, the manifold wisdom of God should be made known to the rulers and authorities in the heavenly realms, 11 according to his eternal purpose which he accomplished in Christ Jesus our Lord.

Eph. 3:20 Now to him who is able to do immeasurably more than all we ask or imagine, **according to his power that is at work within us**, 21 to him be glory in the church and in Christ Jesus throughout all generations, for ever and ever! Amen.

Eph.5:23 For the husband is the head of the wife as Christ is the head of the church, **his body**, of which he is the Savior.

Col.1:18 And **he is the head of the body, the church**; he is the beginning and the firstborn from among the dead, so that in everything he might have the supremacy.

Col. 1:24 Now I rejoice in what was suffered for you, and I fill up in my flesh what is still lacking in regard to Christ's afflictions, **for the sake of his body, which is the church**. 25 I have become its servant by the commission God gave me to present to you the word of God in its fullness-- 26 the mystery that has been kept hidden for ages and generations, but is now disclosed to the saints. 27 To them God has chosen to make known among the Gentiles **the glorious riches of this mystery, which is Christ in you, the hope of glory.**

1Cor.10:15 I speak to sensible people; judge for yourselves what I say. 16 Is not the cup of thanksgiving for which we give thanks a participation in the blood of Christ? And is not the bread that we break a **participation in the body of Christ?** 17 Because there is one loaf, we, who are many, **are one body**, for we all partake of the one loaf.

Rom.12:5 **so in Christ we who are many form one body**, and each member belongs to all the others.

Eph. 5:30 **for we are members of his body.**

Eph. 5:31 "For this reason a man will leave his father and mother and be united to his wife, and the two will become one flesh." 32 This is a profound mystery--but I am talking about Christ and the church.

We see someone who is holding back the revealing of the anti-Christ has to be removed before the anti-Christ can be revealed thus starting the day of the Lord, the tribulation. So what we have just seen is that the Church has to be removed, taken out of the way before the anti-Christ can be revealed. With the tribulation starting with the revealing of the anti-Christ, after the man of lawlessness has been revealed and the Church being removed before the revealing of the anti-Christ, Paul didn't teach any other view other than a pre-trib one.

With the Church now being Jesus to the world, the 'he' that is now holding back the revealing of the anti-Christ, it would make a pre-tribulation view of the rapture the only view that Paul could have taught. A pre-trib rapture is the only one that can work out with all of the above conditions. Only a pre-trib view can work with the rapture occurring at an unknown time with the removal of the one, (The Church) that is holding back the revealing of the anti-Christ thus starting the day of the Lord, the time of God's Wrath. We see the tribulation, the judgments of God start with the first seal in Rev. chapter 6, which is the revealing of the anti-Christ.

> Rev. 6: 1I watched as the Lamb opened the first of the seven seals. Then I heard one of the four living creatures say in a voice like thunder, "Come!" 2I looked, and there before me was a white horse! Its rider held a bow, and he was given a crown, and he rode out as a conqueror bent on conquest.

Those of the other rapture views say that the wrath of God does not start with the first seal in Revelation chapter 6. If the releasing of the worst dictator the world has ever seen is not the wrath of God on a Christ rejecting world I don't know what could be. Look again at how Paul describes him.

> 2 Thes. 2: 9 The coming of the lawless one will be in accordance with the work of Satan displayed in all kinds of counterfeit miracles, signs and wonders, 10 and in every sort of evil that deceives those who are perishing. They perish because they refused to love the truth and so be saved. 11 <u>For this reason God sends them a powerful delusion</u> so that they will believe the lie 12 and so that all will be condemned who have not believed the truth but have delighted in wickedness.

The counterfeit miracles, signs and wonders will be occurring during the first 3 and half years of the tribulation to deceive those that refuse to believe the truth. But it is very probable that these counterfeit miracles, signs and wonders will start after the rapture, before the anti-Christ and the Islamic nations sign the peace agreement with Israel. All those that know the scriptures will know he is the anti-Christ, the man of lawlessness when he signs that peace agreement.

Did you notice verse 11, God sends this man of sin, the anti-Christ. You see this also in the book of Revelation. It is Jesus that takes the scroll from the Father and is opening the seals, not Satan. See Revelation chapter 5 and 6.

Jesus receives the scroll from God the Father and then he proceeds to open it. So everything from the first seal to the last bowl judgment is from God.

Read verse one thru three this way again.

> 2TH 2:1 Concerning the (Rapture), we ask you, brothers, 2 not to become easily unsettled or alarmed by some prophecy, report or letter supposed to have come from us, saying that (the tribulation has already come). 3 Don't let anyone deceive you in any way, for (the tribulation) will not come until the rebellion (falling away) occurs and (the anti-Christ) the man of lawlessness is revealed, the man doomed to destruction.

Remember, the New Testament was written in Greek. They didn't have the word 'Rapture' for Paul to use. Nor did they use the word Tribulation. These words are English translations that came along later by the Church as terms to describe these two events. The Rapture is the "gathering together of the believers in Christ". The "Day of the Lord" is the tribulation.

When you start putting all the scriptures together they point to a pre-tribulation rapture of the Church.

Jesus will catch the Church up before the tribulation, before the Judgments starts. The Church is judged before the tribulation starts, you see this in Rev. chapters 1 through 3. The Church is being judged now. Judgment starts with the house of God.

> 1 Peter 4:17 For it is time for judgment to begin with the family of God; and if it begins with us, what will the outcome be for those who do not obey the gospel of God?

What we see in the first three chapters of the book of Revelation is the Church being judged, which is taking place now, but, it is not the wrath of God as are the judgments of the seals, trumpets and bowls.

I will go into this further later, but I would like to point this out now. Look at how many times the Church is mentioned in the first 3 chapters of the book of Revelation. But there is not another mention of the word Church after the 3rd chapter; there is no mention of the Church all through the tribulation.

To me it is just too much here that suggests that Paul had taught a pre-trib rapture of the Church.

Again, The day of the Lord, the tribulation will not start until the anti-Christ has been revealed and he will not be revealed until the Church is taken out of the way. The revealing of the anti-Christ, when he signs the covenant with Israel will start Israel's last 7 years, Daniel's 70th week. This will start God's prophetic stopwatch. We don't know how much time there will be between the rapture and the anti-Christ bringing about this peace agreement. But the rapture has to occur before they sign this agreement.

We see that the anti-Christ will not be revealed until "He", Jesus has been taken out of the way. The Church is now Jesus to the world. The influence of Jesus, the influence of the Holy Spirit will be taken away when the Church is taken up. The anti-Christ will be revealed after the rapture. The day of the Lord, the tribulation cannot start until all this has happened first.

The evidence points to the day of the Lord, the tribulation being the whole 7 years and the rapture occurring before the tribulation.

With being able to see a falling away from the truth of the bible occurring now and with the rapture taking place before the revealing of the anti-Christ, just how close could we be to the coming of the Lord for the Church.

3. The Last Trumpet in First Corinthians Chapter 15

While this is not part of 1 or 2 Thessalonians it does have to do with the Rapture so I would like to address this now.

> 1CO 15:51 Listen, I tell you a mystery: We will not all sleep, but we will all be changed-- 52 in a flash, in the twinkling of an eye, at the last trumpet. For the trumpet will sound, the dead will be raised imperishable, and we will be changed. 53 For the perishable must clothe itself with the imperishable, and the mortal with immortality. 54 When the perishable has been clothed with the imperishable, and the mortal with immortality, then the saying that is written will come true: "Death has been swallowed up in victory."

Because Paul, in 1 Thes 4:16, said believers would be raptured at the sounding of a trumpet and in 1 Cor. 15:52 he said at the last trumpet many folks have tried to make it appear that the rapture trumpet is the same as the 7th trumpet found in Revelation 11:15-18.

When Paul was writing to the Corinthians, he specifically said "the" last trumpet but he was not referring to the 7th trumpet in the book of Revelation. During the Feast of Trumpets, the Jews blew short trumpet blasts. They would end the feast with a long blast from what is called the last trumpet, which is blown the longest. Judaism has traditionally connected this last trumpet sounding with the resurrection of the dead. Paul also made the connection. For at the rapture the dead in Christ rise first, then those that are alive will be caught up together with those that have just been raised from the dead to meet the Lord in the air. For many Christians, the association between the rapture and the Feast of Trumpets is so strong; they look for the rapture to occur on this feast. See Leviticus 23. But if you jump ahead to Lev. Chapter 25 verse 9 you will see there's another trumpet being blown on the Day of Atonement.

1TH 4:16 For the Lord himself will come down from heaven, with a loud command, with the voice of the archangel and **with the trumpet call of God**, <u>and the dead in Christ will rise first</u>.

Here Paul just referred to it as the trumpet call.

Throughout the Bible there are a number of trumpets being blown for different reasons. For example in Numbers 10 there are trumpets being used in order to give commands to the people of Israel. A trumpet is used to assemble the people for their journey and another trumpet that signals the start of their journey. There were trumpet sounds that would tell the people to stop and another sound telling them to assemble. Depending upon whether the people were moving or getting ready to move, the trumpet would signal them to move or if moving, a trumpet sound would tell them when to stop. So depending on what the purpose was, we see there was more than one "last trumpet." Also notice with Numbers 10 verse 10 it mentions the blowing of trumpets at the different feasts and New Moon festivals.

> Numbers 10: 1 The LORD said to Moses: 2 "Make two trumpets of hammered silver, and use them for calling the community together and for having the camps set out. 3 When both are sounded, the whole community is to assemble before you at the entrance to the Tent of Meeting. 4 If only one is sounded, the leaders—the heads of the clans of Israel—are to assemble before you. 5 When a trumpet blast is sounded, the tribes camping on the east are to set out. 6 At the sounding of a second blast, the camps on the south are to set out. The blast will be the signal for setting out. 7 To gather the assembly, blow the trumpets, but not with the same signal.

> 10 Also at your times of rejoicing—your appointed feasts and New Moon festivals—you are to sound the trumpets over your burnt offerings and fellowship offerings, and they will be a memorial for you before your God. I am the LORD your God."

The last trumpet was the last for which it was associated. The trumpet Paul mentions is the last one for the Church Age. For the Church Age ends with the Rapture. That's why there is no mention of the Church during the tribulation.

You can find many different trumpets throughout the Old Testament. We see Trumpets were often used to assemble the people, to call them together. It will be the same with the Rapture.

In Rev.19 where Jesus is returning there is no mention of a trumpet. In Rev. 11 where it is telling of the 7th trumpet there's not any mention of a resurrection, a gathering or Jesus coming. What you have next are the judgments in Rev. 16, the 7 bowls.

The book of Revelation is laid out in a sequence of events most of which are the results of previous events. They all are part of the scroll you see Jesus opening in Rev. 5. So the last trumpet Paul refers to in 1 Cor.15 is not the 7th trumpet of the book of Revelation. It's just what Paul used to describe how it will be at the rapture not when the rapture would occur.

There seem to be a number of observations that make it impossible for these two trumpets to be the same.

The trumpet of 1 Corinthians 15:52 sounds before the wrath of God descends, while, the chronology of the book of Revelation indicates that the trumpet in Revelation 11:15 sounds toward the end of the time of wrath. In 1 Thessalonians 4 the voice associated with the sounding of the trumpet summons the dead and the living and consequently is heard before the resurrection. In the book of Revelation, while a resurrection is mentioned (11:12) of the two witnesses, the trumpet does not sound until after the resurrection, showing us that two different events must be in view. In 1 Thessalonians the trumpet issues in blessing, while the trumpet in Revelation issues in the finial judgments upon the Christ rejecting world.

A Look at First and Second Thessalonians

The trumpet in 1 Thessalonians is distinctly for the church. Since in the book of Revelation, God is dealing with Israel in particular and Gentiles in general, this seventh trumpet, which falls in the period of the tribulation, could not have reference to the church without losing the distinctions between the church and Israel.

Events at the Rapture are - "In the twinkling of an eye"

Events at the 7th trumpet could take several days, weeks or longer

Result at the Rapture is joy and transformation

Result of the 7th trumpet is "the third woe" (Revelation 11:14) The 7 last plagues

The Rapture is the resurrection of the dead in Christ and those alive in Christ taken up to heaven

The 7th trumpet – no resurrection, no translation of those in Christ mentioned

And this is probably the most important point to whether Paul was referring to the 7th trumpet in the book of Revelation. Paul wrote his letter to the Corinthians in the year 55 a.d. John received the revelation and wrote the book of Revelation in 95 a.d. So Paul wrote this letter some 40 years before John wrote the book of Revelation. So Paul couldn't have been referring to the 7th trumpet in the book of Revelation. The revelation of the trumpets was given to John.

While at first glance it is easy to associate the phrase 'last trumpet' with the 7th trumpet in Revelation being it is the last trumpet, when you compare them you see they cannot be the same. The last trumpet in 1 Corinthians 15 cannot be the 7th trumpet in Revelation.

Conclusion

The contexts of 1 Corinthians 15:52 and that of Revelation 11 are totally different from one another. About the only similarity between the two is that the word "trumpet" is used in both. The respective contexts are totally different. In 1 Corinthians 15:52, there is the context of things related to the church age, while Revelation 11 speaks of judgment during the tribulation.

The last trumpet in 1 Corinthians 15:52 is the final command that Christ gives to His church which sounds the signal to gather us together to meet in the sky and return with him to heaven, to the Father's house.

Chapter Five

The Prophecies in Matthew 24 and 25

1. A STUDY OF MATTHEW 24 Part I

Matthew 24 is considered to be the foundation of end-time prophecy. The link that bridges the Old Testament and the New Testament prophecies together especially Daniel and the Book of Revelation. It is commonly referred to as the Sermon on the Mount. Mark in chapter 13 and Luke in chapter 21 both record Jesus' Sermon on the Mount but Matthew goes into more detail. Jesus goes into great detail concerning the last 7 years allotted to Israel which has now come to be called by the Church the tribulation.

One of the debates over Matthew is the Rapture mentioned in Jesus' Sermon on the Mount. I'll address this when we get to it. With Matthew and the corresponding scriptures in Mark and Luke we will begin to look at the end time prophecies made by Jesus. Where Matthew has the teaching from the Sermon on the Mount in chapters 24 and 25, Luke appears to have it spread out in chapters 12, 17 and 21. I'll reference Luke as well as Mark as we go. Let's now take a look at Matthew 24. I'll start with verse one.

> **MT 24:**1 Jesus left the temple and was walking away when his disciples came up to him to call his attention to its buildings. 2 "Do you see all these things?" he asked. "I tell you the truth, not one stone here will be left on another; every one will be thrown down."

> **MT 24:**3 As Jesus was sitting on the Mount of Olives, the disciples came to him privately. "Tell us," they said, "when will this happen, and what will be the sign of your coming and of the end of the age?"

From the disciple's questions after Jesus' statement about the destruction of the Temple, it would seem that they expected this to happen at the end of the age when Jesus would set up the kingdom, for the first question is connected to the second. They all were hoping that Jesus would be establishing his kingdom soon.

The disciples asked him two questions, "when will this happen, and what will be the sign of your coming and of the end of the age?" Some break this out into three questions. I see it as do other writers I've read as two questions since the disciples would know from the Old Testament Scriptures that the Messiah's coming would mark the end of the age and bring in the Kingdom of God. Mark and Luke only have it as two questions. I don't think it really matters whether it's two or three questions. Jesus addresses both his second coming and the end of the age.

But in verse 4 Jesus doesn't answer the question about there not being one stone left on another, the destruction of the temple that occurred in 70 a.d. and doesn't seem to in the whole Sermon. However, He goes right into addressing their 2nd question, the time during the tribulation, Daniels 70th week.

Although I see it as a reference to the still future time during the tribulation, it could be that Luke has Jesus answering the 70 a.d. destruction in Luke 21.

> Luke 21:20"When you see Jerusalem being surrounded by armies, you will know that its desolation is near. 21Then let those who are in Judea flee to the mountains, let those in the city get out, and let those in the country not enter the city. 22For this is the time of punishment in fulfillment of all that has been written. 23How dreadful it will be in those days for pregnant women and nursing mothers! There will be great distress in the land and wrath against this people. 24They will fall by the sword and will be taken as prisoners to all the nations. Jerusalem will be trampled on by the Gentiles until the times of the Gentiles are fulfilled.

As you will see in a second, with the exception of verse 20 and 24 Luke has the same statements as Matthew, which are clearly referring to the mid-point of the tribulation. It could be that Luke has a dual purpose in his writing and is addressing both the 70 A.D. destruction and the tribulation, as prophecy many times does.

109

Jesus' prophecy concerning the Temple being destroyed in verse 2 came to pass in 70 A.D. when the Romans destroyed the Temple and Jerusalem. Millions of Jews were killed and the other's had to flee to other nations. Jesus had just addressed this. You see this in Chapter 23. Maybe this is why Matthew doesn't address it here in chapter 24.

> MT. 23:33"You snakes! You brood of vipers! How will you escape being condemned to hell? 34Therefore I am sending you prophets and wise men and teachers. Some of them you will kill and crucify; others you will flog in your synagogues and pursue from town to town. 35And so upon you will come all the righteous blood that has been shed on earth, from the blood of righteous Abel to the blood of Zechariah son of Berekiah, whom you murdered between the temple and the altar. 36I tell you the truth, all this will come upon this generation.

You see in verse 36 he said all this, all that he had just told them will come upon them, this generation. Verses 34 thru 36 definitely could apply to the time leading up to the destruction that occurred in 70 a.d.

> MT. 23:37"O Jerusalem, Jerusalem, you who kill the prophets and stone those sent to you, how often I have longed to gather your children together, as a hen gathers her chicks under her wings, but you were not willing. **38Look, your house is left to you desolate.** <u>39For I tell you, you will not see me again until</u> you say, 'Blessed is he who comes in the name of the Lord.

In verse 38 he tells them their house, Jerusalem and the temple will be left to them desolate. This did happen in 70 a.d. With verse 39 he is qualifying the condition of his second coming. It will not happen until Israel accepts him as the Messiah.

Here in Matthew 24 Jesus doesn't seem to address the question of when one stone will not be left on another but the question what will be the sign of your coming and of the end of the age. He goes right to describing the tribulation for it will be the judgment of the tribulation that will bring Israel to the realization that Jesus is the Messiah. You will see this later in his sermon here in Matthew 24. But it could be that Jesus connected the destruction of the temple with the judgment that will occur during the tribulation. Israel would seem to be under judgment ever since they rejected Jesus. Just consider the Nazi concentration camps during World War II. Also notice from Jesus here in Matthew and in the book of Revelation that there will be a third temple built that will be present during the tribulation. We see also in Ezekiel chapter 40 that there will be a temple in Jerusalem during the 1000 year reign of Jesus.

What follows in Matthew 24 are the signs during the tribulation that lead up to Jesus' 2nd coming. For as you will see, the things he describes did not occur during the first century and haven't happened any time in history. Something to take note of, all that Jesus describes here is addressed to the Jewish people. There wasn't a nation of Israel from the destruction by the Babylonians until May of 1948. So what Jesus predicts here couldn't come to pass without there being a nation of Israel and the Jews back in Jerusalem. With the prophecies here as well as the other prophecies that relate to the time just before Jesus returns back down to the earth, there had to be a nation of Israel and the Jews had to have control of the city of Jerusalem. With Israel becoming a nation again in 1948 and with the recapturing of Jerusalem in June 1967, it is a good indication that we are indeed living in the last days, just how close to the beginning of the tribulation we don't know, but with all that is occurring in our world today that is falling in place with bible prophecy, as you will discover in this book, makes one wonder, could it be closer than we actually think. With verse 4 we begin the description of the signs that will lead up to the 2nd coming of Jesus.

> **Mt. 24**: 4Jesus answered: "Watch out that no one deceives you. 5For many will come in my name, claiming, 'I am the Christ, and will deceive many. 6You will hear of wars and rumors of wars, but see to it that you are not alarmed. Such things must happen, but the end is still to come. 7Nation will rise against nation, and kingdom against kingdom. There will be famines

and earthquakes in various places. 8All these are the beginning of birth pains. 9"Then you will be handed over to be persecuted and put to death, and you will be hated by all nations because of me. 10At that time many will turn away from the faith and will betray and hate each other, 11and many false prophets will appear and deceive many people. 12Because of the increase of wickedness, the love of most will grow cold, 13but he who stands firm to the end will be saved. 14And this gospel of the kingdom will be preached in the whole world as a testimony to all nations, and <u>then the end will come</u>.

I believe verses 4 thru 14 Jesus is referring to things during the tribulation, but it sounds like this could have a broader application. Jesus could be describing how conditions will evolve thru history up to and during the tribulation. All the things that he described we can see how they have gotten more severe and more frequent, especially in recent years. Just like birth pains increase in intensity and frequency all these signs are increasing. This will also be true during the tribulation. We see this with the trumpet and bowl judgments in Revelation. We've already had men claiming to be Jesus or the Messiah. We've had wars and are still having wars and rumors of wars. We've had nation against nation, kingdom against kingdom or ethnic group against ethnic group. There have been famines and earthquakes. There is still massive famine all over the world and it's getting worse. We've had more earthquakes since the year 2000 than there has been from the 60's thru the 90's put together. Luke in chapter 21 includes pestilences as does the King James and New King James bible here in Matthew. Verse 7, For nation will rise against nation, and kingdom against kingdom. And there will be famines, pestilences, and earthquakes in various places. Sickness and disease has increased all over the world. There's been more new disease's that have arisen in recent years than any time in history and many that they don't have a cure and vaccine for. And there are more people now who don't believe there's a God and especially believe in Jesus than any time in history. I don't mean because there are more people on the earth. Percentage wise there's more. There have been many false prophets thru history. We are still reaping the effects from some of these false teachers and prophets. Sin and wickedness have greatly increased and love has grown cold. Verse 9 and 10 could apply to the Holocaust. And the most amazing statement from Jesus, this gospel of the kingdom will be preached in the whole world to all nations. No other time in history could this have been fulfilled until Satellite and Cable TV and of course, travel by airplane. And don't forget the Internet. All of these things are a clear indication that we are living in the last days. With the way things appear we might be really close to Jesus returning for the Church and the beginning of the tribulation. With all of these conditions already fulfilled and being fulfilled we should be able to recognize the time in which we live. We should not be blind or close our eyes like the Pharisees and most of the Jews did when Jesus was here the first time.

Look at Matthew 16,

> 1The Pharisees and Sadducees came to Jesus and tested him by asking him to show them a sign from heaven. 2He replied, "When evening comes, you say, 'It will be fair weather, for the sky is red,' 3and in the morning, 'Today it will be stormy, for the sky is red and overcast.' You know how to interpret the appearance of the sky, but you cannot interpret the signs of the times.

So verses 4 thru 14 could have two applications, one of Jesus referring to history from the destruction of Jerusalem in 70 a.d. to the rebirth of Israel in 1948 up to the beginning of the tribulation, and to the tribulation for it appears here in Matthew that Jesus was referring to the tribulation for all these things will be true of the first half of the tribulation. So it appears that verses 4 thru 14 could very easily apply both to history and the tribulation.

But I believe verses 4 thru 8 are ultimately referring to the first 3 ½ years of the tribulation. It appears that during the first half of the tribulation that there may be many claiming to be the Messiah. It's not until the mid-point of the tribulation when Satan indwells the anti-Christ that he persecutes the Jews, enters the temple and desecrates it and claims to be God. He jumps to the middle of the tribulation with

113

verses 9 thru 15 for it is clear that verse 15 occurs at the middle of the tribulation. We know this from Daniel chapter 9. I see verse 15 connected back to verse 9 for he starts verse 15 with "So" when you see standing in the holy place 'the abomination that causes desolation,' spoken of through the prophet Daniel—let the reader understand—

While we can see all these things that Jesus referred to occurring now and have been occurring throughout history, as I will show you here in our look at Matthew 24, I believe his ultimate message was for the time during the tribulation. Verse 13, but he who stands firm to the end will be saved, tends to suggest this for it is a reference to Jesus' 2nd coming. And of course no one entered the 2nd temple as Jesus just described and there hasn't been a temple since 70 a.d.

<u>This gospel of the kingdom will be preached in the whole world as a testimony to all nations.</u> During the Tribulation it will still be that Jesus is the only way to be saved but this gospel of the kingdom will be what Jesus just referred to, the signs, the things happening during the 7 years of the tribulation. It will be what the 2 witnesses and the 144,000 we see in the book of Revelation will be preaching. Again, there has never been a time in history that the message of the Gospel could be preached to the whole world until now.

Some teachers called Preterist like to say all this took place in 70 a.d. But before 70 a.d. no one came claiming to be the Christ. The conditions of verse's 4 thru 14 did not take place before the destruction of the Temple in 70 a.d. At 70 a.d Jews weren't saved, they were scattered, utterly destroyed as a nation. Even Christians living in the area had to flee. Preterist believe that Jesus returned in 70 a.d in the form of the Roman army. I don't mean any disrespect but just how in the world from all the scriptures that describe how Jesus will return can they come up with that. Acts 1 tells exactly how he will return.

> Acts 1: 9After he said this, he was taken up before their very eyes, and a cloud hid him from their sight. 10They were looking intently up into the sky as he was going, when suddenly two men dressed in white stood beside them. 11"Men of Galilee,"

they said, "why do you stand here looking into the sky? This same Jesus, who has been taken from you into heaven, **will come back in the same way you have seen him go into heaven."**

It can't get any plainer than that. Let's continue and compare Matthew with Mark and Luke.

Mark 13:

5Jesus said to them: "Watch out that no one deceives you. 6Many will come in my name, claiming, 'I am he,' and will deceive many. 7When you hear of wars and rumors of wars, do not be alarmed. Such things must happen, but the end is still to come. 8Nation will rise against nation, and kingdom against kingdom. There will be earthquakes in various places, and famines. These are the beginning of birth pains.

9"You must be on your guard. You will be handed over to the local councils and flogged in the synagogues. On account of me you will stand before governors and kings as witnesses to them. 10And the gospel must first be preached to all nations. 11Whenever you are arrested and brought to trial, do not worry beforehand about what to say. Just say whatever is given you at the time, for it is not you speaking, but the Holy Spirit.

12"Brother will betray brother to death, and a father his child. Children will rebel against their parents and have them put to death. 13All men will hate you because of me, but he who stands firm to the end will be saved.

Again, this sounds more like what will occur during the tribulation than it does of the first century leading up to 70 a.d. especially verse 9 thru 13. None of this happened leading up to the 70 a.d. destruction or since.

Luke 21:

> 8He replied: "Watch out that you are not deceived. For many will come in my name, claiming, 'I am he,' and, 'The time is near.' Do not follow them. 9When you hear of wars and revolutions, do not be frightened. These things must happen first, but the end will not come right away." 10Then he said to them: "Nation will rise against nation, and kingdom against kingdom. 11There will be great earthquakes, famines and pestilences in various places, and fearful events and great signs from heaven. 12"But before all this, they will lay hands on you and persecute you. They will deliver you to synagogues and prisons, and you will be brought before kings and governors, and all on account of my name. 13This will result in your being witnesses to them. 14But make up your mind not to worry beforehand how you will defend yourselves. 15For I will give you words and wisdom that none of your adversaries will be able to resist or contradict. 16You will be betrayed even by parents, brothers, relatives and friends, and they will put some of you to death. 17All men will hate you because of me. 18But not a hair of your head will perish. 19By standing firm you will gain life.

This isn't referring to the disciples as some like to suggest, for while they did suffer persecution, not all of this happened to the disciples in their lifetime. All the conditions described here were not present during the time before, during or just after 70 a.d. The conditions mentioned here do not fit with what took place with the destruction in 70 a.d. You have to take all of the verses, all of the conditions together. This is ultimately describing the conditions during the tribulation. We see in Revelation that there will be war during the first half of the tribulation; peace is taken from the earth with the 2nd seal. It will escalate and become worse during the 2nd half of the tribulation. During the 2nd half of the tribulation the Jews as well as anyone that has accepted Jesus will have to flee from the persecution of (Satan) the anti-Christ as you will see next here in Matthew. Verses 10 and 11 appear to be describing the 2nd half of the tribulation. With verse 12 he describes what occurs at the mid-point of the tribulation for he says "but before all this", before nation rises against nation, and kingdom against kingdom, before great earthquakes, famines and pestilences in various places, and fearful events and great signs from heaven. We see in the book of Revelation that these things will occur during the 2nd half of the tribulation during the trumpets and bowl judgments.

Let's continue with Matthew.

> **Mt 24: 15**"So when you see standing in the holy place 'the abomination that causes desolation,' spoken of through the prophet Daniel—let the reader understand— 16then let those who are in Judea flee to the mountains. 17Let no one on the roof of his house go down to take anything out of the house. 18Let no one in the field go back to get his cloak. 19How dreadful it will be in those days for pregnant women and nursing mothers! 20Pray that your flight will not take place in winter or on the Sabbath. 21For then there will be great distress, unequaled from the beginning of the world until now—and never to be equaled again. 22If those days had not been cut short, no one would survive, but for the sake of the elect those days will be shortened. 23At that time if anyone says to you, 'Look, here is the Christ!' or, 'There he is!' do not believe it. 24For false Christs and false prophets will appear and perform great signs and miracles to deceive even the elect—if that were possible. 25See, I have told you ahead of time. 26"So if anyone tells you, 'There he is, out in the desert,' do not go out; or, 'Here he is, in the inner rooms,' do not believe it.

The phrase 'the abomination that causes desolation' comes from an event that took place in the past by Antiochus IV Epiphanes in 168 B.C. He is our closest model of the future anti-Christ. Antiochus was very much opposed to the Jewish religion. He attempted to destroy the Jews and their religion. He desecrated their temple, offering a pig on the altar and installing a statue of a Greek god. This brought about the Maccabean revolt, in which thousands of Jews were killed, including men, women and children. The Maccabeans, who eventually defeated

Antiochus, cleansed the Temple and restored Jewish autonomy, setting up the Hasmonean Dynasty that ruled Israel for about 100 years until the Romans came. We see this was prophesied in Daniel chapter 11.

The fact that Jesus mentions the 'the abomination that causes desolation,' spoken of through the prophet Daniel in chapter 9 as occurring sometime in their future is proof that he was not referring to a past event, that Antiochus IV Epiphanes was not the fulfillment of the prophecy mentioned in chapter 11 of Daniel.

With verse 15 through 20 Jesus is referring to the middle of the tribulation when the anti-Christ enters the Temple and proclaims himself to be God, then from verse 21 he goes thru the last half of the tribulation. You see in verse 15 Jesus says when you see standing in the holy place `the abomination that causes desolation,' spoken of through the prophet Daniel--let the reader understand. This will start the second half of the tribulation. We know from Daniel 9 that this takes place in the middle of the tribulation, after the first 3 ½ years. From this time on there will be 1260 days until the end of the tribulation.

> Daniel 9: 27He will confirm a covenant with many for one 'seven.' In the middle of the 'seven' he will put an end to sacrifice and offering. And on a wing of the temple he will set up an abomination that causes desolation, until the end that is decreed is poured out on him.

Remember, one seven is a period of seven years of 30 days each month and a total of 360 days in a year.

Verse 21 describes how much more severe the second half will be, the great tribulation as it is also called. Again, Preterists like to argue that verse 21 happened in 70 a.d when the Romans destroyed the temple and Jerusalem. While verses 16 thru 20 could apply to the destruction of 70 a.d. the other conditions cannot. The emperor of Rome did not enter the Temple and desecrate it as Jesus describes, even if he was going to, the Temple was destroyed by the soldiers before the emperor could enter it. The destruction in 70 a.d. doesn't fit with all the conditions Jesus mentions. The killing of the Jews by Hitler was much greater than what the Romans did in 70 a.d. So the destruction of the Temple and Jerusalem by the Romans couldn't be what Jesus meant when He said to 'never be equaled again'. This as well as the other conditions of Matthew 24 hasn't happened yet. They will happen during the final 7 years allotted to Israel, the tribulation. And notice something else that Jesus said. He said let the reader understand. The disciples weren't reading this they were hearing it, but those living during the tribulation will have this in the bible to read and understand.

Mark 13:

> 14"When you see 'the abomination that causes desolation' standing where it does not belong—let the reader understand—then let those who are in Judea flee to the mountains. 15Let no one on the roof of his house go down or enter the house to take anything out. 16Let no one in the field go back to get his cloak. 17How dreadful it will be in those days for pregnant women and nursing mothers! 18Pray that this will not take place in winter, 19because those will be days of distress unequaled from the beginning, when God created the world, until now—and never to be equaled again. 20If the Lord had not cut short those days, no one would survive. But for the sake of the elect, whom he has chosen, he has shortened them. 21At that time if anyone says to you, 'Look, here is the Christ or, 'Look, there he is!' do not believe it. 22For false Christs and false prophets will appear and perform signs and miracles to deceive the elect—if that were possible. 23So be on your guard; I have told you everything ahead of time.

During the tribulation there will be the false prophet and the anti-Christ claiming to be the Messiah. Once Satan has entered into him he will be claiming to be God.

Notice that Luke says when you see Jerusalem being surrounded by armies. You see armies are surrounding Israel, Jerusalem now. In the tribulation these armies of the nations will invade Israel. You will see this in our look at Ezekiel 38 and 39.

Luke 21:

20"When you see Jerusalem being surrounded by armies, you will know that its desolation is near.

As I said earlier, there are some that believe Luke is referring to the destruction in 70 a.d. While verse 20 thru 24 could be seen as referring to the destruction of Jerusalem and the Temple by the Roman Army in 70 a.d., it certainly could fit with what happened, I actually believe this is a reference to the tribulation because of all the surrounding verses, they match with Matthew and Mark's description of the tribulation of which the invasion of Israel by Russia and the Islamic nations will be just the beginning. The statement is plural, armies, not just one army as it was in 70 a.d. by just the Romans.

Verse 20 of Luke 21 could fit with Matthew's and Mark's reference to the abomination that causes desolation which will happen in the middle of the tribulation. The Russian and Islamic invasion occurs before the anti-Christ's entering the temple, which is the abomination that causes desolation, so Luke here could be telling all who are in Jerusalem to flee as soon as they see this invasion for this is just the beginning; it's going to get worse. So Luke 21 verse 20 could have the invasion by Russia and the Islamic nations foretold in Ezekiel chapters 38 and 39 in mind. The 2nd seal in Revelation chapter 6 could be this invasion.

While in 70 a.d. the Jews did fall by the sword, they weren't taken as prisoners to all the nations. They had to scatter out into the nations. We know during the tribulation that the Jews as well as anyone that has accepted Jesus are going to have to flee, but many are going to be killed and some are going to be taken as prisoners. We see this described in more detail in Revelation chapter 12 and 13.

So the statement of Jerusalem being surrounded by armies ultimately has to be referring to the time during the tribulation, because the next verses are connected to it. The fact that this is from the Sermon on the Mount as with Matthew 24 and Mark 13 and that they both are referring to the time during the tribulation helps lead me to believe that verse 20 and 21 in Luke 21 are also referring to the time of the tribulation.

But as bible prophecy often does, this could have dual applications, one for the destruction in 70 a.d. and the other for the tribulation for parts of the description could fit both. Read verses 21 through 24.

> Luke 21:21Then let those who are in Judea flee to the mountains, let those in the city get out, and let those in the country not enter the city. 22For this is the time of punishment in fulfillment of all that has been written. 23How dreadful it will be in those days for pregnant women and nursing mothers! There will be great distress in the land and wrath against this people. 24They will fall by the sword and will be taken as prisoners to all the nations. Jerusalem will be trampled on by the Gentiles until the times of the Gentiles are fulfilled.

While the destruction of the temple and the scattering of the Jews was punishment, it was not in fulfillment of all that had been written. Other than one reference in Daniel chapter 9 verse 26, the destruction in 70 a.d. of the temple and Jerusalem could not be seen as foretold in the Old Testament like the destruction that will occur during the tribulation. Jesus is the only one that could be seen as prophesying details of the destruction of the temple in 70 a.d., having said that, the destruction in 70 a.d. could have been the beginning and that the punishment will continue into the tribulation. You see verse 24 says Jerusalem will be trampled on by the Gentiles until the times of the Gentiles are fulfilled.

While I think this is referring to the 2nd half of the tribulation, you could say that Jerusalem is being trampled on by Gentiles now. This will continue until Jesus returns. For the anti-Christ, the Gentiles will take over Jerusalem and the temple at the mid-point of the tribulation.

The other scriptures in Luke 21 are clearly referring to the end times, to the last 7 years before Jesus returns for these statements do not fit with events and conditions during the time leading up to the 70 a.d destruction but fit with the years of the tribulation. When compared with Matthew and Mark this becomes apparent. Children didn't betray their parents nor parents their children. The Jews were not witnesses for Jesus. They did not stand firm. These are conditions that will occur during the tribulation.

We just saw that Matthew referred to the 70 a.d. destruction in chapter 23. Some of the conditions leading up to 70 a.d were a lot like those that will occur during the tribulation. If it was the 70 a.d destruction that Luke had in mind, it could be he just used the same wording that Matthew and Mark used. Matthew and Mark were already in circulation before Luke wrote his gospel so he apparently had read them both. With the exception of Revelation all the New Testament was written before 70 a.d. so Luke wasn't referring to a past event. Don't forget this is the bible; this is a prophecy from Jesus so it could very well be that the statement that Luke used refers to two separate times and events. Again, this could be another example of prophecy having duel fulfillments and purpose.

But as I said before, because this is taken from the Sermon on the Mount, I think it applies more to the tribulation. While this could fit with what took place during the time leading up to a.d. 70, when compared to Matthew and Revelation you see it will also be true of the time of the tribulation. Some of the conditions by Hitler during WWII could fit with these verses from Matthew, Mark and Luke but not all of them. You can see that most of these verse's do not fit with the time leading up to 70 a.d. for they are clearly telling of the events and conditions during the time of the tribulation and Jesus' return. So, while verses 21 thru 23 could seem to fit with what occurred in 70 a.d., I still think being surrounded by armies and when they have to flee applies more to the tribulation. Again, when compared to Matthew and

Mark you see this to be true. For us now, because the past is past, this is now a prophecy about the end times.

So with Luke saying that Jerusalem will be trampled on by the Gentiles until the times of the Gentiles are fulfilled, I believe Jesus was actually referring to the tribulation especially the last 1260 days of the tribulation. But if this is referring to the time from 70 a.d. until when Jesus returns would be fine, it still takes in the last 3 ½ years of the tribulation. It's just that the last 1260 days of the tribulation Satan in the anti-Christ will have total control over Jerusalem and the Temple and the Gentile nations will be persecuting the Jews like never before. This last 3 ½ years is the time that Satan is ruling the world. This is why the last 3 ½ years is referred to as the great tribulation.

> **Mark 13**: 9"You must be on your guard. You will be handed over to the local councils and flogged in the synagogues. On account of me you will stand before governors and kings as witnesses to them. 10And the gospel must first be preached to all nations. 11Whenever you are arrested and brought to trial, do not worry beforehand about what to say. Just say whatever is given you at the time, for it is not you speaking, but the Holy Spirit.

Apparently, this is the Jewish Rabbi's persecuting fellow Jews that have come to believe in Jesus as the Messiah. While this did happen to the disciples and to believing Jews in the first century, the fact that this is connected to the other conditions that were not present in the first century points to this being a condition during the tribulation. With the reinstatement of Judaism and the newly rebuilt temple, the Rabbi's will not like Jews that turn to Jesus. I imagine there will be a great hatred of Jesus all over the world during this time. You can see this already the case now.

With verses 4 thru 8 Matthew seems to have the flow of the events the same as they occur with the seals in Revelation. There in sequence, in the same order like the book of Revelation. This would make sense if Jesus' main focus was on the tribulation. This is another indication that

Jesus had the years of the tribulation in mind. Don't forget, it was Jesus that gave the revelation to John.

When compared to Revelation chapter 6 Matthew 24 verses 4 through 8 appear to occur during the first half of the tribulation and of course the corresponding verses from Mark and Luke.

1st Seal, False Peace, spiritual deception
2nd Seal, War, Peace taken
3rd Seal, inflation
4th Seal, war, famine, plagues, death
5th Seal, divine judgment
6th Seal, Darkness, physical destruction, continuation of wars, great earthquake
7th Seal, Catastrophic events (7 trumpets, 7 bowls) the second half of the tribulation.

The unrolling of the scroll marks the beginning of God's Judgment. Each Seal is a Judgment. Remember it is Jesus that is unrolling and breaking the seals of the scroll. Let's take a look at the first 6 seals in Rev. Chapter 6 and compare them with Matthew.

> **Rev. 6:1** I watched as the Lamb opened the **first of the seven seals**. Then I heard one of the four living creatures say in a voice like thunder, "Come!" 2I looked, and there before me was a white horse! Its rider held a bow, and he was given a crown, and he rode out as a conqueror bent on conquest.

> **Mat. 24:4** Jesus answered: "Watch out that no one deceives you. 5For many will come in my name, claiming, 'I am the Christ,' and will deceive many. 23At that time if anyone says to you, 'Look, here is the Christ!' or, 'There he is!' do not believe it.

With Rev. 6 verse 1 and 2 we can see deception, spiritual deception. The anti-Christ will be the worst deception the world has ever known. After the Rapture there could be many claiming to be the Christ, but

THE anti-Christ will emerge the leader of the world. He will have all the deceptive power of Satan with him.

> **Rev 6:3** When the Lamb opened the **second seal**, I heard the second living creature say, "Come!" 4Then another horse came out, a fiery red one. Its rider was given power to take peace from the earth and to make men slay each other. To him was given a large sword.

The second seal could very well be when Russia and the Islamic nations attack Israel, Ezekiel 38 and 39.

> **Rev. 6:5** When the Lamb opened the **third seal**, I heard the third living creature say, "Come!" I looked, and there before me was a black horse! Its rider was holding a pair of scales in his hand. 6Then I heard what sounded like a voice among the four living creatures, saying, "A quart of wheat for a day's wages, and three quarts of barley for a day's wages, and do not damage the oil and the wine!"

The third seal would be the results of the war in the Middle East, inflation all over the world. Of course the fourth seal, death, famines and earthquakes would be the result of the war.

> **Rev. 6:7** When the Lamb opened the **fourth seal**, I heard the voice of the fourth living creature say, "Come!" 8I looked, and there before me was a pale horse! Its rider was named Death, and Hades was following close behind him. They were given power over a fourth of the earth to kill by sword, famine and plague, and by the wild beasts of the earth.

> **Mat. 24:6** You will hear of wars and rumors of wars, but see to it that you are not alarmed. Such things must happen, but the end is still to come. 7Nation will rise against nation, and kingdom against kingdom. There will be famines and earthquakes in various places. 8All these are the beginning of birth pains.

You see it appears that in Matthew 24 up thru verse 8 Jesus addresses what takes place with the 4 horsemen.

With the fifth seal Jesus addresses those that were killed because of the word of God from the time of Pentecost through the Church age; that they will be rewarded. But notice Jesus tells them that they will have fellow brothers and sisters killed during the tribulation as they had been.

> **Rev. 6: 9**When he opened the **fifth seal,** I saw under the altar the souls of those who had been slain because of the word of God and the testimony they had maintained. 10They called out in a loud voice, "How long, Sovereign Lord, holy and true, until you judge the inhabitants of the earth and avenge our blood?" 11Then each of them was given a white robe, and they were told to wait a little longer, until the number of their fellow servants and brothers who were to be killed as they had been was completed.

> 12I watched as he opened the **sixth seal.** There was a great earthquake. The sun turned black like sackcloth made of goat hair, the whole moon turned blood red, 13and the stars in the sky fell to earth, as late figs drop from a fig tree when shaken by a strong wind. 14The sky receded like a scroll, rolling up, and every mountain and island was removed from its place. 15Then the kings of the earth, the princes, the generals, the rich, the mighty, and every slave and every free man hid in caves and among the rocks of the mountains. 16They called to the mountains and the rocks, "Fall on us and hide us from the face of him who sits on the throne and from the wrath of the Lamb! 17For the great day of their wrath has come, and who can stand?"

The 6th seal is the results of the war that started with the 2nd seal. It looks like nuclear weapons have finally been used. The pestilences that Jesus mentions as well as many of the plaques of the book of Revelation could be caused by radiation fallout from nuclear weapons, as well as chemical and biological weapons.

126

I believe that the 6th seal is at the mid-point of the tribulation and that the 7th seal starts the mid-point when the anti-Christ is indwelt by Satan and enters the temple and desecrates it. This lines up with Matthew 24 verses 15 thru 20. The 7 trumpets are a result of the 7th seal as the 7 bowls are a result of the 7th trumpet.

Since the last 3 ½ years is much more severe, Jesus in Revelation goes into to more detail of the last half of the tribulation with the 7 trumpets and 7 bowls as he does here in Matthew. From the 7th seal the book of Revelation is describing the last 3 ½ years of the tribulation until you get to chapter 20. Here in Matthew chapter 24 with verse 15 through 20 Jesus begins referring to the middle of the tribulation when the anti-Christ enters the Temple and proclaims himself to be God, then from verse 21 he goes thru the last half of the tribulation. We know this by verse 15 when Jesus says "so" when you see standing in the holy place `the abomination that causes desolation,' spoken of through the prophet Daniel--let the reader understand. This will start the second half of the tribulation. We know from Daniel 9 that this takes place in the middle of the tribulation, after the first 3 ½ years. From this time on there will be 1260 days until the end of the tribulation.

So you can see that it appears that up thru verse 8 Jesus has been describing the first half of the tribulation, the first 6 seals of Revelation chapter 6. With verse 9 and especially with verse 15 he begins describing the last half of the tribulation. Verses 15 thru 20 would occur at the 7th seal.

2. A STUDY OF MATTHEW 24 Part II

With Matthew 24 verse 21 thru verse 31 he continues the subject from the mid-point of the tribulation that he started with verse 15 and he starts describing how the last 3 ½ years of the tribulation will be.

> **Mt. 24: 21**For then there will be great distress, unequaled from the beginning of the world until now—and never to be equaled again. 22If those days had not been cut short, no one would survive, but for the sake of the elect those days will be shortened. 23At that time if anyone says to you, 'Look, here is the Christ!' or, 'There he is!' do not believe it. 24For false Christs and false prophets will appear and perform great signs and miracles to deceive even the elect—if that were possible. 25See, I have told you ahead of time. 26"So if anyone tells you, 'There he is, out in the desert,' do not go out; or, 'Here he is, in the inner rooms,' do not believe it. 27For as lightning that comes from the east is visible even in the west, so will be the coming of the Son of Man. 28Wherever there is a carcass, there the vultures will gather.
>
> 29"Immediately after the distress of those days
> "'the sun will be darkened,
> and the moon will not give its light;
> the stars will fall from the sky,
> and the heavenly bodies will be shaken.'
>
> 30"At that time the sign of the Son of Man will appear in the sky, and all the nations of the earth will mourn. They will see the Son of Man coming on the clouds of the sky, with power and great glory. 31And he will send his angels with a loud trumpet call, and they will gather his elect from the four winds, from one end of the heavens to the other.

Here again, you can see that Jesus was referring to the time of the tribulation. The most obvious is verse 27. Jesus is describing how his 2nd coming will be. I would think that if this had happened anytime in past history that there would be some kind of record of it. Someone would have written about it. Since this has not happened you can see with him saying, 'see, I have told you ahead of time' is also a good indication that he was speaking to those that will be living during the time of the tribulation. Remember, this is a prophecy. We see this also with verse 23 when Jesus said 'at that time' referring back to verse 15. Verse 24 mentions false prophets. We know there will be the false prophet from Rev. 13, but these false prophets could be false teachers, false evangelist deceiving people about the anti-Christ. With verse 23 and 26 it's come down to Satan in the man, the anti-Christ.

The anti-Christ will be claiming to be the Messiah and after Satan has entered into him then he will be claiming to be God. During the last half of the tribulation Satan will have indwelt the anti-Christ and will be claiming to be God and you will have the False Prophet backing him up. Jesus is telling everyone how to know the true Messiah. Jesus is giving a clear warning and tells how someone will know if it's really him. They'll be no mistaking the true Messiah. 27For as lightning that comes from the east is visible even in the west, so will be the coming of the Son of Man. Jesus' return with all his angels will be seen in the air by everyone on the earth. And all those that were raptured, both those that were living and those that had died will be returning with him also, the armies of heaven.

Revelation 13 describes the anti-Christ and the false prophet.

> Rev. 13: 5The beast was given a mouth to utter proud words and blasphemies and to exercise his authority for forty-two months. 6He opened his mouth to blaspheme God, and to slander his name and his dwelling place and those who live in heaven. 7He was given power to make war against the saints and to conquer them. And he was given authority over every tribe, people, language and nation. 8All inhabitants of the earth will worship the beast—all whose names have not been written in the book of life belonging to the Lamb that was slain from the creation of the world.

Rev. 13: 11Then I saw another beast, coming out of the earth. He had two horns like a lamb, but he spoke like a dragon. 12He exercised all the authority of the first beast on his behalf, and made the earth and its inhabitants worship the first beast, whose fatal wound had been healed. 13And he performed great and miraculous signs, even causing fire to come down from heaven to earth in full view of men. 14Because of the signs he was given power to do on behalf of the first beast, he deceived the inhabitants of the earth. He ordered them to set up an image in honor of the beast who was wounded by the sword and yet lived. 15He was given power to give breath to the image of the first beast, so that it could speak and cause all who refused to worship the image to be killed. 16He also forced everyone, small and great, rich and poor, free and slave, to receive a mark on his right hand or on his forehead, 17so that no one could buy or sell unless he had the mark, which is the name of the beast or the number of his name.

Revelation chapter 13 is describing the works of the anti-Christ and the false prophet. Verse 11 is describing the false prophet. You see the description of two horns like a lamp, which is commonly used to describe Jesus, but here you see he speaks like a dragon, a description for Satan. With verse 12 you see where the anti-Christ appears to be killed for he receives a fatal wound but this fatal wound had been healed. This is where Satan enters into the man, the anti-Christ. Once Satan has entered into the anti-Christ he will have complete control over the new world order, this 10 region world government will now truly become a beast, the revived Roman Empire of the past. Satan is now here on earth ruling like he has always wanted. You see this described in chapter 12.

Rev. 12: 7And there was war in heaven. Michael and his angels fought against the dragon, and the dragon and his angels fought back. 8But he was not strong enough, and they lost their place in heaven. 9The great dragon was hurled down— that ancient serpent called the devil, or Satan, who leads the whole world astray. He was hurled to the earth, and his angels with him.

This takes place at the mid-point of the tribulation at the 7th seal.

We saw with verse 15, "So when you see standing in the holy place 'the abomination that causes desolation,' spoken of through the prophet Daniel—let the reader understand" takes place at the mid-point of the tribulation.

So Matthew 24 verse 15, the 7th seal of Revelation chapter 8 and the war with the dragon in Revelation chapter 12 and the fatal wound of the anti-Christ in Revelation chapter 13 are occurring around the same time frame, they all occur at the mid-point of the tribulation. With verse 9 of Revelation chapter 12 we see that Satan is cast down to the earth. We see with verse 3 of Revelation chapter 13 that the anti-Christ receives a fatal wound that is healed. Rev. 13: 3One of the heads of the beast seemed to have had a fatal wound, but the fatal wound had been healed. The whole world was astonished and followed the beast. We see this mentioned again with verse 12. All this will take place at the beginning of the 7th seal of Revelation chapter 8. Look at the description of the 7th seal.

> Rev. 8: 1When he opened the seventh seal, there was silence in heaven for about half an hour. 2And I saw the seven angels who stand before God, and to them were given seven trumpets. 3Another angel, who had a golden censer, came and stood at the altar. He was given much incense to offer, with the prayers of all the saints, on the golden altar before the throne. 4The smoke of the incense, together with the prayers of the saints, went up before God from the angel's hand. 5Then the angel took the censer, filled it with fire from the altar, and hurled it on the earth; and there came peals of thunder, rumblings, flashes of lightning and an earthquake.

I can see how the casting down of Satan and all his demons would cause heaven to be silent, like a big gasp for breath.

Now Jesus describes just how he will return back to the earth.

> **Mt. 24:27** For as lightning that comes from the east is visible even in the west, so will be the coming of the Son of Man. **28** Wherever there is a carcass, there the vultures will gather.

With verse 28 we see that Jesus will return to the valley of Megiddo where the last battle of Armageddon will be fought. We see in Revelation chapter 19 what is left of the armies of the world that have fought in this last battle of Armageddon will gather together to fight against Jesus returning.

Compare verse 27 and 28 with Jesus' return in Rev. chapter 19.

The Rider on the White Horse

> Rev. 19:11 I saw heaven standing open and there before me was a white horse, whose rider is called Faithful and True. With justice he judges and makes war. 12His eyes are like blazing fire, and on his head are many crowns. He has a name written on him that no one knows but he himself. 13He is dressed in a robe dipped in blood, and his name is the Word of God. 14The armies of heaven were following him, riding on white horses and dressed in fine linen, white and clean. 15Out of his mouth comes a sharp sword with which to strike down the nations. "He will rule them with an iron scepter." He treads the winepress of the fury of the wrath of God Almighty. 16On his robe and on his thigh he has this name written:
> KING OF KINGS AND LORD OF LORDS.
>
> 17And I saw an angel standing in the sun, who cried in a loud voice to all the birds flying in midair, "Come, gather together for the great supper of God, 18so that you may eat the flesh of kings, generals, and mighty men, of horses and their riders, and the flesh of all people, free and slave, small and great."

19Then I saw the beast and the kings of the earth and their armies gathered together to make war against the rider on the horse and his army. 20But the beast was captured, and with him the false prophet who had performed the miraculous signs on his behalf. With these signs he had deluded those who had received the mark of the beast and worshiped his image. The two of them were thrown alive into the fiery lake of burning sulfur. 21The rest of them were killed with the sword that came out of the mouth of the rider on the horse, and all the birds gorged themselves on their flesh.

MT 24:29 "Immediately after the distress of those days"
the sun will be darkened,
and the moon will not give its light;
the stars will fall from the sky,
and the heavenly bodies will be shaken.'

MT 24:30 "At that time the sign of the Son of Man will appear in the sky, and all the nations of the earth will mourn. They will see the Son of Man coming on the clouds of the sky, with power and great glory.

Verses 27 through 30 are referring to the end of the tribulation and Jesus' second coming that you just read in Revelation chapter 19. Jesus' 2nd coming will be after the tribulation for you see in verse 29 he said Immediately after the distress of those days. The "distress of those days" are the days of the tribulation.

Read from the NKJ version.

Mt: 24: 29 "Immediately after the tribulation of those days the sun will be darkened, and the moon will not give its light; the stars will fall from heaven, and the powers of the heavens will be shaken.

The last battle of Armageddon, the end of WWIII there will be one last massive release of Nuclear weapons all over the world. You see this in Revelation chapter 16 with the 7th bowl. Then Jesus' second coming, as lightning that comes from the east is visible even in the west, so will be the coming of the Son of Man. Everyone on earth will see Him coming. The sun being darkened and the moon not giving its light could be from all the debris and smoke in the air from all the nuclear weapons released at the last battle of Armageddon. The stars falling from the sky couldn't be literal stars for the sun is a star and one of the smaller ones and it is bigger than the earth. The stars falling could be how all the nuclear missiles and debris from explosions will look like coming down. It could also be meteors and asteroids entering the earth's atmosphere. Just think of all the destruction all this will cause, your Sci-Fi movies becoming real. Like John in Revelation, Jesus had to describe what he was telling them in a way that the first century reader could get some kind of picture of it. You see this also with the Old Testament Prophecies. But it could also be that Jesus will supernaturally darken the sun and the moon on the day of his return. It could be just like it was on the day of his crucifixion. The sun and stars were darkened. It was not an eclipse. They knew what an eclipse was. This was a supernatural event from God the Father. Look at how Zechariah describes the day Jesus returns.

> Zech. 14: 6 On that day there will be no light, no cold or frost. 7 It will be a unique day, without daytime or nighttime—a day known to the LORD. When evening comes, there will be light.

Mark also records this.

Mark 13:

> 24"But in those days, following that distress,
>   " 'the sun will be darkened,
>   and the moon will not give its light;
>   25the stars will fall from the sky,
>   and the heavenly bodies will be shaken.'
>   26"At that time men will see the Son of Man coming in clouds with great power and glory.

Take a look at what Luke tells us.

> **Luke 21**: 25"There will be signs in the sun, moon and stars. On the earth, nations will be in anguish and perplexity at the roaring and tossing of the sea. 26Men will faint from terror, apprehensive of what is coming on the world, for the heavenly bodies will be shaken.

This statement in Luke sounds like he is describing the days of distress, the days during the tribulation. For here Luke calls them signs. Just think how the seas will react from being struck by meteors or asteroids or nuclear bombs. You see these things also described in Revelation with the trumpets and bowls, which of course will be occurring before Jesus' return back down to the earth. And notice this; he said there will be signs in the sun, moon and stars. Luke said the nations will be in anguish and perplexity at the roaring and tossing of the sea. The sun and moon affect the tides of the oceans. Remember, these were the words of Jesus.

While just like in Matthew verse 25 and 26 the roaring and tossing of the sea could be seen as already happening, which have been getting worse, the fact is, it will be even worse than it is now during the tribulation. With all the debris in the air from nuclear weapons, meteors and asteroids etc. blocking the sun and moon, striking the seas and earth, the waves will be worse, there will be more tsunamis, larger and more tidal ways. We know now that sun spots and radiation affect the earth's climate. And from recent discoveries, it could be that the signs in the sun, moon and stars could also be astrological signs. With verse 27 and 28 we can see that this is referring to the time during the tribulation. With verse 27 Luke describes Jesus' return.

> **Luke 21**: 27At that time they will see the Son of Man coming in a cloud with power and great glory. 28When these things begin to take place, stand up and lift up your heads, because your redemption is drawing near."

With verse 28 we see all this is to be a sign to those living during the time after the rapture, after the anti-Christ gets the peace agreement signed between Israel and the Islamic nations. When all these signs described begin to take place they are to lift up their heads and stand firm for Jesus' return will be soon.

In Luke 21 verse 28 "these things" refers back to verse 8, to the beginning of the tribulation for he says, "When these things begin take place, stand up and lift up your heads, because your redemption is drawing near." These things that Jesus just mention started in verse 8 of Luke 21 and verse 4 of Matthew 24 with false Christ's and then the deception of the anti-Christ, the 1st seal of Revelation.

Now with verse 31 you see what will take place right after Jesus has returned.

> **Mt.24: 31** And he will send his angels with a loud trumpet call, and they will gather his elect from the four winds, from one end of the heavens to the other.

Read this together,

> **MT 24:29** "Immediately after the distress of those days
> "the sun will be darkened,
> and the moon will not give its light;
> the stars will fall from the sky,
> and the heavenly bodies will be shaken.'
>
> **30** "At that time the sign of the Son of Man will appear in the sky, and all the nations of the earth will mourn. They will see the Son of Man coming on the clouds of the sky, with power and great glory.
>
> **31** And he will send his angels with a loud trumpet call, and they will gather his elect from the four winds, from one end of the heavens to the other.

136

Look at the order in which Jesus puts all this. Verse 29, immediately after the tribulation, verse 30, at that time, after the distress of the tribulation Jesus will return and everyone will see him return. He said 'THEY WILL SEE THE SON OF MAN COMING ON THE CLOUDS OF THE SKY WITH GREAT POWER AND GLORY'.

Again no one will see Jesus come in the air at the Rapture but they will at his 2ⁿᵈ coming. And then after he has returned, Verse 31, he sends his angels to gather his elect.

This is the separation of the sheep and the goats in Matthew 25.

> Mt. 25 31"When the Son of Man comes in his glory, and all the angels with him, he will sit on his throne in heavenly glory. 32All the nations will be gathered before him, and he will separate the people one from another as a shepherd separates the sheep from the goats.

The angels are sent to gather the elect, this takes place after Jesus has returned, notice he said 'AND THEN HE WILL SEND', other words after what he just said, after they have seen the Son of Man return.

Verse 31 is the third time that Jesus mentions the elect. Paul and Peter referred to the Jews as the elect. This could be the angels gathering the Jews back from around the world. These elect could be of the whole house of Israel. Remember, this is not the rapture of the Church. At the rapture of the Church there is no gathering by angels. Read this from Mark.

> **Mark 13: 27** And he will send his angels and gather his elect from the four winds, from the ends of the earth to the ends of the heavens.

Mark also says from the ends of the earth. From the four winds could also be referring to all over the earth. The ends of the heavens could also be just saying that people will be gathered from all over the world, but the ends of the heavens could be referring to those that have died in the Lord during the tribulation. We see in Revelation chapter 20 after Jesus has returned back down to the earth that those that died in the Lord during the tribulation are raised to life.

> Rev. 20: 4I saw thrones on which were seated those who had been given authority to judge. And I saw the souls of those who had been beheaded because of their testimony for Jesus and because of the word of God. They had not worshiped the beast or his image and had not received his mark on their foreheads or their hands. They came to life and reigned with Christ a thousand years.

> **Mt. 24:32** "Now learn this lesson from the fig tree: As soon as its twigs get tender and its leaves come out, you know that summer is near. **33**Even so, when you see all these things, you know that it is near, right at the door. **34**I tell you the truth, this generation will certainly not pass away until all these things have happened. **35**Heaven and earth will pass away, but my words will never pass away.

One major sign that has already taken place is Israel became a nation again in 1948, for without Israel as a nation and Jerusalem once again as the city of David, Jesus' Sermon on the Mount and the whole book of Revelation wouldn't make since. Because Israel was destroyed as a nation and no longer existed is how a lot of the false teachings of the 4th and 5th centuries got stated. That's why the false teaching of replacement theology was able to emerge. Replacement Theology is that the Church has replaced Israel. That all the promises and blessings to Israel now apply to the Church. Oh, but none of the discipline. But the rebirth of Israel should be enough to show that God is not finished with his ancient people of Israel. The rebirth of Israel should show that the prophecies of the bible are to be taken literally.

Preterist, those that believe that Jesus' Sermon on the Mount and the book of Revelation were fulfilled in 70 a.d. have a problem with the date that the book of Revelation was written. As you can imagine they have to date the book before 70 a.d. I won't go here into all the proofs for the date of the writing of the book of Revelation, but it wasn't written until 95 a.d. of which there is more than enough evidence and proof. Israel becoming a nation again and then regaining Jerusalem is definitely a major prophetic sign; for at the time John wrote the book of Revelation there wasn't an Israel, Jerusalem or a Temple in existence. Again, the words of Jesus here in Matthew and in the book of Revelation are prophetic.

Many say that this reference to the fig tree is referring to the rebirth of Israel in 1948 for Israel has often been referred to as a fig tree. Like the symbol for the United States is the Eagle, the bear is the symbol for Russia, the fig tree is the symbol for Israel and that this was fulfilled or began to be fulfilled in 1948 when Israel became a nation again. Remember, there wasn't a nation of Israel from the destruction by the Babylonians until 1948. There wasn't a nation of Israel when Jesus was here, just the city of Jerusalem. The Jews were just living throughout the land. The leaves coming out would be the regaining of Jerusalem. With this being a major sign; the next prophetic fulfillment of verse 32 will be when Israel builds the Temple again.

The re-gathering of the Jews and Israel becoming a nation again and especially the recapture of Jerusalem are definitely fulfillment of bible prophecy and had to occur before the tribulation, but I don't think this statement of the fig tree really has anything to do with Israel becoming a nation again in 1948, although that is a major prophetic event. None of the end time prophecies could occur without Israel as a nation and Jerusalem under Jewish control, which occurred in June of 1967 referred to as the 6-day war. Once again in June of 1967 all the Islamic nations tried to destroy Israel. Though they were greatly outnumbered and against incredible odds it only took Israel 6 days to defeat the Islamic armies. Who does it look like the God of Abraham was helping.

I think Jesus was just using the fig tree as an example of how the signs will be during the tribulation for he said 'when you see all these things', all these things occurring during the 7 years of the tribulation and especially the last 3 ½ years of the tribulation.

139

The reference to a fig tree, its twigs getting tender and its leaves coming out is how you can tell that summer is near. Jesus said, even so, when you see all these things, the things he just described that will be taking place simultaneously, this is how you will know that his return is near, that the kingdom of God is near. All these things will be occurring during the tribulation. We've had all of these things like hurricanes and earthquakes happening throughout history and even more often in the last 50 years. But during the tribulation all these things will be happening together and a lot more severe. All these things include the destruction by the wars, the deception of the anti-Christ and false prophet that Jesus just described. You see in the book of Revelation the progression of the judgments how they get more severe with each series. Jesus said here in Matthew verse 8 it would be like the beginning of birth pains. A woman's birth pains increase until she has given birth. The judgments in the book of Revelation increase until they have given birth to the coming of the Lord and the kingdom of God. I think all the things we see happening now, before the rapture are like false birth pains or like Braxton hicks. Before "true" labor begins, the mother to be may have "false" labor pains, also known as Braxton Hicks contractions. This is her body's way of getting ready for the "real thing" but does not lead to birth. What we are experiencing now does not lead to the birth of the kingdom of God but the signs Jesus gives us here in Matthew do. The true labor pains will start with the signing of the peace agreement between Israel and the Muslim nations. I actually believe the Rapture will be the first birth pain.

Mark also records this, as does Luke.

> Mark 13: 28 "Now learn this lesson from the fig tree: As soon as its twigs get tender and its leaves come out, you know that summer is near. 29Even so, when you see these things happening, you know that it is near, right at the door.

> Luke 21: 29 He told them this parable: "Look at the fig tree and all the trees. 30When they sprout leaves, you can see for yourselves and know that summer is near. 31Even so, when

you see these things happening, you know that the kingdom of God is near.

Notice that Luke included all the trees, not just the fig tree. This, and Jesus saying when you see all these things happening help support that Jesus was relating the fig tree to the things that will be occurring during the tribulation, which will start with the releasing of the Anti-Christ. I just don't think the fig tree is necessarily referring to the rebirth of Israel in 1948.

The message is when you see all these things happening, the things he just described, by all the things that will be happening during the tribulation you will know that the kingdom of God is near. By these signs you will know that you're in the time of Gods judgment. The generation that sees all of these things occurring simultaneously will not pass away; this will be the generation that sees the coming of Jesus back to the earth to establish his kingdom.

I think the example of the fig tree is just to let those living during the tribulation recognize that they are in the tribulation and that the kingdom of God is near. For the budding of the fig tree is linked to these things that he described, the events that are occurring during the tribulation.

Back to Matthew 24

> **34**I tell you the truth, this generation will certainly not pass away until all these things have happened. **35**Heaven and earth will pass away, but my words will never pass away.

Many have used verse 34's statement, 'this generation' to try to put a date on the timing of the Rapture. They usually started with Israel becoming a nation again in 1948. They took a generation to be 40 years for that is how long Israel wondered in the wilderness. I don't think Jesus meant that to be used as how to determine the length of a generation. God chose 40 years because the spies were spying out the land for 40 days. Those that tried to date the rapture added 40 years to

1948 and came up with 1988 to be when the Lord would return for the Church. Well, obviously that wasn't correct. Then they realized that it was more significant when Israel recaptured Jerusalem in 1967. They added 40 years to 1967 and came to 2007 and then subtracted 7 years for the tribulation and came up with the year 2000. Well, when that didn't happen they realized that there wasn't a year between 1 BC and 1 AD so they came to 2001. Of course, that wasn't correct either. I don't think that was the point of Jesus' statement at all. I believe that all he meant was that 'this generation', the generation that sees all these things, all that he had just described happening at the same time, within the 7 year period of the tribulation, Daniel's 70th week will certainly not pass away until he has returned. The generation that sees all these things includes everyone that is living at that time, from the youngest to the oldest. He just said in verse 33 Even so, when you see all these things, you know that it is near, right at the door. That it is near, that his return and the establishment of the kingdom of God is near. He's just letting those that will be living during the tribulation know that it won't be long, to stand firm. The tribulation especially the last 3 ½ years are going to be so bad that Jews as well as those that have accepted Jesus as their Lord thus not taking the mark of the beast and swearing allegiance to the anti-Christ will have to flee from their homes. Jesus is encouraging them not to lose heart, to not lose faith that he is going to return and they will be saved and go into the kingdom of God. From the book of Daniel and Revelation they will be able to calculate just how long it will be till Jesus returns.

> Verse 35, Heaven and earth will pass away, but my words will never pass away. He's letting the reader know that this is a done deal. It's going to come to pass. He has spoken it.

You see in Revelation 21 that the present heavens and earth will pass away and that God will create a new heavens and new earth.

> Rev. 21:5He who was seated on the throne said, "I am making everything new!" Then he said, "Write this down, for these words are trustworthy and true."

So the statement, 'this generation' shouldn't be connected to Israel becoming a nation again just like the fig tree shouldn't be connected either. If anything they should be connected to the peace agreement being signed between Israel the anti-Christ and the Islamic nations.

With this peace agreement Israel will be giving up land and dividing Jerusalem. Remember what Joel prophesied,

> Joel 3: 2 I will gather all nations
> and bring them down to the Valley of Jehoshaphat,
> concerning my inheritance, my people Israel,
> for they scattered my people among the nations
> and divided up my land.

Also Psalm 83:

> 4 "Come," they say, "let us destroy them as a nation,
> that the name of Israel be remembered no more."

Jesus was just letting those that will be here during the tribulation to look at everything that is happening; these things are the signs to know his return is soon. In chapter 21 Luke said, 32"I tell you the truth, this generation will certainly not pass away until all these things have happened. 33Heaven and earth will pass away, but my words will never pass away. Look at what Matthew said in verse 25,
25See, I have told you ahead of time.

Read the warning Luke gives in chapter 21,

> 34"Be careful, or your hearts will be weighed down with dissipation, drunkenness and the anxieties of life, and that day will close on you unexpectedly like a trap. 35For it will come upon all those who live on the face of the whole earth. 36Be always on the watch, and pray that you may be able to escape all that is about to happen, and that you may be able to stand before the Son of Man."

3. A STUDY OF MATTHEW 24 Part III

The Day and Hour Unknown

Mt. 24:36"No one knows about that day or hour, not even the angels in heaven, nor the Son, but only the Father.

This verse is the one that is much debated. Some say this is a reference to the rapture, some say it is not and that there is no mention of the rapture in Matthew 24. Since the rapture will occur at an unknown time you can see how this could be referring to the rapture. But is it or is it referring to the tribulation. I say yes to both. I say he is referring to the rapture and the tribulation. The rapture takes place before the start of the tribulation and it will happen at a time unknown to anyone, but Jesus has been addressing the tribulation. It's the tribulation that he has been talking about. He's been giving signs that will be taking place during the tribulation. But as we will see in a moment it appears that Jesus as does Paul links the rapture with the start of the tribulation, the day of the Lord. It appears that the Rapture starts the day of the Lord but not necessarily the 7-year count down. The 7-year count down will start when the anti-Christ and Israel sign the covenant agreement together with the Palestinians. Just as there was a interval between the death of Jesus ending the Old Testament age and the beginning of the Church age on the day of Pentecost, there will be one between the rapture and the beginning of the 7 years of the tribulation, unless the rapture happens on the day Israel signs this agreement, but I doubt that will be the case.

Jesus is still answering the question, what will be the sign of your coming and of the end of the age. He was just talking about things happening during the tribulation. So Jesus could be saying that no one knows when the tribulation will begin. But as we will see in a second, the rapture will be the first major sign that the tribulation is about to begin. As I just said it appears that both Jesus and Paul links the tribulation and the rapture together, it's just that the 7 year countdown will not start until Israel and the Islamic nations signs the peace agreement with the anti-Christ. It is clear from the scriptures that the rapture, Jesus' coming for the Church will be unknown to anyone, apparently even the angels, but the day and hour for the signing of the peace agreement will be known ahead of time. It will have to be for all the leaders to come together to sign it. So it would appear that Jesus was indeed referring to the rapture here in verse 36 and that the rapture starts the day of the Lord, just not the 7 year peace agreement.

Remember from our study of 1 and 2 Thessalonians, that the day of the Lord would take them by surprise like a thief. In 1 Thessalonians chapter 4 verses 13 thru 18 Paul started out with the Rapture first then in 1 Thessalonians chapter 5 verse 1 he goes into the day of the Lord, the tribulation. The day of the Lord cannot start until after the rapture. The anti-Christ cannot be revealed until after the rapture for the Church is holding his revealing back. You see this from Paul in 2 Thessalonians chapter 2. The 7-year count down will start with the signing of the peace agreement. This will be when the anti-Christ is revealed. The anti-Christ may be in power before the Rapture and will bring order back from all the kayos and confusion caused by the rapture. Even if he isn't in power before the rapture he is going to be the one that will bring order back from all the kayos and confusion that has been caused by the rapture. This could lead to the world being split up into the 10 regions, the 10 toes and horns mentioned in Daniel and Revelation, if it hasn't been already before the rapture.

Let's read First Thessalonians again.

1 Thes. 4:13 Brothers, we do not want you to be ignorant about those who fall asleep, or to grieve like the rest of men, who have no hope. 14We believe that Jesus died and rose again and so we believe that God will bring with Jesus those who have fallen asleep in him. 15According to the Lord's own word, we tell you that we who are still alive, who are left till the coming of the Lord, will certainly not precede those who have fallen asleep. 16For the Lord himself will come down from heaven, with a loud command, with the voice of the archangel and with the trumpet call of God, and the dead in Christ will rise first. 17After that, we who are still alive and are left will be

145

caught up together with them in the clouds to meet the Lord in the air. And so we will be with the Lord forever. 18Therefore encourage each other with these words.

1 Thes. 5:1Now, brothers, about times and dates we do not need to write to you, 2for you know very well that the day of the Lord will come like a thief in the night. 3While people are saying, "Peace and safety," destruction will come on them suddenly, as labor pains on a pregnant woman, and they will not escape.

Most likely it will be that after the signing of the agreement with Israel and the Palestinians and the other Islamic nations that there seems to be peace and safety for the Middle East. The destruction that comes on them suddenly is the 2nd seal when Russia and the Islamic nations attack Israel. So this 7 year agreement doesn't really bring peace at all. We can see here as well as in the book of Revelation that the Islamic nations will not honor this agreement. Notice Paul said 'while people are saying peace and safety'. He didn't say there would be peace. It sounds to me it's more like the world will just be saying now there will finally be peace; they're just hoping this will bring peace.

Peter also describes the tribulation in 2 Peter 3 verse 10, But the day of the Lord will come like a thief. The heavens will disappear with a roar; the elements will be destroyed by fire, and the earth and everything in it will be laid bare. Remember, Paul in 1 Thes. 5 goes on to say: 9For God did not appoint us to suffer wrath but to receive salvation through our Lord Jesus Christ.

Remember from our look at 2 Thessalonians chapter 2.

1Concerning the coming of our Lord Jesus Christ and our being gathered to him, we ask you, brothers, 2not to become easily unsettled or alarmed by some prophecy, report or letter supposed to have come from us, saying that the day of the Lord has already come

146

3Don't let anyone deceive you in any way, for (that day will not come) until the rebellion occurs and the man of lawlessness is revealed, the man doomed to destruction. 4He will oppose and will exalt himself over everything that is called God or is worshiped, so that he sets himself up in God's temple, proclaiming himself to be God. 5Don't you remember that when I was with you I used to tell you these things? 6And now you know what is holding him back, so that he may be revealed at the proper time. 7For the secret power of lawlessness is already at work; but the one who now holds it back will continue to do so till he is taken out of the way. 8And then the lawless one will be revealed, whom the Lord Jesus will overthrow with the breath of his mouth and destroy by the splendor of his coming.

You see with verse 1 he starts off with the rapture, assuring them that the day of the Lord had not started and that they have not missed the rapture. He goes on to remind them that the tribulation does not start until after the rebellion occurs and the anti-Christ is revealed. With verse 6 he shows that the anti-Christ will not be revealed until after the rapture, after the removal of the Church, the one who is now holding his revealing back. The anti-Christ will not be revealed until the one who is holding him back is taken out of the way. Paul is linking the rapture with the start of the day of the Lord, the tribulation. Paul and Peter both said the day of the Lord will come like a thief.

So Mt. 24:36 is a reference to the rapture for the rapture starts the day of the Lord but it is also referring to the beginning of the tribulation. At the time Jesus was speaking this he was still under the time of the Old Testament age. We are now under the time of the Gentiles and the Church age. With the removal of the Church it will go back under the Old Testament age but it will still be the time of the gentiles. You see this from Daniel chapter 9. It will be like things have come full circle back to Israel.

Now we come to what definitely sounds like Jesus is describing the rapture and the beginning of the tribulation.

Mt. 24:37 As it was in the days of Noah, so it will be at the coming of the Son of Man. **38<u>For in the days before the flood</u>**, people were eating and drinking, marrying and giving in marriage, <u>up to the day Noah entered the ark; 39and they knew nothing about what would happen until the flood came and took them all away.</u> That is how it will be at the coming of the Son of Man. 40Two men will be in the field; one will be taken and the other left. 41Two women will be grinding with a hand mill; one will be taken and the other left.

Verses 37 through 39, with the 'days of Noah he is referring to the days before the rapture or the days before the tribulation, and then with the 'at the coming of the Son of Man' he is referring to the rapture and then to the tribulation with the reference to the flood', for the tribulation has been the subject of his preaching so far. In verse 38 he said in the days before the flood. The flood was the judgment. While it has been the tribulation that has been the subject it is like a silent reference to the rapture since the rapture is before the tribulation. Notice how he said "at" the coming of the Son of Man and then mentions the flood, the tribulation. And notice he has the "at" before the flood. The NIV here says "at" the coming, even if you say the coming is meaning his second coming, though I don't believe he is, the "at" could easily be interpreted as meaning at the beginning of the tribulation for the whole 7 years are "at" his second coming. That is the purpose for all the signs. Jesus said this is how you will know it is near, right at the door, Verse 32 and 33. The KJ, NKJ and NAS versions of the bible do not have 'at'. So 'at' the coming of the Son of Man would still be referring to the Rapture. Verse 37 and 38 Jesus referred to the days before the flood, the days of Noah, meaning Noah's days before the flood. The Church age is the days before the judgment of the tribulation. It appears that Jesus is linking the beginning of the tribulation with the rapture just like Paul does in 1 and 2 Thessalonians. Of course, Paul would link them together because he got all this from Jesus.

Verse 37, the days of Noah couldn't be referring to the day's right before his second coming. As we will see, the conditions he describes concerning the days of Noah don't match with the conditions of the tribulation and especially with the end of the tribulation.

The days of Noah, notice that it says "in the days BEFORE the flood". Not the days during the flood. In the days of Noah they were eating and drinking, marrying and giving in marriage. Other words, life was going on as normal. Life won't be normal during the tribulation especially during the last half. By the end of the tribulation right before Jesus' second coming the earth will just about be totally wiped out and destroyed. Life was normal **up to** the day Noah entered the ark. They knew nothing about what would happen UNTIL the flood came and took them **all** away. It's that way now, before the tribulation, before the Rapture. Luke says this also and adds the days of Lot and his family.

> Lk. 17: 26"Just as it was in the days of Noah, so also will it be in the days of the Son of Man. 27People were eating, drinking, marrying and being given in marriage up to the day Noah entered the ark. Then the flood came and destroyed them all.

> 28"It was the same in the days of Lot. People were eating and drinking, buying and selling, planting and building. 29But the day Lot left Sodom, fire and sulfur rained down from heaven and destroyed them all.

Life was going on as usual in Lots day. The fire and sulfur didn't rain down until Lot and his family was out of the way.

Life now is going on as usual and will be up until the Rapture, until the tribulation starts. After the rapture there will be mass confusion and hysteria. Noah entered the ark and closed the door, then the rain came, then the flood. Soon the rapture will come, the shutting of the door, then tribulation.

Life was normal up to the day Noah entered the ark. The illustration is that the floodwaters were the judgment. They knew nothing until the rain started and the flood came. It is the same now.

People do not believe anything is going to happen. They won't until after the Rapture and the Tribulation has started. Verse 39 says, and they knew nothing about what would happen until the flood came and took them all away. They probably will be many that won't think the missing of millions of Christians is anything to be concerned about. I'm sure there will be some kind of explanation for the missing of millions of people. But just think of all the kayos and confusion that will be caused by the rapture. And keep this in mind. The tribulation starts off slowly and builds up in severity. The earth didn't flood when it first started raining. It rained for 40 days and 40 nights. And it didn't start raining until Noah and his family was on the ark and the door was shut. The rain, the tribulation can't start until the Church is on the ark and the door is shut. The main purpose for Jesus giving all these signs and describing things that will be taking place during the tribulation is so they will know that they are in the time of judgment, just like with the rain.

When the angels came to Sodom and Gomorrah they told Lot that they could do nothing until Lot and his family were out. Jesus will return to remove his Church, his bride, get her out then the judgment can start. See Gen. 19:20 - 22.

Another point from Noah and Lot's day is that the people were totally sinful, violent and immoral. You see this is why God destroyed Sodom and Gomorrah and the world of Noah's' day. We see the world is becoming like this more and more, even the United States. Look at what God said about man during Noah's day.

> Genesis 6: 5 The LORD saw how great man's wickedness on the earth had become, and that every inclination of the thoughts of his heart was only evil all the time. 6 The LORD was grieved that he had made man on the earth, and his heart was filled with pain. 11 Now the earth was corrupt in God's sight and was full of violence.

As I mentioned earlier, it could be that after the rapture the anti-Christ will bring order back from all the kayos and confusion that will be caused by the rapture. Just think how it will be. Millions of people just all of a sudden become missing. The anti-Christ will come up with an explanation for this I'm sure, that will calm down most of the people and he will seem to have all the answers. It will seem also, that he is able to bring peace to the world. But once Israel signs that covenant with him it won't be long until all hell will break loose, because with this agreement Israel is ignoring the scriptures and not relying on the God of Abraham, Isaac and Jacob. We don't know how much time will go by between the rapture and the beginning of the tribulation when Israel signs that agreement with the anti-Christ starting Israel's last allotted 7 years, it could be a month, several months, we don't know, but I don't think it will be long. The bible doesn't reveal this. It just lets us know that the tribulation will not start until after the anti-Christ as been revealed, and from what we have seen from the scriptures this will happen when he brings about the 7 year peace agreement.

I think that the rapture will actually be the most important sign that the day of the Lord has begun, couple that with a 7 year covenant agreement signed by Israel, the Islamic nations and the anti-Christ and the fact there has never been a 7 year peace agreement signed between Israel and the Islamic nations, and with the globalization of the world, all this will be clear evidence that the time of Jacobs trouble has come, the time of Gods judgment has begun. There will be many that have not accepted Jesus as their Lord and Savior before the rapture, that have heard the teaching about the rapture, that after the rapture has occurred they will come to believe and accept Jesus as their Savior. They will know that the time of God's judgment has begun. I'm sure that they will be studying the scriptures intently. They will know what to look for as the sign to who the anti-Christ is.

Again, life was going on as normal until the rain started and the flood came. It is the same now, before the rapture.

Mt. 24: 38**For in the days before the flood**, people were eating and drinking, marrying and giving in marriage, up to the day Noah entered the ark; 39and they knew nothing about

<u>what would happen until the flood came and took them **all** away.</u> That is how it will be **at** the coming of the Son of Man. 40Two men will be in the field; one will be taken and the other left. 41Two women will be grinding with a hand mill; one will be taken and the other left.

Luke 17: 26"Just as it was in the days of Noah, so also will it be in the days of the Son of Man. 27People were eating, drinking, marrying and being given in marriage up to the day Noah entered the ark. Then the flood came and destroyed them all. 28"It was the same in the days of Lot. People were eating and drinking, buying and selling, planting and building. 29But the day Lot left Sodom, fire and sulfur rained down from heaven and destroyed them all. 30"It will be just like this on the day the Son of Man is revealed.

Once the rapture as occurred, as I just mentioned, it will be revealed to many that Jesus is the Son of God. Many will turn to Jesus and accept him as their Lord and Savior.

That is how it will be at the coming of the Son of Man. We've just seen that in the days before the flood it was life going on as normal during the days of Noah. The people knew nothing about what would happen until the flood came. The AT the coming of the Son of Man has to be referring to the beginning of the tribulation. The AT therefore is the coming for the Church; this must be what starts it all, the closing of the door. All the signs of the tribulation are AT the second coming of Jesus. With there being 2000 years since Jesus left the earth, the rapture, the beginning of the last 7 years before he returns back down to the earth would be considered AT the second coming.

As for the people of Noah's day not knowing anything about what would happen until the flood came, all the years it took Noah to build the ark he was preaching and warning them the whole time, they just refused to listen and believe, just like most of the world now. People don't believe any of this now. Many won't until after it has come.

You should be able to see the pattern. With Noah and his family as well as with Lot and his family you see the righteous removed before the judgment comes. It will be the same before the judgment of the tribulation. The Church, the righteous of the Lord will be removed, taken out before the judgment of God comes.

Look at this statement by Jesus in Luke 17 verse 22, Then he said to his disciples, "The time is coming when you will long to see one of the days of the Son of Man, but you will not see it.

Just like we are in the days of Noah now, we are in the days of the Son of Man. Jesus couldn't have been just referring to the days in which he was here on earth, he had to be referring to the Church age as the days of the Son of Man. You see with Luke 17 verse 23 he is describing the events during the tribulation just as Matthew and Mark are. With verse 23 he is speaking of the anti-Christ. With verse 24 Jesus is telling how his second coming will be just like in Matthew 24. He is ultimately speaking to those that will be here during the tribulation.

> Luke 17:23Men will tell you, 'There he is!' or 'Here he is!' Do not go running off after them. 24For the Son of Man in his day will be like the lightning, which flashes and lights up the sky from one end to the other.

Luke continues the sermon about the tribulation in chapter 21. So you can see that the tribulation is not the days of Noah or the days of the Son of Man. It's the time of Judgment just like it was during the flood.

> **Mt. 24:40** Two men will be in the field; one will be taken and the other left. 41Two women will be grinding with a hand mill; one will be taken and the other left.

Luke adds,

> Luke 17: 34I tell you, on that night two people will be in one bed; one will be taken and the other left. 35Two women will be grinding grain together; one will be taken and the other left."

What does this one taken and the other left mean? When will this be? Some believe it is when he sits in judgment and sends the angels to harvest the earth, to separate the sheep and the goats, the one taken and one left referring to one taken away in judgment and the other left to enter the kingdom of God. They link the word 'taken' in verses 40 and 41 back with the word 'took' in verse 39, but does this work with all that Jesus said. Notice Jesus started off with referring to the days before the flood.

> Mt.24: 38For in the days before the flood, people were eating and drinking, marrying and giving in marriage, up to the day Noah entered the ark; 39and they knew nothing about what would happen until the flood came and took them all away. That is how it will be at the coming of the Son of Man. 40Two men will be in the field; one will be taken and the other left. 41Two women will be grinding with a hand mill; one will be taken and the other left.

The context of the whole statement doesn't fit that the "took" and "taken" are referring to the same event. The people of Noah's day were left to go through the floodwaters while Noah and his family were taken into the ark. The flood waters took them away in the judgment but Noah and his family was taken into the ark being removed from the judgment of the flood waters. The 'took' in verse 39 is definitely connected to the flood, but the 'taken' in verse 40 and 41 are not. Notice what Jesus said just before verse 40, 'That is how it will be at the coming of the Son of Man'. We've already determined that the 'at the coming of the Son of Man' in verse 37 is a reference to the rapture. Remember how Jesus started the statement, let's read it together again,

> 36"No one knows about that day or hour, not even the angels in heaven, nor the Son, but only the Father. 37As it was in the days of Noah, so it will be at the coming of the Son of Man. 38For in the days before the flood, people were eating and drinking, marrying and giving in marriage, up to the day Noah entered the ark; 39and they knew nothing about what would

154

happen until the flood came and took them all away. That is how it will be at the coming of the Son of Man.

When you but all these scriptures together, that the days of Noah were the days before the flood and that they knew nothing of what was going to happen until the rain started, it would appear that the one taken and the other left have to be referring to what will take place with a pre-tribulation rapture of the Church. Jesus linked his statement at the coming of the Son of Man with the days of Noah and up until the flood came and took them all away. Remember, Noah and his family were already on the ark and the door was shut before the rain started. Lot and his family were out of Sodom then the fire rained down. When Jesus returns at his 2nd coming life will not be very normal. The tribulation won't be the days of Noah or the days of the Son of man but the time of the flood, the time of judgment. And most importantly, he said they knew nothing until the flood came and took them all away. The flood has to be describing the tribulation, not his second coming, remember, they will know Jesus is returning and will be gathered together to make war against him. You can be sure that by the time of the end of the tribulation life hasn't been going on as normal. So the one taken and the other left have to be describing what will take place with the rapture, not his second coming.

Let's look at the Greek Lexicon meaning of the words taken and left.

Taken, Greek Lexicon 3880

The very first translation is 'to take to, to take with one's self, to join to one's self'.

This does not fit with taken in judgment but it does fit with being taken with Jesus back to heaven. So what about the word 'left'?

Left, Greek Lexicon 863

3) to leave, go way from one

- **a)** in order to go to another place
- **b)** to depart from any one
- **c)** to depart from one and leave him to himself so that all mutual claims are abandoned
- **d)** to desert wrongfully
- **e)** to go away leaving something behind
- **f)** to leave one by not taking him as a companion
- **g)** to leave on dying, leave behind one
- **h)** to leave so that what is left may remain, leave remaining
- **i)** abandon, leave destitute

Now doesn't this sound like what will happen when Jesus comes and takes the Church to be with him in the Father's house and leaves those that haven't accepted him behind.

Now compare this with what Jesus said in John 14.

> 1"Do not let your hearts be troubled. Trust in God; trust also in me. 2In my Father's house are many rooms; if it were not so, I would have told you. I am going there to prepare a place for you. 3And if I go and prepare a place for you, I will come back and take you to be with me that you also may be where I am.

The King James, New King James, the New American Standard bibles translate take, receive.

> NKJ. 1 "Let not your heart be troubled; you believe in God, believe also in Me. 2 In My Father's house are many mansions; if *it were* not *so,* I would have told you. I go to prepare a place for you. 3 And if I go and prepare a place for you, I will come again and receive you to Myself; that where I am, *there* you may be also.

Take, Taken and Receive are the same Greek word, Lexicon 3880.

156

This is the same in Luke chapter 17.

Here's something fascinating with these two verses in Luke. "34I tell you, on that night two people will be in one bed; one will be taken and the other left. 35Two women will be grinding grain together; one will be taken and the other left. Some manuscripts 36 Two men will be in the field; one will be taken and the other left.

"Two men are in the field working, two women are at the hand mill working. You do this during the day. But notice there will be two in the bed. You usually sleep at night. When Jesus returns for the Church it will be day on one side of the earth and night on the other. I just thought this statement was interesting.

Verses 40 and 41 here in Matthew 24 are a good indicator that he is referring to the rapture and not his actual second coming, that he at least had the rapture in mind with verse 36. By the time of Jesus' second coming there won't be anyone working in the field. All the green grass has been burned up. Food supplies have been wiped out. This has to be a reference to the rapture.

Remember verse 36 started by saying No one knows about that day or hour, not even the angels in heaven, nor the Son, but only the Father. But we have already seen that Satan, the anti-Christ will know when Jesus' second coming to the earth will be for he assembles the armies of the world that are left to make war against Jesus coming from Heaven. REV 19:19 Then I saw the beast and the kings of the earth and their armies gathered together to make war against the rider on the horse and his army.

As we have just seen, the anti-Christ and the people alive during the last half of the tribulation will be able to determine and know when Jesus is returning to the earth to set up his kingdom.

So what did Jesus mean when he said: No one knows about that day or hour, not even the angels in heaven, nor the Son, but only the Father. No one knows about that day or hour, of the "day of the Lord", the time of judging Israel and the nations. No one knows when the rapture will take place and when the judgment will start. Again, the flood was the judgment. No one knew <u>nothing about what would happen until the flood came and took them all away.</u> Noah had been warning them for over 100 years while he was building the ark. They wouldn't listen. They just made fun of him about like people are now of those in the Church that teaches and believe in the rapture of the Church and a time of judgment afterwards.

No one knows when the rapture will be thus no one knows when the tribulation will begin. There are no signs that point to the rapture. The tribulation won't start until after the rapture, so the one taken and the other left have to be referring to the Rapture of the Church. Again, Jesus here in Matthew as does Paul in First and Second Thessalonians, the rapture and the beginning of the tribulation seems to be linked together.

These scriptures paint a clear picture of a pre-tribulation rapture of the Church. Let me say this again.

Verse 37 says "As it was in the days of Noah." Then we see he says "For in the days before the flood". **The days before the flood were the days of Noah.** Now it's like we are in the days of Noah. Jesus is building his Church. Noah was building his ark. The rain didn't start until Noah had finished the ark. When the bride has made herself ready the bride Groom will come for her. As the bride and groom were in the bridle chamber for 7 days so will the Church, the bride of Christ be in our bridal chamber for 7 years. See "The Rapture and Jewish Wedding."

Read what Paul said again,

> 1TH 5:1 Now, brothers, about times and dates we do not need to write to you, 2 for you know very well that the day of the Lord will come like a thief in the night. 3 While people are saying, "Peace and safety," destruction will come on them

suddenly, as labor pains on a pregnant woman, and they will not escape.

Paul said that the day of the Lord would come like a thief in the night. While people are saying there is peace and safety. Just like in the days of Noah. They knew nothing until it started raining. Noah had already entered the ark and the door was shut. And by the way, the bible says that God closed the door. See Gen. Chapter 7. There will not be peace during the tribulation years, even during the first 3 ½ years. The second seal, the rider on the fiery red horse was given power to take peace from the earth and to make men slay each other. To him was given a large sword. This second seal is probably when Russia and the Muslim nations with her attack Israel; we see this in Ezekiel 38 and 39. Paul was referring to the tribulation when he said 'the day of the Lord.'

Peter also said:

> 2PE 3:10 But the day of the Lord will come like a thief. The heavens will disappear with a roar; the elements will be destroyed by fire, and the earth and everything in it will be laid bare.

With Peter saying 'The heavens will disappear with a roar; the elements will be destroyed by fire, and the earth and everything in it will be laid bare' is a reference to the events that will be occurring during the whole 7 years of the tribulation. You can see the things Peter described happening through reading the book of Revelation. The fires from all of the nuclear weapons and possibly meteors and asteroids will be destroying the earth. The earth will be laid bare. The heavens disappearing with a roar; the elements being destroyed by fire is a good description of nuclear bombs exploding in the atmosphere. But this could include more than just nuclear weapons.

Look at Luke 21 again:

> 25"There will be signs in the sun, moon and stars. On the earth, **nations will be in anguish and perplexity** at the

The Rapture and End Time Prophecies for Beginners

roaring and tossing of the sea. **26Men will faint from terror, apprehensive of what is coming on the world,** for the heavenly bodies will be shaken.

Notice he said "what IS coming on the world". Put this with "begin" in verse 28.

27At that time they will see the Son of Man coming in a cloud with power and great glory. 28When these things **begin** to take place, stand up and lift up your heads, because your redemption is drawing near."

You just can't get away from the fact that at the end of the tribulation, right before Jesus' second coming life won't be normal and that they will be expecting him, gathered together to make war against him and his army. Rev. 19:19.

Jesus' 2nd coming will not be like a thief as the rapture will be. Remember what Jesus said:

MT 24: 27 For as lightning that comes from the east is visible even in the west, so will be the coming of the Son of Man.

MT 24:30 "At that time the sign of the Son of Man will appear in the sky, and all the nations of the earth will mourn. They will see the Son of Man coming on the clouds of the sky, with power and great glory

You see further evidence for a pre-trib rapture with verses 42 thru 44.

Mt. 24:42"Therefore keep watch, because you do not know on what day your Lord will come. 43But understand this: If the owner of the house had known at what time of night the thief was coming, he would have kept watch and would not have let his house be broken into. 44So you also must be ready, because the Son of Man will come at an hour when you do not expect him.

160

So with verse 36 referring to the rapture and the beginning of the tribulation you can see that verse 42 is also a reference to the rapture. Verses 37 thru 39 are about the days before the tribulation, before the rapture. Verses 40 and 41 are referring to the Rapture.

He starts verse 42 with 'Therefore' keep watch because you do not know on what day your Lord will come. This is true only for a pre-trib rapture of the Church, not of his second coming. He said 'Therefore' meaning because of what he just said. No one knows of that day or hour, therefore keep watch.

So with verses 42 thru 44 he has to be referring to a pre-trib rapture. You see we are told to be ready and to keep watch for we don't know when our Lord will come. This is true for the rapture but not true for his second coming. His second coming will not be as a thief but the rapture before the tribulation will occur as a thief. By the way, Satan doesn't know either when Jesus will return for the Church.

The point to keep in mind is people living during the tribulation will know when Jesus is returning. They will know it is near and getting nearer by all the signs during the tribulation. But the rapture, none of us knows when it will occur.

> **Mt. 24 44**So you also must be ready, because the Son of Man will come at an hour when you do not expect him.

Again, there are not many now that expect him, but at the end of the tribulation they all will be expecting him, some with open arms and love, some with guns and hatred.
Mark also records this.

> **Mark 13**: 32"No one knows about that day or hour, not even the angels in heaven, nor the Son, but only the Father. 33Be on guard! Be alert! You do not know when that time will come. 34It's like a man going away: He leaves his house and puts his servants in charge, each with his assigned task, and tells the one at the door to keep watch. 35"Therefore keep watch because

The Rapture and End Time Prophecies for Beginners

you do not know when the owner of the house will come back—whether in the evening, or at midnight, or when the rooster crows, or at dawn. 36If he comes suddenly, do not let him find you sleeping. 37What I say to you, I say to everyone: 'Watch!' "

So yes Matthew 24 does reference the rapture. The days of Noah are the days of the Church, the days we are in now. We're in the days before the flood.

Read what Luke adds to this.

> **Luke 21**: 34"Be careful, or your hearts will be weighed down with dissipation, drunkenness and the anxieties of life, and that day will close on you unexpectedly like a trap. 35For it will come upon all those who live on the face of the whole earth. 36Be always on the watch, and pray that you may be able to escape all that is about to happen, and that you may be able to stand before the Son of Man."

Notice Jesus here in Luke said to pray that you may be able to escape ALL that is about to happen. He didn't say pray that you will survive through it. The rapture will be the means of escape. Also notice he said escape and stand before the Son of Man. With the Rapture we will escape and stand before Jesus. While after Jesus' second coming those that lived through the tribulation will stand before Jesus, they did not escape. After Jesus' second coming, they will stand before him to be judged. Verse 36 sounds like the standing is more one of joy and adulation than judgment. Also with him saying 'pray that you will be able to escape' places the escaping the tribulation before standing before him. With the second coming they will stand before him after the tribulation.

As we have seen from Revelation chapter 19, Jesus' second coming will not close on them unexpectedly like a trap but the rapture and the tribulation, that day will. The tribulation will come upon all those that live on the face of the whole earth.

Verse 36 of Luke 21 he said to always be on the watch and pray that you may be able to escape all that is about to happen and that you may be able to stand before the Son of Man. This has to be referring to the tribulation not his second coming. The tribulation is what you would want to escape, not his second coming. All this is about to happen, so pray that you will be able to escape.

Luke 21:36 from the New King James.

> 36 Watch therefore, and pray always that you may be counted worthy to escape all these things that will come to pass, and to stand before the Son of Man."

You see it says here from the New King James version "escape all these things that **will** come to pass". These things to escape are the events that will be occurring during the tribulation. The only way to escape them is to be taken out of this world first, for we just saw from Luke 21 verse 35, For it will come upon all those who live on the face of the whole earth.

The escaping and the standing before Jesus are together. This will only happen with the rapture. Jesus left going back to heaven 2000 years ago and put his servants in charge. Luckily we do have some at the door and watching. We have some watchman on the walls trying to warn everyone just as Noah did in his day. He tells everyone to Watch.

The Rapture will be sudden. Don't let him find you sleeping, catch you unaware. Don't let the rapture close on you unexpectedly. If you're not living for the Lord you may find yourself in the flood.

Come Lord Jesus.

4. A STUDY OF MATTHEW 24 Part IV

The subject that started with verse 36 continues with verse 45.

> **MT 24:45** "Who then is the faithful and wise servant, whom the master has put in charge of the servants in his household to give them their food at the proper time? 46 It will be good for that servant whose master finds him doing so when he returns. 47 I tell you the truth, he will put him in charge of all his possessions. 48 But suppose that servant is wicked and says to himself, `My master is staying away a long time,' 49 and he then begins to beat his fellow servants and to eat and drink with drunkards. 50 The master of that servant will come on a day when he does not expect him and at an hour he is not aware of. 51 He will cut him to pieces and assign him a place with the hypocrites, where there will be weeping and gnashing of teeth.

Matthew 24 verses 45 thru 50 sound more like our time now than it does anytime during the tribulation. While verse 51, the cutting him to pieces and assigning him a place with the hypocrites, where there will be weeping and gnashing of teeth probably are referring to hell, it could also be meaning the tribulation as well.

> Matthew 24: 48But suppose that servant is wicked and says to himself, 'My master is staying away a long time,' 49and he then begins to beat his fellow servants and to eat and drink with drunkards. 50The master of that servant will come on a day when he does not expect him and at an hour he is not aware of.

Notice in verse 48 the statement of the master staying away a long time. This has to be referring to our time now and not anytime during the tribulation. Once the anti-Christ has signed the covenant with Israel and the Islamic nations there will be only 7 years until his return to the Earth, so the statement 'My master is staying away a long time,' could not apply to the 7 years of the tribulation. And notice how many times here in Matthew that Jesus says he will come at a time when no one is expecting him and at a time they are not aware of. He has to be

164

referring to the rapture of the Church for this does not apply to his second coming. Remember you can calculate the time of his second coming. As we see in Revelation chapter 19 Satan, the anti-Christ obviously does this.

Verse 50, the master of that servant will come on a day when he does not expect him and at an hour he is not aware of. Those that are not saved are not expecting him and are not looking for him; they are not and won't be watching. Sadly, there are many in the Church that are not expecting him or watching for his return for the Church. Verse 48, the servant, like many today even in the Church, because it's been so long since Jesus left for the Father's house don't believe that Jesus will literally return for his Church. Many Pastors are beating their flocks by teaching there is no Rapture and teaching things taught by demons.

> 1 Timothy 4: 1The Spirit clearly says that in later times some will abandon the faith and follow deceiving spirits and things taught by demons.

I'm not saying that those in the Church that are teaching there's no rapture are not saved, but it is a teaching from Satan himself.

Luke 12:35 thru 48 parallels with Matthew 24:42 - 51 as does Mark 13:32-37.

Luke 12:35-48

Watchfulness

> 35"Be dressed ready for service and keep your lamps burning, 36like men waiting for their master to return from a wedding banquet, so that when he comes and knocks they can immediately open the door for him. 37It will be good for those servants whose master finds them watching when he comes. I tell you the truth, he will dress himself to serve, will have them recline at the table and will come and wait on them. 38It will be good for those servants whose master finds them ready, even if

he comes in the second or third watch of the night. 39But understand this: If the owner of the house had known at what hour the thief was coming, he would not have let his house be broken into. 40You also must be ready, because the Son of Man will come at an hour when you do not expect him."

Notice again he describes this coming as a thief that comes when no one is aware of. This is true of the rapture and not of Jesus' second coming. He goes on to say if the owner of the house new what time the thief was coming he would be waiting for him to stop him. This is not what will take place with the rapture but is exactly what we see of Jesus' second coming in Revelation chapter 19. Satan has the armies of the world gathered together waiting to prevent his house from being broken into. Rev. 19: 19Then I saw the beast and the kings of the earth and their armies gathered together to make war against the rider on the horse and his army. The rapture will come at a time no one is aware of, like a thief. The second coming they will know he is coming.

41Peter asked, "Lord, are you telling this parable to us, or to everyone?" 42The Lord answered, "Who then is the faithful and wise manager, whom the master puts in charge of his servants to give them their food allowance at the proper time? 43It will be good for that servant whom the master finds doing so when he returns. 44I tell you the truth, he will put him in charge of all his possessions. 45But suppose the servant says to himself, 'My master is taking a long time in coming,' and he then begins to beat the menservants and maidservants and to eat and drink and get drunk. 46The master of that servant will come on a day when he does not expect him and at an hour he is not aware of. He will cut him to pieces and assign him a place with the unbelievers.

Again, you can see that this is describing the conditions with the rapture and not Jesus' second coming. It will be those that are unbelievers now; that are not taken up in the rapture that will go into the tribulation, are assigned their place with unbelievers.

47"That servant who knows his master's will and does not get ready or does not do what his master wants will be beaten with many blows. 48But the one who does not know and does things deserving punishment will be beaten with few blows. From everyone who has been given much, much will be demanded; and from the one who has been entrusted with much, much more will be asked.

Mark 13:32-37.

32"No one knows about that day or hour, not even the angels in heaven, nor the Son, but only the Father.

33Be on guard! Be alert! You do not know when that time will come. 34It's like a man going away: He leaves his house and puts his servants in charge, each with his assigned task, and tells the one at the door to keep watch.

35"Therefore keep watch because you do not know when the owner of the house will come back—whether in the evening, or at midnight, or when the rooster crows, or at dawn. 36If he comes suddenly, do not let him find you sleeping.

37What I say to you, I say to everyone: 'Watch!' "

We're in the days of the Son of Man, (the days of the Church), the days of Noah, the days of Lot. The days of Noah ended when Noah entered the ark. The days of Lot as far as Sodom was concerned ended when Lot left. **We're in the days of the Church, the days of the Son of Man**. The days of the Son of Man, the days of the Church will end when the Church leaves and enters the bridle chamber.

So Matthew 24, the Sermon on the Mount as it is called, from what we have read from all these verses lends support that Jesus was indeed referring to the rapture, he just didn't come right out directly, for the Church was still kept hidden. The Jews were only expecting the coming kingdom. Jesus had told the disciples that he would build his

Church and that the gates of hell would not be able to prevail against it but he hadn't taught them much about the Church for you see no other mention of the Church other than him telling them he would build his Church. The only mention of the Church is in Matthew 16 and 18. The disciples didn't understand that the Church Jesus was talking about would be made up of Jews and Gentiles. Like many things the disciples didn't come to understand about the Church until after Pentecost.

Look at Acts 1

This is after Jesus has risen from the dead, right before he ascends back to heaven.

> 6So when they met together, they asked him, "Lord, are you at this time going to restore the kingdom to Israel?"
> 7He said to them: "It is not for you to know the times or dates the Father has set by his own authority.
> 8But you will receive power when the Holy Spirit comes on you; and you will be my witnesses in Jerusalem, and in all Judea and Samaria, and to the ends of the earth."
> 9After he said this, he was taken up before their very eyes, and a cloud hid him from their sight.
> 10They were looking intently up into the sky as he was going, when suddenly two men dressed in white stood beside them.
> 11"Men of Galilee," they said, "why do you stand here looking into the sky? This same Jesus, who has been taken from you into heaven, will come back in the same way you have seen him go into heaven."

Right before Jesus ascends up to heaven, they still have the kingdom on their minds. For those that don't believe that Jesus will come back literally or that there will be a literal kingdom of God on Earth notice Verse 6. Jesus didn't deny that the kingdom would come literally hear on earth; because the kingdom wasn't coming right then he went to addressing the birth of the Church. He tells them it's not for them to know the times or dates the Father has set. If he was not returning literally or if there wasn't going to be a literal kingdom here on earth I think Jesus would have told them. He wouldn't have let them go on believing something that wasn't true and not going to happen.

Notice verse 11. The angels said to them of his second coming that Jesus would come back in the same way that he left, literally and visibly in the sky. Everyone will see him. The Rapture will not be visible. The Rapture is what kicks all of this off. It won't start until after he has removed his bride.

Here's a word from the Apostle Paul.

Romans 13

> 11And do this, understanding the present time. The hour has come for you to wake up from your slumber, because our salvation is nearer now than when we first believed. 12The night is nearly over; the day is almost here. So let us put aside the deeds of darkness and put on the armor of light. 13Let us behave decently, as in the daytime, not in orgies and drunkenness, not in sexual immorality and debauchery, not in dissension and jealousy. 14Rather, clothe yourselves with the Lord Jesus Christ, and do not think about how to gratify the desires of the sinful nature.

The fact is that the Rapture is going to catch most of the world by surprise, and unfortunately most of the Church too unless they wake up. At the Rapture Jesus comes like a thief and it is going to be like he steals us away. There will be many that will be caught sleeping, not aware of the signs of the times, they won't be watching and ready and the Rapture will come upon them like a thief. Don't let this happen to you. Be ready. Get to know Jesus now before it's too late. Not only because of the rapture, but your life could be required of you tonight.

5. A STUDY OF MATTHEW 25.

The Sermon on the Mount of chapter 24 continues into chapter 25.

> MT 25:1 "At that time the kingdom of heaven will be like ten virgins who took their lamps and went out to meet the bridegroom. 2 Five of them were foolish and five were wise. 3 The foolish ones took their lamps but did not take any oil with them. 4 The wise, however, took oil in jars along with their lamps. 5 The bridegroom was a long time in coming, and they all became drowsy and fell asleep. 6 "At midnight the cry rang out: `**Here's the bridegroom! Come out to meet him**!'

Jesus is continuing the subject he started with verse 36 in chapter 24. You see with verse 4 the statement about the bridegroom being gone a long time like the master in verse 48 of chapter 24. He's still on the same subject just presenting it in a different way.

Verses 1 thru 6 are an illustration again taken from the Jewish Wedding custom. The bride and her attendants, bridesmaids, here the 10 virgins would wait and watch for the Groom. When the cry rang out that the Groom was coming they all would go out to meet him. This usually occurred late at night or around midnight.

> MT 25:7 "Then all the virgins woke up and trimmed their lamps. 8 The foolish ones said to the wise, `Give us some of your oil; our lamps are going out.' 9" `No,' they replied, `there may not be enough for both us and you. Instead, go to those who sell oil and buy some for yourselves.' 10 "But while they were on their way to buy the oil, the bridegroom arrived. The virgins who were ready went in with him to the wedding banquet. And the door was shut. 11"Later the others also came. `Sir! Sir!' they said. `Open the door for us!' 12 "But he replied, `I tell you the truth, I don't know you.'

> 13"Therefore keep watch, because you do not know the day or the hour.

As you can see from verse 13 he is continuing what he started with Matthew 24 verse 36 and verse 45, also verse 1 says, 'At That Time', referring back to verse 36 in chapter 24. Remember Mt. 24 verse 36, No one knows the day or hour. Verses 1 thru 13 are a picture of how it will be with a pre-trib rapture of the Church. No other rapture view can parallel with the Jewish wedding custom like the pre-tribulation view.

In verse 5 with them saying that the bridegroom was a long time in coming also makes this sound like a pre-trib rapture. If the rapture occurs any time after the signing of the treaty between the anti-Christ and Israel the most it would be is 3 ½ years to 7 years until his coming. Everyone saved will be longing and looking for his coming. They will know that it's not far away.

Remember from The Jewish Wedding Custom.

The Groom and his Father go to the bride's house and makes the covenant with her and pays her father the price for her. (Jesus did this on the cross). Then the Groom would return to his Father's house to build the bridal chamber. (Jesus returned to his father's house, heaven and is preparing a place for us). This is most likely the heavenly city, the New Jerusalem. Rev. 21. When all has been made ready and the allotted amount of time had passed the Father of the Groom would tell his son to go get his bride. No one would know when the Groom would return, not even the Groom. His Father would let him know when all has been made ready and tell him to go get his bride. (Matthew 24:36). The Groom returns to the bride's house and gets his bride, again, at a time unknown to her. (Jesus will do this when he returns for the Church at the rapture). The bride and the bridesmaids go out to meet him. The bride and groom go to his Father's house and enter into the bridal chamber for 7 days and then after the 7 days are complete they come out for the wedding feast or supper. (We will be in heaven, the Fathers house for the 7 years of the tribulation in the bridle chamber, room).

The Jewish wedding custom is a perfect picture of Jesus returning for his Church, taking us to his Father's house for 7 years and then after the 7 years returning for the wedding supper/feast. Again, only the pre-trib rapture fits the picture of the Jewish wedding custom.

> John 14: 1"Do not let your hearts be troubled. Trust in God; trust also in me. 2In my Father's house are many rooms; if it were not so, I would have told you. I am going there to prepare a place for you. 3And if I go and prepare a place for you, I will come back and take you to be with me that you also may be where I am.

Here in verse 10 he mentions the 'wedding banquet'. The wedding banquet and the feast or supper are not the same. During the 7 days the bride and Groom are in the bridle chamber, these 7 days are also known as the bride's week, the family and friends would have a weeklong celebration, the wedding banquet. Then after the 7th day the bride and groom would come out to the wedding supper/feast. You see this first mentioned in Genesis chapter 29 with the story of Jacob, Leah and Rachael. This all fits with a pre-trib rapture of the Church. Again, no other rapture view will parallel with the Jewish wedding custom.

I think the point or lesson of the 10 virgins is that 5 were prepared, had oil in their lamps, that they were either saved or not saved. They all fell asleep but the 5 wise woke up and had oil in their lamps. The Church was a sleep to the rapture as well as many doctrines of the bible for thousands of years until the reformation. Unfortunately, there are still many even in the Church that hasn't woken up to the truth concerning the rapture. Oil is often used as a reference to the Holy Spirit. The five wise will go with the Lord in the rapture while the five unwise will be left behind, to go through the tribulation. Unless you are born again you will not have the Holy Spirit, the oil. The 5 foolish are told to go and buy some oil from those who sell oil. After the rapture there probably will be many that will be going to Pastors to get saved and to see if they could still be taken up to heaven. Unfortunately any Pastors left after the rapture will have to get saved also. I'm sure after the rapture a lot of people will be crying out to the Lord to take them up. He'll say I don't know you. If they ask for forgiveness and are then saved they will be born again but will have to go through the tribulation. Notice verse 11, they asked for the door to be open. The door has been shut just like to door on Noah's ark. Since they didn't prove their loyalty to Jesus during their life they will now have to prove it through the tribulation, unfortunately, some with their lives. Rev. 12:11 They overcame him (the anti-Christ, Satan) by the blood of the Lamb and by the word of their testimony; they did not love their lives so much as to shrink from death.

Some also believe the 10 virgins represent the Church and with verse 7 the 5 wise woke up to the fact that the Lord's coming for the Church is near, by knowing the signs of the times. They were ready, watching, while the 5 unwise were not. Because we are told to be ready and watching, the 5 wise were waiting and watching for his return in faith while the 5 unwise were not ready or watching, because they do not believe that Jesus will return to rescue us from his coming wrath. So those that don't believe he is returning or believe in the rapture will not take part in the rapture so they will be left behind. They are the scoffers that Peter and Jude referred to being in the last days. It would be just like having to have faith to be saved and faith to be healed. Anything we receive from the Lord is by faith, so if someone does not have the faith to believe in the rapture then they will not take part in the catching up of the Church.

There are others that believe the 10 virgins are referring to Christians, they believe the 5 wise were filled with the Spirit and living for the Lord while the unwise had backslid and are not living for the Lord. The 5 unwise will be living their lives' their way without any concern for the Lord. The unwise won't go up in the Rapture. As I said, I think this is more a point of being saved or not. I have always assumed that if you were saved you would go up in the rapture. While none of us are perfect or sinless we should be living for the Lord, have the Lord Jesus in our lives. Jesus should be a priority in your life, not just someone you think about on Sunday or on Easter. So then I'm sure that just like with salvation, by the grace of God all true Christians will be caught up at the rapture. But Jesus must be in your life. If your sin does not concern you and Jesus has no place in your life then you should be concerned that you're not saved. The Holy Spirit will convict you of sin, unless of course he is not in you. There are many in Church today that think they are saved but are not. If there is not a true commitment from your heart then it doesn't matter if you've walked down an Isle and have been baptized, and it doesn't matter how much you serve in the Church, Jesus will say to you, MT 25:12 "But he replied, `I tell you the truth, I don't know you.'

Jesus said in Matthew 7:

> 21"Not everyone who says to me, 'Lord, Lord,' will enter the kingdom of heaven, but only he who does the will of my Father who is in heaven. 22Many will say to me on that day, 'Lord, Lord, did we not prophesy in your name, and in your name drive out demons and perform many miracles?' 23Then I will tell them plainly, 'I never knew you. Away from me, you evildoers!'

See also Matthew 13.

We will look at Matthew 13 in a moment, but to the point from those that believe the 10 virgins represent the whole Church, those ready and living for the Lord and those that are not ready or living for the Lord. They do have scriptures that sound like that's what could be meant here. Let's look at some.

> Luke 21: 34"Be careful, or your hearts will be weighed down with dissipation, drunkenness and the anxieties of life, and that day will close on you unexpectedly like a trap. 35For it will come upon all those who live on the face of the whole earth.

This will come upon those not living for the Lord unexpectedly like a trap. Thus they won't go with Jesus to the Father's house.

Luke 12: 45But suppose the servant says to himself, 'My master is taking a long time in coming,' and he then begins to beat the menservants and maidservants and to eat and drink and get drunk. 46The master of that servant will come on a day when he does not expect him and at an hour he is not aware of. He will cut him to pieces and assign him a place with the unbelievers.

This does appear to be a born again Christian for it says he is a servant. He is not living for the Lord; he has no concern for the things of the Lord. He is living carelessly, eating and drinking, going on with normal daily life, enjoying the pleasures of life without regard for the Lord or to the soon-approaching rapture. He is also found mistreating his fellowman. What happens? He is assigned his place with the unbelievers. He is left to go through the tribulation. This man does not lose his salvation for that is a gift to all who truly believe on the Lord Jesus Christ, but he loses his reward. For this Scripture would indicate that the Rapture is the reward of readiness.

Look at verses 47 and 48.

47"That servant who knows his master's will and does not get ready or does not do what his master wants will be beaten with many blows. 48But the one who does not know and does things deserving punishment will be beaten with few blows.

Notice it says "that servant who knows his master's will and does not get ready or does not do what his master wants". It does say his master, so this sounds like he is a Christian, so he has been saved. This also sounds like it could be referring to the tribulation. The one not living for the Lord now will have to prove him or herself through the tribulation.

Look at Revelation chapter 3.

14"To the angel of the church in Laodicea write: These are the words of the Amen, the faithful and true witness, the ruler of

God's creation. 15I know your deeds, that you are neither cold nor hot. I wish you were either one or the other! 16So, because you are lukewarm—neither hot nor cold—I am about to spit you out of my mouth. 17You say, 'I am rich; I have acquired wealth and do not need a thing.' But you do not realize that you are wretched, pitiful, poor, blind and naked.

There are Christians that are lukewarm.

Could the parable of the 10 virgins be that a born again Christian not ready for his coming for the Church, one not living for the Lord, living his life with no regard or no concern for the Lord, living a sinful life style, could such a person not go with the Church in the rapture and be left to go into the tribulation? I just don't know. Like I said earlier, I have always just assumed that if you were born again that would be what gets you taken up in the rapture just like that is what gets you into heaven. But those that teach that a Christian could be left behind have a point. Look again at what Luke said.

> Luke 21: 34"Be careful, or your hearts will be weighed down with dissipation, drunkenness and the anxieties of life, and that day will close on you unexpectedly like a trap. 35For it will come upon all those who live on the face of the whole earth. 36Be always on the watch, and pray that you may be able to escape all that is about to happen, and that you may be able to stand before the Son of Man."

If their view is correct it doesn't mean you have to be sinless to go up in the rapture. None of us are going to be perfect. We all sin and fall sort of the glory of God. It would be the one living for the Lord would repent daily of their sins, where the one not living for the Lord would not. He most likely wouldn't even think anything about it. You should examine yourself. Is Jesus part of your 'daily' life?

There are those that believe that the 10 virgins are a reference to the guests that are invited to the wedding supper which takes place here on earth after Jesus' return, thus believing this is referring to Jesus' second coming, the same as the separation of the sheep and the goats and Jesus sending the angels to gather the elect in Revelation, with the 'at that time' referring back to Matt. 24 verse 51. This view doesn't work for one; the wedding supper of the Lamb will be here on earth after Jesus returns, Revelation 19.

This view also doesn't work because you see in verse 1 the virgins went out to meet the Groom when he is first returning from his Father's house <u>for</u> his bride not when the bride and groom are coming out of the bridle chamber after the 7 days, as would be the case at his second coming.

The guests are invited to the wedding supper that happens after the 7 days the bride and groom have been in the bridle chamber. This will be the case for all those that have survived the tribulation. There could be guests present at the Grooms Fathers house when they arrived. There would be guests, friends and family that have gathered from hearing the announcement and those that are part of the procession with the groom, Angels could be these guests, but here the guests are not the virgins that are let into the wedding banquet. The point of the verse is that the Groom was coming <u>for</u> his bride from the Fathers house, not coming out of the bridle chamber with his bride. Verse 10 says wedding banquet, which happens during the 7 days the bride and groom are in the bridle chamber, not after they come out of the bridle chamber. Again, the guests were not waiting and watching with the bride. Guests are invited to the wedding super after the bride and groom have come out of the bridle chamber. The 10 virgins being a reference to his second coming at the end of the tribulation doesn't work with all the statements Jesus made, which seem to be an example from the Jewish Wedding Custom.

Verse 1, they are waiting for the Groom to come for his bride.

Verse 5, the bridegroom was a long time in coming. If this were referring to when he came out of the bridle chamber then it would have only been 7 days. They would not have fallen asleep during the wedding banquet. I'm sure people won't fall asleep during the tribulation. Plus the bride is no longer waiting for her groom when they are in the bridle chamber.

Verse 10, they went into the banquet which is during the 7 days the bride and groom are in the bridle chamber.

Verse 13 they are told to keep watch. This was for him to come for his bride to take her to his Father's house, not watching for the groom to come out of the bridle chamber, after he had been together with his bride for 7 days and nights.

So when he said in verse 1 "at that time". This is referring back to Matthew 24 verse 36 "No one knows about that day or hour" where he was referring to the Rapture and to the beginning of the tribulation. Verse 50, The master of that servant will come on a day when he does not expect him and at an hour he is not aware of.

In verse 6 he said

> "At midnight the cry rang out: `Here's the bridegroom! Come out to meet him!'

This would be referring to when the Groom first returns from his Father's house for his bride. The bridesmaids would keep watch with the bride for the Groom and go out to meet him. At Jesus' 2nd coming he is returning with his bride. Just like with the wedding custom, at the end of the 7 days of being in the bridle chamber the groom comes out with his bride, then there's the wedding super/feast.

I think Jesus was just using the 10 virgins as a point for being saved, ready and watching.

Notice there isn't any mention of the bride. This is why I think this is just an example of how people will be at Jesus' coming for his bride, the Church. He's just distinguishing between believers and unbelievers. Here I think we should look at the lesson he was giving.

With the parable of the Talents Jesus gives another example of how it will be during the days before the rapture.

The Parable of the Talents

14"Again, it will be like a man going on a journey, who called his servants and entrusted his property to them. 15To one he gave five talents of money, to another two talents, and to another one talent, each according to his ability. Then he went on his journey. 16The man who had received the five talents went at once and put his money to work and gained five more. 17So also, the one with the two talents gained two more. 18But the man who had received the one talent went off, dug a hole in the ground and hid his master's money.

19"After a long time the master of those servants returned and settled accounts with them. 20The man who had received the five talents brought the other five. 'Master,' he said, 'you entrusted me with five talents. See, I have gained five more.'
21"His master replied, 'Well done, good and faithful servant! You have been faithful with a few things; I will put you in charge of many things. Come and share your master's happiness!' 22"The man with the two talents also came. 'Master,' he said, 'you entrusted me with two talents; see, I have gained two more.' 23"His master replied, 'Well done, good and faithful servant! You have been faithful with a few things; I will put you in charge of many things. Come and share your master's happiness!'

24"Then the man who had received the one talent came. 'Master,' he said, 'I knew that you are a hard man, harvesting where you have not sown and gathering where you have not scattered seed. 25So I was afraid and went out and hid your talent in the ground. See, here is what belongs to you.' 26"His master replied, 'You wicked, lazy servant! So you knew that I harvest where I have not sown and gather where I have not scattered seed? 27Well then, you should have put my money on deposit with the bankers, so that when I returned I would have received it back with interest. 28" 'Take the talent from him and give it to the one who has the ten talents. 29For everyone who has will be given more, and he will have an abundance. Whoever does not have, even what he has will be taken from him. 30And throw that worthless servant outside, into the darkness, where there will be weeping and gnashing of teeth.'

With verse 14 he said "Again, it will be like" referring back to verse 1 and Mt. 24 verse 36. Verse 14 thru 18 also sounds like the times we're in now, the Church age, the time since Pentecost, for notice again with verse 19, after a long time the master returned to settle accounts with them. For those that live through the tribulation this sounds like the judgment that will happen here on earth after Jesus has returned, but it also sounds like the judgment seat of Christ. For Christians, living or dead, after the rapture, will be the judgment seat of Christ in heaven where all those that were caught up in the rapture will have their deeds judged and receive their rewards. For the non-believer that has already died; the final judgment.

Look at what Luke has in chapter 19. It's a lot like what Matthew says here, Luke seems to be addressing what will take place after Jesus' second coming, he may be giving us a look at just what we may be doing during the millennium reign of Jesus. Notice how it sounds just like when Jesus came from heaven to be appointed king and the Jews rejecting him as king then returning.

Luke 19:

The Parable of the Ten Minas

> 11While they were listening to this, he went on to tell them a parable, because he was near Jerusalem and the people thought that the kingdom of God was going to appear at once. 12He said: "A man of noble birth went to a distant country to have himself appointed king and then to return. 13So he called ten of his servants and gave them ten minas. 'Put this money to work,' he said, 'until I come back.'

14"But his subjects hated him and sent a delegation after him to say, 'We don't want this man to be our king.'

15"He was made king, however, and returned home. Then he sent for the servants to whom he had given the money, in order to find out what they had gained with it.

16"The first one came and said, 'Sir, your mina has earned ten more.' 17" 'Well done, my good servant!' his master replied. 'Because you have been trustworthy in a very small matter, take charge of ten cities.'

18"The second came and said, 'Sir, your mina has earned five more.' 19"His master answered, 'You take charge of five cities.'

Could it be that we are going to be put in charge of cities during the millennium?

20"Then another servant came and said, 'Sir, here is your mina; I have kept it laid away in a piece of cloth. 21I was afraid of you, because you are a hard man. You take out what you did not put in and reap what you did not sow.'

22"His master replied, 'I will judge you by your own words, you wicked servant! You knew, did you, that I am a hard man, taking out what I did not put in, and reaping what I did not sow? 23Why then didn't you put my money on deposit, so that when I came back, I could have collected it with interest?' 24"Then he said to those standing by, 'Take his mina away from him and give it to the one who has ten minas.'

25" 'Sir,' they said, 'he already has ten!'

26"He replied, 'I tell you that to everyone who has, more will be given, but as for the one who has nothing, even what he has will be taken away. 27But those enemies of mine who did not want me to be king over them—bring them here and kill them in front of me."

Though a little different, you can see how this is saying the same thing as in Matthew chapter 25. Luke could have gotten this from a different sermon for I'm sure Jesus taught on this on more than one occasion. Here, Luke could have been addressing the Jews.

Paul on the judgment seat of Christ.

> 2 Corinthians 5: 9So we make it our goal to please him, whether we are at home in the body or away from it. 10For we must all appear before the judgment seat of Christ, that each one may receive what is due him for the things done while in the body, whether good or bad.

All those that have been saved since the day of Pentecost will be judged and receive their rewards in heaven after the rapture. The judgment after his second coming is where he will raise and judge those that lived and died during the tribulation that accepted Jesus, we see this in Revelation chapter 20. All those that were righteous during the Old Testament times are also raised at this time. Those that are found righteous from the Old Testament Times and the Tribulation will enter into the Kingdom here on earth to rule and reign with the Church age saints as immortals. You see this in the last chapter of Daniel.

> Daniel 12: 1 "At that time Michael, the great prince who protects your people, will arise. There will be a time of distress such as has not happened from the beginning of nations until then. But at that time your people—everyone whose name is found written in the book—will be delivered. 2 Multitudes who sleep in the dust of the earth will awake: some to everlasting life, others to shame and everlasting contempt. 3 Those who are wise will shine like the brightness of the heavens, and those who lead many to righteousness, like the stars for ever and ever.

Isaiah in chapter 26 and Ezekiel in chapter 37 also speak of this resurrection.

> Isa. 26:19 But your dead will live; their bodies will rise. You who dwell in the dust, wake up and shout for joy Your dew is like the dew of the morning; the earth will give birth to her dead.

> Ez. 37: 12 Therefore prophesy and say to them: 'This is what the Sovereign LORD says: O my people, I am going to open your graves and bring you up from them; I will bring you back to the land of Israel. 13 Then you, my people, will know that I am the LORD, when I open your graves and bring you up from them. 14 I will put my Spirit in you and you will live, and I will settle you in your own land. Then you will know that I the LORD have spoken, and I have done it, declares the LORD.' "

Jesus will also judge those that lived through the tribulation to see if they are righteous and are worthy to enter the kingdom. You will see this with the separation of the sheep and the goats in verse 31 of Matthew 25.

The driving theme here is that 2 of the servants served the Lord, bore fruit, did something with their lives for the Lord while one didn't. He knew of the Lord but didn't have him in his heart, didn't serve him, just lived his life without any thought of the Lord. Just buried his talent and just went on with his life not thinking any more about it until it was too late. He's making the same point as with the 10 virgins. The talents could also be referring to how much someone has grown in the Lord. Some people don't go to Church or read their bibles to learn anything. They never gain any more knowledge concerning the things in the bible. They never get to know the Lord.

So from the statements made here with the parables of the talents, and the 10 minas, they both fit with the time we are in now, the Church age, though Luke seems to include the time of the tribulation also. The point is, everyone will be judged.

Matt. 25:31– 46.

This is the end time harvest when Jesus returns. With verse 31 he goes back to referring to his second coming. You see He doesn't start it with again or at that time as when he referred back to Matthew 24:36. He goes into describing what will take place after he returns for the establishing of the kingdom of God.

The Sheep and the Goats

> MT 25:31 "When the Son of Man comes in his glory, and all the angels with him, he will sit on his throne in heavenly glory. 32 All the nations will be gathered before him, and he will separate the people one from another as a shepherd separates the sheep from the goats. 33 He will put the sheep on his right and the goats on his left.

> 34 "Then the King will say to those on his right, `Come, you who are blessed by my Father; take your inheritance, the kingdom prepared for you since the creation of the world.

First notice in verse 31 when he comes in glory all the angels come with him. At the rapture no angels come. After his 2nd coming He sits on his throne ready to Judge.

Second, verse 32 all the nations are gathered before him and he separates the people. This doesn't happen at the rapture.

Third, verses 33 and 34 he separates the sheep and the goats. He tells the sheep to come and take their inheritance, the kingdom prepared for them. The goats go into eternal punishment. Where there will be weeping and gnashing of teeth.

Let's read Matthew chapter 13 from verse 24. He goes into more detail.

Matthew 13.

The Parable of the Weeds

24Jesus told them another parable: "The kingdom of heaven is like a man who sowed good seed in his field. 25But while everyone was sleeping, his enemy came and sowed weeds among the wheat, and went away. 26When the wheat sprouted and formed heads, then the weeds also appeared 27"The owner's servants came to him and said, 'Sir, didn't you sow good seed in your field? Where then did the weeds come from? 28" 'An enemy did this,' he replied. "The servants asked him, 'Do you want us to go and pull them up?'29" 'No,' he answered, 'because while you are pulling the weeds, you may root up the wheat with them. 30Let both grow together until the harvest. At that time I will tell the harvesters: First collect the weeds and tie them in bundles to be burned; then gather the wheat and bring it into my barn.' "

The Parable of the Weeds Explained

36Then he left the crowd and went into the house. His disciples came to him and said, "Explain to us the parable of the weeds in the field."

37He answered, "The one who sowed the good seed is the Son of Man. 38The field is the world, and the good seed stands for the sons of the kingdom. The weeds are the sons of the evil one, 39and the enemy who sows them is the devil. The harvest is the end of the age, and the harvesters arc angels.

40"As the weeds are pulled up and burned in the fire, so it will be at the end of the age. 41The Son of Man will send out his angels, and they will weed out of his kingdom everything that causes sin and all who do evil. 42They will throw them into the fiery furnace, where there will be weeping and gnashing of teeth. 43Then the righteous will shine like the sun in the kingdom of their Father. He who has ears, let him hear.

The Parable of the Net

> 47"Once again, the kingdom of heaven is like a net that was let down into the lake and caught all kinds of fish. 48When it was full, the fishermen pulled it up on the shore. Then they sat down and collected the good fish in baskets, but threw the bad away. 49This is how it will be at the end of the age. The angels will come and separate the wicked from the righteous 50and throw them into the fiery furnace, where there will be weeping and gnashing of teeth.

At the Rapture there are no angels involved, only Jesus. Also, with the rapture first the righteous, the Church are called up and the wicked are left behind, after the 2nd coming it's the wicked that are separated first and then the righteous left to go into the kingdom. The two cannot be the same event or happen at the same time. Here we see only the righteous will enter into the Kingdom.

Let's continue with Matthew 25.

> 35 For I was hungry and you gave me something to eat, I was thirsty and you gave me something to drink, I was a stranger and you invited me in, 36 I needed clothes and you clothed me, I was sick and you looked after me, I was in prison and you came to visit me.' 37 "Then the righteous will answer him, `Lord, when did we see you hungry and feed you, or thirsty and give you something to drink? 38 When did we see you a stranger and invite you in, or needing clothes and clothe you? 39 When did we see you sick or in prison and go to visit you?'

> 40 "The King will reply, `I tell you the truth, whatever you did for one of the least of these brothers of mine, you did for me.'

> 41 "Then he will say to those on his left, `Depart from me, you who are cursed, into the eternal fire prepared for the devil and his angels. 42 For I was hungry and you gave me nothing to eat, I was thirsty and you gave me nothing to drink, 43 I was a

186

stranger and you did not invite me in, I needed clothes and you did not clothe me, I was sick and in prison and you did not look after me.' 44 "They also will answer, `Lord, when did we see you hungry or thirsty or a stranger or needing clothes or sick or in prison, and did not help you?'

45 "He will reply, `I tell you the truth, whatever you did not do for one of the least of these, you did not do for me.'
46 "Then they will go away to eternal punishment, but the righteous to eternal life."

Verses 31 thru 34 obviously takes place after Jesus has returned to the earth, after his second coming. This is when he judges those that lived through the tribulation.

Verses 35 thru 45 are during the tribulation. Jesus here seems to be showing how those that were living during the tribulation treated the 144,000 Jewish evangelists and anyone else that are righteous during the tribulation. Only those that have accepted Jesus would risk their lives for another believer during this last half of the tribulation.

Those that accepted Jesus will go into the earthly kingdom, those that did not accept Jesus will not enter the kingdom. They will die. The earthly kingdom of God will start with only the righteous, those that have believed in and have accepted Jesus.

Jesus mentions this also in chapter 16 of Matthew.

MT. 16:27 For the Son of Man is going to come in his Father's glory with his angels, and then he will reward each person according to what he has done.

Notice the progression here in chapter 25, first the Rapture verse 1 through 13. Next those that lived during the Church age being judged and receiving their rewards, verse 14 thru 23. Verses 24 thru 30 are the outcome of those that hide their talent. To me this also sounds like those that have heard the gospel, know all about Jesus but didn't do anything, just ignored it, they just kept putting it off, they never accepted Jesus as Lord and Savior. Again, the same point and message as the 10 virgins. Then his second coming, verses 31 through 46 and the judgment of those that lived through the tribulation.

My advice to everyone is to take a look at your on life, do you have the Lord Jesus in your life, are you serving him or have you buried him in the ground with no thought or concern for him. Judge yourself now before it's too late.

2 Corinthians 13

> 5Examine yourselves to see whether you are in the faith; test yourselves. Do you not realize that Christ Jesus is in you—unless, of course, you fail the test?

We see the same theme through all these scriptures. Those that believe and have accepted Jesus into their lives will take part in the blessed hope of being taken back to the Father's house at the rapture. All those that have not will be left to go through the tribulation. It's each person's decision. The rapture is a reward of accepting him now.

Don't wait until the Church disappears. Come to Jesus now. Pray where you are. Make things right between you and God. Confess your sins. Believe on the Lord Jesus. Welcome Him into your heart and prepare to go with the Church. Because you do not know at what hour Jesus will come. But more important than being ready for the Rapture, if you died now, are you ready to stand before the Lord.

Jesus is coming for the Church; it could be sooner than you think. Are you ready for it?

Maranatha
Our Lord Comes.

Chapter Six

The End Time Prophecies
of Ezekiel

1. Ezekiel 36

Ezekiel has many prophecies, some that have been fulfilled and many that have not. Ezekiel takes us into the kingdom of God here on earth, the 1000 year reign of Christ. Here we will look at the prophecies that deal with the re-gathering of the Jews back to Israel and with chapters 38 and 39 an end time invasion of Israel by Russia and her allies.

Ezekiel was from the tribe of Levi and he was trained as a priest and would have become one if he hadn't been taken captive to Babylon in the 2nd siege of Jerusalem in 597 B.C. Daniel was taken captive 8 years earlier in 605 B.C. with the first siege of Nebuchadnezzar. There would be one more finial siege, which began in 586 B.C. that caused the desolation and destruction of Jerusalem and the Temple.

After the death of Solomon the 12 tribes of Israel split with 10 of the tribes being to the North, which were called Israel, and 2 tribes to the South called Judah. Jerusalem was part of the Southern kingdom of Judah. The southern kingdom of Judah was all that was left of Israel since Assyria had conquered the northern kingdom over 100 years earlier.

The people of Judah by abandoning God for the pagan deities of their neighbors, they had not only become unclean as a people, but had defiled the temple, the city, and the land. They had ignored the warnings of the earlier prophets like Isaiah, as they were Jeremiah and now Ezekiel. God's only choice now was to withdraw Himself, send the people into captivity and destroy the nation of Judah as he had done to the Kingdom of Israel in the North.

It was in the fifth year of his captivity that Ezekiel was called as a prophet. The Book of Ezekiel speaks both of judgment and of restoration. The first 24 chapters deal mostly with the Lord's warnings against His people, and His efforts to convince them that Jerusalem would be destroyed, and their temple would be burned to the ground. Ezekiel tried to persuade them to turn away from their idols and back to God. History shows us that when the people of Israel turned away from God he would have to bring disaster on them to get them to turn back to him. We can see this is the purpose for the judgments in the book of Revelation, only then it will be for the whole world.

In Chapters 25-32 Ezekiel pronounced judgment on Israel's neighbors for their treatment of His people. In Chapter 33 the fall of Jerusalem was announced and explained, and in Chapter 34 the Lord said that since Israel's leaders didn't take care of the people, He would send His Servant David to lead them. David had been dead for 400 years, so this is interpreted to mean the Messiah, the son of David, of which is a Messianic prophesy of the earthly kingdom of God. He foretells the scattering of the Jews throughout the world which found its fulfillment in a.d. 70, then of their re-gathering back to the land of Israel and finally of Jesus' earthly reign. Then in chapter 35 follows a final pronouncement against Edom. The people of Edom were descendants of Esau and therefore cousins of the Israelites. Because of their treatment of the people of Judah, God decreed the total desolation of Edom, which was accomplished by the Nabateans. The Arab people of today are descendants of Ishmael, Abraham's son by his wife's handmaiden (servant girl) Hagar. The descendants of Esau and Ishmael had intermarried but today there is no direct trace of the descendants of Esau. Today, Edom would refer to all the Arab people. While chapter 35 concerning the descendants of Esau could be seen as having been fulfilled in the past, there are verses that point to a yet future fulfillment. The Jews are descendants of Abraham's son Isaac through his wife Sarah of whom the promised Messiah would come, of which we now know is Jesus. This promise was made to Abraham and his wife Sarah, not to Hagar.

You will see here in our look at Ezekiel the future outcome of the judgment of God against those that come against Israel. You will see this also in the book of Revelation.

That brings us to chapter 36, where Ezekiel shifted to a promise of restoration and while there are other end time prophecies throughout Ezekiel this is where the major End Time Prophecies of Ezekiel begin and continue till the end which takes us into the Earthly Kingdom of God here on earth. Here in Ezekiel you will see one of the major prophecies of the return of the Jews back to their home land that began after World War One that eventually resulted in the rebirth of Israel as a nation.

Ezekiel 36

A Prophecy to the Mountains of Israel

> 1 "Son of man, prophesy to the mountains of Israel and say, 'O mountains of Israel, hear the word of the LORD. 2 This is what the Sovereign LORD says: The enemy said of you, "Aha! The ancient heights have become our possession." ' 3 Therefore prophesy and say, 'This is what the Sovereign LORD says: Because they ravaged and hounded you from every side so that you became the possession of the rest of the nations and the object of people's malicious talk and slander,

> 4 therefore, O mountains of Israel, hear the word of the Sovereign LORD : This is what the Sovereign LORD says to the mountains and hills, to the ravines and valleys, to the desolate ruins and the deserted towns that have been plundered and ridiculed by the rest of the nations around you- 5 this is what the Sovereign LORD says: In my burning zeal I have spoken against the rest of the nations, and against all Edom, for with glee and with malice in their hearts they made my land their own possession so that they might plunder its pastureland.' 6 Therefore prophesy concerning the land of Israel and say to the mountains and hills, to the ravines and valleys: 'This is what the Sovereign LORD says: I speak in my jealous wrath because you have suffered the scorn of the nations. 7 Therefore this is what the Sovereign LORD says: I swear with uplifted hand that the nations around you will also suffer scorn.

> 8 " 'But you, O mountains of Israel, will produce branches and fruit for my people Israel, for they will soon come home. 9 I am concerned for you and will look on you with favor; you will

be plowed and sown, 10 and I will multiply the number of people upon you, even the whole house of Israel. The towns will be inhabited and the ruins rebuilt. 11 I will increase the number of men and animals upon you, and they will be fruitful and become numerous. I will settle people on you as in the past and will make you prosper more than before. Then you will know that I am the LORD. 12 I will cause people, my people Israel, to walk upon you. They will possess you, and you will be their inheritance; you will never again deprive them of their children.

13 " 'This is what the Sovereign LORD says: Because people say to you, "You devour men and deprive your nation of its children," 14 therefore you will no longer devour men or make your nation childless, declares the Sovereign LORD. 15 No longer will I make you hear the taunts of the nations, and no longer will you suffer the scorn of the peoples or cause your nation to fall, declares the Sovereign LORD.' "

This prophecy could be seen as being fulfilled after the Israelites returned from captivity by the Babylonians. But since they were completely driven from the land again in 70 A.D. following their rejection of the Jesus we know its complete fulfillment was yet still in the future. One clue that this has to be referring to the re-gathering that began after WWI is in verse 10 where it says' "even the whole house of Israel". The Jews didn't have control of all the land of Israel after the Babylonian return only the city of Jerusalem and the temple. There wasn't a nation of Israel even during the time Jesus was here. We see also with verse 12 that the Lord said "you will never again deprive them of their children". The people of Israel weren't in the land to have children from 70 a.d. until really 1948 when they became a nation again and the Jews started returning by the hundreds of thousands.

This prophecy began to be fulfilled when the Jews began returning to the land after World War 1 and then in 1948 when Israel became a nation again. The promise made to Israel in verse 15 does not describe Israel today; the requirements of the promises given here will find their complete fulfillment in the future. The final restoration of Israel will occur after Jesus has returned.

> 16 Again the word of the LORD came to me: 17 "Son of man, when the people of Israel were living in their own land, they defiled it by their conduct and their actions. Their conduct was like a woman's monthly uncleanness in my sight. 18 So I poured out my wrath on them because they had shed blood in the land and because they had defiled it with their idols. 19 I dispersed them among the nations, and they were scattered through the countries; I judged them according to their conduct and their actions. 20 And wherever they went among the nations they profaned my holy name, for it was said of them, 'These are the LORD's people, and yet they had to leave his land.' 21 I had concern for my holy name, which the house of Israel profaned among the nations where they had gone.

The word of the Lord started in verse 16 sounds like it could be referring to the dispersion that took place in 70 a.d. Where the Babylonian destruction caused the Jews to mostly be taken captive into Babylon, the 70 a.d. destruction caused them to be scattered out into many nations. God not only judged them for rejecting Jesus, but the religious rulers and teachers had become corrupt.

> 22 "Therefore say to the house of Israel, 'This is what the Sovereign LORD says: It is not for your sake, O house of Israel, that I am going to do these things, but for the sake of my holy name, which you have profaned among the nations where you have gone. 23 I will show the holiness of my great name, which has been profaned among the nations, the name you have profaned among them. Then the nations will know that I am the LORD, declares the Sovereign LORD, when I show myself holy through you before their eyes.

You see it said repeatedly that it is for the Lord's namesake that he will do this, not because of the people of Israel. This is why the Jews have survived as a people all these thousands of years even though they didn't have a country from the Babylonian destruction until 1948.

The remaining verses here in chapter 36 sounds like they are referring more to the latter day re-gathering than to the one after the Babylonian captivity.

> 24 "'For I will take you out of the nations; I will gather you from all the countries and bring you back into your own land.

Many believe that verse 24 has already started with the rebirth of Israel as a nation in 1948 and Jews coming back to their homeland from all over the world. Every year there are more and more Jews returning to Israel. The re-gathering since 1948 is the first phase; it actually continues through the first half of the tribulation and is completed after Jesus has returned. With Israel being lost as a nation for thousands of years and then suddenly becoming a nation again we can see that the words of these prophecies are the word of the Lord. Oh, notice he said back to their on land. The land belongs to the Jews.

There's an amazing verse in Isaiah that describes the rebirth of Israel as a nation that took place in 1948.

Isaiah 66

> 8 Who has ever heard of such a thing?
> Who has ever seen such things?
> Can a country be born in a day
> or a nation be brought forth in a moment?
> Yet no sooner is Zion in labor
> than she gives birth to her children.

In 1948 the United Nations assembled to vote on establishing Israel as a nation again. Israel became a nation again the moment the United Nations proclaimed it. This took place on a single day.

While here in chapter 36 we can see the beginning of verse 24 has started; verses 25 thru 36 will not be accomplished until Jesus has returned and sets up the earthly Kingdom of God, for we cannot fit the descriptions of these verses with the condition of Israel now. The final re-gathering of the Jews to Israel will be completed after Jesus has returned. Jesus will bring all the Jews from all over the world that have not already returned, back to their homeland, Israel.

> Ez. 36: 25 I will sprinkle clean water on you, and you will be clean; I will cleanse you from all your impurities and from all your idols. 26 I will give you a new heart and put a new spirit in you; I will remove from you your heart of stone and give you a heart of flesh. 27 And I will put my Spirit in you and move you to follow my decrees and be careful to keep my laws. 28 You will live in the land I gave your forefathers; you will be my people, and I will be your God. 29 I will save you from all your uncleanness. I will call for the grain and make it plentiful and will not bring famine upon you. 30 I will increase the fruit of the trees and the crops of the field, so that you will no longer suffer disgrace among the nations because of famine. 31 Then you will remember your evil ways and wicked deeds, and you will loathe yourselves for your sins and detestable practices. 32 I want you to know that I am not doing this for your sake, declares the Sovereign LORD. Be ashamed and disgraced for your conduct, O house of Israel!

We can see from verses 22 thru 32 that the incorrect teaching of Replacement Theology, that the Church has replaced Israel, is totally false. This shows that it's not because of anything the Jews have done but because of and for the name of the Lord that's he's going to do this. God is going to keep his promises to Israel for his names sake.

Again, while this could be seen as referring to the return from the Babylonian captivity, which I'm sure those that returned back from Babylon would see their return as fulfilling this prophecy, we can see statements that did not apply to or were fulfilled with the return from the Babylonian captivity. We can see clues here that suggest that this is also referring to the return from all the countries that began with the return after World War 1. Remember, a prophecy can refer to more than one event and time or its complete fulfillment can be separated by thousands of years. First clue is being brought back from the nations and countries they had been scattered into. During the Babylonian captivity they were mainly taken into captivity into Babylon, not many nations like was the case after the 70 a.d. destruction by the Romans. Second clue, they will remove all the vile images and detestable idols, this would be a reference to the Temple that will be present during the tribulation. Remember, the Temple and all of Jerusalem were destroyed a second time by the Romans. This could be referring to the image of the anti-Christ that will be set up in the temple during the second half of the tribulation. Third, verses 25 thru 27, "25 I will sprinkle clean water on you, and you will be clean; I will cleanse you from all your impurities and from all your idols. 26 I will give you a new heart and put a new spirit in you; I will remove from you your heart of stone and give you a heart of flesh. 27 And I will put my Spirit in you and move you to follow my decrees and be careful to keep my laws." This will take place after Jesus has returned.

These verses suggest that this is not referring to the return from Babylon but to a yet future time. These promises were not possible with the return from Babylon because Jesus hadn't come yet. Now that Jesus has died and Rose again, this promise will be fulfilled by the Holy Spirit, the New Birth. It will be fulfilled for Israel once they have accepted Jesus as the Messiah and he has returned.

> 33 " 'This is what the Sovereign LORD says: On the day I cleanse you from all your sins, I will resettle your towns, and the ruins will be rebuilt. 34 The desolate land will be cultivated instead of lying desolate in the sight of all who pass through it. 35 They will say, "This land that was laid waste has become like the garden of Eden; the cities that were lying in ruins, desolate and destroyed, are now fortified and inhabited." 36 Then the nations around you that remain will know that I the LORD have rebuilt what was destroyed and have replanted what was desolate. I the LORD have spoken, and I will do it.'

37 "This is what the Sovereign LORD says: Once again I will yield to the plea of the house of Israel and do this for them: I will make their people as numerous as sheep, 38 as numerous as the flocks for offerings at Jerusalem during her appointed feasts. So will the ruined cities be filled with flocks of people. Then they will know that I am the LORD."

Again, with verses 33 thru 38 you can see that they were not fulfilled with the return from Babylon or with the return after WWI and WWII, they have to be for a future time. While it could appear they were at least partially fulfilled with the return from Babylon, the fact that Israel was destroyed in 70 A.D. by the Romans and were drove out into the nations, and the land was desolate until after 1948 when Israel was proclaimed a nation again, rules out that he was only referring to the return from Babylon. Starting with verse 33 he said "On the day I cleanse you from all your sins" and then with verse 35, "This land that was laid waste has become like the garden of Eden" will take place after Jesus has returned. While the land of Israel is great you wouldn't say it's like the Garden of Eden. You will see in our look at Revelation that after Jesus has returned he will restore the earth from all the destruction that has occurred during the tribulation. We see from verse 36 that the Lord will rebuild and replant what has been destroyed. And notice this from verse 36, "Then the nations around you that remain will know that I the LORD have rebuilt what was destroyed and have replanted what was desolate". He said the nations that remain, remain from what? From the destruction that takes place during the tribulation. This is not just a description of the Babylonian or Roman destruction of which only Jerusalem and the Temple were destroyed. The countries that now surround Israel will be destroyed during the tribulation. Those that remain will know Jesus is Lord after he returns. This shows that this prophecy takes us to the return of Christ back down to the Earth.

Also with him saying 'on the day I cleanse you from all your sins, I will resettle your towns'. This will only happen after Jesus has returned. Most likely Israel and Jerusalem will be laid waste during the 2nd half of the tribulation for we know the Jews are going to have to flee from the anti-Christ during this time. We also know that there is going to be massive nuclear explosions throughout Israel and Jerusalem especially at the last battle of Armageddon. Again, the condition of Israel today does not fit with the promises. You have to take all the promises and conditions into account for the complete fulfillment of these prophecies.

The Jews haven't had the Old Testament means for their sins to be cleansed since the destruction of the first Temple. The Shekinah Glory departed the Temple before Jerusalem was destroyed by the Babylonians. You see this in Ezekiel 10 and 11. The Shekinah Glory (the presence of the Lord) has never returned and won't until the beginning of the Millennium with Jesus. See Ezekiel 43. The time period of the Second Temple took place without the Spirit of God hovering between the Cherubim above the Ark in the Holy of Holies. This was the case even when Jesus was here. There was no Ark of the Covenant along with the Mercy Seat and Cherubim present in the Holy of Holies. There wasn't even any furniture present, just a stone platform, called the foundation stone, on which the Ark had rested in the 1st Temple. It was just an empty room. The Ark of the Covenant wasn't present for the High Priest to sprinkle the blood on which was the requirement for the forgiveness of the sins of the people. For several hundred years they conducted the ceremony as if the Lord was there, sprinkling the blood on the foundation stone and hoping He would forgive them. After the 2nd Temple was destroyed in 70 a.d. they haven't even been able to do that.

Ezekiel 36 is an overview of the re-gathering of the Jews back to Israel that extends from that which actually started in the early 1900's and really began in 1948 and will be completed after Jesus has returned, at the beginning of the earthly Kingdom of God.

Other Old Testament scriptures about the re-gathering of Israel.

Jeremiah 31

8 See, I will bring them from the land of the north
and gather them from the ends of the earth.
Among them will be the blind and the lame,
expectant mothers and women in labor;
a great throng will return.
9 They will come with weeping;
they will pray as I bring them back.
I will lead them beside streams of water
on a level path where they will not stumble,
because I am Israel's father,
and Ephraim is my firstborn son.
10 "Hear the word of the LORD, O nations;
proclaim it in distant coastlands:
'He who scattered Israel will gather them
and will watch over his flock like a shepherd.'
11 For the LORD will ransom Jacob
        and redeem them from the hand of those stronger than they.

Isaiah 43

5 Do not be afraid, for I am with you;
I will bring your children from the east
and gather you from the west.
6 I will say to the north, 'Give them up!'
and to the south, 'Do not hold them back.'
Bring my sons from afar
and my daughters from the ends of the earth-
7 everyone who is called by my name,
whom I created for my glory,
whom I formed and made."

Since 1948 Jews from the North, from Russia, Germany and other parts of Europe along with Jews from the South, from Northern Africa have moved to Israel.

Isaiah 65

> 8 This is what the LORD says:
> "As when juice is still found in a cluster of grapes and men say,
> 'Don't destroy it, there is yet some good in it,' so will I do in
> behalf of my servants; I will not destroy them all. 9 I will bring
> forth descendants from Jacob, and from Judah those who will
> possess my mountains; my chosen people will inherit them, and
> there will my servants live.

The return of the Jews to the land and there being a nation of Israel is essential to end time prophecies. None of the prophecies that concern the time just before the return of Jesus to establish his kingdom here on earth could be fulfilled until the Jews were back in the land as a nation again. They also had to have control of Jerusalem again.

With seeing the prophecy of Israel becoming a nation again being fulfilled in 1948 let us know that we are living in the last days. With the way the condition and attitude of the Middle East and the world concerning Israel has become shows us that we are indeed close to all these prophecies being fulfilled. It lets us know that just like all the other prophecies from the past were literally fulfilled, these prophecies are to be taken literally also. We can see all that is prophesied falling into place right before our eyes.

2. Ezekiel 37

The Valley of Dry Bones

1 The hand of the LORD was upon me, and he brought me out by the Spirit of the LORD and set me in the middle of a valley; it was full of bones. 2 He led me back and forth among them, and I saw a great many bones on the floor of the valley, bones that were very dry. 3 He asked me, "Son of man, can these bones live?" I said, "O Sovereign LORD, you alone know."

4 Then he said to me, "Prophesy to these bones and say to them, 'Dry bones, hear the word of the LORD! 5 This is what the Sovereign LORD says to these bones: I will make breath enter you, and you will come to life. 6 I will attach tendons to you and make flesh come upon you and cover you with skin; I will put breath in you, and you will come to life. Then you will know that I am the LORD.' "

7 So I prophesied as I was commanded. And as I was prophesying, there was a noise, a rattling sound, and the bones came together, bone to bone. 8 I looked, and tendons and flesh appeared on them and skin covered them, but there was no breath in them.

9 Then he said to me, "Prophesy to the breath; prophesy, son of man, and say to it, 'This is what the Sovereign LORD says: Come from the four winds, O breath, and breathe into these slain, that they may live.' " 10 So I prophesied as he commanded me, and breath entered them; they came to life and stood up on their feet—a vast army.

Have you seen pictures of the dead bodies that had been thrown into ditches or were in the gas chambers during the holocaust, I wonder if this is a picture of that? While many believe this could also be a reference to the re-gathering of the Jews back to the land of Israel, this prophecy has more than that in view. Israel as they are now have no life in them, they don't have the Spirit of God. They lost the Spirit and their life when they rejected Jesus. They actually lost it with the destruction by the Babylonians. But after Jesus has returned he will pour out his Spirit and they will have the breath of God in them. They will be filled with life once again. They will be filled with the Holy Spirit of the New Covenant. We see this again with verse 14. We also see this foretold by Joel.

> Joel 2: 28 "And afterward,
> I will pour out my Spirit on all people.
> Your sons and daughters will prophesy,
> your old men will dream dreams,
> your young men will see visions.
> 29 Even on my servants, both men and women,
> I will pour out my Spirit in those days.

And afterward, that is after the tribulation. We see in Daniel chapter 12 that after Jesus has returned all of the Old Testament Saints will be raised to life, we see this also here and again with verse 12 and 13. This will also include those that died during the holocaust and those that have died during the tribulation. We see this in Revelation chapter 20. All the righteous throughout all the generations will be raised back to life by Jesus after he has returned.

> 11 Then he said to me: "Son of man, these bones are the whole house of Israel. They say, 'Our bones are dried up and our hope is gone; we are cut off.' 12 Therefore prophesy and say to them: 'This is what the Sovereign LORD says: O my people, I am going to open your graves and bring you up from them; I will bring you back to the land of Israel. 13 Then you, my people, will know that I am the LORD, when I open your graves and bring you up from them. 14 I will put my Spirit in you and you will live, and I will settle you in your own land. Then you will know that I the LORD have spoken, and I have done it, declares the LORD.' "

Again, the re-gathering of the Jews back to the land of Israel will be completed after Jesus has returned.

Take a look at these scriptures that are describing what Jesus will do after he has returned.

> Zechariah 8: 3 This is what the LORD says: "I will return to Zion and dwell in Jerusalem. Then Jerusalem will be called the City of Truth, and the mountain of the LORD Almighty will be called the Holy Mountain." 7 This is what the LORD Almighty says: "I will save my people from the countries of the east and the west. 8 I will bring them back to live in Jerusalem; they will be my people, and I will be faithful and righteous to them as their God."

> Isaiah 11: 10 In that day the Root of Jesse will stand as a banner for the peoples; the nations will rally to him, and his place of rest will be glorious. 11 In that day the Lord will reach out his hand a second time to reclaim the remnant that is left of his people from Assyria, from Lower Egypt, from Upper Egypt, from Cush, from Elam, from Babylonia, from Hamath and from the islands of the sea. 12 He will raise a banner for the nations and gather the exiles of Israel; he will assemble the scattered people of Judah from the four quarters of the earth.

The root of Jesse is Jesus.

Verses 1 thru 14 here in Ezekiel 37 sounds like they are describing the resurrection of the Old Testament and tribulation Saints after Jesus' second coming. Again, you see this also in chapter 12 of Daniel. The time of distress is what occurs during the tribulation. Compare verse one of Daniel 12 with Matthew 24 verse 21, "For then there will be great distress, unequaled from the beginning of the world until now—and never to be equaled again".

> Dan. 12: 1 "At that time Michael, the great prince who protects your people, will arise. There will be a time of distress such as has not happened from the beginning of nations until then. But

at that time your people—everyone whose name is found written in the book—will be delivered.

2 Multitudes who sleep in the dust of the earth will awake: some to everlasting life, others to shame and everlasting contempt.

The rest of chapter 37 is describing what Jesus will do after he has returned and has set up his earthly kingdom. When he is referring to them being under one king, his servant David this is actually a reference to Jesus. At that time they didn't know what the Messiah's name would be so the Old Testament Scriptures when referring to the Messiah during the kingdom of God on earth would refer to him as God's servant David. David was promised that one of his descendants would sit on the thrown forever during the kingdom of God. Jesus, through Mary is a descendant of David. Jesus is even a descendant of David's through Joseph's family line.

One Nation Under One King

15 The word of the LORD came to me: 16 "Son of man, take a stick of wood and write on it, 'Belonging to Judah and the Israelites associated with him.' Then take another stick of wood, and write on it, 'Ephraim's stick, belonging to Joseph and all the house of Israel associated with him.' 17 Join them together into one stick so that they will become one in your hand.

18 "When your countrymen ask you, 'Won't you tell us what you mean by this?' 19 say to them, 'This is what the Sovereign LORD says: I am going to take the stick of Joseph—which is in Ephraim's hand—and of the Israelite tribes associated with him, and join it to Judah's stick, making them a single stick of wood, and they will become one in my hand.' 20 Hold before their eyes the sticks you have written on 21 and say to them, 'This is what the Sovereign LORD says: I will take the Israelites out of the nations where they have gone. I will gather them

from all around and bring them back into their own land. 22 I will make them one nation in the land, on the mountains of Israel. There will be one king over all of them and they will never again be two nations or be divided into two kingdoms. 23 They will no longer defile themselves with their idols and vile images or with any of their offenses, for I will save them from all their sinful backsliding, and I will cleanse them. They will be my people, and I will be their God.

24 " 'My servant David will be king over them, and they will all have one shepherd. They will follow my laws and be careful to keep my decrees. 25 They will live in the land I gave to my servant Jacob, the land where your fathers lived. They and their children and their children's children will live there forever, and David my servant will be their prince forever. 26 I will make a covenant of peace with them; it will be an everlasting covenant. I will establish them and increase their numbers, and I will put my sanctuary among them forever. 27 My dwelling place will be with them; I will be their God, and they will be my people. 28 Then the nations will know that I the LORD make Israel holy, when my sanctuary is among them forever.' "

Remember after the death of Solomon the 12 tribes of Israel was split, the 10 tribes that followed Jeroboam became the kingdom of Israel, sometimes also referred to as Ephraim. See Isaiah 11:13. The two remaining tribes of Judah and Benjamin became the kingdom of Judah, in the New Testament referred to as Judea by the Greeks. The 10 tribes of Israel were carried off into to Assyria in 722 B.C. Between 605 B.C. and 586 B.C the Babylonians carried the two tribes of Judah off into captivity. You could say that the first part of this prophecy has already been fulfilled because Israel is one nation, but other than those with a last name of Levi, the Jews don't know which tribe they are from. I'm sure after Jesus has returned he is perfectly capable of telling them which tribe they are from. We see a reference to this in Revelation chapter 7 concerning the 144,000 Jewish servants of God. After Jesus returns the 12 tribes will once again be one kingdom. See also (Jer. 3:18, 23:5-6, 30:3; Hosea 1:11; Amos 9:11). The fact that there is no record of this ever happening in history points to a yet future fulfillment. As I said, currently most Jews don't even know which tribe they are descendant from. It is still believed that the 10 tribes of Israel are lost. While they may be lost to us, they are not lost to God.

Ezekiel in chapter 34 also describes what will take place after Jesus has returned.

Ezekiel 34:

> 11 " 'For this is what the Sovereign LORD says: I myself will search for my sheep and look after them. 12 As a shepherd looks after his scattered flock when he is with them, so will I look after my sheep. I will rescue them from all the places where they were scattered on a day of clouds and darkness.

The day of clouds and darkness sounds like it is referring to the days of the tribulation. This will become clear after our look at the book of Revelation.

> 13 I will bring them out from the nations and gather them from the countries, and I will bring them into their own land. I will pasture them on the mountains of Israel, in the ravines and in all the settlements in the land. 14 I will tend them in a good pasture, and the mountain heights of Israel will be their grazing land. There they will lie down in good grazing land, and there they will feed in a rich pasture on the mountains of Israel. 15 I myself will tend my sheep and have them lie down, declares the Sovereign LORD. 16 I will search for the lost and bring back the strays. I will bind up the injured and strengthen the weak, but the sleek and the strong I will destroy. I will shepherd the flock with justice.

> 17 " 'As for you, my flock, this is what the Sovereign LORD says: I will judge between one sheep and another, and between rams and goats.

The Rapture and End Time Prophecies for Beginners

Remember the parable of the weeds in Matthew chapter 13 and of the separation of the sheep and goats in Matthew chapter 25.

> 22 I will save my flock, and they will no longer be plundered. I will judge between one sheep and another. 23 I will place over them one shepherd, my servant David, and he will tend them; he will tend them and be their shepherd. 24 I the LORD will be their God, and my servant David will be prince among them. I the LORD have spoken.
> 25 " 'I will make a covenant of peace with them and rid the land of wild beasts so that they may live in the desert and sleep in the forests in safety.

Compare to Isaiah chapter 11:

> 6 The wolf will live with the lamb,
> the leopard will lie down with the goat,
> the calf and the lion and the yearling together;
> and a little child will lead them.
>
> 7 The cow will feed with the bear,
> their young will lie down together,
> and the lion will eat straw like the ox.
>
> 8 The infant will play near the hole of the cobra,
> and the young child put his hand into the viper's nest.
>
> 9 They will neither harm nor destroy
> on all my holy mountain,
> for the earth will be full of the knowledge of the LORD
> as the waters cover the sea.

Holy Mountain refers to his Holy Kingdom.

Compare also with Isaiah 65:

> 25 The wolf and the lamb will feed together,
> and the lion will eat straw like the ox,
> but dust will be the serpent's food.

They will neither harm nor destroy on all my holy mountain," says the LORD.

28 They will no longer be plundered by the nations, nor will wild animals devour them. They will live in safety, and no one will make them afraid. 29 I will provide for them a land renowned for its crops, and they will no longer be victims of famine in the land or bear the scorn of the nations. 30 Then they will know that I, the LORD their God, am with them and that they, the house of Israel, are my people, declares the Sovereign LORD.

You see here Ezekiel as does Isaiah, are referring to the Kingdom of God after Jesus has returned. Verse 31 explains who the sheep are.

31 You my sheep, the sheep of my pasture, are people, and I am your God, declares the Sovereign LORD.'

Next in chapter 38 we see a new vision and word is given to Ezekiel. After giving a word of restoration, the resurrection of Israel and of the kingdom of God, with chapters 38 and 39 the visions step back and give a prophecy of a future invasion of Israel by all the nations that surround her. It's like the word of the Lord first says it's going to turn out o.k. before revealing what is going to happen first. With chapter 40 he goes back to revealing the kingdom of God here on earth.

3. Ezekiel 38

Now with Chapter 38 we come to a prophecy of an end time war, an invasion of Israel by several nations.

A Prophecy Against Gog

> 1 The word of the LORD came to me: 2 "Son of man, set your face against Gog, of the land of Magog, the chief prince of Meshech and Tubal; prophesy against him 3 and say: 'This is what the Sovereign LORD says: I am against you, O Gog, chief prince of Meshech and Tubal. 4 I will turn you around, put hooks in your jaws and bring you out with your whole army—your horses, your horsemen fully armed, and a great horde with large and small shields, all of them brandishing their swords. 5 Persia, Cush and Put will be with them, all with shields and helmets, 6 also Gomer with all its troops, and Beth Togarmah from the far north with all its troops—the many nations with you.

Ezekiel didn't include all the events of the End Times, but what he did include is in the proper sequence with how they would occur. Falling between Israel's modern re-birth and the beginning of the re-gathering of the Jews in 1948, prophesied in Ezekiel chapters 36-37, and the Millennium, covered in Ezekiel chapters 40-48, is the battle of Ezekiel in chapters 38-39 which has to take place after Israel's rebirth in 1948 but before Jesus' 2nd coming.

Ezekiel 38 and 39 are prophecies of an end time invasion and war against Israel. These prophecies in these two chapters haven't happened in history so they have to be for a future time. We see with verse 8 that it says after many days and in future years, it's a way of letting them know it is for the distant future, like Daniel was told in Dan. 12 verse 4 "But you, Daniel, close up and seal the words of the scroll until the time of the end" and verse 9 "He replied, "Go your way, Daniel, because the words are closed up and sealed until the time of the end." With verses 1 through 6 Ezekiel is naming many of the nations that will come against Israel in the last days.

210

Later I will identify these nations.

> 7 "'Get ready; be prepared, you and all the hordes gathered about you, and take command of them. 8 After many days you will be called to arms. In future years you will invade a land that has recovered from war, whose people were gathered from many nations to the mountains of Israel, which had long been desolate. They had been brought out from the nations, and now all of them live in safety. 9 You and all your troops and the many nations with you will go up, advancing like a storm; you will be like a cloud covering the land.

As we saw in chapter 36, the first phase of the re-gathering of the Jews to the land of Israel began after WWI and WWII. Israel became a nation again in 1948. There hadn't been a nation of Israel since the Babylonian destruction. Even now there are still Jews returning to Israel by the thousands. I believe there will be a continuation of the re-gathering while the temple is being rebuilt.

Verse 8 says that Gog of Magog will invade a land that has recovered from war and that the people were gathered from many nations. Israel, the Jews have recovered from war. Israel has recovered from the destruction it incurred in 70 a.d. by the Romans. And the Jews have recovered from the war and persecution of WWII by the Nazi's and they have been re-gathered back to the land of Israel from many nations. Once the anti-Christ has at least seemed to have brought peace between the Jews and the Muslims, Israel, so it will appear, will be living in safety. But as we will see, this peace won't last long.

We see that this prince, Gog of Magog is told to get ready, to be prepared and all the hordes, nations with him. He is to take command of them. We see again with verse 8 that it will be after many days and in future years that they will be called to arms to invade Israel. Again with verse 9 we see there will be many nations coming against Israel.

Later we will look at who all these nations are, but let me give you a hint, the characteristic these nations have in common coming with

Magog is their religion, they're all Muslim. Magog is Russia and Gog is the prince or president of Russia. This is Russia and the Islamic nations coming to invade Israel. We can see that Russia has now already allied itself with Iran and most of the other Islamic nations.

> 10 " 'This is what the Sovereign LORD says: On that day thoughts will come into your mind and you will devise an evil scheme. 11 You will say, "I will invade a land of unwalled villages; I will attack a peaceful and unsuspecting people—all of them living without walls and without gates and bars. 12 I will plunder and loot and turn my hand against the resettled ruins and the people gathered from the nations, rich in livestock and goods, living at the center of the land." 13 Sheba and Dedan and the merchants of Tarshish and all her villages will say to you, "Have you come to plunder? Have you gathered your hordes to loot, to carry off silver and gold, to take away livestock and goods and to seize much plunder?" '

> 14 "Therefore, son of man, prophesy and say to Gog: 'This is what the Sovereign LORD says: In that day, when my people Israel are living in safety, will you not take notice of it? 15 You will come from your place in the far north, you and many nations with you, all of them riding on horses, a great horde, a mighty army. 16 You will advance against my people Israel like a cloud that covers the land. In days to come, O Gog, I will bring you against my land, so that the nations may know me when I show myself holy through you before their eyes.

Most scholars believe this invasion will take place in the first half of the tribulation after the rapture, after the anti-Christ has come to power and seemingly to have brought peace to the Middle East and made it possible for Israel to rebuild the temple, after the anti-Christ, the Islamic nations and Israel have signed the 7 year covenant peace agreement. This would be why the anti-Christ and his army come to Israel's aid although there are indications that God may also intervene himself through an earthquake and the earth opening up. In Daniel chapter 9 verse 27 it says that this covenant is not only with Israel but also with many, indicating many other nations. This will have to be with the Islamic nations since the conflict over Israel and Jerusalem is with the Muslims. After the anti-Christ has brought about the peace agreement between Israel and the Islamic nations, Israel will be living at peace and not expecting to be attacked. Most likely this invasion will be too much for Israel to defend on their own. So because of the agreement signed by the anti-Christ, the head of the revived Roman Empire, his army will come to Israel's aid.

But there are some that believe this will occur before the tribulation. Some believe it could be before the rapture then there are those that believe it could be after the Rapture but before the tribulation. We don't know how long it will be between the Rapture and the beginning of the tribulation when the anti-Christ gets the peace agreement signed between Israel and the Islamic nations. It could be that a prominent political leader, which becomes the anti-Christ, will now be able to bring peace to the Middle East thus setting the stage for him to make a 7 year covenant with Israel. But from the indications of what I just mentioned above, that Israel would be living in safety and at peace before this invasion, verse 14, it sounds to me that this will occur after the rapture, after the signing of the covenant between Israel and the Islamic nations. This would go along with what the Apostle Paul said in 1 Thes. 5:2. For Israel is not at peace and living in safety now. I don't expect them to be at peace until this agreement has been signed. Then there are those that believe this will happen at the beginning of the tribulation. They get this from verse 9 of Ezekiel 39, that Israel will be burning the weapons for fuel during the 7 years of the tribulation. I will explain latter why I don't see how this will be the case. You see, the bible doesn't tell us exactly when this battle will happen. But from similar verses in Revelation to those we see here in Ezekiel I still tend to think it will happen after the tribulation, during the first 3 ½ years, possibly with the 2nd seal of Revelation chapter 6. I guess this is another one of the things we will just have to wait and see.

When Israel gives in and gives up the west bank and the Golan Heights, the mountainous areas, it will open up the way for these nations to march into Israel. Thus the statement in verse 11, "I will invade a land of unwalled villages; I will attack a peaceful and unsuspecting people—all of them living without walls and without gates and bars. When this invasion happens the anti-Christ with his army will come to Israel's rescue only to betray them later. But this is not the end of this prophecy. This is just the beginning; this is most likely the beginning of WWIII. Like Jesus said, wars are degreed till the end.

With verse 17 thru 23 it sounds like it's describing the tribulation.

> 17 " 'This is what the Sovereign LORD says: Are you not the one I spoke of in former days by my servants the prophets of Israel? At that time they prophesied for years that I would bring you against them. 18 This is what will happen in that day: When Gog attacks the land of Israel, my hot anger will be aroused, declares the Sovereign LORD. 19 In my zeal and fiery wrath I declare that at that time there shall be a great earthquake in the land of Israel. 20 The fish of the sea, the birds of the air, the beasts of the field, every creature that moves along the ground, and all the people on the face of the earth will tremble at my presence. The mountains will be overturned, the cliffs will crumble and every wall will fall to the ground. 21 I will summon a sword against Gog on all my mountains, declares the Sovereign LORD. Every man's sword will be against his brother. 22 I will execute judgment upon him with plague and bloodshed; I will pour down torrents of rain, hailstones and burning sulfur on him and on his troops and on the many nations with him. 23 And so I will show my greatness and my holiness, and I will make myself known in the sight of many nations. Then they will know that I am the LORD.'

As verse 17 indicates, all of the Old Testament Prophets prophesied about the battles and destruction and judgment of the tribulation. With verses 19 thru 22 it sounds like nuclear warfare and its effects like that of which we see in Revelation.

This could very well be what causes the earthquakes and the mountains to be overturned, the cliffs to crumble and the walls in the city to fall mentioned in verses 19 and 20. If this invasion takes place after the rapture then this could be what we see in Revelation chapter 6 that starts with the 2nd seal.

> Rev. 6: 3When the Lamb opened the second seal, I heard the second living creature say, "Come!" 4Then another horse came out, a fiery red one. Its rider was given power to take peace from the earth and to make men slay each other. To him was given a large sword.

As I've already mentioned, this could very well be the beginning of WWIII when Russia and the Islamic nations attack Israel.

> Rev. 6: 5When the Lamb opened the third seal, I heard the third living creature say, "Come!" I looked, and there before me was a black horse! Its rider was holding a pair of scales in his hand. 6Then I heard what sounded like a voice among the four living creatures, saying, "A quart of wheat for a day's wages, and three quarts of barley for a day's wages, and do not damage the oil and the wine!"

A war in the Middle East will affect the Oil production and supply. We can see now that any disturbance in the Middle East causes the cost of Oil to skyrocket and this in turn affects the prices of everything. This war will cause massive inflation.

> Rev. 6: 7When the Lamb opened the fourth seal, I heard the voice of the fourth living creature say, "Come!" 8I looked, and there before me was a pale horse! Its rider was named Death, and Hades was following close behind him. They were given power over a fourth of the earth to kill by sword, famine and plague, and by the wild beasts of the earth.

The last statement in verse 8 tells us that this will only affect a fourth of the earth, not the whole world as will be the case later.

This is another indication that this will be the beginning, the evasion of Russia and the Islamic nations against Israel spoken of here in Ezekiel 38 and 39. With the disruption in food supplies there will be mass famine. The plagues could very well be caused from not only nuclear weapons but chemical and biological weapons also.

> Rev. 6: 12I watched as he opened the sixth seal. There was a great earthquake. The sun turned black like sackcloth made of goat hair, the whole moon turned blood red, 13and the stars in the sky fell to earth, as late figs drop from a fig tree when shaken by a strong wind. 14The sky receded like a scroll, rolling up, and every mountain and island was removed from its place. 15Then the kings of the earth, the princes, the generals, the rich, the mighty, and every slave and every free man hid in caves and among the rocks of the mountains. 16They called to the mountains and the rocks, "Fall on us and hide us from the face of him who sits on the throne and from the wrath of the Lamb! 17For the great day of their wrath has come, and who can stand?"

Compare with Ezekiel 38 again, 19 In my zeal and fiery wrath I declare that at that time there shall be a great earthquake in the land of Israel. 20 The fish of the sea, the birds of the air, the beasts of the field, every creature that moves along the ground, and all the people on the face of the earth will tremble at my presence. The mountains will be overturned, the cliffs will crumble and every wall will fall to the ground. 22 I will execute judgment upon him with plague and bloodshed; I will pour down torrents of rain, hailstones and burning sulfur on him and on his troops and on the many nations with him.

This seems to bring us to the mid-point of the 7 years of the tribulation. So if this invasion starts with the 2nd seal it may continue up to the mid-point of the tribulation. We see in Ezekiel and especially in Revelation with verses 12 thru 14 of chapter 6 that nuclear weapons have finally been used.

That would explain the response we see in verses 15 thru 17 of Revelation chapter 6. What the world has feared has finally happened. With the 7th seal containing the 7 trumpets we see the aftermath and effects of the radiation fallout from these nuclear explosions. Unfortunately, this is not the last of the nuclear warfare that we will see. It is also after this that the anti-Christ breaks the covenant with Israel and enters the temple causing the 'abomination of desolation' that Daniel and Jesus spoke of and then goes out to kill all the Jews and anyone calling on the name of Jesus. It's after this that he cause's everyone that will swear allegiance to him and worship him, to take the mark of the beast thus denying Jesus. Look at the words of Jesus again.

Mt. 24: 15"So when you see standing in the holy place 'the abomination that causes desolation, 'spoken of through the prophet Daniel—let the reader understand— 16then let those who are in Judea flee to the mountains. 17Let no one on the roof of his house go down to take anything out of the house. 18Let no one in the field go back to get his cloak. 19How dreadful it will be in those days for pregnant women and nursing mothers! 20Pray that your flight will not take place in winter or on the Sabbath. 21For then there will be great distress, unequaled from the beginning of the world until now—and never to be equaled again.

Luke 21: 20"When you see Jerusalem being surrounded by armies, you will know that its desolation is near. 21Then let those who are in Judea flee to the mountains, let those in the city get out, and let those in the country not enter the city. 22For this is the time of punishment in fulfillment of all that has been written. 23How dreadful it will be in those days for pregnant women and nursing mothers! There will be great distress in the land and wrath against this people. 24They will fall by the sword and will be taken as prisoners to all the nations. Jerusalem will be trampled on by the Gentiles until the times of the Gentiles are fulfilled.

4. Ezekiel 39

Chapter 39 continues with the prophecy started in chapter 38.

> **1** "Son of man, prophesy against Gog and say: 'This is what the Sovereign LORD says: I am against you, O Gog, chief prince of Meshech and Tubal. 2 I will turn you around and drag you along. I will bring you from the far north and send you against the mountains of Israel. 3 Then I will strike your bow from your left hand and make your arrows drop from your right hand. 4 On the mountains of Israel you will fall, you and all your troops and the nations with you. I will give you as food to all kinds of carrion birds and to the wild animals. 5 You will fall in the open field, for I have spoken, declares the Sovereign LORD. 6 I will send fire on Magog and on those who live in safety in the coastlands, and they will know that I am the LORD.

One of the clues as to the location of Magog is found here in verse 2 saying they will come from the far North. Russia is in the far North from Israel. On a map if you draw a straight line North from Jerusalem you go right through Moscow. As I will show you later, Meshech is an ancient name for Moscow.

This is describing the first part of WWIII. It also sounds like with verse 6 that Russia and those that are living in safety in the coastlands will be struck with nuclear missiles. Russia and the other northern countries and the many Islamic nations with them will be completely destroyed. With verse 2 saying that "I will turn you around and drag you along" it sounds like Russia will be forced into this. It could be that although Russia has always hated the Jews, the Islamic nations will somehow force Russia into leading this invasion to destroy Israel. They most likely will not think that they would be able to defeat Israel on there on. They have tried it in the past, like during the 6-day war in June of 1967 and again in 1973 but they failed. Because Russia has allied itself with the Islamic nations they will be able to convince Russia in leading them in this invasion to destroy Israel. But it could be that it will be God himself that drags Russia into this. It just shows that no matter how it comes about, God is in control. This actually continues until the end of the tribulation with the last battle of Armageddon. After Russia and the Islamic nations have been defeated, China will team up with Russia and come against the anti-Christ that now has his headquarters in Jerusalem. China and Russia are already allies. Russia and China will come against the anti-Christ's army at the last battle of Armageddon.

This all could indeed start after the anti-Christ has signed the 7 year covenant with Israel allowing them to rebuild the temple.

With the Jews being able to rebuild the temple, you can be assured that all the Muslims will not like this and will hate and want to destroy Israel even more than they do now. Remember, they believe Jerusalem is theirs and it is a vow of the Muslims to wipe the Jews off the face of the earth. It sounds like they will finally try to do it.

> **7** "'I will make known my holy name among my people Israel. I will no longer let my holy name be profaned, and the nations will know that I the LORD am the Holy One in Israel. 8 It is coming! It will surely take place, declares the Sovereign LORD. This is the day I have spoken of.

Will there actually be a WWIII. You can count on it. The Lord has declared it. God will make the holy name of Jesus known among the Jews after they realize that the anti-Christ is not the messiah. All the nations of the world will know that Jesus is Lord once he has returned. Verse 8, It is coming! It will surely take place, declares the Sovereign LORD.

Verses 9 thru 16 are telling us what will happen after the tribulation, after Jesus has returned and during the first 7 years of the Millennium. Israel will have to clean up all the debris that has been left through the destruction of the tribulation. With verse 9 it appears that Ezekiel jumps to the end of the tribulation.

It sounds like it is also describing what they will have to clean up from the valley of Megiddo, after the last battle of Armageddon.

Keep this in mind. From reading the words of prophecies it many times sounds like all the events described are going to happen back to back without any delay in time between them, but this often is not the case. The events described here in Ezekiel as were the prophecies concerning Jesus' first and second comings have many years between the beginning and the end. It's now been 2000 years since Jesus' first coming to the Earth.

> 9 " 'Then those who live in the towns of Israel will go out and use the weapons for fuel and burn them up—the small and large shields, the bows and arrows, the war clubs and spears. For seven years they will use them for fuel. 10 They will not need to gather wood from the fields or cut it from the forests, because they will use the weapons for fuel. And they will plunder those who plundered them and loot those who looted them, declares the Sovereign LORD. 11 " 'On that day I will give Gog a burial place in Israel, in the valley of those who travel east toward the Sea. It will block the way of travelers, because Gog and all his hordes will be buried there. So it will be called the Valley of Hamon Gog.
>
> 12 " 'For seven months the house of Israel will be burying them in order to cleanse the land. 13 All the people of the land will bury them, and the day I am glorified will be a memorable day for them, declares the Sovereign LORD.
>
> 14" 'Men will be regularly employed to cleanse the land. Some will go throughout the land and, in addition to them, others will bury those that remain on the ground. At the end of the seven months they will begin their search. 15 As they go through the land and one of them sees a human bone, he will set up a marker beside it until the gravediggers have buried it in the Valley of Hamon Gog. 16 (Also a town called Hamonah will be there.) And so they will cleanse the land.'

He says that it will take Israel 7 months to bury the dead and that they will use the weapons for fuel for 7 years. With this saying that they will use the weapons for fuel for 7 years many want to place this before the rapture since the tribulation is for 7 years. This statement of using the weapons for fuel for 7 years is not connected to the 7 years of the tribulation. It's not the same 7 years. The indication here is that after Jesus has returned they will use the weapons for fuel just as it will be after Jesus has returned that they will be burying the dead for 7 months. We see this start with verse 7. "I will make known my holy name among my people Israel. I will no longer let my holy name be profaned, and the nations will know that I the LORD am the Holy One in Israel." This will not happen until after Jesus has returned. The burning the weapons for fuel couldn't be during the 7 years of the tribulation because after the Russian, Islamic invasion, at the mid-point of the tribulation the Jews will have to flee from the persecution of the anti-Christ. They will not be able to bury the dead. There won't be anyone in Jerusalem to bury the dead. It could be that the bodies will lie there, rotting until after the tribulation when Jesus returns and destroys the anti-Christ and those gathered with him. We also see in Revelation 19 verses 17 and 18, after the last battle of Armageddon that there will be a great super for all the birds of the air of all the bodies in the valley of Megiddo. We see in verse 4 that God said of Russia and the nations with them, "I will give you as food to all kinds of carrion birds and to the wild animals. The war and fighting will only get worse with more nuclear exchanges and continue till the end. It appears that Russia is not completely destroyed until the last battle of Armageddon. Since the anti-Christ stopped them from invading Israel Russia unites with China and comes against the anti-Christ and his army in the valley of Megiddo at the last battle of Armageddon.

Once Jesus has returned the Jews will be able to return to Jerusalem. The statement in verse 15 that when they find a human bone they will set up a marker beside it until the gravediggers come and get it to bury it shows that this will not take place immediately after this battle.

It will be during the first 7 months and the first 7 years of the Millennium that they will be using the weapons for fuel. It could be that it will be the fuel in the tanks and vehicles that they will use. Another clue as to it being after Jesus has returned is that he says that they will plunder those who plundered them and loot those who looted them. This will not take place anytime during the tribulation. And he says the day I (Jesus) am glorified will be a memorable day for them. This is after Jesus has returned. We get more insight to this from Zechariah:

> Zech. 25: 30 "Now prophesy all these words against them and say to them:" 'The LORD will roar from on high; he will thunder from his holy dwelling and roar mightily against his land. He will shout like those who tread the grapes, shout against all who live on the earth.

> 31 The tumult will resound to the ends of the earth, for the LORD will bring charges against the nations; he will bring judgment on all mankind and put the wicked to the sword,' " declares the LORD.

> 32 This is what the LORD Almighty says:
> "Look! Disaster is spreading from nation to nation; a mighty storm is rising from the ends of the earth."

> 33 At that time those slain by the LORD will be everywhere— from one end of the earth to the other. They will not be mourned or gathered up or buried, but will be like refuse lying on the ground.

First notice that it says the Lord is bringing charges against all the nations and judgment on all mankind, from nation to nation, from the ends of the earth. The slain will be everywhere. The whole world will be affected by what will become WWIII. Now notice the last part of verse 33, "They will not be mourned or gathered up or buried, but will be like refuse lying on the ground". It says they will not be buried, but we just saw that Ezekiel says that they will be buried and it will take 7 months. The statement of Zechariah 25 verse 33 is occurring during the tribulation, so the statement of Ezekiel sounds like it is of the first

7 months and 7 years of the Millennium. This also is another indication that this invasion of Russia and the Islamic nations most likely occurs after the rapture.

Next, verses 17 thru 24 are about the day that the Lord Jesus returns. The description in Revelation 19 is what leads me to believe this prophecy of Ezekiel actually continues on till the end. We can see not only could the Jews be burying the dead from the attack from Russia and the nations with them but they will be burying the dead from the last battle of Armageddon.

> Rev. 19: 17And I saw an angel standing in the sun, who cried in a loud voice to all the birds flying in midair, "Come, gather together for the great supper of God, 18so that you may eat the flesh of kings, generals, and mighty men, of horses and their riders, and the flesh of all people, free and slave, small and great."

The valley of Megiddo will become a lake of blood filled with dead soldiers and horses. Russia and China both have a horse Calvary. Revelation 14 verse 20 says that the blood will flow as high as a horses bridle for a distance of about 180 miles.

> **Ez. 39:** 17 "Son of man, this is what the Sovereign LORD says: Call out to every kind of bird and all the wild animals: 'Assemble and come together from all around to the sacrifice I am preparing for you, the great sacrifice on the mountains of Israel. There you will eat flesh and drink blood. 18 You will eat the flesh of mighty men and drink the blood of the princes of the earth as if they were rams and lambs, goats and bulls—all of them fattened animals from Bashan. 19 At the sacrifice I am preparing for you, you will eat fat till you are glutted and drink blood till you are drunk. 20 At my table you will eat your fill of horses and riders, mighty men and soldiers of every kind,' declares the Sovereign LORD.

21 "I will display my glory among the nations, and all the nations will see the punishment I inflict and the hand I lay upon them. 22 From that day forward the house of Israel will know that I am the LORD their God. 23 And the nations will know that the people of Israel went into exile for their sin, because they were unfaithful to me. So I hid my face from them and handed them over to their enemies, and they all fell by the sword. 24 I dealt with them according to their uncleanness and their offenses, and I hid my face from them.

25 "Therefore this is what the Sovereign LORD says: I will now bring Jacob back from captivity and will have compassion on all the people of Israel, and I will be zealous for my holy name. 26 They will forget their shame and all the unfaithfulness they showed toward me when they lived in safety in their land with no one to make them afraid. 27 When I have brought them back from the nations and have gathered them from the countries of their enemies, I will show myself holy through them in the sight of many nations. 28 Then they will know that I am the LORD their God, for though I sent them into exile among the nations, I will gather them to their own land, not leaving any behind. 29 I will no longer hide my face from them, for I will pour out my Spirit on the house of Israel, declares the Sovereign LORD."

While we know that the re-gathering of Israel started in 1948 when Israel became a nation again, it will be completed after Jesus has returned.

The Jews will have to flee again in the middle of the tribulation when the anti-Christ turns on them and enters the temple proclaiming himself to be God. After Jesus has returned he will bring all of the Jews back to Israel, none will be left behind. Remember, Jesus spoke of the Jews having to flee at the mid-point of the tribulation in Matthew chapter 24 verses 15 thru 21 and in Luke chapter 21 verses 20 thru 24, also in Revelation chapter 12.

We know from the description given here with the last verses of Ezekiel 39 that these verses are referring to after Jesus has returned. We see the Lord will have compassion on Israel, we see the Jews will forget their shame and unfaithfulness of rejecting Jesus. Verse 27 says that the Lord will show himself holy through Israel in the sight of many nations, a description of the Millennium. Verse 28 says that they will then know that Jesus is the Lord their God. He says he will not leave any behind. Verse 29 says the Lord will no longer hide his face from them and he will pour out his Spirit on the house of Israel. Compare Ezekiel with Joel. Afterwards is referring to after the tribulation.

Joel 2:

28 "And afterward, I will pour out my Spirit on all people. Your sons and daughters will prophesy, your old men will dream dreams, your young men will see visions. 29 Even on my servants, both men and women, I will pour out my Spirit in those days.

Joel 3:

17 "Then you will know that I, the LORD your God,
dwell in Zion, my holy hill. Jerusalem will be holy;
never again will foreigners invade her.

Read Joel chapters 1, 2 and 3, but for now notice these verses and compare with Ezekiel. When you compare Joel to Revelation you can see that Joel is describing what will be taking place during the tribula**tion.**

Joel 1:

6 A nation has invaded my land, powerful and without number;
it has the teeth of a lion, the fangs of a lioness.

Compare this with Isaiah,

225

Isaiah 1:

> 7 Your country is desolate, your cities burned with fire; your fields are being stripped by foreigners right before you, laid waste as when overthrown by strangers.

> 9 Unless the LORD Almighty had left us some survivors, we would have become like Sodom, we would have been like Gomorrah.

Joel 2:

> 1 Blow the trumpet in Zion; sound the alarm on my holy hill. Let all who live in the land tremble, for the day of the LORD is coming. It is close at hand-

> 2 a day of darkness and gloom, a day of clouds and blackness. Like dawn spreading across the mountains a large and mighty army comes, such as never was of old nor ever will be in ages to come.

> 18 Then the LORD will be jealous for his land and take pity on his people.

> 19 The LORD will reply to them:
> "I am sending you grain, new wine and oil, enough to satisfy you fully; never again will I make you an object of scorn to the nations.

> 20 "I will drive the northern army far from you, pushing it into a parched and barren land, with its front columns going into the eastern sea and those in the rear into the western sea. And its stench will go up; its smell will rise." Surely he has done great things.

Notice verse 20 says "and its stench will go up; its smell will rise". This will be from all the dead bodies lying on the ground decaying.

As I've mentioned already, from the scriptures it sounds like the anti-Christ will defeat this northern army, Russia and those with them. This is not unlike times in the past when God would use an army for his purpose whether for or against Israel.

Now Joel is describing the last battle of Armageddon.

Joel 3:

> 1 "In those days and at that time,
> when I restore the fortunes of Judah and Jerusalem,
>
> 2 I will gather all nations and bring them down to the Valley of Jehoshaphat. There I will enter into judgment against them concerning my inheritance, my people Israel,
> <u>for they scattered my people among the nations</u>
> <u>and divided up my land.</u>
>
> 11 Come quickly, all you nations from every side, and assemble there. Bring down your warriors, O LORD!
> 12 "Let the nations be roused;
> let them advance into the Valley of Jehoshaphat,
> for there I will sit to judge all the nations on every side.
> 13 Swing the sickle, for the harvest is ripe.
> Come, trample the grapes, for the winepress is full
> and the vats overflow— so great is their wickedness!"
> 14 Multitudes, multitudes in the valley of decision!
> For the day of the LORD is near in the valley of decision.
> 15 The sun and moon will be darkened,
> and the stars no longer shine.
> 16 The LORD will roar from Zion and thunder from Jerusalem;
> the earth and the sky will tremble. But the LORD will be a refuge
> for his people, a stronghold for the people of Israel.

Compare with the book of Revelation,

Rev. 14: 14I looked, and there before me was a white cloud, and seated on the cloud was one "like a son of man" with a crown of gold on his head and a sharp sickle in his hand.15Then another angel came out of the temple and called in a loud voice to him who was sitting on the cloud, "Take your sickle and reap, because the time to reap has come, for the harvest of the earth is ripe." 16So he who was seated on the cloud swung his sickle over the earth, and the earth was harvested.

17Another angel came out of the temple in heaven, and he too had a sharp sickle. 18Still another angel, who had charge of the fire, came from the altar and called in a loud voice to him who had the sharp sickle, "Take your sharp sickle and gather the clusters of grapes from the earth's vine, because its grapes are ripe." 19The angel swung his sickle on the earth, gathered its grapes and threw them into the great winepress of God's wrath. 20They were trampled in the winepress outside the city, and blood flowed out of the press, rising as high as the horses' bridles for a distance of 1,600 stadia. "That is 180 miles".

Jesus said,

Mt. 24: 27For as lightning that comes from the east is visible even in the west, so will be the coming of the Son of Man. 28Wherever there is a carcass, there the vultures will gather.

29"Immediately after the distress of those days "'the sun will be darkened, and the moon will not give its light; the stars will fall from the sky, and the heavenly bodies will be shaken.'

30"At that time the sign of the Son of Man will appear in the sky, and all the nations of the earth will mourn. They will see the Son of Man coming on the clouds of the sky, with power and great glory.

The End Time Prophecies of Ezekiel

We can see from Joel as well from Matthew and Revelation that the prophecy here in Ezekiel continues until the end of the tribulation. It also sounds like the war starts with the Russian invasion. The Valley of Jehoshaphat is the valley of Megiddo where the last battle of Armageddon will be fought.

But the prophecy and visions of Ezekiel do not end here with chapter 39. Beginning with Chapter 40 he is describing the 1000 year kingdom of God and the temple here on earth with Jesus ruling and reigning as King. We get insight into the millennium Temple with Ezekiel 47 that started in chapter 40. In chapter 43 we see the glory returns to the Temple. Read the rest of Ezekiel starting with chapter 40.

It should be obvious that it isn't a coincidence that Russia and Iran are allies and that Russia and China are allies. The Islamic nations want to wipe Israel off the map. We see here in Ezekiel that they will try it and that it will be what starts Word War III. It will become the worst war man has every fought. You will see in our look at Revelation that it will become nuclear, biological and chemical. But the destruction of the tribulation, the judging of Israel and the nations will lead us into the earthly kingdom of God here on earth. Jesus will purge and purify the earth of all uncleanness and unrighteousness. Later we will look at scriptures that tell us what the earthly kingdom of God will be like.

Next we will look at who the nations are that Ezekiel mentions. I think you will be amazed when you see who these nations are and that they exist today, and at what these nations are saying concerning Israel. We can see today that the whole world is turning against Israel, even the United States. And all this is foretold in the word of God. The bible is the word of God.

5. Who are the nations in Ezekiel chapters 38 and 39?

Now let us identify these nations that Ezekiel is referring to and how we know this.

First, why would God be so against Gog of Magog. Well, this leader and country is against God. I will show you in a second how they have identified Magog as to being Russia, but know and understand that when it is referring to Russia it is referring to the government. It is Russia's leader and leaders; it's government that is opposed to God. Unfortunately, most of the Russian people don't believe in God. But many have come to believe in Jesus and hopefully many more will. It's not that God is against every single Russian, only its leader, Gog who is intent on destroying his people.

As I mentioned earlier, one of the clues to whom and where Magog is, is its geographic location in relation to Israel. Ezekiel said this army would come from the far North. If you take a map and draw a line straight up from Jerusalem you will come to Russia and Moscow.

For the sake of space I'm not going to go into a lot of detail on how all this has been traced back in history, it's been done by bible scholars as well as historians already. If you want to see more detail on how all this has been traced, there are several articles on RaptureReady.com. All the other prophecy scholars I've mentioned have also written how these nations have been traced back in history. I'll just give enough to show that the modern nations we see today that surround Israel, all that we see forming today was prophesied here by Ezekiel.

Magog is Russia

"Magog" is an ancient name for the nation now known as Russia. "Gog" means "the chief prince of Magog," the chief prince of Meshech and Tubal. (Ez. 38:2-3; 39:1). "Gog" signifies a prince, or head, today we would say president or prime minister.

The name "Moscow" derives from the tribal names "Meshech," and "Tobolsk," the name from "'Tubal." Magog became "Rosh," then "Russ," and today is known as "Russia." The word translated "chief" in Ezekiel 38:2-3 literally means in Hebrew the "top" or "head". In this name we have the first historical trace of the Russ or Russian nation. Genesis 10 gives the descendants of Noah's son's. Genesis 10 and 1 Chron. 1 helps to establish the identity of these people. Magog, Gomer, Meshech, and Tubal are four of the seven sons of Japheth. Magog was the second son of Japheth. Tubal and Meshech were the fifth and sixth sons of Japheth. "Meshech" was founder of the Moshci who dwelt in the Moschian mountains. "Moschi," derived from the Hebrew name Meshech is the source of the name for the city of Moscow. "Tubal" was the founder of the Tebereni people. Magog, Meshech, and Tubal make up the modern Russian people and compose the present land of Russia.

The Nations with Russia in the coming Attack on Israel

Ez. 38: 5 Persia, Cush and Put will be with them, all with shields and helmets, 6 also Gomer with all its troops, and Beth Togarmah from the far north with all its troops—the many nations with you. 7 " 'Get ready; be prepared, you and all the hordes gathered about you, and take command of them.

1. Persia is Iran (Persia included the areas of Iraq and Afghanistan)

All authorities agree on who Persia is today. It is modern Iran.

2. Cush is now Ethiopia (Black African Nations)

Ethiopia is a translation of the Hebrew word, "Cush." Cush is translated "Ethiopia" twenty-one times in the King James Version of the Bible, which is somewhat misleading. It is certain that the ancient Ethiopians are made up of Cushites though they do not represent all of them, according to history. Cush would also represent the Sudan.

231

Many of the African nations will be united and allied with the Russians in the invasion of Israel. This is seen in Daniel chapter 11. Russia is called "the King of the North" and the African nations (Cush) is called "the King of the South." I'll explain this in our look at Daniel.

3. Put is now Libya (Arabic African Nations)

Libya is the translation of the original Hebrew word, "Put." The descendants of Put migrated to the land west of Egypt and became the source of the North African Arab nations, such as Libya, Algeria, Tunisia, and Morocco. "Persia, Ethiopia, and Libya with them; all of them with shield and helmet" (Ezek. 38:5). KJV. Russia's ally, Put, certainly included more than what is now called Libya.

4. Gomer with all Its Troups(Hordes) (Old Iron Curtain Countries)

The modern Jews understand it to be Germany, and call that country by this Hebrew name." It also includes the area of modern Poland, Czechoslovakia, and East Germany. Gomer and all its troops are a part of all the area of modern Eastern Europe that was totally behind the Iron Curtain. This includes East Germany and the Slovak countries.

5. Togarmah from the far north with all its troops(Hordes)

(Southern Russia and the Cossacks)

Ezekiel 38:6; also Gomer with all its troops, and Beth Togarmah from the far north with all its troops. King James, "of the north quarters, and all his bands." Togarmah is part of modern South-Russia and is probably the origin of the Cossacks and other people of the Eastern part of Russia. Togarmah would also represent modern day Turkey.

6. The Many Nations with You

> Ezekiel indicates that he hasn't given a complete list of allies. This Russian ruler is commanded to 'Get ready; be prepared, you and all the hordes gathered about you, and take command of them (Ezek. 38:7). NIV. This Russian ruler is to equip the nations with him and to take command of them.

It is amazing that all of these countries that are mentioned in Ezekiel hate Israel and are already allied with Russia today or soon to be, and that almost all of the countries predicted here are already armed with weapons created and manufactured in Russia. Other than the northern countries, all the Middle Eastern and northern African nations mentioned as coming with Russia, the one main characteristic all these nations have in common is their religion, they're all Muslim.

Look at what Psalm 83 says,

> 3 With cunning they conspire against your people;
> they plot against those you cherish.
>
> 4 "Come," they say, "let us destroy them as a nation, that the name of Israel be remembered no more." 5 With one mind they plot together; they form an alliance against you

Remember what Joel said,

> Joel 3: 2 I will gather all nations and bring them down to the Valley of Jehoshaphat. There I will enter into judgment against them concerning my inheritance, my people Israel, for they scattered my people among the nations and divided up my land.

What we see here from Psalm 83, "let us destroy them as a nation, that the name of Israel be remembered no more" and Joel 3, to "divided up the land of Israel" is exactly what we see the Islamic nations are saying and want today.

All the world is saying divide the land and give it to the Palestinians, even the United States.

I can't go into it all now, but if you research history you will find that the land was never the Palestinians. The Jews occupied it until the Roman dispersion. The land was desolate until the Jews started returning after WWI. There never were an actual Palestinian people. Those referred to as Palestinians are mostly Jordanian refugees. All the land was referred to as Palestine by the Romans. You know even the Koran says that Jerusalem and the land belong to the Jews. Go to Hal Lindsey's website. He has a teaching on this.

Take a look at these other scriptures and the nations they mention.

Isaiah 17:

> 1 An oracle concerning Damascus:
> "See, Damascus will no longer be a city
> but will become a heap of ruins.
>
> 14 In the evening, sudden terror!
> Before the morning, they are gone!

Jeremiah 49:

> 24 Damascus has become feeble, she has turned to flee
> and panic has gripped her; anguish and pain have seized her, pain
> like that of a woman in labor.
>
> 26 Surely, her young men will fall in the streets;
> all her soldiers will be silenced in that day,"
> declares the LORD Almighty.
>
> 27 "I will set fire to the walls of Damascus;
> will consume the fortresses of Ben-Hadad."

Amos 1:

> 5 I will break down the gate of Damascus;
> I will destroy the king who is in the Valley of Aven
> and the one who holds the scepter in Beth Eden.
> The people of Aram will go into exile to Kir,"
> says the LORD.

> 7 I will send fire upon the walls of Gaza
> that will consume her fortresses.
> 10 I will send fire upon the walls of Tyre
> that will consume her fortresses."

Damascus is the oldest existing city in the world. These verses would tend to point to a future event due to the fact that Damascus has never been totally destroyed as Isaiah 17 describes. It sounds like it will be destroyed by a nuclear strike. Could it be that there will be a battle between Syria, Gaza, Lebanon and Jordan against Israel before the invasion by Russia mentioned here in Ezekiel before the tribulation and before the Rapture. They could be part of the "many nations with you" Ezekiel 38 verse 6. But if there is a pre-Russian attack on Israel Iran could be part of it or at least backing them up. This pre-Russian attack will be defeated. That could be why Russia winds up leading the invasion described here in Ezekiel. So keep your eye on Damascus.

Isn't it interesting that all three of these countries have terrorist groups. Hamas is in Gaza and Hezbollah is in Lebanon. Damascus is the capital of Syria which has thousands of terrorist. All these terrorist groups are a threat to Israel. Israel has already given up Gaza and what do they get in return for it, thousands of rocket missiles shot into Israel from Gaza. This should show that Israel giving up land is not going to bring peace.

With the threat that these terrorist groups pose to Israel it just seems like Israel is going to have to do something and before these groups get nuclear weapons, especially before Iran does. Iran's supreme leader has been publicly saying that he wants to wipe Israel off the map and when he gets a nuclear missile he will use it against Israel. With Obama becoming president, even the United States government is no longer backing Israel and calling for Israel to give up land and divide Jerusalem, giving land and part of Jerusalem to the Palestinians. And you see all of this foretold in the bible.

Before we leave our look at Ezekiel I would like to make mention of the fact that there are those that because Revelation 20 mentions Gog and Magog that they say that the prophecy of Ezekiel will take place after the 1000 years of Christ's reign here on earth. I, as do most disagree with this.

> Rev. 20: 7When the thousand years are over, Satan will be released from his prison 8and will go out to deceive the nations in the four corners of the earth—Gog and Magog—to gather them for battle. In number they are like the sand on the seashore. 9They marched across the breadth of the earth and surrounded the camp of God's people, the city he loves. But fire came down from heaven and devoured them. 10And the devil, who deceived them, was thrown into the lake of burning sulfur, where the beast and the false prophet had been thrown. They will be tormented day and night for ever and ever.

We see in Revelation chapter 20 that there is no battle at all. But God sends fire down from heaven and devours them. The conditions and description of the battles mentioned in Ezekiel 38 and 39 don't match up or compare to that of the conditions present during or at the end of the Millennium. Read Ezekiel 38 verses 16 thru 23; they are a description of the tribulation. Verse 16 says, "so that the nations may know me when I show myself holy through you before their eyes" and verse 23 ends saying, "I will make myself known in the sight of many nations. Then they will know that I am the LORD.'" This is taking place during the tribulation. We see during the Millennium that all the nations know that Jesus is Lord. In chapter 39 verse 4 says, "I will give you as food to all kinds of carrion birds and to the wild animals." This happens at the battle of Armageddon. Again we see with verse 7, "'I will make known my holy name among my people Israel. I will no longer let my holy name be profaned, and the nations will know that I the LORD am the Holy One in Israel." Again, this will have already happened before the end of the 1000 years of the earthly Kingdom of God. This takes place at the beginning of the Millennium; during the 1000 year earthly kingdom of God everyone on earth knows that Jesus is the Lord. Read verse 9 thru the end of chapter 39. They are describing what happens after the battle of Armageddon, burying the dead for 7 months and burning the fuel for 7 years etc. All this does not fit with or occur after the 1000 years of peace.

What we see next in Revelation chapter 20 is the devil thrown into the lake of burning sulfur where the beast and the false prophet had already been thrown and then the great white throne judgment. The fact that this happens after all that was described in Revelation, that we can see links Revelation together with Ezekiel and Daniel as well as other Old Testament prophecies should make it clear that this here in Revelation 20 is not the same reference to Gog and Magog of Ezekiel 38 and 39. It is just a reference to the fact that this will start from the same geographic location, that it will be led by the same country as that of the battle of Ezekiel. John was just using the statement of Gog and Magog to show where this will start. Russia as a whole has always been a country that hasn't believed in God. Fortunately, there have been some in Russia that have believed in God and Jesus.

Chapter Seven

The Visions and Prophecies of Daniel

1. The Book of Daniel.

Introduction:

All the peoples of the earth were worshiping pagan gods. The truth of the one true God was going to be lost so God chose Abram, changed his name to Abraham and called him and his descendants to keep the truth of the one true God alive. We see this promise was made to Abraham and his wife Sarai whose name was later changed to Sarah. Because of God's love for Abraham, and because of Abrahams Faith, God chose the descendants of Abraham and his wife Sarah to be His representatives on Earth. And of course it was through Abraham and Sarah that the Messiah was to come. See Genesis chapter 17. This is why the Jews were chosen to be the people of God. Israel was to be a nation of priests; they were to be God's representatives throughout the earth. They were to be a light to the world demonstrating the wisdom of God's laws and to show he is a loving and just God. But as we know, Israel continually rebelled and turned away from their loving God. So finally as was foretold by Jeremiah and other prophets God was forced to sit in judgment against Israel and sent the Babylonian army against them.

Jer. 5: 15 O house of Israel," declares the LORD,
"I am bringing a distant nation against you—
an ancient and enduring nation,
a people whose language you do not know,
whose speech you do not understand.

16 Their quivers are like an open grave;
all of them are mighty warriors.

17 They will devour your harvests and food,
devour your sons and daughters;
they will devour your flocks and herds,
devour your vines and fig trees.
With the sword they will destroy
the fortified cities in which you trust.

18 "Yet even in those days," declares the LORD, "I will not destroy you completely. 19 And when the people ask, 'Why has the LORD our God done all this to us?' you will tell them, 'As you have forsaken me and served foreign gods in your own land, so now you will serve foreigners in a land not your own.'

Jer. 19: 15 "This is what the LORD Almighty, the God of Israel, says: 'Listen! I am going to bring on this city and the villages around it every disaster I pronounced against them, because they were stiff-necked and would not listen to my words.' "

Jer. 20: 4 For this is what the LORD says: 'I will make you a terror to yourself and to all your friends; with your own eyes you will see them fall by the sword of their enemies. I will hand all Judah over to the king of Babylon, who will carry them away to Babylon or put them to the sword. 5 I will hand over to their enemies all the wealth of this city—all its products, all its valuables and all the treasures of the kings of Judah. They will take it away as plunder and carry it off to Babylon.

Jer. 25: 8 Therefore the LORD Almighty says this: "Because you have not listened to my words, 9 I will summon all the peoples of the north and my servant Nebuchadnezzar king of Babylon," declares the LORD, "and I will bring them against this land and its inhabitants and against all the surrounding nations. I will completely destroy them and make them an object of horror and scorn, and an everlasting ruin.

If you read Jeremiah you will see that he pleaded and pleaded with the people to turn back to God, but they would not. So God was forced to bring about all the judgments that Jeremiah prophesied.

We see this described in 2 Chronicles also.

2 Chron. 36:

The Fall of Jerusalem

> 15 The LORD, the God of their fathers, sent word to them through his messengers again and again, because he had pity on his people and on his dwelling place. 16 But they mocked God's messengers, despised his words and scoffed at his prophets until the wrath of the LORD was aroused against his people and there was no remedy. 17 He brought up against them the king of the Babylonians, who killed their young men with the sword in the sanctuary, and spared neither young man nor young woman, old man or aged. God handed all of them over to Nebuchadnezzar. 18 He carried to Babylon all the articles from the temple of God, both large and small, and the treasures of the LORD's temple and the treasures of the king and his officials. 19 They set fire to God's temple and broke down the wall of Jerusalem; they burned all the palaces and destroyed everything of value there. 20 He carried into exile to Babylon the remnant, who escaped from the sword, and they became servants to him and his sons until the kingdom of Persia came to power.

We see here that the nation of Israel rebelled against God and they did it again when they rejected Jesus. The Romans destroyed the temple and Jerusalem again in 70 a.d. We can see from history that God's patience with sin and rebellion has a limit. We also can see that before God unleashes his judgment he will give warning after warning, he will plea and plea until he can plea no more. We see this here with Jeremiah and the other prophets that were warning Israel and we see that Jesus did also before the destruction in 70 a.d.

> Mt. 23: 37"O Jerusalem, Jerusalem, you who kill the prophets and stone those sent to you, how often I have longed to gather your children together, as a hen gathers her chicks under her

242

wings, but you were not willing. 38Look, your house is left to you desolate. 39For I tell you, you will not see me again until you say, 'Blessed is he who comes in the name of the Lord.

They had almost 40 years after they crucified Jesus to repent and accept him as the Messiah before the Temple was destroyed.

Now we have all the Old and New Testaments prophecies warning the world of the coming judgments because of the rebellion against God. Just as in the days of Noah and in the days of Lot, people still won't listen and believe.

We cannot understand the Book of Revelation until we understand the Book of Daniel. Daniel along with Revelation is talking about 4 Kingdoms that have ruled the world (Babylon, Medo-Persia, Greece, and Rome) and a future Roman or European empire that will have 10 kings. Daniel records the kingdoms from his time looking forward into the future while in Revelation John records them looking back through the past. Daniel's prophecies are probably the most wide spanning prophecies in the bible. He not only describes the succeeding kingdoms but also foretells of both Jesus' first and second comings. He also describes a future world leader that will control the whole world. He goes into great detail of the wars that have occurred that affected Israel but also a war that will be WWIII. When you study Daniel, then the prophecies of the book of Revelation becomes much clearer.

Here in this chapter, we will look at the visions and prophecies of Daniel. Daniel prophesied about each kingdom that would rule the known world. Since we are able to look back on history, we can see just how accurate these predictions were. Daniel also prophesied about a kingdom that will cover the whole earth. That kingdom or government is still in the future. We will look at both the prophecies of the past kingdoms and the one still in the future, at least it is at the time of this writing.

While I will focus on the prophecies of Daniel, go and read the rest of Daniel. It will show you just how God used and worked through Daniel, Shadrach, Meshach and Abednego to be a witness to the Babylonians.

The Magi, (the wise men) that came and gave gifts to Jesus were from Babylon. See the second chapter of Matthew. Undoubtedly they would have known about the coming birth of the Messiah from what had been handed down through the centuries from the teachings that they got from Daniel and his prophecies.

People who do not believe in a personal God and His supernatural involvement in human affairs, that don't believe that prophecy is possible or those that don't believe that bible prophecy is to be taken literally have a hard time with the idea that the book of Daniel is a sixth-century B.C. document. The accuracy of the prophecies of Daniel are so clear and accurate that in the third century B.C. a pagan writer, after reading Daniel said that it was so accurate it was like reading history, that the Book of Daniel was a forgery that someone who assumed the name of Daniel wrote this later after the fact and not by the 6th century B.C. Today liberal scholars and unbelievers are claiming this to. History doesn't record anyone criticizing or doubting the authorship of the book of Daniel until this pagan scholar in the third century B.C. All of these events were spelled out in such great detail and match so well with what occurred during the fourth, third, and second centuries B.C. that nonbelievers insist that these sections of the book had to be written during the second century B.C. But with the finding of many copies of Daniel with the Qumran scrolls or the Dead Sea scrolls, it has been proven that the book of Daniel was written well before history records these events.

The discovery of excellent manuscript copies among the Dead Sea Scrolls makes it almost mandatory to accept the earlier date for its composition. Among these copies of Daniel were all the books of the Old Testament except for Esther.

Why would the Qumran Jews view the book as inspired and make copies of it if they knew it was a contemporary forgery? **Two fragments of the book are said by paleographers to be as old as the large Isaiah scroll, which everyone admits was copied several centuries before 160 BC.**

Interestingly, the Jews in the Qumran community, which flourished in the first century before Christ and produced the Dead Sea Scrolls, prized Daniel so highly that they may have had more copies of it than any other book. They left eight complete copies and many fragments.

The style of the Hebrew language in which most of it was written and the Aramaic of a few sections, points to sixth-century B.C. authorship.

Flavius Josephus a Jewish Historian writing in 75 a.d. tells us that when Alexander the Great was coming into Jerusalem to destroy it because of the Jews refusal to submit to him, the High Priest came out in all his Priestly garments to meet Alexander the Great. He showed him from the book of Daniel that it had been foretold that he would conquer the Persian kingdom and of the establishment of his Grecian empire. Alexander was so impressed that he went into the Temple, forgave the Jews of their rebellion and did not destroy the city.

Daniel is indeed a prophetic book that accurately predicted what is now past history. Since it foretold future events that have now been fulfilled, we can be assured that the events that are still future will also come true just as literally as those of the past.

Before I continue I would like to give credit where credit is due. As I said in the beginning of this book I've learned a lot of this from several different bible prophecy teachers and authors. I lot of this information I got from articles on RaptureReady.com. If you want to study more you really should go to this site, your one stop for the Rapture and Bible prophecy.

2. Daniel Chapter 2.

The Northern Kingdom of Israel was conquered in 701BC by Assyria and then the Southern Kingdom was conquered and carried away into slavery 100 years later by the King of Babylon. Babylon was the country located where we know today as Iraq.

In the first Chapter of Daniel it starts off with the story of Daniel and the people of Israel after going into captivity by the Babylonians. If you read the book of Jeremiah you will see that he had been warning them that Judah, the southern part of Israel was going to go into captivity by the Babylonians for their sin.

To give you an understanding and the back ground about Daniel, let's look at the first few verses of chapter 1. To get insight into just how strong and devoted Daniel was, read all of Daniel.

> Dan. 1: 1 In the third year of the reign of Jehoiakim king of Judah, Nebuchadnezzar king of Babylon came to Jerusalem and besieged it. 2 And the Lord delivered Jehoiakim king of Judah into his hand, along with some of the articles from the temple of God. These he carried off to the temple of his god in Babylonia and put in the treasure house of his god.
>
> 3 Then the king ordered Ashpenaz, chief of his court officials, to bring in some of the Israelites from the royal family and the nobility- 4 young men without any physical defect, handsome, showing aptitude for every kind of learning, well informed, quick to understand, and qualified to serve in the king's palace. He was to teach them the language and literature of the Babylonians. 5 The king assigned them a daily amount of food and wine from the king's table. They were to be trained for three years, and after that they were to enter the king's service. 6 Among these were some from Judah: Daniel, Hananiah, Mishael and Azariah. 7 The chief official gave them new names: to Daniel, the name Belteshazzar; to Hananiah, Shadrach; to Mishael, Meshach; and to Azariah, Abednego.

The Visions and Prophecies of Daniel

In chapter 2 of Daniel we find the first vision and prophecy given to Daniel. Here we find the foundation of which the other visions are built on.

From reading the descriptions given in these prophecies of Daniel and looking back on history we can see that not only does God know the future, he predetermines it.

> Isaiah 46: 10 I make known the end from the beginning, from ancient times, what is still to come I say: My purpose will stand, and I will do all that I please.

> Rev. 22: 13I am the Alpha and the Omega, the First and the Last, the Beginning and the End.

As I mentioned at the beginning of this book, God often uses types and patterns. He also uses numbers to show that it is he that is in charge and in control. Like with the number 7. The number seven is considered to be the number of God and to suggest fullness or completion. We can see this with the prophecies of Daniel.

For example, in Daniel and Revelation there are seven kingdoms, seven heads, seven eyes, seven horns, seven thunders, seven seals, seven trumpets, seven churches, seven bowls and seven angels who stand before God. The bible only records Jesus speaking seven times when He was on the cross. Consider things in our physical world, there are seven continents, seven colors in the rainbow, seven days in a week; there are seven notes in our musical scale. These are signs to show that God is the creator of the universe. God is in everything! The use of seven in Daniel and Revelation is deliberate and important.

The kingdoms presented in Daniel 2 foretell the total history of man from the Babylonian kingdom up to the kingdom of God.

We see that God destroys the rebellious kingdom of man before He establishes His kingdom on Earth!

247

Daniel Chapter 2.

Nebuchadnezzar's Dream

1 In the second year of his reign, Nebuchadnezzar had dreams; his mind was troubled and he could not sleep. 2 So the king summoned the magicians, enchanters, sorcerers and astrologers to tell him what he had dreamed. When they came in and stood before the king, 3 he said to them, "I have had a dream that troubles me and I want to know what it means."

4 Then the astrologers answered the king in Aramaic, "O king, live forever! Tell your servants the dream, and we will interpret it."

5 The king replied to the astrologers, "This is what I have firmly decided: If you do not tell me what my dream was and interpret it, I will have you cut into pieces and your houses turned into piles of rubble. 6 But if you tell me the dream and explain it, you will receive from me gifts and rewards and great honor. So tell me the dream and interpret it for me."

7 Once more they replied, "Let the king tell his servants the dream, and we will interpret it."

8 Then the king answered, "I am certain that you are trying to gain time, because you realize that this is what I have firmly decided: 9 If you do not tell me the dream, there is just one penalty for you. You have conspired to tell me misleading and wicked things, hoping the situation will change. So then, tell me the dream, and I will know that you can interpret it for me."
10 The astrologers answered the king, "There is not a man on earth who can do what the king asks! No king, however great and mighty, has ever asked such a thing of any magician or enchanter or astrologer. 11 What the king asks is too difficult. No one can reveal it to the king except the gods, and they do not live among men."

12 This made the king so angry and furious that he ordered the execution of all the wise men of Babylon. 13 So the decree was issued to put the wise men to death, and men were sent to look for Daniel and his friends to put them to death.

14 When Arioch, the commander of the king's guard, had gone out to put to death the wise men of Babylon, Daniel spoke to him with wisdom and tact. 15 He asked the king's officer, "Why did the king issue such a harsh decree?" Arioch then explained the matter to Daniel. 16 At this, Daniel went in to the king and asked for time, so that he might interpret the dream for him.

17 Then Daniel returned to his house and explained the matter to his friends Hananiah, Mishael and Azariah. 18 He urged them to plead for mercy from the God of heaven concerning this mystery, so that he and his friends might not be executed with the rest of the wise men of Babylon. 19 During the night the mystery was revealed to Daniel in a vision. Then Daniel praised the God of heaven 20 and said:

"Praise be to the name of God forever and ever; wisdom and power are his.

21 He changes times and seasons; he sets up kings and deposes them. He gives wisdom to the wise and knowledge to the discerning.

22 He reveals deep and hidden things; he knows what lies in darkness, and light dwells with him.

23 I thank and praise you, O God of my fathers:
You have given me wisdom and power,
you have made known to me what we asked of you,
you have made known to us the dream of the king."

Daniel Interprets the Dream

24 Then Daniel went to Arioch, whom the king had appointed to execute the wise men of Babylon, and said to him, "Do not execute the wise men of Babylon. Take me to the king, and I will interpret his dream for him."

25 Arioch took Daniel to the king at once and said, "I have found a man among the exiles from Judah who can tell the king what his dream means."

26 The king asked Daniel (also called Belteshazzar), "Are you able to tell me what I saw in my dream and interpret it?"

27 Daniel replied, "No wise man, enchanter, magician or diviner can explain to the king the mystery he has asked about, 28 but there is a God in heaven who reveals mysteries. He has shown King Nebuchadnezzar what will happen in days to come. Your dream and the visions that passed through your mind as you lay on your bed are these:

29 "As you were lying there, O king, your mind turned to things to come, and the revealer of mysteries showed you what is going to happen. 30 As for me, this mystery has been revealed to me, not because I have greater wisdom than other living men, but so that you, O king, may know the interpretation and that you may understand what went through your mind.

31 "You looked, O king, and there before you stood a large statue—an enormous, dazzling statue, awesome in appearance. **32** The head of the statue was made of pure gold, its chest and arms of silver, its belly and thighs of bronze, **33** its legs of iron, its feet partly of iron and partly of baked clay. **34** While you were watching, a rock was cut out, but not by human hands. It struck the statue on its feet of iron and clay and smashed them.

35 Then the iron, the clay, the bronze, the silver and the gold were broken to pieces at the same time and became like chaff on a threshing floor in the summer. The wind swept them away without leaving a trace. But the rock that struck the statue became a huge mountain and filled the whole earth.

36 "This was the dream, and now we will interpret it to the king. **37** You, O king, are the king of kings. The God of heaven has given you dominion and power and might and glory; **38** in your hands he has placed mankind and the beasts of the field and the birds of the air. Wherever they live, he has made you ruler over them all. You are that head of gold.

39 "After you, another kingdom will rise, inferior to yours. Next, a third kingdom, one of bronze, will rule over the whole earth. **40** Finally, there will be a fourth kingdom, strong as iron—for iron breaks and smashes everything—and as iron breaks things to pieces, so it will crush and break all the others.

41 Just as you saw that the feet and toes were partly of baked clay and partly of iron, so this will be a divided kingdom; yet it will have some of the strength of iron in it, even as you saw iron mixed with clay. **42** As the toes were partly iron and partly clay, so this kingdom will be partly strong and partly brittle. **43** And just as you saw the iron mixed with baked clay, so the people will be a mixture and will not remain united, any more than iron mixes with clay.

44 "In the time of those kings, the God of heaven will set up a kingdom that will never be destroyed, nor will it be left to another people. It will crush all those kingdoms and bring them to an end, but it will itself endure forever. **45** This is the meaning of the vision of the rock cut out of a mountain, but not by human hands—a rock that broke the iron, the bronze, the clay, the silver and the gold to pieces "The great God has shown the king what will take place in the future. The dream is true and the interpretation is trustworthy."

251

46 Then King Nebuchadnezzar fell prostrate before Daniel and paid him honor and ordered that an offering and incense be presented to him. 47 The king said to Daniel, "Surely your God is the God of gods and the Lord of kings and a revealer of mysteries, for you were able to reveal this mystery."

48 Then the king placed Daniel in a high position and lavished many gifts on him. He made him ruler over the entire province of Babylon and placed him in charge of all its wise men. 49 Moreover, at Daniel's request the king appointed Shadrach, Meshach and Abednego administrators over the province of Babylon, while Daniel himself remained at the royal court.

Daniel lists the chronological progression of these world empires, the 4 Kingdoms that have ruled the world from Daniels day (Babylon, Medo-Persia, Greece, and Rome) and a future Revival of the Roman or European empire, the feet with 10 toes, then finally the kingdom of God. The vision occurred around 600 B.C., but it spans a time period up to the return of Jesus and the kingdom of God here on earth. So the vision has not been totally fulfilled yet. The vision begins with the kingdom of Babylon as the head of gold and the vision ends when Jesus, The Rock of Ages, the King of kings and Lord of lords, destroys the kingdom that will be ruling over the world at the time of Jesus' Second Coming. (See Revelation 17:12, 13; 19:11-21.) This will be the revived Roman Empire that the anti-Christ will be ruling. The world will have been divided into 10 regions and the anti-Christ (Satan) will appoint 10 kings over these regions, the 10 toes of Daniel's vision.

Rev. 17: 12"The ten horns you saw are ten kings who have not yet received a kingdom, but who for one hour will receive authority as kings along with the beast. 13They have one purpose and will give their power and authority to the beast.

Apparently these 10 kings only purpose is to sign their authority over to the anti-Christ.

Looking back on history this can be accurately interpreted. Babylon was conquered by the Medes (today's Kurds) and the Persians (Iran) at the end of the seventy year period set aside for Israel's captivity. They are the chest and arms of silver. The Greek armies under Alexander the Great conquered Persia and are represented by the belly and thighs of bronze. The legs of iron are the Eastern and Western divisions of the Roman Empire that displaced the Greeks. The Roman Empire was never really conquered, but collapsed from within from the weight of its own decay.

1) The Head of Gold, **BABYLON** 605 B.C.-538 B.C.
2) The Chest and Arms of Silver, **The MEDES and PERSIANS** 538 B.C.-331 B.C
3) The Belly and Thighs of Bronze, **Empire of Greece** 331 B.C.-146 B.C
4) The Legs of Iron, **Empire of ROME** 146 B.C.-500 A. D
5) A Gap in Time of many centuries. This is the time we are now living in, the Church age.
6) The Feet partly of Iron and Partly of baked Clay, The 10 Toes, **The Future Revived Roman Empire, the coming one world government.**
7) The Rock, The Stone cut without hands, **The Kingdom of God** on earth with Jesus as King.

Isn't this amazing, God not only showed Daniel the future of the world but he also showed Nebuchadnezzar. I'm sure it was to show the king and people of Babylon that the God of Israel is the true God. But this isn't the last time that Daniel will be given a vision of the future kingdoms.

With the feet and 10 toes partly of iron and partly of baked clay we switched from what is now history to prophecy. This will be what is referred to as the Revived Roman Empire, which will emerge from the European Union. This last world empire will divide up the world into 10 regions. We see from the mixture of the iron and clay that this last empire will be a mixture that will not stay united; it will be a divided kingdom that will have a hard time staying in agreement. We can look at the world today and see how this would be so true.

With verse 35 "Then the iron, the clay, the bronze, the silver and the gold were broken to pieces at the same time" it would appear that the last kingdom of the feet and 10 toes will have characteristics of all of the previous kingdoms. We can see that this is true of the nations of the world today.

But we see that Jesus destroys this kingdom.

> 44 "In the time of those kings, the God of heaven will set up a kingdom that will never be destroyed, nor will it be left to another people. It will crush all those kingdoms and bring them to an end, but it will itself endure forever.

This prophetic vision makes it clear that the kingdom of God here on earth is not a spiritual kingdom which by spiritual processes will gradually conquer the earth, but rather by a catastrophic judgment from heaven destroying the political kingdoms of Man thus paving the way for the millennial kingdom of God, which occurs with the second coming of Jesus. The revelation given here gives no support to either the amillennial view that the kingdom of God is only a spiritual kingdom that exists now here on earth or to the postmillennial view that the Church, which they see as the kingdom of God will gradually gain control over the whole earth spiritually and then Jesus will return. Since it's now been 2000 years since the Church started, they say this could take an undetermined amount of time. The destruction of the last world power is an event, not a process and will be fulfilled by Jesus at his second coming.

3. Daniel Chapter 7

In chapter 5 we see that Nebuchadnezzar has died and his son Belshazzar is king.

Historians say the first year of Belshazzar was about 552 B.C. If so, this vision occurs about fifty years after the vision recorded in Daniel 2 and about 14 years before the Medes and Persians conquered Babylon. Daniel had already had this vision when Belshazzar held his feast in chapter 5. Daniel having been taken into captivity as a teenager is now a man getting on up in years. I didn't want to say old man, if he was in his 60's that's not an old man. You've got to be in at least in your 90's to be old.

Daniel's Dream of Four Beasts

1 In the first year of Belshazzar king of Babylon, Daniel had a dream, and visions passed through his mind as he was lying on his bed. He wrote down the substance of his dream.

2 Daniel said: "In my vision at night I looked, and there before me were the four winds of heaven churning up the great sea. 3 Four great beasts, each different from the others, came up out of the sea.

4 "The first was like a lion, and it had the wings of an eagle. I watched until its wings were torn off and it was lifted from the ground so that it stood on two feet like a man, and the heart of a man was given to it.

5 "And there before me was a second beast, which looked like a bear. It was raised up on one of its sides, and it had three ribs in its mouth between its teeth. It was told, 'Get up and eat your fill of flesh!'

6 "After that, I looked, and there before me was another beast, one that looked like a leopard. And on its back it had four wings like those of a bird. This beast had four heads, and it was given authority to rule.

7 "After that, in my vision at night I looked, and there before me was a fourth beast—terrifying and frightening and very powerful. It had large iron teeth; it crushed and devoured its victims and trampled underfoot whatever was left. It was different from all the former beasts, and it had ten horns.

8 "While I was thinking about the horns, there before me was another horn, a little one, which came up among them; and three of the first horns were uprooted before it. This horn had eyes like the eyes of a man and a mouth that spoke boastfully.

9 "As I looked,
"thrones were set in place,
and the Ancient of Days took his seat.
His clothing was as white as snow;
the hair of his head was white like wool.
His throne was flaming with fire,
and its wheels were all ablaze.

10 A river of fire was flowing,
coming out from before him.
Thousands upon thousands attended him;
ten thousand times ten thousand stood before him.
The court was seated,
and the books were opened.

11 "Then I continued to watch because of the boastful words the horn was speaking. I kept looking until the beast was slain and its body destroyed and thrown into the blazing fire. 12 (The other beasts had been stripped of their authority, but were allowed to live for a period of time.)

13 "In my vision at night I looked, and there before me was one like a son of man, coming with the clouds of heaven. He approached the Ancient of Days and was led into his presence. 14 He was given authority, glory and sovereign power; all peoples, nations and men of every language worshiped him. His

dominion is an everlasting dominion that will not pass away, and his kingdom is one that will never be destroyed.

The Interpretation of the Dream

15 "I, Daniel, was troubled in spirit, and the visions that passed through my mind disturbed me. 16 I approached one of those standing there and asked him the true meaning of all this. "So he told me and gave me the interpretation of these things: 17 'The four great beasts are four kingdoms that will rise from the earth. 18 But the saints of the Most High will receive the kingdom and will possess it forever—yes, for ever and ever.'

19 "Then I wanted to know the true meaning of the fourth beast, which was different from all the others and most terrifying, with its iron teeth and bronze claws—the beast that crushed and devoured its victims and trampled underfoot whatever was left. 20 I also wanted to know about the ten horns on its head and about the other horn that came up, before which three of them fell—the horn that looked more imposing than the others and that had eyes and a mouth that spoke boastfully. 21 As I watched, this horn was waging war against the saints and defeating them, 22 until the Ancient of Days came and pronounced judgment in favor of the saints of the Most High, and the time came when they possessed the kingdom.

23 "He gave me this explanation: 'The fourth beast is a fourth kingdom that will appear on earth. It will be different from all the other kingdoms and will devour the whole earth, trampling it down and crushing it. 24 The ten horns are ten kings who will come from this kingdom. After them another king will arise, different from the earlier ones; he will subdue three kings. 25 He will speak against the Most High and oppress his saints and try to change the set times and the laws. The saints will be handed over to him for a time, times and half a time. (Or *for a year, two years and half a year*)

257

26 " 'But the court will sit, and his power will be taken away and completely destroyed forever. 27 Then the sovereignty, power and greatness of the kingdoms under the whole heaven will be handed over to the saints, the people of the Most High. His kingdom will be an everlasting kingdom, and all rulers will worship and obey him.'

28 "This is the end of the matter. I, Daniel, was deeply troubled by my thoughts, and my face turned pale, but I kept the matter to myself."

Daniel is shown the same kingdoms of the future that he had seen in his first vision recorded in chapter 2 but this time he is given more details about the 4th beast.

Compare Daniel chapters 2 and 7.

Daniel 2	Daniel 7
605 B.C.-538 B.C. Gold - Nebuchadnezzer's **BABYLON**	1st Beast - LION with wings of an eagle **BABYLON**
538 B.C.-331 B.C. Silver – Dual Empire of the **MEDES and PERSIANS**	2nd Beast - BEAR raised up on one side **MEDES and PERSIANS**
331 B.C.-146 B.C. Bronze Empire of **GREECE**	3rd Beast - LEOPARD with 4 wings & 4 heads Empire of **GREECE**
146 B.C.-500 A. D. Iron Empire of **ROME**	4th Beast - BEAST with iron teeth Empire of **ROME**
GAP IN TIME OF MANY CENTURIES, The Church age	GAP IN TIME OF MANY CENTURIES, The Church age
Iron and Clay 10 toes (2:42) **Future Revived Roman Empire** "Stone cut without hands" is Jesus. Strikes feet at His 2nd coming	10 horns (7:7) **Future Revived Roman Empire** "Little horn" is the AntiChrist (7:8) "Son of Man" is Jesus (7:13)

Daniel saw four great beasts rise up from the sea and he was told these beasts represented four empires that would rise at their appointed time. (Daniel 7:15-16)

Dan. 7: 3 Four great beasts, each different from the others, came up out of the sea. 4 "The first was like a lion, and it had the wings of an eagle. I watched until its wings were torn off and it was lifted from the ground so that it stood on two feet like a man, and the heart of a man was given to it.

The first beast to rise up was a lion, and it represents the empire of Babylon. Just as gold is the king of metals, so the lion is the king of beasts. The eagle's wings indicate a military prowess that none can escape. The ancients regarded the eagle's keen vision and its ability to swoop down on its prey as a fitting symbol of military power. (Deuteronomy 28) Babylon's symbol was the winged lion. Being made into a man makes it represent Nebuchadnezzar.

> Deut. 28: 49 The LORD will bring a nation against you from far away, from the ends of the earth, like an eagle swooping down, a nation whose language you will not understand, 50 a fierce-looking nation without respect for the old or pity for the young.

As Daniel watched, its wings were torn off. The lion lost its power and ability to subdue nations. In this vision, the lion received a man's heart, a heart that is subject to vanity, arrogance, and pride. This transition uniquely describes the arrogance of the kings of Babylon. God had to humiliate King Nebuchadnezzar by taking him from the throne and giving him the mind of an animal for seven years because of pride and arrogance. (See Daniel 4) Unfortunately, Belshazzar King of Babylon did not learn from Nebuchadnezzar's humiliation and Babylon ultimately was conquered because of arrogance and vanity. (Daniel 5:22)

> Dan. 7: 5 "And there before me was a second beast, which looked like a bear. It was raised up on one of its sides, and it had three ribs in its mouth between its teeth. It was told, 'Get up and eat your fill of flesh!'

The second beast represented the Medo-Persian Empire, which conquered Babylon in 539 B.C. (Dan. 5). Two features stand out about this ferocious bear. First, Daniel observed that it was raised up on one of its sides. This feature corresponds with the fact that the Persians became the dominant side of the Medo-Persian Empire. We see in Daniel's vision of the statue in chapter 2 that the image of the chest had two arms suggesting the two kingdoms. Second, the three ribs represented Lydia, Egypt and Babylon. The three ribs are Persia's three major conquests, Lydia in 546BC, Babylon in 539BC, and Egypt in

525BC. After the Medes and Persians subdued these three kingdoms, they controlled the known world

> Dan. 7: 6 "After that, I looked, and there before me was another beast, one that looked like a leopard. And on its back it had four wings like those of a bird. This beast had four heads, and it was given authority to rule.

The third beast, the leopard represented the kingdom of Greece, the empire that swallowed up Medo-Persia. The leopard is a swift and cunning hunter that easily kills prey larger than itself. The leopard in this vision had four wings indicating its conquest would be incredibly swift. The four wings represent the speed with which Alexander the Great conquered the known world. He conquered the Medo-Persian Empire in a mere ten years! At the peak of his conquests and military prowess, Alexander died of "swamp fever" (probably malaria) at the age of 33 as he and his armies had returned from a conquest of India to Babylon to celebrate. He died in 323 B.C. He had no offspring to inherit his kingdom. It was eventually divided between his four leading generals: Ptolemy, who was given Egypt, Palestine, and Arabia; Cassander, who was given Macedonia and Greece; Lysimachus who was given Thrace and Bithynia; and Seleucus who was given Syria, Babylonia, and land to the east. The four heads of the leopard represent these four kings. Isn't bible prophecy amazing.

> Dan. 7: 7 "After that, in my vision at night I looked, and there before me was a fourth beast—terrifying and frightening and very powerful. It had large iron teeth; it crushed and devoured its victims and trampled underfoot whatever was left. It was different from all the former beasts, and it had ten horns.
>
> 8 "While I was thinking about the horns, there before me was another horn, a little one, which came up among them; and three of the first horns were uprooted before it. This horn had eyes like the eyes of a man and a mouth that spoke boastfully.

With Rome's victory over Greece, the Romans finally gained control of the known world. The Roman military was known for its use of iron and its policy of devouring and destroying everything in its path. You see this when they destroyed Jerusalem and the Temple in 70 a.d. The Romans were skillful manufacturers of iron weapons. Their ironclad warriors and chariots of iron were legendary. Rome fell after a series of civil wars within its borders; the empire crumbled during the last half of the fifth century A.D. One interesting fact from history to take notice of is that of all the world empires that have existed, they all were conquered by the next succeeding empire, but not Rome. It became so corrupt that it fell from within. It has not been conquered or defeated.

Did you notice the fourth beast has teeth of iron? This feature parallels the "legs of iron" mentioned in Daniel 2. The legs are the strongest part of the body representing the strength of Rome.

We see this fourth beast is different than all the other beasts in that it has 10 horns. This parallels the feet with 10 toes of iron and clay from Daniels first vision in chapter 2. With the 10 horns we once again jump from history to prophecy. This is where, with the description in verses 7 and 8 and with the description of the feet with 10 toes in chapter 2 bible scholars find that the last world empire will be a revived form of the old Roman Empire.

Notice the description in the 2nd chapter of the legs and feet, there as one. Dan. 2: 33 its legs of iron, its feet partly of iron and partly of baked clay. But you see that the two feet is a kingdom that is made up of the 10 toes.

Dan. 2: 41 Just as you saw that the feet and toes were partly of baked clay and partly of iron, so this will be a divided kingdom; yet it will have some of the strength of iron in it, even as you saw iron mixed with clay. 42 As the toes were partly iron and partly clay, so this kingdom will be partly strong and partly brittle.

And you see here in the 7th chapter verse 7 that the beast here has 10 horns. But they are described with the 4th kingdom. Rome was the 4th kingdom, so we can see that the last world kingdom of the feet with 10 toes and the 10 horns of the 4th beast is a continuation of Rome. Another amazing fact with this prophecy showing two legs and two feet is that in the later years of the Roman Empire it was split up into Western and Eastern Europe. Could it be that this last revived form of the Roman Empire, with the representation of the two feet of Iron mixed with clay be the European Continents and the American Continents?

These visions are not only of Rome but also of the future revived Roman Empire of the last days of the tribulation.

The description here in chapter 7 is much broader than the vision in chapter 2. Here with the description of this beast it describes in more detail the characteristics of the last world empire before the return of Christ. We see this with the 10 horns and with the little horn, the anti-Christ coming up among the 10 horns. Notice this little horn is not one of the 10 but emerges from among them and uproots three of the first horns. This little horn represents a ruler who will come up last in the fourth kingdom who will be a world conquer. Just as the image was destroyed in Daniel 2, so this forth beast will be destroyed and thrown into the blazing fire (Dan. 2:44, 7:11), the lake of fire in Rev. 19:20.

With verse 8 we see a depiction of the anti-Christ in the little horn. Compare this with the book of Revelation.

> Rev. 13: 1 And I saw a beast coming out of the sea. He had ten horns and seven heads, with ten crowns on his horns, and on each head a blasphemous name. 2The beast I saw resembled a leopard, but had feet like those of a bear and a mouth like that of a lion. The dragon gave the beast his power and his throne and great authority. 3One of the heads of the beast seemed to have had a fatal wound, but the fatal wound had been healed. The whole world was astonished and followed the beast. 4Men worshiped the dragon because he had given authority to the

beast, and they also worshiped the beast and asked, "Who is like the beast? Who can make war against him?" 5The beast was given a mouth to utter proud words and blasphemies and to exercise his authority for forty-two months. 6He opened his mouth to blaspheme God, and to slander his name and his dwelling place and those who live in heaven. 7He was given power to make war against the saints and to conquer them. And he was given authority over every tribe, people, language and nation. 8All inhabitants of the earth will worship the beast—all whose names have not been written in the book of life belonging to the Lamb that was slain from the creation of the world.

Compare also with Revelation chapter 17.

Rev. 17: 3Then the angel carried me away in the Spirit into a desert. There I saw a woman sitting on a scarlet beast that was covered with blasphemous names and had seven heads and ten horns.

The 10 horns parallel with the 10 toes of Daniels first vision.

Rev. 17:7Then the angel said to me: "Why are you astonished? I will explain to you the mystery of the woman and of the beast she rides, which has the seven heads and ten horns. 8The beast, which you saw, once was, now is not, and will come up out of the Abyss and go to his destruction. The inhabitants of the earth whose names have not been written in the book of life from the creation of the world will be astonished when they see the beast, because he once was, now is not, and yet will come. 9"This calls for a mind with wisdom. The seven heads are seven hills on which the woman sits. 10They are also seven kings. Five have fallen, one is, the other has not yet come; but when he does come, he must remain for a little while. 11The beast who once was, and now is not, is an eighth king. He belongs to the seven and is going to his destruction.

The seven heads are 7 kingdoms for we see they are 7 kings. Five have fallen; this would include the kingdoms that were before Babylon, Assyria and Egypt. The one that is would be Rome, for it was the ruling empire at the time John was receiving and writing the book of Revelation. So we have had, 1)Egypt, 2)Assyria, 3)Babylon, 4)the Meds and Persians, 5)Greece and 6)Rome. The one that has not yet come would be the revived form of the Old Roman Empire for verse 3 says, "One of the heads of the beast seemed to have had a fatal wound, but the fatal wound had been healed". Now isn't that amazing. Remember how numbers are important and how God uses them to make a point and how the number 7 means total and complete. We have had 6 ruling empires. With the finial revived Roman Empire, that will make man's 7th attempt at ruling the world. Now you can't believe that this is just a coincidence.

The 8th king is the little horn in Daniel 7. The beast who once was, and now is not, is an eighth king. This is Satan in the anti-Christ. The man, who will be the anti-Christ, will be the 7th king, but will apparently be killed somehow and then indwelt by Satan at the middle of the tribulation, thus Satan in the man, in the anti-Christ will be the 8th king. This is why here in Daniel and in Matthew 24 and in the book of Revelation you see so much more detail about the last half of the tribulation.

Again, the reference in verse 3 "One of the heads of the beast seemed to have had a fatal wound, but the fatal wound had been healed", this could represent the old Roman Empire falling and being revived with the anti-Christ, the little horn being in control. It also refers to the anti-Christ being killed and then indwelt by Satan. So again we can see how prophecy could have dual implications.

Revelation 12:7 tells us about Satan entering the anti-Christ.

> Rev. 12: 7And there was war in heaven. Michael and his angels fought against the dragon, and the dragon and his angels fought back. 8But he was not strong enough, and they lost their place in heaven. 9The great dragon was hurled down—that ancient

serpent called the devil, or Satan, who leads the whole world astray. He was hurled to the earth, and his angels with him.

Rev. 12: 13When the dragon saw that he had been hurled to the earth, he pursued the woman who had given birth to the male child. 14The woman was given the two wings of a great eagle, so that she might fly to the place prepared for her in the desert, where she would be taken care of for a time, times and half a time, out of the serpent's reach. 15Then from his mouth the serpent spewed water like a river, to overtake the woman and sweep her away with the torrent. 16But the earth helped the woman by opening its mouth and swallowing the river that the dragon had spewed out of his mouth. 17Then the dragon was enraged at the woman and went off to make war against the rest of her offspring—those who obey God's commandments and hold to the testimony of Jesus.

Daniel mentioned this 3 ½ period of time in verse 25.

Dan. 7: 25 He will speak against the Most High and oppress his saints and try to change the set times and the laws. The saints will be handed over to him for a time, times and half a time.

The eighth king is Satan in the anti-Christ.

Another clue that this is a form of the Old Roman Empire is that he belongs to the seven. We also see that this king and his kingdom will be a short-lived one; it will not last as long as the others. This last world empire will only last 7 years.

Rev. 17: 12"The ten horns you saw are ten kings who have not yet received a kingdom, but who for one hour will receive authority as kings along with the beast. 13They have one purpose and will give their power and authority to the beast. 14They will make war against the Lamb, but the Lamb will overcome them because he is Lord of lords and King of kings—and with him will be his called, chosen and faithful followers."

You can see that the 10 horns in Daniel 7 and Revelation are the same as the 10 toes of Daniel chapter 2. Look back at Chapter 2.

Again, you can see that as the feet are a continuation of the legs so also this last world kingdom or government will be a continuation of the Old Roman Empire.

In Revelation 17 verse 12 and 13 you see that these kings will receive authority as kings just to give their power and authority over to the anti-Christ.

The world will be divided up into 10 regions. An organization of the European Union called the club of Rome already has the plans for this in place. There will be 10 kings or presidents appointed over each of these regions. What are we hearing world leaders talk about, even here in the United States, a New World Order? Well, this is it.

The world may be divided into 10 regions or controlling nations before the anti-Christ comes on the seen for it says he comes from among the 10 horns, we see this in verses 7 and 8. It will at least already have been divided up before the mid-point of the tribulation, before Satan has entered into the anti-Christ, for the little horn in verse 8 is Satan. The anti-Christ appointing 10 kings over these regions or nations could happen at the mid-point of the tribulation, after Satan has entered into the man, the anti-Christ.

In the past and still some today have seen the 10 toes and 10 horns as representing 10 nations, but from the descriptions given, especially with the 10 kings only being given authority for one hour showing that they did not have this authority before the anti-Christ gives it to them and with the fact that there are already plans to have the world divided up into ten regions leads me as well as others I have read to believe it is referring to a world kingdom or government of ten regions. There are more than 10 nations that are members of the European Union now.

But those that see it as referring to 10 European nations see it as 10 prominent nations that will have the most power, the ones that have the controlling, decision making power. They believe there will be 5 Eastern European nations and 5 Western European nations thus representing the two feet of Daniels vision.

With verse 8 here in Daniel chapter 7 we see that three of the first kingdoms that come under the anti-Christ's rule, the little horn, don't do it willingly, they will be uprooted, forced to comply. This most likely happens after satan has entered the man, the anti-Christ.

> 8 "While I was thinking about the horns, there before me was another horn, a little one, which came up among them; and three of the first horns were uprooted before it. This horn had eyes like the eyes of a man and a mouth that spoke boastfully.

We see in chapter 2 of Daniel that verses 41 thru 43 says that the 10 toed kingdom will not have the same power that its legs had, that it will be divided. Like I said before, you can see how this will be true of the nations of the world today.

Next in Daniels vision here in chapter 7 he sees into heaven.

> Dan. 7: 9 "As I looked,
> "thrones were set in place,
> and the Ancient of Days took his seat.
> His clothing was as white as snow;
> the hair of his head was white like wool.
> His throne was flaming with fire,
> and its wheels were all ablaze.

Look at John's description of Jesus in the first chapter of Revelation.

> Rev.1: 12I turned around to see the voice that was speaking to me. And when I turned I saw seven golden lampstands, 13and among the lampstands was someone "like a son of man,"

dressed in a robe reaching down to his feet and with a golden sash around his chest.

14His head and hair were white like wool, as white as snow, and his eyes were like blazing fire. 15His feet were like bronze glowing in a furnace, and his voice was like the sound of rushing waters. 16In his right hand he held seven stars, and out of his mouth came a sharp double-edged sword. His face was like the sun shining in all its brilliance.

And the thrones set in place

> Rev. 4: 4Surrounding the throne were twenty-four other thrones, and seated on them were twenty-four elders. They were dressed in white and had crowns of gold on their heads.

At the beginning of the tribulation God and 24 elders will sit in judgment over what is about to come upon the world. These 24 thrones and elders are not mentioned anywhere in the Old Testament other than here with Daniel seeing thrones (plural) set in place at the end of the age. None of the other Old Testament views of God's Throne mention these thrones. The fact that they don't appear in Old Testament accounts, but do when the End of the Age is the context implies that they have been added since the cross. It could only be a reference to the Church.

> Dan. 7: 10 A river of fire was flowing,
> coming out from before him.
> Thousands upon thousands attended him;
> ten thousand times ten thousand stood before him.
> The court was seated,
> and the books were opened.

Ten thousand was the biggest number they had in those days, so Daniel used that number multiplied by itself to describe a multitude no one could count.

Also compare with

> Rev. 5: 11 Then I looked and heard the voice of many angels, numbering thousands upon thousands, and ten thousand times ten thousand. They encircled the throne and the living creatures and the elders.

Fire has often been used to symbolize judgment. John in Rev. 1 verse 14 said his eyes were like blazing fire and in verse 15 his feet were like bronze glowing in a furnace. This is showing that God is about to judge the world.

Now with verse 11 of Daniel chapter 7, we come to the return of Jesus and what he does to the little horn, the anti-Christ and his kingdom. We saw also with verse 44 of chapter 2 that Jesus destroys this kingdom when he returns.

> Dan. 2: 44 "In the time of those kings, the God of heaven will set up a kingdom that will never be destroyed, nor will it be left to another people. It will crush all those kingdoms and bring them to an end, but it will itself endure forever.

> Dan. 7: 11 "Then I continued to watch because of the boastful words the horn was speaking. I kept looking until the beast was slain and its body destroyed and thrown into the blazing fire. 12 (The other beasts had been stripped of their authority, but were allowed to live for a period of time.)

Apparently this last kingdom, this last one world government will be stripped of its authority over the world but will be allowed to remain for a while, probably just until Jesus gets things in order. It could be the structure and organization of the 10 regions is allowed to remain for a period of time.

Compare this with the book of Revelation

Rev. 13: 5The beast was given a mouth to utter proud words and blasphemies and to exercise his authority for forty-two months. 6He opened his mouth to blaspheme God, and to slander his name and his dwelling place and those who live in heaven.

Rev. 19 19Then I saw the beast and the kings of the earth and their armies gathered together to make war against the rider on the horse and his army. 20But the beast was captured, and with him the false prophet who had performed the miraculous signs on his behalf. With these signs he had deluded those who had received the mark of the beast and worshiped his image. The two of them were thrown alive into the fiery lake of burning sulfur. 21The rest of them were killed with the sword that came out of the mouth of the rider on the horse, and all the birds gorged themselves on their flesh.

Now we come to the second coming of the Lord,

Dan. 7: 13 "In my vision at night I looked, and there before me was one like a son of man, coming with the clouds of heaven. He approached the Ancient of Days and was led into his presence. 14 He was given authority, glory and sovereign power; all peoples, nations and men of every language worshiped him. His dominion is an everlasting dominion that will not pass away, and his kingdom is one that will never be destroyed.

The coming of the Son of man in verse 13 is understood to refer to the coming of Jesus as the Messiah in His second coming, as Jesus himself used this expression "Son of man" in many references to Himself in the Gospel of Matthew (8:20; 9:6; 10:23; 11:19; 12:8, 32, 40; etc). This verse referred to Jesus in His incarnation approaching "the Ancient of Days", an obvious reference to God the Father. The reference in verse 14 of him being given authority, glory and power over all peoples and nations will be fulfilled in the millennial kingdom.

It sounds like Jesus will go before the Father and will be told to go and end the destruction of the earth and to destroy the anti-Christ and his government. We see with verse 14 that Jesus is given the authority of the kingdom of God.

Compare this with

> Rev. 1: 7Look, he is coming with the clouds,
> and every eye will see him,
> even those who pierced him;
> and all the peoples of the earth will mourn because of him. So shall it be! Amen.

And

> Mt. 24: 30"At that time the sign of the Son of Man will appear in the sky, and all the nations of the earth will mourn. They will see the Son of Man coming on the clouds of the sky, with power and great glory.

Finally, we come to the culmination of human history, the dominion over Planet Earth, which Adam lost to Satan, has now been re-gained by the Son of God. We come to the kingdom of God, which Jesus will rule and reign with His Church for a 1000 years, until God the Father makes all things new, the New Heavens and New Earth.

Next with Daniel chapter 7 verse 15 we come to the interpretation of the dream. We see that Daniel was particularly concerned about the meaning of the fourth beast, which was given special emphasis in the vision.

> 15 "I, Daniel, was troubled in spirit, and the visions that passed through my mind disturbed me. 16 I approached one of those standing there and asked him the true meaning of all this. "So he told me and gave me the interpretation of these things: 17 'The four great beasts are four kingdoms that will rise from the

earth. 18 But the saints of the Most High will receive the kingdom and will possess it forever—yes, for ever and ever.'

19 "Then I wanted to know the true meaning of the fourth beast, which was different from all the others and most terrifying, with its iron teeth and bronze claws—the beast that crushed and devoured its victims and trampled underfoot whatever was left. 20 I also wanted to know about the ten horns on its head and about the other horn that came up, before which three of them fell—the horn that looked more imposing than the others and that had eyes and a mouth that spoke boastfully. 21 As I watched, this horn was waging war against the saints and defeating them, 22 until the Ancient of Days came and pronounced judgment in favor of the saints of the Most High, and the time came when they possessed the kingdom.

We see it is mentioned repeatedly that the saints of the Most High will receive the kingdom.

We can see that this is not only a description of the Old Roman Empire of the past but it is also of the future revived Roman Empire. We can see that this hasn't been fulfilled yet by the fact that the Roman empire of the past did not have control over all the earth; just the known part of Europe and the Middle East and it was not made up of 10 kingdoms or 10 worldly regions like the future empire will be. There hasn't been one man ruling the whole word, especially Satan here in a man. And we certainly have not had Jesus returning and destroying this 10 toed, 10-horn kingdom. Remember, Jesus himself said everyone will see him return at his second coming.

In another vision of Daniel in the 11th chapter he is shown and describes this little horn again.

Dan. 11: 36 "The king will do as he pleases. He will exalt and magnify himself above every god and will say unheard-of things against the God of gods. He will be successful until the time of wrath is completed, for what has been determined must take place.

Look again at Paul's description of the anti-Christ, this little horn.

2 Thessalonians 2

The Man of Lawlessness

1Concerning the coming of our Lord Jesus Christ and our being gathered to him, we ask you, brothers, 2not to become easily unsettled or alarmed by some prophecy, report or letter supposed to have come from us, saying that the day of the Lord has already come. 3Don't let anyone deceive you in any way, for (that day will not come) until the rebellion occurs and the man of lawlessness is revealed, the man doomed to destruction.

4He will oppose and will exalt himself over everything that is called God or is worshiped, so that he sets himself up in God's temple, proclaiming himself to be God.

5Don't you remember that when I was with you I used to tell you these things? 6And now you know what is holding him back, so that he may be revealed at the proper time. 7For the secret power of lawlessness is already at work; but the one who now holds it back will continue to do so till he is taken out of the way.

8And then the lawless one will be revealed, whom the Lord Jesus will overthrow with the breath of his mouth and destroy by the splendor of his coming.

9The coming of the lawless one will be in accordance with the work of Satan displayed in all kinds of counterfeit miracles, signs and wonders, 10and in every sort of evil that deceives those who are perishing. They perish because they refused to love the truth and so be saved. 11For this reason God sends them a powerful delusion so that they will believe the lie 12and so that all will be condemned who have not believed the truth but have delighted in wickedness.

Compare all this with

Mt. 24: 15"So when you see standing in the holy place 'the abomination that causes desolation,' spoken of through the prophet Daniel—let the reader understand—

With this Jesus is telling us when Satan indwells the anti-Christ, he becomes the little horn, he becomes the 8th king. The time factor for his rule was represented by Daniel and John in Revelation as a 'time, times and half a time' referring to 3 ½ years. This will be the last 3 ½ years of the tribulation.

We can see that the descriptions of the anti-Christ by John in the book of Revelation and Paul are the same as Daniel's description of the little horn.

The description given here of the end time, the forth beast, and the ten horns followed by the eleventh horn in verse 7 and 8, that gained control of the first three horns has never been fulfilled in history.

It is obvious that the kingdoms of the Medes and Persians, Greece and Rome are gone to past history. The last stage of the Old Roman Empire, described here, as the ten-horn stage has never been fulfilled.

Some interpreters of this prophecy have attempted to find fulfillment of all of this in the past. Some have attempted to find ten kings of the past and the eleventh king who would arise to somehow fulfill this prophecy, but there is nothing corresponding to this in the history of the Roman Empire. Furthermore, the 10 horns do not reign one after the other, but they reign simultaneously. Further, the 10 horns were not the world empire of the little horn, but they were the forerunner to the world empire of the little horn, which the little horn after subduing three of the ten horns will go on to become a world dictator. This little horn eventually becomes Satan himself in the anti-Christ.

The amillennial interpretation which holds there is no millennial kingdom often claims fulfillment of the chapter completely in history. A complete fulfillment however, would require first, a ruler who would rule the entire earth and secondly, a ten king confederacy in which the ruler conquered three of the ten kings. No ruler in the past has been singled out in a 3 ½ year period to be the persecutor of Israel and to bring in the special period that in the Old Testament was placed before the Second Coming. If such a ruler could be identified, he and his rule would have had to be destroyed forever by Jesus himself and would need to be followed by the kingdom of God here on earth. Furthermore, since we see that Jesus while referring back to Daniel as a description, is referring to a future event in Matthew 24, and with seeing the book of Revelation is a continuation of Daniel, this would have to have happened since Jesus was here and since John received and wrote the book of Revelation.

Although the destruction of 70 a.d. does not meet with the conditions given here, the Preterist claim this took place with the destruction of Jerusalem by the Romans and that Jesus returned in the form of the Roman army. They also say we are in the Kingdom of God now. Again, the conditions the world is in today do not meet with the conditions given of the kingdom of God not to mention how Jesus said in Matthew 24 his return would be.

Any attempt to interpret the little horn as a Catholic Pope is also faulty. No King or Pope can be identified in history fulfilling these prophecies. The Papacy is still active in the world and was not limited to 3 ½ years, and the papacy has not been destroyed, especially by the Second Coming as the prophecy requires. If this prophecy is to be understood in its literal fulfillment, it must be interpreted parallel to chapter 2 where the prophecy of the destruction of the feet and toes of the image and of the whole image itself has not been fulfilled in history.

We see in this prophecy that this final world ruler has not emerged, and the various circumstances surrounding his rule have not been fulfilled in history.

In view of the fact that the prophecies of the past kingdoms have been fulfilled so literally, a literal fulfillment of the unfulfilled end time prophecies is the only satisfactory approach we can take, this holds that there is still yet a future world empire when the end-time prophecies will be fulfilled.

We can see the beginnings of the formation of this last world empire now with the European Union. We see the whole world is calling for a new one world government.

> Dan. 7: 26 "'But the court will sit, and his (the anti-Christ's) power will be taken away and completely destroyed forever.
>
> 27 Then the sovereignty, power and greatness of the kingdoms under the whole heaven will be handed over to the saints, the people of the Most High. His kingdom will be an everlasting kingdom, and all rulers will worship and obey him.'
>
> 28 "This is the end of the matter. I, Daniel, was deeply troubled by my thoughts, and my face turned pale, but I kept the matter to myself."

We see that the end of this matter will be the kingdom of God with Jesus ruling and reigning.

The bible is the Word of God and Jesus is Lord.

4. Daniel Chapter 8

It's been 2 years since the vision of the 4 beasts we saw in chapter 7. Now he's had another vision, this one of a ram and a goat. As we'll see, it was intended to give both him and us more detail on the things to come, because the vision has a dual fulfillment. For Daniel this vision was all in the future, but for us the first fulfillment is now history, assuring us the final fulfillment is still in our future.

The year was 551 BC. It was 12 years before the fall of Babylon to the Medes and Persians. This vision preceded the final destruction of Babylon in 539 BC. The prophecy in this vision, however, has to do with the second and third kingdoms we saw in the image of Daniel chapter 2 with the chest and arms of silver and the belly and thighs of bronze. In this vision Daniel recorded in detail how the second and third kingdoms would come on the scene.

Daniel's Vision of a Ram and a Goat

1 In the third year of King Belshazzar's reign, I, Daniel, had a vision, after the one that had already appeared to me. 2 In my vision I saw myself in the citadel of Susa in the province of Elam; in the vision I was beside the Ulai Canal.

Susa was about 200 to 230 miles east of Babylon in modern day Iran and would become the capital of the Persian Empire. Nehemiah lived there, as did Queen Esther. Today it's known as Shush. Later, after the Medo-Persians had conquered Babylon Xerxes built a great palace in this city, which was the scene of the Book of Esther and where Nehemiah served as King Artaxerxes' cupbearer. (Neh. 1:11).

3 I looked up, and there before me was a ram with two horns, standing beside the canal, and the horns were long. One of the horns was longer than the other but grew up later. 4 I watched the ram as he charged toward the west and the north and the south. No animal could stand against him, and none could rescue from his power. He did as he pleased and became great.

278

The ram with two horns represents Medo-Persia. The King of Persia wore a ram's head crown into battle. By now you should be able to see how this parallels with the chest and arms of silver in chapter 2 and with the bear that was raised up on its side in chapter 7. The longer horn that grew up later is Persia that eventually became dominant. (The Angel Gabriel will confirm the identities of both animals for us later in the chapter.) As I've noted before Media was home to the Kurds of today while Persia has become Iran. There was a Royal Road that ran from Susa all the way to Sardis in Western Turkey bringing goods from the Mediterranean to the capital city.

Together these two conquered an area extending from Pakistan in the East to Greece in the West and to the shores of the Black and Caspian Seas in the North and ruled it until Alexander the Great came on the scene 200 years later, in about 330 BC.

Although Daniel was alive to see the fulfillment of the prophecies surrounding the destruction of Babylon by the Medes and Persians, he did not live long enough to see the outcome of the Persian kingdom, as the prophecy will reveal.

> Dan. 8: 5 As I was thinking about this, suddenly a goat with a prominent horn between his eyes came from the west, crossing the whole earth without touching the ground. 6 He came toward the two-horned ram I had seen standing beside the canal and charged at him in great rage. 7 I saw him attack the ram furiously, striking the ram and shattering his two horns. The ram was powerless to stand against him; the goat knocked him to the ground and trampled on him, and none could rescue the ram from his power. 8 The goat became very great, but at the height of his power his large horn was broken off, and in its place four prominent horns grew up toward the four winds of heaven.

Again, you can see the parallel with descriptions of Greece in chapters 2 and 7. The one horned goat was the symbol of Phillip of Macedon, father to Alexander the Great. Alexander defeated the Persians in 331

B.C. When Alexander died his kingdom was divided up amongst his 4 generals, Cassander was given (Macedonia and Greece), Lysimachus was given (Thrace, Bithynia and Asia Minor), Ptolemy took (Israel, Jordon 'Palestine and Arabia Petrea' and Egypt) and Seleucus (Turkey, Syria, Lebanon and later 'Babylon' Iran and Iraq).

Although another leader under Alexander, Antigonus, attempted to gain power, he was easily defeated. This is another testimony to the accuracy of Daniel's prophetic vision that the conquests of Alexander the Great were divided into four sections, not three or five. As I mentioned earlier the accuracy of this prophecy is so clear that liberal scholars want to say the book is a forgery, that one who assumed the name of Daniel wrote this later after the fact. Liberal scholars hold that prophecy of the future was/is impossible. But with the finding of many copies of Daniel with the Qumran scrolls it has been proven that the book of Daniel was written well before history records these events. The bible tells us that God reveals the future.

Dan. 2: 22 He reveals deep and hidden things;
he knows what lies in darkness,
and light dwells with him.

Det. 29: 29 The secret things belong to the LORD our God, but the things revealed belong to us and to our children forever,

Amos 3: 7 Surely the Sovereign LORD does nothing
without revealing his plan
to his servants the prophets.

Isaiah 46: 10 I make known the end from the beginning,
from ancient times, what is still to come.
I say: My purpose will stand,
and I will do all that I please.

Dan. 8: 9 Out of one of them came another horn, which started small but grew in power to the south and to the east and toward the Beautiful Land. 10 It grew until it reached the host of the heavens, and it threw some of the starry host down to the earth and trampled on them. 11 It set itself up to be as great as the Prince of the host; it took away the daily sacrifice from him, and the place of his sanctuary was brought low. 12 Because of rebellion, the host of the saints and the daily sacrifice were given over to it. It prospered in everything it did, and truth was thrown to the ground.

13 Then I heard a holy one speaking, and another holy one said to him, "How long will it take for the vision to be fulfilled—the vision concerning the daily sacrifice, the rebellion that causes desolation, and the surrender of the sanctuary and of the host that will be trampled underfoot?"

14 He said to me, "It will take 2,300 evenings and mornings; then the sanctuary will be reconsecrated."

There is a distinction between the horn here and the little horn of Daniel 7:8. The little horn of Daniel 7 came out of the fourth empire and in its final stage which is still future. By contrast, the horn here in chapter 8 came out of the third kingdom, the goat and refers to prophecy that now for us has already been fulfilled.

Now we move forward in history to 175 BC and a descendant of Seleucus named Antiochus IV, called another horn here, who gave himself the name Epiphanes, or Divine One. By now the Seleucid Empire had grown substantially and included Israel (the Beautiful Land) taken from descendants of Ptolemy. Antiochus Epiphanes hated the Jews and swore to wipe their religion off the face of the Earth. He almost succeeded. Arranging to have Israel's last legitimate High Priest, Onais III, murdered, he began selling the office of high priest to the highest bidder, a moneymaker that the Romans later adopted as well. He invaded Israel and took control of Jerusalem and the Temple Mount. He banned circumcision, the speaking or reading of Hebrew, and possession of Hebrew Scriptures, burning every copy he could find. He converted the Temple into a pagan worship center, erecting a statue of Zeus (Jupiter) in the Temple with his own face on it, requiring the Jews to worship it or be put to death. He slaughtered a pig on the holy altar and ordered the priests to do likewise. He fulfilled the requirements of throwing truth to the ground. History has recorded that Antiochus by taking the name Epiphanes, which means Divine or glorious one, assumed that he was God; much like the little horn of Daniel 7 will do in the future Great Tribulation. He is a picture of what the future anti-Christ will be like.

This defilement of the Temple rendered it unfit for use by the Jews. It became known as the Abomination of Desolation and triggered the Maccabean revolt, a successful 3 yearlong guerrilla action led by Judeas Maccabeas (Judah the Hammer.) to oust the forces of Antiochus from Israel and restore the Temple for worship. Because of it, Antiochus Epiphanes has become the clearest type of the anti-Christ. For 3 years, 1150 days (2300 evening and morning sacrifices, the Jews had a morning and evening sacrifice, thus 2300 divided by 2 equals 1150, 1150 divided by 360 days equals 3 years 19 days), the sanctuary laid desolate until it was consecrated again. It's ceremonially celebrated today as the Feast of Hanukkah. It's interesting that from the time Antiochus defiled the temple until it was consecrated again was 3 ½ years, just like the last half of the tribulation will be when the future anti-Christ will do the same thing.

With this we have another example how at times prophecy can have a dual meaning and purpose. While this act has been fulfilled by Antiochus, it also sounds just like what the anti-Christ will do; we know that this is not the final fulfillment of this vision or the ones in chapters 2 and 7. In just a moment in verse 17 Daniel is told to "understand that the vision concerns the time of the end."

There are those that want to say this is the fulfillment of the anti-Christ, that there is no future anti-Christ coming that will defile the temple and that this is proof that all bible prophecy has been fulfilled. But we see in Matthew 24 and the parallel scriptures in Mark and Luke that Jesus spoke of this "Abomination of Desolation" happening in the future and in 2 Thessalonians Paul spoke of a future anti-Christ, the man of sin. So we know from Jesus' on words that this will happen again.

It will happen at the mid-point of the tribulation but next time it will be much worse. So, all bible prophecy has not been fulfilled. Read these scriptures again.

Mt. 24: 15"So when you see standing in the holy place 'the abomination that causes desolation,' spoken of through the prophet Daniel—let the reader understand— 16then let those who are in Judea flee to the mountains. 17Let no one on the roof of his house go down to take anything out of the house. 18Let no one in the field go back to get his cloak. 19How dreadful it will be in those days for pregnant women and nursing mothers! 20Pray that your flight will not take place in winter or on the Sabbath. 21For then there will be great distress, unequaled from the beginning of the world until now—and never to be equaled again. 22If those days had not been cut short, no one would survive, but for the sake of the elect those days will be shortened.

See also Mark chapter 13 verses 14 thru 20 and Luke chapter 21 verses 20 thru 24.

2 Thes. 2: 3Don't let anyone deceive you in any way, for (that day will not come) until the rebellion occurs and the man of lawlessness is revealed, the man doomed to destruction. 4He will oppose and will exalt himself over everything that is called God or is worshiped, so that he sets himself up in God's temple, proclaiming himself to be God.

It also shows that Satan has nothing new. Everything he has done in the past he is going to try again. The conditions of the destruction that happened in 70 a.d. do not meet with the conditions mentioned here, so the future prophecy of the 'the abomination that causes desolation,' was not fulfilled in 70 a.d.

The Interpretation of the Vision

> Dan.8: 15 While I, Daniel, was watching the vision and trying
> to understand it, there before me stood one who looked like a
> man. 16 And I heard a man's voice from the Ulai calling,
> "Gabriel, tell this man the meaning of the vision." 17 As he
> came near the place where I was standing, I was terrified and
> fell prostrate. "Son of man," he said to me, "understand that
> the vision concerns the time of the end." 18 While he was
> speaking to me, I was in a deep sleep, with my face to the
> ground. Then he touched me and raised me to my feet.
>
> 19 He said: "I am going to tell you what will happen later in the
> time of wrath, because the vision concerns the appointed time
> of the end. 20 The two-horned ram that you saw represents the
> kings of Media and Persia. 21 The shaggy goat is the king of
> Greece, and the large horn between his eyes is the first king. 22
> The four horns that replaced the one that was broken off
> represent four kingdoms that will emerge from his nation but
> will not have the same power.

We see that the angel Gabriel is told to go and explain to Daniel the
meaning of this vision. With verses 20 thru 22 Gabriel gives a brief
explanation of who the ram and the goat are and who the 4 horns are.
We see this corresponds to visions of chapter 2 and 7. Isn't it amazing
how accurate this was. We now know that Gabriel's interpretation has
been confirmed by history. But we see that with verse 19 He said: "I
am going to tell you what will happen later in the time of wrath,
because the vision concerns the appointed time of the end". The vision
concerns the appointed time of the end, that's why the visions are
beginning to go into more detail about the last kingdom upon the earth
and the anti-Christ. After the brief description in verses 20 thru 22,
with verse 23 he is not only describing what happened with Antiochus
Epiphanes but he goes to the end times he started with verse 19 and
describes the anti-Christ, the little horn of Daniel 7 verse 8 and the
end-times fulfillment of the one called a stern-faced king, a master of
intrigue.

23 "In the latter part of their reign, when rebels have become completely wicked, a stern-faced king, a master of intrigue, will arise. 24 He will become very strong, but not by his own power. He will cause astounding devastation and will succeed in whatever he does. He will destroy the mighty men and the holy people. 25 He will cause deceit to prosper, and he will consider himself superior. When they feel secure, he will destroy many and take his stand against the Prince of princes. Yet he will be destroyed, but not by human power.

The description here of this wicked ruler is very similar to what history records concerning Antiochus Epiphanes. While this is a prophecy concerning Antiochus Epiphanes, it is also of the little horn from chapter 7, the anti-Christ. As I've mentioned before, it sounds like it could be another example of a dual meaning because of the similarities between Antiochus Epiphanes and the end-time world ruler. Antiochus did have great power over the Holy Land and Syria and for a time had power in Egypt until he had to withdraw because of pressure from the Roman Empire. He devastated Hebrew worship and desecrated the temple. He killed thousands of Jews who attempted to continue their worship in opposition to him. He considered himself above others; he even proclaimed himself to be God, thus the name Epiphanes which means "divine or glorious one". Antiochus died in 164 B.C. while on a military campaign, but his death was by natural causes, so it could be said that it fulfilled "he will be destroyed, but not by human power". As we see in Revelation 19, Jesus will destroy the future anti-Christ, so this will also fulfill being "destroyed, but not by human power".

While this can be seen as to being fulfilled by Antiochus it is also typical of the description of the future role of the coming Antichrist, the man of sin, during the last half of the tribulation. Like Antiochus, the final world ruler will claim to be God, will persecute the Jews, will stop Jewish sacrifices and will be evil, much worse than Antiochus, Hitler or anyone else have been.

As we saw with our look at chapters 2 and 7, characteristics of all the kingdoms will be present in the end times. You see that he has jumped to the end times with verse 23 for he said "in the latter part of their reign". And back with verse 19 He said: "I am going to tell you what will happen later in the time of wrath, because the vision concerns the appointed time of the end. So he is referring to a ruler during the time of the end. We see that at the end times a king will arise like Antiochus but this end time king will not be acting on his own, he will be empowered by Satan and will eventually be indwelt by him. So with verse 23 he has actually jumped to the end-times fulfillment by Satan in the anti-Christ. Don't forget the biggest evidence that this prophecy is of the future anti-Christ and not just of Antiochus Epiphanes is the fact that Jesus in Matthew said this is still to come. Mt. 24: 15"So when you see standing in the holy place 'the abomination that causes desolation, 'spoken of through the prophet Daniel—let the reader understand. As I mentioned earlier, this did not occur historically with the Roman general Titus who destroyed the Temple in 70 A.D. He did not enter the temple and set up the 'abomination that causes desolation'. The Temple was completely destroyed by his soldiers.

So it would appear hear that because the subject was about the other horn that sprang up that Gabriel jumps ahead to describing the future end time ruler, the anti-Christ. It's just what history records of Antiochus Epiphanes fits that of the future man of sin, the anti-Christ. As I've said before, prophecy can often refer to more than one time and event. Concerning the anti-Christ read 2 Thessalonians chapter 2 and Revelation chapters 12 and 13 again.

This future world leader will start out appearing like he is the best politician of all time. He will start out a peacemaker but will turn into the worst dictator the world has ever known. He will make Hitler seem like a grade school child. He will turn out to hate the Jews and all those that have accepted Jesus after the rapture.

> 26 "The vision of the evenings and mornings that has been given you is true, but seal up the vision, for it concerns the distant future."

Again, we see he said that this concerns the distant future; it is referring to the time right before Jesus returns.

> 27 I, Daniel, was exhausted and lay ill for several days. Then I got up and went about the king's business. I was appalled by the vision; it was beyond understanding

Gabriel concluded his explanation of the vision by saying "The vision of the evenings and mornings that has been given you is true" implying that the 2300 evenings and mornings will surely come true, but the vision's ultimate fulfillment is for the End Times for Daniel is told to "seal up the vision, for it concerns the distant future." The Temple's desolation by Antiochus Epiphanes fulfilled the prophecy of the evenings and mornings. This has been verified in history.

The second half of the Tribulation, the coming Abomination of Desolation is said to last at least 1260 days, a time, times and half a time, as we will see in chapter 12. We see this also in the book of Revelation.

Isn't it interesting that the 2300 evenings and mornings were about 3 ½ years and that the last half of the tribulation, when satan is in the anti-Christ will be also.

I know I've said this before but it bears repeating. History tells us that the first part of this prophecy was fulfilled literally, so we should assume that the last half will be fulfilled literally also.

5. Daniel Chapter 9 Introduction.

With chapter 9 it's now about 13 years later, 538 B.C. since the vision of chapter 8. Daniel is probably in his 80's and has been in Babylon for nearly 70 years.

The Persian Empire overthrew the Babylonians in 605 BC as predicted in (Isa. 41:25-26; 44:26-45:3; Dan. 5:25-31). Jeremiah's prophecy (Jer. 25:11; 29:10) had prophesied the exile would last for 70 years (Dan. 9:2). Daniel having now been in exile for 67 years realized the day of Israel's release was at hand. He longed for the day when the Jewish people could once again possess the city of Jerusalem and worship in their temple.

But he wasn't sure that the starting point for the 70 years of judgment that was foretold by Jeremiah was 605 BC. There was another group of exiles deported in 597 BC, and the final, complete devastation of Jerusalem did not occur until 586 BC. If the 70-year period was reckoned from these dates, the restoration of the Jewish people could be another 20 years away. Troubled by these uncertainties, Daniel began to pray. Recognizing that the ultimate fulfillment of restoration depended on national repentance (Jer. 29:10-14), Daniel sought to personally intercede for Israel through a prayer of petition with its focus on the restoration of Jerusalem and the Temple (Dan. 9:3-19). While Daniel was still in prayer, the angel Gabriel appeared with a prophecy from God. As we will see, this message had in view far more than the 70 years of judgment Daniel was concerned about.

First, I would like to look at how God came up with 70 years for Israel's captivity and the 490 years allotted to Israel that we see from verse 24 and then the message that Gabriel brings him.

Jeremiah prophesies Israel's time of captivity.

Jeremiah 25

Seventy Years of Captivity

1 The word came to Jeremiah concerning all the people of Judah in the fourth year of Jehoiakim son of Josiah king of Judah, which was the first year of Nebuchadnezzar king of Babylon. 2 So Jeremiah the prophet said to all the people of Judah and to all those living in Jerusalem: 3 For twenty-three years—from the thirteenth year of Josiah son of Amon king of Judah until this very day—the word of the LORD has come to me and I have spoken to you again and again, but you have not listened.

4 And though the LORD has sent all his servants the prophets to you again and again, you have not listened or paid any attention. 5 They said, "Turn now, each of you, from your evil ways and your evil practices, and you can stay in the land the LORD gave to you and your fathers for ever and ever. 6 Do not follow other gods to serve and worship them; do not provoke me to anger with what your hands have made. Then I will not harm you."

7 "But you did not listen to me," declares the LORD, "and you have provoked me with what your hands have made, and you have brought harm to yourselves."

8 Therefore the LORD Almighty says this: "Because you have not listened to my words, 9 I will summon all the peoples of the north and my servant Nebuchadnezzar king of Babylon," declares the LORD, "and I will bring them against this land and its inhabitants and against all the surrounding nations. I will completely destroy them and make them an object of horror and scorn, and an everlasting ruin. 10 I will banish from them the sounds of joy and gladness, the voices of bride and bridegroom, the sound of millstones and the light of the lamp.

11 This whole country will become a desolate wasteland, and these nations will serve the king of Babylon seventy years.

12 "But when the seventy years are fulfilled, I will punish the king of Babylon and his nation, the land of the Babylonians, for their guilt," declares the LORD, "and will make it desolate forever. 13 I will bring upon that land all the things I have spoken against it, all that are written in this book and prophesied by Jeremiah against all the nations. 14 They themselves will be enslaved by many nations and great kings; I will repay them according to their deeds and the work of their hands."

Isaiah also prophesied this.

Isa. 39: 5 Then Isaiah said to Hezekiah, "Hear the word of the LORD Almighty: 6 The time will surely come when everything in your palace, and all that your fathers have stored up until this day, will be carried off to Babylon. Nothing will be left, says the LORD. 7 And some of your descendants, your own flesh and blood who will be born to you, will be taken away, and they will become eunuchs in the palace of the king of Babylon."

Isaiah also prophesied of the return to Jerusalem to rebuild it.

Isa. 44: 24 "This is what the LORD says—
your Redeemer, who formed you in the womb:
I am the LORD,
who has made all things,
who alone stretched out the heavens,
who spread out the earth by myself
25 who foils the signs of false prophets
and makes fools of diviners,
who overthrows the learning of the wise
and turns it into nonsense,
26 who carries out the words of his servants
and fulfills the predictions of his messengers,

who says of Jerusalem, 'It shall be inhabited,'
of the towns of Judah, 'They shall be built,'
and of their ruins, 'I will restore them,'

27 who says to the watery deep, 'Be dry,
 and I will dry up your streams,'
28 who says of Cyrus, 'He is my shepherd
 and will accomplish all that I please;
he will say of Jerusalem, "Let it be rebuilt,"
and of the temple, "Let its foundations be laid."'

Isa. 45: 1 "This is what the LORD says to his anointed,
to Cyrus, whose right hand I take hold of
to subdue nations before him
and to strip kings of their armor,
to open doors before him
so that gates will not be shut:

Cyrus was the king of Persia that issued the first decree for Jerusalem to be rebuilt. Isaiah prophesied this some 200 years before it would happen.

While the judgment on Israel came because of their evil ways and their evil practices, and because they followed other gods and served and worship them, the duration of 70 years came from the fact that for 490 years they had neglected to let their farmland rest for one year out of every seven as God had commanded.

Leviticus 25

The Sabbath Year

1 The LORD said to Moses on Mount Sinai, 2 "Speak to the Israelites and say to them: 'When you enter the land I am going to give you, the land itself must observe a sabbath to the LORD. 3 For six years sow your fields, and for six years prune your vineyards and gather their crops. 4 But in the seventh year

the land is to have a sabbath of rest, a sabbath to the LORD. Do not sow your fields or prune your vineyards. 5 Do not reap what grows of itself or harvest the grapes of your untended vines. The land is to have a year of rest. 6 Whatever the land yields during the sabbath year will be food you—for yourself, your manservant and maidservant, and the hired worker and temporary resident who live among you, 7 as well as for your livestock and the wild animals in your land. Whatever the land produces may be eaten.

Because they neglected the Sabbath year rest for the land, by sending them to Babylon for 70 years, God would give the land the 70 years of rest that were due it.

2 Chronicles 36:

15 The LORD, the God of their fathers, sent word to them through his messengers again and again, because he had pity on his people and on his dwelling place. 16 But they mocked God's messengers, despised his words and scoffed at his prophets until the wrath of the LORD was aroused against his people and there was no remedy. 17 He brought up against them the king of the Babylonians, who killed their young men with the sword in the sanctuary, and spared neither young man nor young woman, old man or aged. God handed all of them over to Nebuchadnezzar. 18 He carried to Babylon all the articles from the temple of God, both large and small, and the treasures of the LORD's temple and the treasures of the king and his officials. 19 They set fire to God's temple and broke down the wall of Jerusalem; they burned all the palaces and destroyed everything of value there.

20 He carried into exile to Babylon the remnant, who escaped from the sword, and they became servants to him and his sons until the kingdom of Persia came to power.

21 The land enjoyed its sabbath rests; all the time of its desolation it rested, until the seventy years were completed in fulfillment of the word of the LORD spoken by Jeremiah.

Remember when I said that numbers have meaning and how God uses numbers as patterns. In the story of Moses and the people of Israel in Numbers chapters 13 and 14, the spies spied out the Promised Land for 40 days, when the people heard about the giants they did not believe Moses, that God would deliver the land to them and they rebelled, so God caused them to wander in the wilderness for 40 years, 1 year for each day the spies were in the land. We can see a pattern with how God comes up with the time of judgment. We see this with this prophecy in chapter 9. It's interesting how Israel didn't obey God for 490 years and as we will see, God gives them a total of 490 years to accomplish his purposes?

Verse 24 "Seventy 'sevens' are decreed for your people and your holy city to finish transgression, to put an end to sin, to atone for wickedness, to bring in everlasting righteousness, to seal up vision and prophecy and to anoint the most holy. Remember, the 70 'sevens or weeks' is a period of 490 years (70 x 7).

Now let's get to the prophecy.

6. Daniel Chapter 9

Daniel's Prayer

> 1 In the first year of Darius son of Ahasuerus (a Mede by descent), who was made ruler over the Babylonian kingdom- 2 in the first year of his reign, I, Daniel, understood from the Scriptures, according to the word of the LORD given to Jeremiah the prophet, that the desolation of Jerusalem would last seventy years. 3 So I turned to the Lord God and pleaded with him in prayer and petition, in fasting, and in sackcloth and ashes.

For the sake of space I won't put here Verse's 4 thru 19, they tell us Daniels prayer, but go and read them. They give us insight into Daniels heart.

The Seventy "Sevens"

> 20 While I was speaking and praying, confessing my sin and the sin of my people Israel and making my request to the LORD my God for his holy hill- 21 while I was still in prayer, Gabriel, the man I had seen in the earlier vision, came to me in swift flight about the time of the evening sacrifice. 22 He instructed me and said to me, "Daniel, I have now come to give you insight and understanding. 23 As soon as you began to pray, an answer was given, which I have come to tell you, for you are highly esteemed. Therefore, consider the message and understand the vision:

> 24 "Seventy 'sevens' are decreed for your people and your holy city to finish transgression, to put an end to sin, to atone for wickedness, to bring in everlasting righteousness, to seal up vision and prophecy and to anoint the most holy.

25 "Know and understand this: From the issuing of the decree to restore and rebuild Jerusalem until the Anointed One, the ruler, comes, there will be seven 'sevens,' and sixty-two 'sevens.' It will be rebuilt with streets and a trench, but in times of trouble. **26** After the sixty-two 'sevens,' the Anointed One will be cut off and will have nothing. The people of the ruler who will come will destroy the city and the sanctuary. The end will come like a flood: War will continue until the end, and desolations have been decreed.

27 He will confirm a covenant with many for one 'seven.' In the middle of the 'seven' he will put an end to sacrifice and offering. And on a wing of the temple he will set up an abomination that causes desolation, until the end that is decreed is poured out on him.

Many consider verses 24 thru 27 to be the most important prophecy in the Bible. It lays the future foundation of Israel and of all human history. The understanding of end time prophecy cannot be understood until you understand this prophecy. We cannot understand the Book of Revelation until we understand the Book of Daniel.

Chapter 9 begins with Daniel praying because he understood from reading Jeremiah that Israel's captivity in Babylon would last for 70 years and then Babylon would be defeated and the Jews set free to rebuild the city of Jerusalem and the Temple. When the Angel Gabriel gave this message to Daniel, Jerusalem had been in ruins for nearly 70 years and the Jewish people were still captive in Babylon. Daniel not being sure just where the start date was to accurately calculate Israel's captivity, didn't know just how close to the end of the 70 years Israel was, so he began to pray on behalf of Israel. From Daniel's prayer it appears that he expected the immediate and full fulfillment of Israel's restoration with the conclusion of the seventy-year captivity. The message from Gabriel had far more in mind than just the release of the Israelites from the Babylonian captivity. As we will see, the complete fulfillment of the finial restoration program for Israel by the Messiah would be for the distant future and progressive in nature.

Remember, The Hebrew word translated weeks (or sevens) refers to a period of 7 years, like our word decade refers to a period of 10 years. It literally means "a week of years."

So 70 weeks (or sevens) is 70 x 7 years or 490 years. This period is divided into three parts, 7 sevens (49 years) and then 62 sevens (434 years) for a total of 69 sevens or 483 years. Then there's the last week (or seven), 7 years. Gabriel's revelation to Daniel was that the full allotted amount of time would extend for "seventy "weeks", 490 years (verse 24). The final "week," the "seventieth week" of verse 27 will be fulfilled when the Temple is rebuilt and later desecrated by the abomination of desolation. Since all the conditions of the prophecies concerning the abomination of desolation cannot be found in history, this requires that the seventieth week of Daniel be understood as eschatological, that is, having its fulfillment in the end time. This is made clear by Jesus' reference to verse 27 in Matthew 24.

We can see there is a clear prophecy of the Coming of the Messiah. Counting forward for 7 weeks of years (49 years) and 62 weeks of years (434 years), each from a decree giving the Jews permission to restore and rebuild Jerusalem and its walls, they should expect the Messiah. That's a total of 483 years after the decree is issued. It was 483 years from this decree of (444 B.C.) that Jesus rode into Jerusalem and proclaimed himself to be the Messiah. That same week he was crucified, cut off.

The Bible records the issuing of three decrees by Gentile kings authorizing the Jews in exile to return to their homeland. The first one was by Cyrus in 539 BC (**2 Chr. 36:22 & 23; Ezra 1:2-4**). But this cannot be the decree that the angel Gabriel had in mind when he revealed this to Daniel. It referred only to the temple and makes no mention of the city.

The second royal decree involving the Jews and Jerusalem was made by Artaxerxes in **458 BC** (**Ezra 7:11-26**). Like the decree of Cyrus, no specific mention is made of rebuilding the city of Jerusalem or its walls.

Artaxerxes also issued the third royal decree involving the Jews and the city of Jerusalem in **444 BC** (**Neh. 2:5-8,17-18**). This is specific in authorizing the rebuilding of the city walls. With this the Jews completed the rebuilding of the city of Jerusalem and its walls.

With Cyrus' decree the Jews were released to return to Jerusalem. Many of the Jews returned to Jerusalem but only the foundation was laid during Cyrus' reign. You see this recorded in Ezra. If you read Ezra you will see that there was much opposition to rebuilding the temple.

You see in Ezra chapter 4 that Artaxerxes is now king and the temple has not been rebuilt. Read Ezra chapters 5 and 6 and you will see, because it had been almost a hundred years, king Darius had to refer to the old records "the royal archives" of Cyrus to find his decree before he made his decision to let the rebuilding continue. Ezra 6 verses 14 and 15, "They finished building the temple according to the command of the God of Israel and the decrees of Cyrus, Darius and Artaxerxes, kings of Persia. The temple was completed on the third day of the month Adar, in the sixth year of the reign of King Darius."

So it all started with the decree from Cyrus but it was the third decree by King Artaxerxes that allowed the rebuilding to be completed, thus making it the starting point, the decree that Gabriel was referring to here in chapter 9. You see this decree in Ezra chapter 7 by King Artaxerxes and also in Nehemiah chapter 2.

With the **444 BC** decree of Artaxerxes, If one uses "prophetic years" of 360 days each, it is exactly 483 years (173,880 days) from the day of Artaxerxes decree in 444 BC (Neh. 2:1) to the day of Christ's triumphal entry into Jerusalem during the last week of His earthly life (Mt. 21). It was on that day in AD 33 that Jesus officially announced to the Israelites that He was the Messiah. Later that week He was "cut off" or crucified. The use of a 360-day prophetic year is taken from the Jewish calendar.

Scholars differ as to whether the exact date is the last month of 445 B.C. or the first month of 444 B.C. Some prophecy teachers use the date 445 BC. Though scholars continue to differ on the subject, the most plausible explanation is the 444 B.C. date because this works out precisely to the fulfillment of the prophecy and also coincides with the actual rebuilding of the city. The use of either of these start dates brings us remarkably to Jesus.

The text says, verse 25 "Know and understand this: From the issuing of the decree to restore and rebuild Jerusalem until the Anointed One, the ruler, comes, there will be seven 'sevens,' and sixty-two 'sevens.' It will be rebuilt with streets and a trench, but in times of trouble. 26 After the sixty-two 'sevens,' the Anointed One will be cut off and will have nothing.

These 69 "sevens or weeks" culminate in "the Messiah, the Anointed One." But what does this mention of 7 weeks before the 62 weeks mean? The answer is expressed in the last words of verse 25, "It will be rebuilt with streets and a trench, but in times of trouble." The 7 weeks or 49 years that precede the 62 weeks, the 434 years is undoubtedly the time period it took for Ezra, Nehemiah, and others to rebuild the city. According to verse 25, in the first 7 sevens, the first 49 years the rebuilding of Jerusalem will be in times of trouble. We see this described in Ezra. This was the fulfillment of the first seven sevens, the first 49 years. The last week or 7 years of this prophecy has not been fulfilled yet.

Notice the requirements of the vision that had to be met in the fulfillment of the seventy weeks that were outlined to Daniel in verse 24.

According to Daniel there are 6 major requirements that will serve to establish the time of the prophecy's fulfillment.

(1) "to finish transgression"
(2) "to put an end to sin"
(3) "to atone for wickedness"
(4) "to bring in everlasting righteousness"
(5) "to seal up vision and prophecy"
(6) "to anoint the most holy"

They will be fulfilled after the completion of the 490 years and they relate to people of Israel and Jerusalem. Verse 24 says that they "are decreed for your people and your holy city". In other words, the fulfillment of the seventy weeks prophecy must occur with respect to Daniel's "people, national Israel and the Holy City Jerusalem".

Some commentators argue that although these requirements were once future they have now all been fulfilled historically by Jesus. In this case the entire prophecy of the seventy weeks is viewed as being fulfilled consecutively without interruption within the first century. Whether you take these 6 requirements as to only relating to Israel or you see them relating universally to everyone, the only one that could be said that Jesus fulfilled, is that by dying on the cross and being raised from the dead he atoned for wickedness or iniquity. The others have yet to be accomplished. Furthermore, the climax of Gabriel's prophecy to Daniel in verse 27 was that the one who would one day desolate the Temple would himself be destroyed completely. This did not occur historically with the Roman general Titus who destroyed the Second Temple. Rather, he and his emperor father Vespasian enjoyed parading the Temple vessels through the streets of Rome. Furthermore the destruction of Jerusalem and the temple occurred almost 40 years after Jesus' resurrection. So there appears there is a gap in time before the last 7 years. I will explain this gap in a second. So the final week has not been fulfilled. Jesus will finally accomplish the rest of the requirements in the future kingdom of God here on earth when He returns.

Let's take a look at these six accomplishments of the 490 years that have been allotted to Israel.

1. To Finish Transgression. The 70 weeks will "finish the transgression." The Hebrew word translated 'transgression' carries the idea of rebellion against God. Jews and Christians take this to mean that rebellion against God will end. They also agree that only true believers in God whether Jew or Gentile will enter the messianic kingdom of God here on earth. But Christians believe that "to finish the transgression" also includes a national acceptance from all Israel of Jesus as Messiah.

2. To Put an End to Sin / Sin Sealed Up. Daniel also predicted that the 70-week period would "put an end of sins." The word translated 'sins' refers to sins other than revolt or rebellion, general immorality, dishonesty, and the like. The verb in the Hebrew text translated "put an end to" in NIV literally means "to seal up." Among those living during the kingdom, sin will be rare by today's standards. Satan will be bound and there will be no demons to temp anyone. Sin will be from just man's sinful nature. Jews and Christians alike believe that this will occur when the Messiah rules the world.

3. To Atoned For Wickedness. This 70-week program is "to make reconciliation for iniquity" (KJ) or "to atone for wickedness" (NIV). The verb in this sentence is **kaphar**, the Old Testament term used to denote the covering of sin by making a sacrifice. Christians see this as having been fulfilled in the death of Jesus, who according to the New Testament gave Himself to die on the cross as the perfect sacrifice. With Jesus this atonement has been accomplished but it could also refer to what Jesus will do when he establishes his earthly kingdom.

4. To Bring In Everlasting Righteousness. The conclusion of the 70-week period will also "bring in everlasting righteousness." This undoubtedly points to the justice and peace of the earthly kingdom of God that Israel has been waiting for since the days of the prophets. It is a mark of the messianic age, which corresponds to what other prophets have also predicted.

According to the prophet Isaiah,

> Isa. 2: 2 In the last days the mountain of the LORD's temple will be established as chief among the mountains; it will be raised above the hills, and all nations will stream to it. 3 Many peoples will come and say, "Come, let us go up to the mountain of the LORD, to the house of the God of Jacob. He will teach us his ways, so that we may walk in his paths." The law will go out from Zion, the word of the LORD from Jerusalem.

> 4 He will judge between the nations and will settle disputes for many peoples. They will beat their swords into plowshares and their spears into pruning hooks. Nation will not take up sword against nation, nor will they train for war anymore.

5. To Seal up Vision and Prophecy. When the messianic age begins, all that was promised through visions and prophecies will be accomplished. Finally the whole world will understand prophecies going back to when God first spoke to Abraham and said,

"all peoples on earth will be blessed through you." (**Gen. 12:1-3**).

6. To Anoint The Most Holy. Some Jews see this as being fulfilled in the consecration of the future rebuilt temple in the days of a yet undisclosed Messiah. Some Christians also believe "the Most Holy" refers to a rebuilt temple. They base this on the temple description of **Ezekiel 40-44** and believe that animal sacrifices will once again be offered at the holy place but this time, however, the sacrifices will be seen as memorials to Jesus. In the Old Testament they pointed forward to what the Messiah would do, during the earthly Kingdom they will point back to what he has done. Other Christians, while agreeing that Christ's second coming will usher in this kingdom age, believe Jesus Himself will be anointed as "the Most Holy." When he was here before he was not anointed as the "Most Holy" by the Jews.

While there is much disagreement among Jewish and Christian scholars about how all of this will work out, some things are clear. According to Daniel's prophecy, God has a 70-week (490 year) program that will culminate in an age when spiritual rebellion against God will end, sin as we know it will have ended 'there will be no more demons to temp people', reconciliation will have been accomplished, righteousness will prevail, prophecy will have been fulfilled, and God's anointing of either a new temple and/or His Messiah will occur.

What Daniel's prophecy clearly reveals is that the Messiah had to come in the time predicted in verses 25-26, that is, 483 years into the 490 years.

The religious leaders and the Jewish people of Jesus' time knew this time frame of 483 years given in Daniel. That's why through reading the gospels we can see that the leaders and the people had an expectancy of the coming of the Messiah. Here are just a couple of scriptures.

> Luke 19: 11While they were listening to this, he went on to tell them a parable, because he was near Jerusalem and the people thought that the kingdom of God was going to appear at once.

Look at this from John about John the Baptist,

> John 1: 19Now this was John's testimony when the Jews of Jerusalem sent priests and Levites to ask him who he was. 20He did not fail to confess, but confessed freely, "I am not the Christ" 21They asked him, "Then who are you?
> Are you Elijah?" He said, "I am not."
> "Are you the Prophet?" He answered, "No."

They were not repeating themselves, they asked him two questions. Was he Elijah or was he the prophet? Who is this prophet that they asked about? This comes from Moses in Deuteronomy chapter 18.

Deut. 18: 15 The LORD your God will raise up for you a prophet like me from among your own brothers. You must listen to him. 16 For this is what you asked of the LORD your God at Horeb on the day of the assembly when you said, "Let us not hear the voice of the LORD our God nor see this great fire anymore, or we will die."

17 The LORD said to me: "What they say is good. 18 I will raise up for them a prophet like you from among their brothers; I will put my words in his mouth, and he will tell them everything I command him. 19 If anyone does not listen to my words that the prophet speaks in my name, I myself will call him to account.

This prophet was to be the Messiah. There are many more scriptures like this in the gospels that show they had an expectancy of the Messiah.

Because they refused to believe Jesus was the Messiah, we see Jesus said to them,

Mt. 16: 2He replied, "When evening comes, you say, 'It will be fair weather, for the sky is red,' 3and in the morning, 'Today it will be stormy, for the sky is red and overcast.' You know how to interpret the appearance of the sky, but you cannot interpret the signs of the times. 4A wicked and adulterous generation looks for a miraculous sign, but none will be given it except the sign of Jonah." Jesus then left them and went away.

Of course we now know that the sign of Jonah that Jesus gave them was, like Jonah was in the belly of a great fish for 3 days and nights, Jesus was in the grave for three days and 3 nights and then rose from the dead.

Luke 19: 41 Now as He drew near, He saw the city and wept over it, 42 saying, "If you had known, even you, especially in this your day, the things that make for your peace! But now they are hidden from your eyes. 43 For days will come upon you when your enemies will build an embankment around you, surround you and close you in on every side, 44 and level you, and your children within you, to the ground; and they will not leave in you one stone upon another, because you did not know the time of your visitation." NKJ

Almost 40 years later the Romans destroyed Jerusalem and the Temple. Till this day there still hasn't been one stone from the temple found.

Notice in verse 26 of Daniel chapter 9 that it says the Messiah would come before the city and the sanctuary are destroyed. Again, this happened in 70 A.D. So the Messiah had to come before this destruction. Jesus is the only one in history that can be pointed to as fulfilling this. This is still a puzzle to the Jews.

The religious leaders and the people of Israel new the scriptures, yet they still rejected him. The scriptures paint two pictures of the Messiah, one coming as a suffering servant and the other of one coming as a conquering king. They wanted the conquering King. See Isaiah 52: 13 thru 15 and Isaiah 53. They didn't think they were as spiritually dead as they were to need a spiritual redeemer. Jesus said of the religious leaders that they were full of dead men's bones. Mt. 23:27.

So we see with Jesus' triumphant entry into Jerusalem that 483 years of the 490 years prophesied had past leaving 7 years.

The words in verse 26 "and will have nothing" added after the words "cut off" may mean "without inheriting the messianic kingdom". This fulfillment of the Kingdom, as declared by Jesus in Acts 1:6-7 awaits the future, or the end of the final week when the finial requirements for the establishment of the messianic kingdom are completed, and the overthrow of the Temple desolator (the Antichrist) (verse 27).

So we see that there would be 483 years after the issuing of the decree to rebuild and restore Jerusalem that the Messiah would come. In this period the Messiah, the Anointed One, is born and is cut off after the conclusion of the 483rd year as stated in verse 26. The prophecy continues in verse 26 with an event after the 69th seven and before the 70th seven, "The people of the ruler who will come will destroy the city and the sanctuary. The end will come like a flood: War will continue until the end, and desolations have been decreed", as we know, this took place in 70 A.D.

Obviously, if the fulfillment of the last 7 years immediately followed the 483 years, then you could not consider the destruction of Jerusalem as part of the fulfillment. So once again, this shows that the last 7 years does not immediately follow the 483rd year. There are 7 years still yet in the future. As we know, wars and desolations have been continuing and they will continue right up until the end. And notice, it says the "people of the ruler who will come". Of the destruction of 70 a.d. it doesn't say the ruler, the anti-Christ will destroy the city and the temple but the people of the ruler who would come. This is another clue as to the future empire of the anti-Christ being a revived form of the Old Roman Empire.

We see another event that relates to the temple and to the people (the Romans) who destroyed the Second Temple must occur during the last week. A ruler will make a covenant with "the many", Israel and other nations. While the specific nature of this "covenant" is not made clear here, it is clear that it relates to the Temple in some way. Verse 27 "He (the ruler to come, the anti-Christ) will confirm a covenant with many for one 'seven.' In the middle of the 'seven' he will put an end to sacrifice and offering. And on a wing *of the temple* he will set up an abomination that causes desolation, until the end that is decreed is poured out on him." This did not occur historically with the Roman general Titus who destroyed the Temple in 70 A.D. They destroyed the Temple and Jerusalem. And he did not make a covenant with Israel and the many. The rebuilding of the Temple with its renewed worship will be a direct result of the covenant that the Antichrist (ruler) makes with Israel for the "one seven," the seven years of the Tribulation period. Since the Temple marked the beginning and the end of the 69 weeks, the beginning and end of the 483 years, then it should be expected to be involved with the beginning of the last week as well, the last 7 years, especially when it would appear to mark a revival of God's direct dealing with Israel as a Nation. With the anti-Christ entering the temple and stopping the daily sacrifice in the middle of the tribulation, it would appear that he will have something to do with its rebuilding.

Remember, the purpose of the Tribulation is not just to judge Israel and the nations, to weed out all that are unrighteous, but also to prepare Israel for the fulfillment of its promises in the Millennium where the Temple is prominent.

The fulfillment of the phrase "to bring in everlasting righteousness" refers to the millennial restoration or "age of righteousness" (see Isaiah 1:26; 11:2-5; 32:17; Jeremiah 23:5-6; 33:15-18)

The eschatological restoration of Israel may also be intended in the requirement "to seal up vision and prophecy," which has the fulfillment of Jeremiah's prophecy in view. The final requirement "to anoint the most holy" must also look to the future, and specifically a future dedication of the Temple's Holy of Holies. We see the millennial Temple in Ezek. 40-48. It will be filled with the Presence of God (Ezek. 43:1-7), and will be consecrated for use throughout the messianic age (Ezek. 43:11, 18-27; 44:11-28; 45:13-46:15; Isa. 56:6-7; 60:7; Jer. 33:18; Zech. 14:16-21).

Daniel describes the Messiah's mission to Israel beginning with His crucifixion as Israel's Savior and culminating with His reign as Israel's king. Thus, Daniel's prophecy can only be fulfilled when all of the requirements from the angel Gabriel are realized, and this can only be accomplished in the coming age of the Messiah's reign in the earthly kingdom of God.

So with Jesus' death on the cross, the prophetic stopwatch stopped leaving a gap in time, which we know as the Church age. In this prophecy there is no indication that the last 7 years were to happen right after the 483 years. The concept that there is a time gap between verse 26 and 27 has a great deal of scriptural confirmation. We see this also with the Statue in chapter 2. One of the most important confirmations is the fact that the Old Testament seems to present the first and second comings of Jesus as occurring at the same time.

If the entire Church age can be interposed between references to the first and second comings of Jesus in the Old Testament, it certainly sets a precedent for having a time gap between the 69th 'seven' and the 70th 'seven of Daniel. See Isaiah 61. He foretells Jesus' first and second comings and the earthly kingdom of God all in one prophecy. And remember, this present Church age of Jews and Gentiles being one was a mystery to the Old Testament Saints and Prophets. Just like with Isaiah's prophecy, Daniels prophecy spans the time from the issuing of the decree in 444 B.C. to the second coming of Jesus.

There seems to be a clue to the time gap with the descriptions after the second part of verse 26. First notice, after the 483 years have completed it says, "The people of the ruler who will come will destroy the city and the sanctuary". Notice he said 'the people' of the ruler, not the ruler, not the anti-Christ. As I have just mentioned, this would be referring to the destruction in 70 a.d. by the Romans. Remember what we have seen from the other chapters of Daniel, that the kingdom of the anti-Christ will be a revival of the old Roman Empire. So here it saying 'the people of the ruler' is referring to the people of the old Roman Empire of which the anti-Christ will come out of. The anti-Christ will come out of the people of the Old Roman Empire. Rome's influence is seen in the governments of Europe and America today. Second notice he said, the end will come like a flood: War will continue until the end, and desolations have been decreed. Then with verse 27 he goes into describing the last 7 years. He will confirm a covenant with many for one 'seven.' In the middle of the 'seven' he will put an end to sacrifice and offering. And on a wing *of the temple* he will set up an abomination that causes desolation, until the end that is decreed is poured out on him. This is what Jesus referred to in Matthew 24.

So we see there are events described that take place after the 483 years but before the last 7 years. It just doesn't tell us how long this will be.

Since the destruction in 70 a.d. happened almost 40 years after the end of the 483 years, we see there is a gap of time.

Since there has not been a 7 year peace agreement made with Israel and other nations by 'the ruler that will come' this gap is still continuing today, this gap is The Church age.

Remember what we saw earlier that Paul said that the Church was a mystery to the Old Testament saints. This is why there is no mention in Daniel of the time period between the 483 years and the last 7 years. What we do have are numerous scriptures on the last 7 years allotted to Israel and the Holy City Jerusalem. The prophetic stopwatch for Israel's last 7 years will start ticking again when Israel signs the covenant with the little horn, the anti-Christ.

It is with this prophecy that bible scholars find that the tribulation, in which Revelation gives details of with the 7 seals, 7 trumpets and the 7 bowls, will be 7 years. As we have seen, there are numerous scriptures that give us details of this last 7 years, Daniel's 70th week.

In Matthew 24 Jesus gave numerous signs that will let the people of Israel know that they are in the time of distress mentioned in Daniel chapter 12. With Jesus' reference to the 'abomination of desolation' foretold by Daniel, the people will know that they are in the last half of the tribulation, the last 1260 days. The Apostle Paul in 2 Thessalonians tells us that the day of the Lord, this last 7 years allotted to Israel will not come until the man of lawlessness is revealed. With the first seal in the 6th chapter of Revelation we see the releasing of the anti-Christ. Daniel was told that this would occur in the end times, and with the final act of the Temples desolation comes Gods final judgment against the Gentile powers.

With the destruction of the Antichrist and his armies by Jesus we see in Rev. 19:20, and the national repentance of Israel (Rom. 11:26-27), the final restoration of Israel for which Daniel prayed will be fulfilled, and then Israel's realization of all the promises of God will be accomplished.

Take a look at this from Jeremiah.

Jeremiah 31

36 "Only if these decrees vanish from my sight,"
declares the LORD,
"will the descendants of Israel ever cease
to be a nation before me."

37 This is what the LORD says:
"Only if the heavens above can be measured
and the foundations of the earth below be searched out
will I reject all the descendants of Israel
because of all they have done,"
declares the LORD.

Did you see what he said in verse 36 and 37? As I mentioned before, this again blows replacement theology that the Church has replaced Israel out of the water. God will not break his promises to Israel.

38 "The days are coming," declares the LORD, "when this city will be rebuilt for me from the Tower of Hananel to the Corner Gate. 39 The measuring line will stretch from there straight to the hill of Gareb and then turn to Goah. 40 The whole valley where dead bodies and ashes are thrown, and all the terraces out to the Kidron Valley on the east as far as the corner of the Horse Gate, will be holy to the LORD. The city will never again be uprooted or demolished."

This all will be fulfilled with Jesus' 2nd coming and the establishment of the millennium kingdom of God here on earth.

So it should be clear that there are 7 more years allotted to Israel. These last 7 years are the 7 years just before Jesus returns back down to the earth. These are the 7 years of the tribulation that the book of Revelation gives us the details of. With these 7 years being Israel's last 7 years, this is why the Church is removed before these 7 years. That is why we see no mention in the book of Revelation of the Church as to being present here on earth during these last 7 years.

In our look at the book of Revelation I will explain more why the Church is not present during the time of the 7 years of the tribulation.

We saw that this prophecy foretold exactly when the Messiah would come and that Jesus is the only one that was here that could have fulfilled this. Put this together with all the other prophecies that Jesus fulfilled concerning the Messiah and there should be no doubt that Jesus is the Messiah. As I have said many times before, with the first part of this prophecy coming true literally we can be assured that the rest will come true just as literally as the first.

7. Daniel Chapter 11.

Read Chapter 10, it is actually the lead in to chapters 11 and 12. In the 10th chapter we see he had a revelation (vision) about future wars. Chapter 10 tells us what lead to the Angel coming to explain to Daniel the meaning of the revelation that he had received. Chapter 10 begins by saying, 1 In the third year of Cyrus king of Persia, a revelation was given to Daniel (who was called Belteshazzar). Its message was true and it concerned a great war. The understanding of the message came to him in a vision. When Daniel received this vision he was probably 85. This is the last revelation or vision that Daniel receives. One thing to notice from chapter 10, the Angel mentions the kings of Persia and Greece, the next two succeeding empires that would come after Babylon. These kings aren't the human kings but the demonic spiritual kings over these kingdoms for he says in verse 13; the prince of the Persian kingdom resisted me twenty-one days. This could not be a human king he is referring to for no human could stand up against an angel, especially if it was Gabriel. Remember Ephesians chapter 6 verse 12 says, For our struggle is not against flesh and blood, but against the rulers, against the authorities, against the powers of this dark world and against the spiritual forces of evil in the heavenly realms.

The details of the interpretation of the revelation are given in chapters 11 and 12. Chapter 10 flows right into chapter 11.

Daniel Chapter 11.

1 And in the first year of Darius the Mede, I took my stand to support and protect him.)

The Kings of the South and the North

2 "Now then, I tell you the truth: Three more kings will appear in Persia, and then a fourth, who will be far richer than all the others. When he has gained power by his wealth, he will stir up everyone against the kingdom of Greece. 3 Then a mighty king will appear, who will rule with great power and do as he

pleases. 4 After he has appeared, his empire will be broken up and parceled out toward the four winds of heaven. It will not go to his descendants, nor will it have the power he exercised, because his empire will be uprooted and given to others.

This is the same description as we saw in chapters 2, 7, 8 and 9. Here it goes into more detail.

In identifying the four kings it is probable that the explanation excluded Darius the Mede and Cyrus II (550 – 530 B.C). The four kings who would follow Cyrus as King of Persia were Cambyses (530-522 B.C.) who was not mentioned in the Old Testament, Pseudo-Smerdis (522-521 B.C.), Darius 1 (521-486 B.C., see Ezra 5-6) and Xerxes 1 (486-465 B.C., see Ezra 4:6). He's the king who chose the young Jewish girl Esther to be his wife. Her story is told in the Book of Esther.

As Daniel indicated, Xerxes I or sometimes-spelled Zerxes I was the ruler who attempted to conquer Greece at the time of the greatest power of the Persian Empire. Xerxes I gathered an army of several hundred thousand and began a war against Greece in which his fleets as well as his troops were defeated. Persia never rose to great power after this. The disastrous expedition against Greece probably occurred between Esther 1 and Esther 2. You can find additional facts furnished in Ezra, Nehemiah, and Esther and by Haggai, Zechariah and Malachi.

As we know now from history, Daniel prophesied the coming of Alexander the Great. 130 years later Alexander the Great defeated the Persian King Darius III at the Battle of Guagamela, conquering the Persian Empire. When Alexander died a few years later in 323 B.C., as history records, his conquest was divided among his four commanding generals. All this must have really baffled Daniel; at the time Daniel wrote this prophecy Greece was a small and relatively insignificant nation.

Daniel continues with the prophecy with even more detail than the previous prophecies. Now the prophecy will focus on two of his

Generals, see Daniel chapter 7. Those from the family of Seleucus are called the "King of the North", and those of Ptolemy are called the "King of the South." The kings of the North and South are determined from their location in relation to Jerusalem. Jerusalem was in the middle of this fighting between Seleucus and Ptolemy.

Remember from our previous study that Seleucus took parts of Turkey, Syria, Lebanon, and later Iran and Iraq, while Ptolemy got Egypt, Israel, and Jordan.

This next section of verses 5 thru 35 I got off of RaptureReady.com from an article by Jack Kelly called 'The End Times According to Daniel Part 3'. These verses' cover past history that were prophetic at Daniels time. I like the way he inserted (in bold) the names of the kings and dates in with the verses so we can get a clearer picture of the history. As he said, this will give us a hint of the incredible accuracy of the prophecies in Daniel 11, and prepare us for the shift from history to prophecy. Of course all the dates are B.C.

Dan. 11: 5 "The king of the South **(Ptolemy I Soter, 323-285)** will become strong, but one of his commanders **(Seleucus I Nicator, 311-280)** will become even stronger than he and will rule his own kingdom **(Babylon)** with great power. 6 After some years, they will become allies. The daughter of the king of the South **(Berenice, daughter of Ptolemy II Philadelphus, 285-246)** will go to the king of the North **(Antiochus II Theos, 261-246)** to make an alliance, but she will not retain her power, and he and his power will not last. In those days she will be handed over, together with her royal escort and her father and the one who supported her.

(Antiochus left his wife Laodice for Berenice, but Laodice conspired to have Antiochus, Berenice, and her father Ptolemy II killed. The city of Laodicea in Rev. 3 is named after her.)

7 "One from her family line will arise to take her place. **(Berenice's brother Ptolemy III Euergetes, 246-221. He**

killed Laodice to avenge his sister and father.) He will attack the forces of the king of the North **(Seleucus II Callinicus, 246-226)** and enter his fortress; he will fight against them and be victorious. 8 He will also seize their gods, their metal images and their valuable articles of silver and gold and carry them off to Egypt. For some years he will leave the king of the North alone. 9 Then the king of the North will invade the realm of the king of the South but will retreat to his own country. 10 His sons **(Seleucus III Ceranus, 226-223 and Antiochus III, called the Great, 223-187)** will prepare for war and assemble a great army, which will sweep on like an irresistible flood and carry the battle as far as his fortress.

11 "Then the king of the South **(Ptolemy IV Philopator, 221-203)** will march out in a rage and fight against the king of the North **(Antiochus the Great),** who will raise a large army, but it will be defeated **(The Battle of Raphia in 217).** 12 When the army is carried off, the king of the South will be filled with pride and will slaughter many thousands **(10,000 according to the historian Polybius),** yet he will not remain triumphant. 13 For the king of the North **(still Antiochus)** will muster another army, larger than the first; and after several years, he will advance with a huge army fully equipped.

14 "In those times many will rise against the king of the South. **(Ptolemy V Epiphanes, 203-181).** The violent men among your own people will rebel in fulfillment of the vision, but without success. **(Ptolemy's general Scopas crushed the rebellion in 200)** 15 Then the king of the North **(still Antiochus the Great)** will come and build up siege ramps and will capture a fortified city. The forces of the South will be powerless to resist; even their best troops will not have the strength to stand. 16 The invader will do as he pleases; no one will be able to stand against him. He will establish himself in the Beautiful Land **(Israel, captured from the King of the South in 197)** and will have the power to destroy it. 17 He will determine to come with the might of his entire kingdom and

will make an alliance with the king of the South. And he will give him a daughter **(Cleopatra I married Ptolemy V in 194)** in marriage in order to overthrow the kingdom, but his plans will not succeed or help him. **(Don't confuse this Cleopatra with the later one, Cleopatra II, consort to both Julius Caesar and Marc Anthony)** 18 Then he will turn his attention to the coastlands and **(teaming up with the famous Carthaginian General Hannibal)** will take many of them, but a commander **(Roman Consul Lucius Cornelius Scipio Asiaticus, with whom Cleopatra and Ptolemy had sided)** will put an end to his insolence and will turn his insolence back upon him. 19 After this, he will turn back toward the fortresses of his own country but will stumble and fall, to be seen no more. **(Antiochus the Great died in battle in 187)**

20 "His successor **(Seleucus IV Philopator)** will send out a tax collector to maintain the royal splendor. In a few years, however, he will be destroyed, yet not in anger or in battle. **(Heliodorus engineered a coup against him)**

21 "He will be succeeded by a contemptible person **(Antiochus IV Epiphanes, 175-164)** who has not been given the honor of royalty. **(Antiochus Epiphanes mounted a palace revolt against his young cousin and rightful heir Demetrius I).** He will invade the kingdom when its people feel secure, and he will seize it through intrigue. 22 Then an overwhelming army will be swept away before him; both it and a prince of the covenant **(Onias III, the last legitimate High Priest, who was murdered in 170)** will be destroyed. 23 After coming to an agreement with him, he will act deceitfully, and with only a few people he will rise to power. 24 When the richest provinces feel secure, he will invade them and will achieve what neither his fathers nor his forefathers did. He will distribute plunder, loot and wealth among his followers. He will plot the overthrow of fortresses—but only for a time.

25 "With a large army he will stir up his strength and courage against the king of the South. **(Ptolemy VI)**. The king of the South will wage war with a large and very powerful army, but he will not be able to stand because of the plots devised against him. 26 Those who eat from the king's provisions **(Ptolemy's family)** will try to destroy him; his army will be swept away, and many will fall in battle. 27 The two kings **(Antiochus and Ptolemy)**, with their hearts bent on evil, will sit at the same table and lie to each other, but to no avail, because an end will still come at the appointed time. 28 The king of the North will return to his own country with great wealth, but his heart will be set against the holy covenant. He will take action against it and then return to his own country. **(On his way back to Syria in 169 Antiochus Epiphanes plundered the Temple in Jerusalem and killed many priests)**

29 "At the appointed time he will invade the South again, but this time the outcome will be different from what it was before. 30 Ships of the western coastlands **(Rome)** will oppose him, and he will lose heart. Then he will turn back and vent his fury against the holy covenant. He will return and show favor to those who forsake the holy covenant. **(As Antiochus stood in Egypt on the shore of the Mediterranean, the Roman Commander Popilius Laenas drew a circle around him in the sand, telling him that if he stepped out of the circle for any other reason than to surrender and go home, he would be killed. Humiliated and furious he took out his rage on the Jews, prompting the Maccabean revolt.)**

31 "His armed forces will rise up to desecrate the temple fortress and will abolish the daily sacrifice. Then they will set up the abomination that causes desolation. **(168)** 32 With flattery he will corrupt those who have violated the covenant, but the people who know their God will firmly resist him. **(The Hasidim, who remained faithful to God, were the ancestors of today's Hasidic Jews. They are world renowned for their trade in diamonds)**

33 "Those who are wise will instruct many, though for a time they will fall by the sword or be burned or captured or plundered. 34 When they fall, they will receive a little help, and many who are not sincere will join them. **(The Maccabeans, who defeated Antiochus, cleansed the Temple and restored Jewish autonomy, setting up the Hasmonean Dynasty that ruled Israel for about 100 years until the Romans came.)** 35 Some of the wise will stumble, so that they may be refined, purified and made spotless until the time of the end, for it will still come at the appointed time.

As I said earlier, I like the way Jack inserted some about the history in with the scriptures. It is amazing looking back on history and seeing how these prophecies came true so accurately and literally. Since the first part of this prophecy came true literally, we can be assured that the second part will also.

The first part of the prophecy is now history, which is easily verified, with the last part still being future. The actions of the future anti-Christ will not be unlike that of some of the past kings of the nations that invaded Israel. Because of his persecution of the Jews during the period of his reign, Antiochus IV Epiphanes is our closest model of the anti-Christ, called "the king" in verse 36. Antiochus was very much opposed to the Jewish religion. He desecrated their temple, offering a pig on the altar and installed a statue of a Greek god. This brought about the Maccabean revolt, in which thousands of Jews were killed, including men, women and children. The attempt to destroy the Jews and their religion is described in verse 31 "His armed forces will rise up to desecrate the temple fortress and will abolish the daily sacrifice. Then they will set up the abomination that causes desolation."

This is not the fulfillment of what Daniel prophesied in chapter 9. One major requirement of Daniel chapter 9 is that there is to be a 7 year covenant agreement made. We see no such agreement here in chapter 11. With this and other requirements of Daniel 9 we know that this prophesy of the abomination of desolation that Daniel 9 refers to has not happened. In Matthew 24 we see that the conditions Jesus describes didn't occur with this prophecy here in chapter 11. Furthermore Jesus tells us that all this will happen again in the future. Have you heard the phrase, history repeats itself? This again could be a case where prophecy is foretelling two similar yet separate events.

We can see from all the wars that have been fought and from reading the book of Revelation that man hasn't learned anything from the past. And we can see that Satan has nothing new, he tries the same things over and over again.

> Ecclesiastes 1: 9 What has been will be again, what has been done will be done again; there is nothing new under the sun.

We see with verse 35 there seems to be a shift in what he was saying, that he is no longer referring to the kings he had just been describing. We see that he says that the conditions of verse 35 will continue until the "time of the end" so we see a jump in time, that there's a gap of time like there is in chapter 9. Verse 35 "Some of the wise will stumble, so that they may be refined, purified and made spotless until the time of the end, for it will still come at the appointed time."

The reference to "the time of the end" referred to in the remaining prophecy of Daniel beginning in verse 36 was not the immediate outcome of the reign of Antiochus IV Epiphanes. The chronological gap between Antiochus IV Epiphanes (verses 21-35) and the end time (verses 36-45) was common in the Old Testament as many prophecies concerning the first and second comings of the Messiah though presented together are separated so far now by two thousand years in there fulfillment. The prophecy given in verses 36 thru 45 have not been fulfilled yet and, it fact, relate to the period just before the Second Coming.

So the message has now jumped to the end time period of the tribulation and the anti-Christ. As we will see verses 36 thru 45 are clearly about the future anti-Christ of the tribulation. Since the nations that will be involved will be from the same geographic locations he flows right into talking about the anti-Christ, the king at verse 36. We also see with verse 36 that it says that this king will be successful until the time of wrath has been completed. This clearly shows us that it is the tribulation being referred to now; for the tribulation is called the time of wrath and that it is now **the** anti-Christ, the little horn of the previous visions that is being referred to. We see again in verse 40 that he says it is the time of the end.

The King Who Exalts Himself

36 "The king will do as he pleases. He will exalt and magnify himself above every god and will say unheard-of things against the God of gods. He will be successful until the time of wrath is completed, for what has been determined must take place. 37 He will show no regard for the gods of his fathers or for the one desired by women, nor will he regard any god, but will exalt himself above them all. 38 Instead of them, he will honor a god of fortresses; a god unknown to his fathers he will honor with gold and silver, with precious stones and costly gifts. 39 He will attack the mightiest fortresses with the help of a foreign god and will greatly honor those who acknowledge him. He will make them rulers over many people and will distribute the land at a price.

While Antiochus IV Epiphanes could also be seen as fulfilling this, this King in verse 36 is referring to the Little Horn of Daniel 7:8, 21-24 as well as to the beast out of the Sea in Revelation 13:1-10, the anti-Christ.

Rev. 13:.5The beast was given a mouth to utter proud words and blasphemies and to exercise his authority for forty-two months. 6He opened his mouth to blaspheme God, and to slander his name and his dwelling place and those who live in heaven.

Daniel also said of this ruler "He will be successful until the time of wrath is completed, for what has been determined must take place". This is in keeping with Daniel 7:27-28 and also the destruction of the final world ruler in Revelation 19:20. He will fulfill the prophecy of

319

speaking "against the God of gods" as mentioned also in Revelation chapter 13.

The description of Antiochus IV Epiphanes in verses 21 and 23 of how he came into power "a contemptible person who has not been given the honor of royalty and with only a few people he will rise to power" may even turn out to be a description of how the future anti-Christ rises to power.

With it here in Daniel 11 verse 39 saying that this King will "greatly honor those who acknowledge him. He will make them rulers over many people and will distribute the land at a price." It sounds like what the anti-Christ might do with the 10 regions that the world has been divided up into.

> Rev. 17: 12"The ten horns you saw are ten kings who have not yet received a kingdom, but who for one hour will receive authority as kings along with the beast.

Remember what Paul said of the anti-Christ,

> 2 Thes. 2: 3Don't let anyone deceive you in any way, for (that day will not come) until the rebellion occurs and the man of lawlessness is revealed, the man doomed to destruction. 4He will oppose and will exalt himself over everything that is called God or is worshiped, so that he sets himself up in God's temple, proclaiming himself to be God.

The anti-Christ will not only deny the God of Israel, he will deny Jesus and he will deny the god of all religions and will proclaim himself to be god. Here in chapter 11 he said, verse 37, He will show no regard for the gods of his fathers or for the one desired by women, nor will he regard any god, but will exalt himself above them all. 38 Instead of them, he will honor a god of fortresses; a god unknown to his fathers he will honor. The phrase, (the one desired by women) referred to the Messiah for all Jewish women wanted to be the one that would give birth to the Messiah. From this and from the statement gods of his fathers some believe the anti-Christ will be Jewish. But from the statement in verse 38, (Instead of them) leads me to believe the reference is of two, that the gods of his fathers and the one desired by women aren't the same. This isn't referring to just the God of the Jews. The Jews only have one God, not gods as verse 37 says.

Until Mohammad the Arab peoples had come to have many gods. Allah was the moon god at the time. So, if the anti-Christ's fathers were Muslim's, the statement, (gods of his fathers) could refer to Allah. Some believe the anti-Christ will be a Muslim. Christianity, Judaism and Islam are the most prominent religions in the world today. Of course Christianity's origins are from Judaism. This could be saying that the anti-Christ will have a Muslim background on his father's side and a Jewish or Christian, at least will claim, seem to be Christian, background on his mother's side. There are also those that believe the anti-Christ will be from Rome and there those that believe he will be from Greece. The Romans and Greeks also had many gods. No one will actually know for sure until the 7 year peace agreement is signed, though you could have a pretty good suspicion as that time approaches.

Again, while Antiochus IV Epiphanes could be seen as fulfilling this, the fact that from the words of Jesus and Paul and from John in Revelation, we can see that this is indeed referring to a future end time ruler, it is clear that Daniel was not just describing one of the rulers that reigned between the time of Daniel and Jesus. And since there has not been any event or anyone that could be said to as fulfilling all the requirements from Daniel chapter 9 and Matthew 24, this prophecy has to be for yet a future time. Again, notice how he uses the phrase, 'the time of the end'.

40 "At the time of the end the king of the South will engage him in battle, and the king of the North will storm out against him with chariots and cavalry and a great fleet of ships. He will invade many countries and sweep through them like a flood. 41 He will also invade the Beautiful Land. Many countries will fall,

but Edom, Moab and the leaders of Ammon will be delivered from his hand. 42 He will extend his power over many countries; Egypt will not escape. 43 He will gain control of the treasures of gold and silver and all the riches of Egypt, with the Libyans and Nubians in submission. 44 But reports from the east and the north will alarm him, and he will set out in a great rage to destroy and annihilate many. 45 He will pitch his royal tents between the seas at the beautiful holy mountain. Yet he will come to his end, and no one will help him.

I've read different interpretations of verse 40. The different interpretations are over who the king of the North is and who the Him and He in verse 40 is, who is the king of the South engaging in battle? Identifying who these are here is in how you read verse 40.

"At the time of the end the king of the South will engage him in battle, and the king of the North will storm out against him with chariots and cavalry and a great fleet of ships."

Is the king of the North the anti-Christ or is it Russia? Is the king of the North the same king mentioned in verse 36?

The problem comes from verse 44 "But reports from the east and the north will alarm him" If the king of the north in verse 40 is the anti-Christ that is storming out against the king of the south then there's another king of the north introduced in verse 44, which could be plausible for the king of the North in verse 44 would be Russia.

Of course, China, along with the other Asian countries will be the king of the East. The king of the South would be Egypt and the northern African nations, and the other Islamic nations that will be part of the Russian Invasion of Israel.

One interpretation is that the King of the North is the anti-Christ and his army of the revived Roman Empire. This would have the king of the north the same king referred to in verse 36 and the 'King of the North' in verse 40. This interpretation seems to make sense because it flows with the fact that the prophecy has been referring to the kings of the south and north fighting each other and the king of the North was not Russia. With the mention of another king of the north in verse 44 leads to there being another king introduced. Russia is called the king of the Far North in Ezekiel 38 and 39, Russia is farther north from Israel than any other country. The king of the north in verse 44 doesn't appear that it can be the anti-Christ, the revived Roman Empire, because that would require the revived Roman Empire and China uniting together, this is not what the scriptures in Revelation describes. China will come against the anti-Christ and his army after the anti-Christ has defeated Russia and the Islamic nations. This really makes sense with the fact that Russia and China are now already allied together as are the Islamic nations are with Russia, especially Iran. So here as well as in Revelation it sounds like Russia wasn't totally destroyed when the anti-Christ stops Russia and the Islamic nations from invading Israel, it sounds like Russia will be with China in this attack against the anti-Christ's army at the last battle of Armageddon. So it appears the King and the 'Him' in verse 36 and 'King of the North' in verse 40 is the anti-Christ. The King of the North in verse 44 would be Russia.

Let me insert into the verse's the anti-Christ and Russia to see if this makes it clearer.

First verse 36 "The (anti-Christ) will do as he pleases. He will exalt and magnify himself above every god and will say unheard-of things against the God of gods. He (The anti-Christ) will be successful until the time of wrath is completed, for what has been determined must take place.

Now verses 40 thru 45,

> 40 "At the time of the end the king of the South will engage (the anti-Christ, the king of the North) in battle, and the (anti-Christ, the king of the North) will storm out against him with chariots and cavalry and a great fleet of ships. He (the anti-Christ) will invade many countries and sweep through them like a flood. 41 He (the anti-Christ) will also invade the Beautiful

Land. Many countries will fall, but Edom, Moab and the leaders of Ammon will be delivered from his hand. 42 He (the anti-Christ) will extend his power over many countries; Egypt will not escape. 43 He (the anti-Christ) will gain control of the treasures of gold and silver and all the riches of Egypt, with the Libyans and Nubians in submission.

44 But reports from the east (China) and the north (Russia) will alarm him, and he will set out in a great rage to destroy and annihilate many. 45 He (the anti-Christ) will pitch his royal tents between the seas at the beautiful holy mountain. Yet he will come to his end, and no one will help him.

This seems to flow with the previous verses and with what we've already read about the anti-Christ from the previous chapters, especially with verse 45 that he will come to his end and no one will help him. No one will be able to help him when Jesus returns.

It also would agree with Ezekiel 38 and 39 having Russia and the Islamic nations attacking Israel and then the Revived Roman Empire, the anti-Christ coming to Israel's aid. This also lines up with what we see in the book of Revelation.

We know that the anti-Christ with his army will come to Israel's rescue and attack Russia and the nations with Russia. The armies of Russia and all the Islamic nations might prove to be too much for Israel to handle on there on. The anti-Christ and his forces will defeat Russia and the Islamic nations. After the anti-Christ and his army have defeated the Islamic nations and Russia he decides to make Jerusalem his headquarters. From Revelation chapters 12 and 13 it sounds like he will be killed somehow and then Satan will enter into him raising him from the dead. Now the anti-Christ will actually be Satan, of course no one will know this unless they know the bible. He will set himself up as God in the temple desecrating it, the abomination that causes desolation. This will be the mid-point of the tribulation. The Jews will flee Jerusalem and go to Petra, the place prepared for them. See

Revelation chapter 12 and 13. I will explain a little about Petra in a second.

Then the Euphrates River will be dried up allowing the Kings of the East, China and the other Asian countries to come into the Middle East to attack the anti-Christ there. China could be pulled into this because of its ties with Russia. Again, China and Russia are allies today. While the drying up of the Euphrates River could be done supernaturally by God or by a nuclear bomb, it can be done easily today. In Turkey there is a dam called the Atatuak Dam that can be closed thus causing the river to be dried up. With the anti-Christ now controlling the Middle East oil supplies, if China defeats the anti-Christ and his army then they will have control of all the oil, and the world to. The Kings of the East will attack the anti-Christ just outside Jerusalem. China already has a highway to be used for military purposes that leads from China to the Middle East. The anti-Christ through satanic help, remember, it's actually Satan now, will deceive all the other nations of the world that were not part of the invasion of Israel by Russia and the Muslims to unit with him and they will meet the Kings of the East in the valley of Megiddo, the battle of Armageddon.

So the scenario would be,

The king of the South will engage him, the anti-Christ, the king of the North, in battle and the king of the North, the anti-Christ will storm out against him the king of the South which will include Egypt and the northern African nations along with the other Islamic nations. When Egypt and the other Islamic nations begin to come against Israel, the anti-Christ, the king of the North will come against them because of the agreement he has made with Israel. Again, this could be what we see starting in Revelation Chapter 6 with the 2nd seal. Russia, the other king of the North from verse 44 will be pulled into this. Ezekiel 38 and 39 tells us that Russia leads this. If Russia starts this then it could be that the anti-Christ's army will be split to come against the south and north at the same time. It could all possibly first start with the Islamic nations that border Israel that are not mentioned in Ezekiel Chapters 38 and 39, which could very well take place before the tribulation and even before the Rapture. These nations will be defeated. Then later will be the war we see here in Daniel and in Ezekiel and also in the book of Revelation. That could be what forces Russia to get involved.

Verse 40 and 41 tells us that this king will "invade many countries and sweep through them like a flood. He will also invade the Beautiful Land. Many countries will fall". Again, the king of the north here sounds more like the acts of the anti-Christ that we have seen from the other prophecies of Daniel than they do of Russia. With the invasion of Ezekiel 38 and 39 the anti-Christ's army will have gone through Israel into Egypt and North Africa defeating them along with Russia, then when he hears reports that China is uniting with Russia and are going to come against him, he will turn back to make his stand in Jerusalem.

China will not come into this until later at the end of the tribulation at the battle of Armageddon, after the anti-Christ has defeated Russia and the Islamic nations. We see this with verse 44, But reports from the east and the north will alarm him, and he will set out in a great rage to destroy and annihilate many. 45 He will pitch his royal tents between the seas at the beautiful holy mountain. Yet he will come to his end, and no one will help him.

From what we see from Ezekiel, Russia will not have been totally destroyed yet and from what we see here in Daniel Russia will come with China against the anti-Christ in the last battle of Armageddon, thus the reports of the king of the east and north.

Another possible interpretation is that the king of the North is Russia in verse 40 and 44 thus allowing for only one king of the north and that the "he" and "him" that is referred to in verse 40 is the anti-Christ, the king from verse 36.

This would be the king of the south (Egypt) and north (Russia) coming against the anti-Christ.

40 "At the time of the end the king of the South will engage him (the anti-Christ, the king from verse 36) in battle, and the king of the North (Russia) will storm out against him (the anti-Christ) with chariots and cavalry and a great fleet of ships. He (the anti-Christ) will invade many countries and sweep through them like a flood.

41 He (the anti-Christ) will also invade the Beautiful Land. Many countries will fall, but Edom, Moab and the leaders of Ammon will be delivered from his hand. 42 He (the anti-Christ) will extend his power over many countries; Egypt will not escape. 43 He (the anti-Christ) will gain control of the treasures of gold and silver and all the riches of Egypt, with the Libyans and Nubians in submission. 44 But reports from the east and the north (China and Russia) will alarm him, and he will set out in a great rage to destroy and annihilate many. 45 He (the anti-Christ) will pitch his royal tents between the seas at the beautiful holy mountain. Yet he will come to his end, and no one will help him.

The two interpretations are not all that different for the outcome is the same for both. It's just who do you see the King of the North in verse 40 being, Russia or the anti-Christ. It will work either way.

The interpretation that the king of the North in verse 40 is the anti-Christ and the king of the North in verse 44 is Russia seems to keep the flow from the previous verses because of the fact that it has been the king of the North and South warring against each other. Antiochus IV Epiphanes the king of the North was a type of anti-Christ. From all the other prophecies we've read from Daniel, the focus has all been about the anti-Christ, not Russia. With these prophecies and with what happened in the past, the king of the North was not Russia. So the king of the North mentioned in verse 44 would be Russia, the king of the far North of Ezekiel 38 and 39. With either interpretation it is still that China will be allied with Russia. Again, in either case the outcome is the same. The different interpretations come to the same conclusion concerning Russia, the Islamic nations and of course with China and other eastern nations that make up the king of the East.

About Petra, Petra which means rock is located 180 miles south of Amman in Jordan and about 60 to 100 miles to the south of Jerusalem in a mountain chain. This is where it is believed the Jews will flee during the second half of the tribulation. It is here where it is believed Isaiah refers to when he says in Isaiah 26, 20 Go, my people, enter your rooms and shut the doors behind you; hide yourselves for a little while until his wrath has passed by. 21 See, the LORD is coming out of his dwelling to punish the people of the earth for their sins. The earth will disclose the bloodshed upon her; she will conceal her slain no longer. What makes this city so unique is that it remains hidden--its main entrance being a narrow cleft in the rock called "the Siq." An interesting feature about this mysterious city (of about 20 square miles) was that the rose-red city was lost to the world for hundreds of years until it was re-discovered by John Burckhardt in 1812. So it could very well be that the rock city of Petra could become a hiding place for the one-third of the Jews - the Remnant of Israel - during the second half of the tribulation. Scholars interpret the one-third as believing Israel of Romans chapter 11 and the godly remnant that God supernaturally protects in a specially prepared hiding place. Go to the Internet and Google Petra to learn more and see pictures of this city. It's really amazing.

We know from Ezekiel and Daniel that Russia along with the King of the South, Egypt and the Northern African nations along with the other Islamic nations will attack Israel. The Islamic nations will not like the agreement the anti-Christ has made allowing Israel to rebuild the Temple. We see now that the Muslims see the rebuilding of the Temple as a major threat. Russia and the Islamic nations will come against Israel. Though the nations that border Israel could be of "the many nations with you" in Ezekiel chapter 38, as I said earlier, an invasion could start with the Islamic nations that border Israel. Israel will defeat them and because of Russia's ties with these nations; Russia will be forced into leading this invasion we see here in Daniel and Ezekiel. It could be that the Islamic nations like Iran will not have the power to come against Israel on their own so they will pressure Russia into invading Israel. We saw in Ezekiel 38 that God said of Russia, verse 4 "I will turn you around, put hooks in your jaws and bring you out with your whole army", verse 9 "You and all your troops and the many nations with you will go up, advancing like a storm; you will be like a cloud covering the land." But with verse 10 saying that Russia will devise an evil scheme it could be that Russia instigates the whole thing, and assures the Islamic nations that they will give them all the land of Israel. Russia's plan could be to double cross the Islamic nations. If they are defeated then Russia would have control of most of the world's oil supply, and what if Israel finds oil. They are drilling trying to find oil now. If Israel strikes oil this could cause a major problem for the OPEC countries. Israel could cause the cost of oil to dramatically drop, what a blessing that would be for the world.

I tend to believe that the invasion by Russia and the Islamic nations will happen after the Rapture, after the anti-Christ has signed the agreement with Israel and the Islamic nations, and that we see this with the 2nd seal in Revelation chapter 6. But there are those that believe it will happen before the rapture and before the anti-Christ signs the agreement with Israel, so it happens before the tribulation. If this becomes the case then the war we see in Revelation chapter 6 with the 2nd seal would have to be another conflict starting. You can see how this could go either way. If it is after the rapture, after the anti-Christ and Israel have signed the covenant then that would be why the anti-Christ comes to Israel's aid. If it happens before the anti-Christ and Israel have signed the covenant, then this could be why Israel signs it. Daniel 9 verse 27 says that the anti-Christ signs the covenant with the many. To me that sounds like he signs it with Israel and the Islamic nations. And the agreement will include Israel rebuilding the Temple. I believe that is why Israel will be willing to give up land and divide up Jerusalem. The Muslims (Palestinians) will not agree to a peace treaty without getting at least part of Jerusalem and getting the West Bank and the Golan Heights. This is another one of those things we will just have to wait and see. The outcome is the same either way. But to me it appears that it will happen after the rapture. The signing of the 7-year covenant is what starts the countdown to Armageddon, the countdown of the tribulation.

Verse 45 says "He will pitch his royal tents between the seas at the beautiful holy mountain. Yet he will come to his end, and no one will help him." Just as we see in Chapter 7, the anti-Christ will be defeated, but it will be by Jesus, we see this in Revelation 19. We will look at the anti-Christ again in our look at the book of Revelation.

You can see how all the scriptures agree and say the same thing. With putting Ezekiel, Daniel as well as other prophecies together with the book of Revelation, you can get a clear picture of what will take place during the time of the tribulation. We can see there will indeed be a World War III.

But, the good news is that we can see that Jesus will return again, and he will rule and reign. Chapter 12 will pick up after the battle of Armageddon and go into the return of Jesus.

8. Daniel Chapter 12

Once again with chapter 12 we can see that this is referring to the tribulation. Here he is continuing with the interpretation in chapter 11. Chapter 11 ended with a great battle, the climax of WWIII. We begin first with verse 1 referring to the 2nd half of the tribulation, and then to the return of Jesus.

The End Times

> 1 "At that time Michael, the great prince who protects your people, will arise. There will be a time of distress such as has not happened from the beginning of nations until then. But at that time your people—everyone whose name is found written in the book—will be delivered.

Compare verse 1 with what Jesus said of when the anti-Christ enters the temple,

> Mt. 24: 15"So when you see standing in the holy place 'the abomination that causes desolation,' spoken of through the prophet Daniel—let the reader understand— 16then let those who are in Judea flee to the mountains. 17Let no one on the roof of his house go down to take anything out of the house. 18Let no one in the field go back to get his cloak. 19How dreadful it will be in those days for pregnant women and nursing mothers! 20Pray that your flight will not take place in winter or on the Sabbath. 21For then there will be great distress, unequaled from the beginning of the world until now—and never to be equaled again.

> 2 Multitudes who sleep in the dust of the earth will awake: some to everlasting life, others to shame and everlasting contempt. 3 Those who are wise will shine like the brightness of the heavens, and those who lead many to righteousness, like the stars for ever and ever.

With verses 2 and 3 he is referring to the resurrection of all the Old Testament saints after the second coming of Jesus. Those that were righteous will be raised after Jesus' second coming while those that were not righteous will not be raised until 1000 years later, at the Great White Throne Judgment. This will be true of all those that their names are not found written in the Lambs book of Life, from both the Old and New Testament times. We see in Revelation chapter 20 that those who were killed during the tribulation for Jesus and the word of God will also come to life after Jesus returns.

> Rev. 20: 4I saw thrones on which were seated those who had been given authority to judge. And I saw the souls of those who had been beheaded because of their testimony for Jesus and because of the word of God. They had not worshiped the beast or his image and had not received his mark on their foreheads or their hands. They came to life and reigned with Christ a thousand years. 5(The rest of the dead did not come to life until the thousand years were ended.) This is the first resurrection. 6Blessed and holy are those who have part in the first resurrection. The second death has no power over them, but they will be priests of God and of Christ and will reign with him for a thousand years.

In Isaiah chapter 26 Isaiah also prophesied about this resurrection after Jesus' 2nd coming.

> 19 But your dead will live; their bodies will rise.
> You who dwell in the dust, wake up and shout for joy.
> Your dew is like the dew of the morning;
> the earth will give birth to her dead.

Anyone who's names are not written in the Lambs book of Life, after the Great White Throne judgment will go through death once more, the second death, for they have already died once.

Rev. 20: 11Then I saw a great white throne and him who was seated on it. Earth and sky fled from his presence, and there was no place for them. 12And I saw the dead, great and small, standing before the throne, and books were opened. Another book was opened, which is the book of life. The dead were judged according to what they had done as recorded in the books. 13The sea gave up the dead that were in it, and death and Hades gave up the dead that were in them, and each person was judged according to what he had done. 14Then death and Hades were thrown into the lake of fire. The lake of fire is the second death. 15If anyone's name was not found written in the book of life, he was thrown into the lake of fire.

4 But you, Daniel, close up and seal the words of the scroll until the time of the end. Many will go here and there to increase knowledge."

Many will go here and there to increase knowledge. How true this is today. With the ability to travel all over the world, with books and the Internet, knowledge has been greatly increased. Even with me, my knowledge of the rapture and end time prophecy have been greatly increased and increased much quicker than it could have been without books and especially without the internet. I know I've said this before, but isn't the bible amazing, isn't it just amazing how accurate the prophecies of the bible are.

5 Then I, Daniel, looked, and there before me stood two others, one on this bank of the river and one on the opposite bank. 6 One of them said to the man clothed in linen, who was above the waters of the river, "How long will it be before these astonishing things are fulfilled?"

7 The man clothed in linen, who was above the waters of the river, lifted his right hand and his left hand toward heaven, and I heard him swear by him who lives forever, saying, "It will be for a time, times and half a time. When the power of the holy

people has been finally broken, all these things will be completed."

We see this mentioned in the book of Revelation of the last 3 ½ years of the tribulation. Remember, a time was one year, times was two years and of course half a time, half a year, the same as 1260 days and 42 months. Remember, all this is based on a prophetic year of 360 days for a year. This is the amount of time it will take to break the Jewish people of their human pride and soften their hearts to accept Jesus as the Messiah.

Rev. 12: 13When the dragon saw that he had been hurled to the earth, he pursued the woman who had given birth to the male child. 14The woman was given the two wings of a great eagle, so that she might fly to the place prepared for her in the desert, where she would be taken care of for a time, times and half a time, out of the serpent's reach.

Rev. 13: 5The beast was given a mouth to utter proud words and blasphemies and to exercise his authority for forty-two months.

8 I heard, but I did not understand. So I asked, "My lord, what will the outcome of all this be?"

9 He replied, "Go your way, Daniel, because the words are closed up and sealed until the time of the end.

We see here that these prophecies are for the time of the end. From the previous chapters we have seen all this ends with the second coming of Jesus.

All these thousands of years these words have been sealed up. People reading this and other prophecies concerning the end times especially the book of Revelation haven't been able to understand what it all could mean. But since the end of WWII and with modern technology and with current world events the words of these prophecies are

334

beginning to be opened up. This is another sign that we are living in the end times, close to all this being fulfilled.

Look at what the Apostle John was told about the prophecy of the book of Revelation.

> Rev 22: 10Then he told me, "Do not seal up the words of the prophecy of this book, because the time is near.

During the years of the tribulation these prophecies will become totally unsealed. They will be clear to those that are living it. They will be able to look at what's happening and relate it to these prophecies of Daniel and all the other prophecies concerning the time of the end, the years of the tribulation. But unfortunately, there will be those that will ignore it, dismiss it. They still won't believe. We see in Revelation that John tells us twice that they still would not repent.

> 10 Many will be purified, made spotless and refined, but the wicked will continue to be wicked. None of the wicked will understand, but those who are wise will understand.

We see that many will be purified and made spotless, but the wicked will continue to be wicked right up to the end. We see that the wicked will not understand any of this, but the wise will. This would mean that those in Jesus, those that know the bible would understand, but those that are not saved, those that are not in Jesus will not understand; they will continue to be totally sinful. Look at how the Message Bible words this.

> Dan. 9-10 "'Go on about your business, Daniel,' he said. 'The message is confidential and under lock and key until the end, until things are about to be wrapped up. The populace will be washed clean and made like new. But the wicked will just keep on being wicked, without a clue about what is happening. Those who live wisely and well will understand what's going on.'

This alone blow's Amillennialism and Postmillennialism views out of the water, since they believe the Church will eventually evangelize the world so that the whole world will be saved and righteous and then Jesus can return. Haven't they read this? The bible makes it clear that the world will get worse and worse, it will not be righteous until after Jesus has returned and establishes his kingdom.

> 11 "From the time that the daily sacrifice is abolished and the abomination that causes desolation is set up, there will be 1,290 days. 12 Blessed is the one who waits for and reaches the end of the 1,335 days.

No explanation is given here on the 1290 or 1335 days mentioned. Because Revelation mentions 1260 days it's been a puzzle to bible scholars so there's been many different possible explanations for the difference of the days here and in Revelation.

So I'll give you my thoughts on it. I could be just as wrong or right as anybody else.

As I've mentioned earlier in this book, it could be that the battle of Armageddon will take place after 1260 days from the time of the abomination that causes desolation, the anti-Christ entering into the temple and defiling it. We see in Revelation that the last battle of Armageddon does not start when Jesus returns, but before.

> Rev. 14: 19The angel swung his sickle on the earth, gathered its grapes and threw them into the great winepress of God's wrath. 20They were trampled in the winepress outside the city, and blood flowed out of the press, rising as high as the horses' bridles for a distance of 1,600 stadia. (About 180 miles).

This will be when China and the other Asian nations along with Russia come together against the anti-Christ and the nations of the earth at the last battle of Armageddon.

Rev. 16: 12The sixth angel poured out his bowl on the great river Euphrates, and its water was dried up to prepare the way for the kings from the East.

Rev. 16: 16Then they gathered the kings together to the place that in Hebrew is called Armageddon. 17The seventh angel poured out his bowl into the air, and out of the temple came a loud voice from the throne, saying, "It is done!" 18Then there came flashes of lightning, rumblings, peals of thunder and a severe earthquake. No earthquake like it has ever occurred since man has been on earth, so tremendous was the quake. 19The great city split into three parts, and the cities of the nations collapsed. God remembered Babylon the Great and gave her the cup filled with the wine of the fury of his wrath. 20Every island fled away and the mountains could not be found. 21From the sky huge hailstones of about a hundred pounds each fell upon men. And they cursed God on account of the plague of hail, because the plague was so terrible.

Like I have already mentioned, this sounds like there's a massive nuclear exchange amongst the nations. When Jesus returns he won't be using nuclear weapons. From what is said in verse 21, it doesn't sound like this is the end, when Jesus returns. We see Jesus returning in Revelation chapter 19. Verse 21 of Revelation 19 says it is by the sword of his mouth that kills those that are gathered together to make war against him returning, his just speaking the word kills them.

We see that after the nations of the world have just about destroyed themselves and everything on the earth, the anti Christ is able to get them to now come together to fight against Jesus. He most likely will somehow be blaming Jesus for all the destruction.

Rev.19: 11I saw heaven standing open and there before me was a white horse, whose rider is called Faithful and True. With justice he judges and makes war. 12His eyes are like blazing fire, and on his head are many crowns. He has a name written on him that no one knows but he himself. 13He is dressed in a

robe dipped in blood, and his name is the Word of God. 14The armies of heaven were following him, riding on white horses and dressed in fine linen, white and clean. 15Out of his mouth comes a sharp sword with which to strike down the nations. "He will rule them with an iron scepter." He treads the winepress of the fury of the wrath of God Almighty. 16On his robe and on his thigh he has this name written:
KING OF KINGS AND LORD OF LORDS.

17And I saw an angel standing in the sun, who cried in a loud voice to all the birds flying in midair, "Come, gather together for the great supper of God, 18so that you may eat the flesh of kings, generals, and mighty men, of horses and their riders, and the flesh of all people, free and slave, small and great."

19Then I saw the beast and the kings of the earth and their armies gathered together to make war against the rider on the horse and his army. 20But the beast was captured, and with him the false prophet who had performed the miraculous signs on his behalf. With these signs he had deluded those who had received the mark of the beast and worshiped his image. The two of them were thrown alive into the fiery lake of burning sulfur. 21The rest of them were killed with the sword that came out of the mouth of the rider on the horse, and all the birds gorged themselves on their flesh.

Just think of all the dead bodies of soldiers and animals that will be in this valley. Bodies of dead left from the first battles of Russia and the Islamic nations to the battle of Armageddon to finally the return of Jesus. You can see how the birds and animals will be able to gorge themselves on their flesh.

So the 1260 days could be the last battle when all the nations come together fighting each other. We see this described in Daniel. Then 30 days later Satan, the anti-Christ has what is left of the armies of the world gathered together to make war against Jesus when he returns.

The next 45 days, could be that during these 45 days the temple will be cleansed making it ready for Jesus and the kingdom, and Jesus will be judging Israel and those that have survived the tribulation. After this last 45 days Jesus will officially start the kingdom of God.

> Mt. 19: 28Jesus said to them, "I tell you the truth, at the renewal of all things, when the Son of Man sits on his glorious throne, you who have followed me will also sit on twelve thrones, judging the twelve tribes of Israel.

> Mt. 25: 31"When the Son of Man comes in his glory, and all the angels with him, he will sit on his throne in heavenly glory. 32All the nations will be gathered before him, and he will separate the people one from another as a shepherd separates the sheep from the goats. 33He will put the sheep on his right and the goats on his left. 34"Then the King will say to those on his right, 'Come, you who are blessed by my Father; take your inheritance, the kingdom prepared for you since the creation of the world.

> 41"Then he will say to those on his left, 'Depart from me, you who are cursed, into the eternal fire prepared for the devil and his angels.

As I've said before, I guess the meaning of the 1290 days and the 1335 days is another one of those things we will just have to wait and see for sure.

> 13 "As for you, go your way till the end. You will rest, and then at the end of the days you will rise to receive your allotted inheritance."

We see with this last statement that Daniel is told that he will die before all this takes place, but at the end of all this he will be raised up to receive his allotted inheritance.

Take a look at what the first three verses' of the last chapter of the Old Testament says.

Malachi 4

> 1 "Surely the day is coming; it will burn like a furnace. All the arrogant and every evildoer will be stubble, and that day that is coming will set them on fire," says the LORD Almighty. "Not a root or a branch will be left to them.

This is referring to the tribulation, but verse 2 and 3 are referring to the Millennium reign of Christ.

> 2 But for you who revere my name, the sun of righteousness will rise with healing in its wings. And you will go out and leap like calves released from the stall. 3 Then you will trample down the wicked; they will be ashes under the soles of your feet on the day when I do these things," says the LORD Almighty.

With verse 5 you can see how a prophecy can span thousands of years. You can see another example of how a scripture that mentions more than one prophecy in one verse can be separated by thousands of years.

> 5 "See, I will send you the prophet Elijah before that great and dreadful day of the LORD comes. 6 He will turn the hearts of the fathers to their children, and the hearts of the children to their fathers; or else I will come and strike the land with a curse."

Jesus said this was fulfilled in John the Baptist. John the Baptist did indeed come before the great and dreadful day of the Lord, he has come before the tribulation. Many also believe this could have a duel meaning, that it also could refer to one of the two witnesses that we see mentioned in the book of Revelation for we know that one of them could very well be Elijah. Most believe the two witnesses will be either Enoch or Moses and Elijah.

Next we will look at the book of Revelation and you will see how all these prophecies come together and find there fulfillment in the Revelation, during the time of the tribulation.

Chapter Eight

A Look at the book of Revelation

1. Revelation Introduction:

The book of Revelation is like a continuation of Daniel for it reveals the details of the time period during Daniel's 70th week in chapter 9 as well as the details of the vision in chapter 11. The first three chapters fill in the time between the 69th week and the 70th week, the Church age. This was not revealed to Daniel because the Church was not revealed to the Old Testament Prophets. Revelation also gives more details of Jesus' Sermon on the Mount. We saw in Matthew 24 that Jesus' intent was to address those that would be going through Daniel's 70th week, the 7 years of the Tribulation. All the Old Testament prophecies concerning the time just before the return of Christ find there fulfillment in the book of Revelation.

First let me say that this is not an attempt to be a complete study of the book of Revelation or to explain everything in Revelation chapter by chapter or verse by verse; that would be a book in itself. I just want to point out some significant things to help you understand the symbolism used in the book of Revelation and help with what we have already studied become clearer, and to show how modern technology has made the book of Revelation become clearer. You will see that the book of Revelation couldn't be addressing any other generation until this generation. The description of modern technology of today proves this.

If you go and read Revelation after reading this you should have a better understanding and a clearer picture to what is being revealed. You will see that the symbols and images used aren't that mysterious or hard to understand. You will see that the explanations are either explained in Revelation or in the Old Testament.

Now concerning the dating of the book of Revelation in 95 a.d., remember Irenaeus (120-202), he was a disciple of Polycarp (69-155) who had been personally taught by the Apostle John. He wrote that John was exiled to the Isle of Patmos under the emperor Domitian. Papias (60 -130) is another early Church father that was taught by the Apostle John. He was 10 years old when Jerusalem and the Temple were destroyed. If anyone would know when John was on the Isle of Patmos and wrote the book of Revelation these three men would. All early Church fathers and writers point towards the end of the Emperor Domitian's reign. He reigned from 81 to 96. With Domitian reigning from 81 to 96, the amillennialist and preterist claims that the book was written around 68 A.D is proven to be false. They have to date the book before the fall and destruction of Jerusalem in 70 A.D. for their views to work. There are no historical writings for the 68 date until around 367 when the teaching started that all bible prophecy had been fulfilled. There is no account of anyone claiming John was on the Isle of Patmos during Nero's reign (54-68) until A.D. 550.

There is no scripture evidence that John was on Patmos during Nero's reign, just the opposite. John was an old man while on the Isle of Patmos. If he was around 15 to 20 when Jesus started his ministry, then he would have been around 53 to 58 with the 68 date, that's not an old man even today. But he would have been in is 80's with the 95 dating. Also, it wasn't Nero's way to exile anyone to Patmos, which was Domitian's way of doing things.

For more on the evidence for the 95 or 96 date for the writing of the book of Revelation read Grant Jeffrey's book Triumphant Return.

When you read the book of Revelation the first thing to notice from the very first verse in chapter one is that this is the revelation of Jesus Christ. Prophecy is ultimately about Jesus. We see that Jesus sent an angel to John. John makes a point of letting the reader know that he literally saw all that they are about to read. In verse 19 we see John was told to write down what he will see.

> Rev. 1: 1The revelation of Jesus Christ, which God gave him to show his servants what must soon take place. He made it known by sending his angel to his servant John, 2who testifies to everything he saw—that is, the word of God and the testimony of Jesus Christ.

Jesus testifies concerning himself,

> 8"I am the Alpha and the Omega," says the Lord God, "who is, and who was, and who is to come, the Almighty."

> 18I am the Living One; I was dead, and behold I am alive for ever and ever! And I hold the keys of death and Hades.

Alpha and Omega are the first and last letters in the Greek alphabet. Jesus is saying that he is the beginning and the end.

We see in verse 1 of chapter 4 that John was taken up to heaven where he saw things in and from heaven. Later you will see that he was literally transported into the future.

> Rev. 4: 1After this I looked, and there before me was a door standing open in heaven. And the voice I had first heard speaking to me like a trumpet said, "Come up here, and I will show you what must take place after this." 2At once I was in the Spirit, and there before me was a throne in heaven with someone sitting on it.

Now take a look at what verse 3 of chapter 1 says,

> Rev. 1: 3Blessed is the one who reads the words of this prophecy, and blessed are those who hear it and take to heart what is written in it, because the time is near.

No other book in the bible says that the reader would be blessed from reading its words and taking them to heart. Of course we are blessed from reading any of the books of the bible but with prophecy, especially with the prophecies in the book of Revelation there is a special blessing. This has been true for everyone through all the generations but its special blessing is even truer for us now. There has been no generation that has seen so many of these prophecies beginning to fall in place than our generation. Since 1948 when Israel became a nation again there has been more prophecies being fulfilled than any time since Jesus ascended up to heaven.

Modern technology has now made it possible for these prophecies to literally come true. When we read these prophecies and see the condition the world is in today and getting worse, when we see that the bible foretold this, and with seeing how things in the world are beginning to line up with these prophecies it further strengthens the faith of the believer and should move the non-believer to come to realize that the bible is the word of God and come to believe in who the bible says Jesus is. The believer and non-believer alike should see that God indeed revealed these things to his prophets and if we can see that these things are true then we can be assured that the things that are said about Jesus and eternal life are true also. I've said it before and I'll say again, the Bible is the word of God and Jesus is Lord.

In the book of Revelation the main theme we can see is that Jesus is in control and he is going to return and establish the kingdom of God here on Earth of which he will rule and reign and remove Satan and all the demons. Then at the end of the 1000 years of the kingdom of God Jesus will finally destroy Satan and all evil and is going to create a New Heavens and New Earth.

The first 3 chapters refer to and deal with the Church, but notice after chapter three, all throughout the book of Revelation from the 4th chapter you have no mention of the Church. The only witnesses, messengers you see are the two witnesses and the 144,000 from the 12 tribes of Israel. If the Church is here during the tribulation we sure are keeping our mouths quiet. Surely if the Church was still here we would have some mention of it. There would be something about the Church since the book starts off with so much on the Church. But it would make since not to mention the Church after the 3rd chapter if the Church is not here.

I've read an argument that the reference to the 'saints' refers to or is a synonym for the Church but this is not the case. The word saint or saints is found all in the Old Testament, just read the Psalms, but the Church was not born until the day of Pentecost. These saints of the Old Testament were not part of the Church. The saints of the tribulation are not part of the Church. The tribulation is Daniels last week that was allotted to Israel, Daniel's people, the Jews.

In the book of Revelation there are pauses in the descriptions of the judgments. From the pauses between the seals and the trumpets and the trumpets and the bowls and between the bowls and the return of Jesus we can see that the book of Revelation is organized into three sections.

Before we look at the Seal, Trumpet and Bowl judgments, I would first like to look ahead and explain some things we find with these pauses, we will come across these later in our look at the book of Revelation. This will allow me to go from the seal and trumpet judgments right into the bowl judgments for they all flow one into the next. After reading this book you should have a good foundation to begin your studying of bible prophecy. The intent is that after you read this you will go and read the book of Revelation. You can use this book to refer back to. You should read this book more than once.

Before we get started with our look at the book of Revelation I would like to remind you that the Church, the true believers in Christ will be taken out of this world before the events of the tribulation begin. We will see this here in Revelation also.

So don't let the things you read here scare you. If you are a true born again Christian you won't be here to experience these things. There is really no excuse for anyone to be here after the rapture seeing how everyone has been given a chance to hear the gospel and accept Jesus into their lives. Christians are to study and know these things to warn those that haven't accepted Jesus yet, to give them a chance to repent and escape all these things. (Luke 21:36). That's the purpose of the judgments of the tribulation. To give everyone living during the tribulation, the last 7 years before Jesus returns a chance to accept him and to be worthy to go into the Kingdom of God. Prophecy is not only meant to warn the people, seeing bible prophecy being fulfilled shows that the bible is the word of God and that Jesus is Lord

2. Absence of the Church

In Revelation chapters 1 through 3 there are constant references to the Church. The word "church" is found every few verses: angels of the seven churches, messages to the seven churches, He who has an ear, let him hear what the Spirit says to the churches etc. Go read chapters 1 thru 3.

Where is the church during the Tribulation? It is missing! "Church" is not mentioned during the entire Tribulation period, Chapters 4 to 19. There is no message to the church. What you do have is Two Witnesses from Israel's past and you have the 144,000 who are sealed from the twelve tribes of Israel. It is the last seven years of Israel's history before the end of this age. Israel was the vehicle of God's blessing to the whole earth. They were not the "Chosen People" because God was playing favorites. They were chosen that through them, God could get the message out to others and to keep his written word intact. When they did not do well with being witnesses and messengers, He set them aside and put the Church in. (Romans 16:25-26; Ephesians 3:1-11). And of course, they were to be the people from which Jesus the messiah would come.

The Church has been here for almost 2000 years now but there are still seven years of Israel's allotted time from Daniels prophecy in Daniel chapter 9 that remain to be fulfilled. We believers of today are the spiritual seed of Abraham, but we are not Israel. God has temporarily grafted us in, but the time will come when Israel is grafted back into her own tree. (Romans 11:13-27).

> RO 11:13 I am talking to you Gentiles. Inasmuch as I am the apostle to the Gentiles, I make much of my ministry 14 in the hope that I may somehow arouse my own people to envy and save some of them. 15 For if their rejection is the reconciliation of the world, what will their acceptance be but life from the dead? 16 If the part of the dough offered as first fruits is holy, then the whole batch is holy; if the root is holy, so are the branches.

RM 11:17 If some of the branches have been broken off, and you, though a wild olive shoot, have been grafted in among the others and now share in the nourishing sap from the olive root, 18 do not boast over those branches. If you do, consider this: You do not support the root, but the root supports you. 19 You will say then, "Branches were broken off so that I could be grafted in." 20 Granted. But they were broken off because of unbelief, and you stand by faith. Do not be arrogant, but be afraid. 21 For if God did not spare the natural branches, he will not spare you either.

RM 11:22 Consider therefore the kindness and sternness of God: sternness to those who fell, but kindness to you, provided that you continue in his kindness. Otherwise, you also will be cut off. 23 And if they do not persist in unbelief, they will be grafted in, for God is able to graft them in again. 24 After all, if you were cut out of an olive tree that is wild by nature, and contrary to nature were grafted into a cultivated olive tree, how much more readily will these, the natural branches, be grafted into their own olive tree!

RM 11:25 I do not want you to be ignorant of this mystery, brothers, so that you may not be conceited: Israel has experienced a hardening in part until the full number of the Gentiles has come in. 26 And so all Israel will be saved, as it is written:

"The deliverer will come from Zion;
he will turn godlessness away from Jacob.
27And this is my covenant with them
when I take away their sins."

So you can see that the purpose of the Tribulation is not just to judge the nations, weeding out all the unrighteous, but also to bring Israel back in. In verse 15 Paul said their acceptance will be life from the dead. When Jesus returns he will raise those that were righteous during the Old Testament times as well as those that were killed during the tribulation. See Daniel chapter 12 and Revelation chapter 20. Again notice he said that this is a mystery. The Church was a mystery to the Old Testament saints. The full number of Gentiles was a mystery. It all fits together perfectly.

The absent church also accounts for the rise in lawlessness during The Tribulation period. (2 Thessalonians 2:3-8).

The Church is absent because,

The Church is Promised Deliverance from Wrath

Luke 21:36

"Be always on the watch, and pray that you may be able to escape all that is about to happen, and that you may be able to stand before the Son of Man."

1 Thessalonians 5:9

For God did not appoint us to suffer wrath but to receive salvation through our Lord Jesus Christ

2 Peter 2

6if he condemned the cities of Sodom and Gomorrah by burning them to ashes, and made them an example of what is going to happen to the ungodly; 7and if he rescued Lot, a righteous man, who was distressed by the filthy lives of lawless men 8(for that righteous man, living among them day after day, was tormented in his righteous soul by the lawless deeds he saw and heard)— 9if this is so, then the Lord knows how to rescue godly men from trials and to hold the unrighteous for the day of judgment, while continuing their punishment on the day of judgment.

Message to the Church of Philadelphia

In the third chapter of Revelation we see a special promise made to the Church in Philadelphia, which is prophetic of the true Church that will be present just before the tribulation.

> Rev. 3: 10Since you have kept my command to endure patiently, I will also keep you from the hour of trial that is going to come upon the whole world to test those who live on the earth.

I've read one of the other views argument that this means to keep through, not from as the pre-tribulation view says. Well, the Strong's Greek Lexicon translation of the word 'from' is G1537 (out of, from, by, away from). So we see there is a promise to those that are truly part of the Church will be kept from the hour of trial. Put this together with all the other scriptures and we see that the Church will be taken out before the hour of trial comes on all those that are living on the earth.

We are plainly told that we who trust in Christ are not under condemnation (Romans 8:1). Whenever God judges the unrighteous, He delivers those who trust in Him. This is seen in the Biblical stories of the Flood in the days of Noah, the judgment of Sodom and Gomorrah (Lot and his family saved).

The events of the Tribulation are judgments from God, and as such, it would be consistent for Him to deliver the Church before it begins.

It should be obvious that the book of Revelation is addressing events that will concern Israel and the world, not the Church, the bride of Christ. Revelation 4 through 19 is addressing the time of the tribulation, the last 7 years allotted to Israel.

Again, this is strong evidence for a pre-tribulation rapture of the Church.

The Church is not mentioned during the tribulation because the Church, his ambassadors, the bride of Christ has been removed before the start of Israel's last seven years.

Jew and Gentile

Something else to notice in the book of Revelation is he distinguishes between the Jew and a Gentile, Israel and the nations. You see believing Jews and unbelieving Jews, believing Gentiles and unbelieving Gentiles.

But of the time we are in now, the Church age Paul said:

GAL 3:28 There is neither Jew nor Greek, slave nor free, male nor female, for you are all one in Christ Jesus.

With the book of Revelation distinguishing between Jew and Gentile and from the fact the Church is not mentioned at all as being here during the time of God's judgments, it is a good indication that the Church is not present during the tribulation. There isn't a reference to the Church after chapter 3 until chapter 19 as the bride coming with Jesus from heaven. Remember, the Church is considered the body of Christ, we are ambassadors for Christ. Believers while here on earth are ambassadors, we make up the body of Christ, but once we have been taken up to heaven with Jesus, we are the bride of Christ. It's while we are in heaven during the tribulation that the wedding takes place.

Notice the phrase that references the Church that is found in the first 3 chapters of Revelation but not once after Rev. 4:1. (He who has an ear, let him hear what the Spirit says to the churches.) Look at what you have after Rev. 4:1. Rev. 13:9 He who has an ear, let him hear. No reference to the Church. Notice how Jesus used the phrase before the establishment of the Church, before the day of Pentecost.
See Matthew 11:15, 13:9, 13:43, Mark 4:9, 4:23, Luke 8: 8, 14:35.

MT 11: 15 He who has ears, **let him hear,**

353

MT 13: 9 He who has ears, **let him hear**. And Mark 4:9, Luke 8:8

MT 13:40 "As the weeds are pulled up and burned in the fire, so it will be at the end of the age. 41 The Son of Man will send out his angels, and they will weed out of his kingdom everything that causes sin and all who do evil. 42 They will throw them into the fiery furnace, where there will be weeping and gnashing of teeth. 43 Then the righteous will shine like the sun in the kingdom of their Father. He who has ears, **let him hear.**

Notice how he is talking about the end of the tribulation. Rev. 14:14-19

There was not yet a Church when Jesus made these statements. This is good evidence that the Church is not present during the Tribulation or John would have used the same phrase 'to the churches' in chapter 13.

If the Church is not here during the tribulation then it would make since not to say (He who has an ear, let him hear what the Spirit says to the churches.) If John was also addressing the Church he would not have changed his statement.

Because of all this it is believed that Rev. 4:1 is a reference as to where the Rapture fits in with the timing of the events in the book of Revelation. We see that it is before the opening of the Seals, the judgments of God, thus it is evidence for a pre-trib rapture of the Church.

Rev. 4: 1After this I looked, and there before me was a door standing open in heaven. And the voice I had first heard speaking to me like a trumpet said, "Come up here, and I will show you what must take place after this."

After what, after what he had just described in the first 3 chapters, after the Church age.

Rev. 1: 19"Write, therefore, what you have seen, what is now and what will take place later.

In verse 19 John is told to write what he has seen, the things he had seen when Jesus was here, what is now, the Church and the Roman Empire, and the main focus of the revelation, what will take place later. What will take place later is a good indicator that what we read in Revelation was not what was taking place through Rome at the time of Johns writing. That would fit under the now. And since the revelation was received and written around 95 A. D. after Jerusalem had been destroyed by the Romans, that leaves us with no other conclusion than the book of Revelation is prophetic of a yet future time.

Don't lose sight that this last 7 years before Jesus returns are Israel's last week, the last 7 years allotted to Daniel's people, the Jews. Daniel 9:24-27.

This is Israel's last chance to evangelize the world, to be the witness that they were called to be. With the two witnesses and with the 144,000 being called servants of God many believe they will be witnesses for the gospel. This will be for preparing Israel and the surviving gentiles that have accepted Jesus as the Lord to enter into the Kingdom of God. We do see that Israel will recognize and accept Jesus as the Messiah before he returns back down to the earth, thus all Israel will be saved. Jesus said he would not return until this happens.

Matthew 23: 39For I tell you, you will not see me again until you say, 'Blessed is he who comes in the name of the Lord.

Luke 13: 35Look, your house is left to you desolate. I tell you, you will not see me again until you say, 'Blessed is he who comes in the name of the Lord.

During the 1000 year reign of Christ Israel will once again be God's chosen nation. Jesus will rule the nations, the whole world from Jerusalem.

RO 11:25 I do not want you to be ignorant of this mystery, brothers, so that you may not be conceited: Israel has experienced a hardening in part until the full number of the Gentiles has come in. 26 And so all Israel will be saved, as it is written:

"The deliverer will come from Zion; he will turn godlessness away from Jacob. 27 And this is my covenant with them when I take away their sins."

While the Gospel will always be that Jesus is the only way for salvation, I imagine the gospel will be quite different during the time of the tribulation. We see in Matthew 24 Jesus reveals things that will be occurring during the tribulation. Then he says that this gospel concerning the things occurring during the tribulation that he referred to as signs of his return will be preached in the whole world as a testimony to all nations. The gospel will include the things that are occurring, and about the man called the anti-Christ, that he is not the Messiah, that these things are judgments from God and will culminate in the return of Jesus down to earth and the establishment of the kingdom of God.

Mt. 24: 14And this gospel of the kingdom will be preached in the whole world as a testimony to all nations, and then the end will come.

If you haven't already, get your bible and read chapters 1 thru 3. For the sake of space I'm not going to address the messages to all the Churches. But I would like you to read the messages to the Church and notice how he uses the word 'Church' when addressing the Church. Again, you don't see the word 'Church' used again after the 3rd chapter. It should be clear; the Church is no longer here.

3. Pre-Tribulation Rapture at Rev. 4:1

Rev. 4. John

> 1After this I looked, and there before me was a door standing open in heaven. And the voice I had first heard speaking to me like a trumpet said, "**Come up here**, and I will show you what must take place after this." 2At once I was in the Spirit, and there before me was a throne in heaven with someone sitting on it.

This verse is considered to be the place in the book of Revelation that the rapture takes place for from here on there's no mention of the Church. This being where the rapture takes place is also supported by the statement "and I will show you what must take place after this". After what? After John was taken up to heaven but also after the judgment of the Church we see in chapters 2 and 3. He will show John what must take place after the Church age.

Look again at what John was told in Chapter 1,

> 19"Write, therefore, what you have seen, what is now and what will take place later.

I've been using the NIV bible but look also at the New King James.

> Rev. 4: 1 <u>After these things</u> I looked, and behold, a door standing open in heaven. And the first voice which I heard was like a trumpet speaking with me, saying, "Come up here, and I will show you things which must take place after this."

> Rev. 1: 19 Write the things which you have seen, and the things which are, and the things which will take place after this.

Jesus told John to write about three things: First, In Chapter 1 "the things which you have seen" we see his description of Jesus in His glory, the things he'd seen in the glorified Person of Jesus; Second,

Chapters 2 & 3 "the things which are" we see the spiritual condition of the church through the ages, the things that were spiritually significant of the churches of John's day, and the things that will be spiritually significant of the churches at the time of the rapture, we see churches whose experiences would typify conditions throughout church history until Jesus returns for His people. We can also see these 7 different spiritual conditions in church denominations and in individual believers.

But now in Rev. 4 begins the story of John's travel to heaven where he saw the things that will take place both there and on earth following the close of church history. Third, are the things that would take place NKJ "after this" NASB "after these things", NIV "take place later" Rev. 1:19, in other words, events that take place later, at the end of the age. "After this or after these things" refers to the events after the church age. John has been called up into heaven to be shown the things, which must happen after the Rapture, both in heaven and on earth.

As I mentioned in the last chapter, it is very interesting that the word "church", which is used repeatedly in the first three chapters, is completely missing after this point. "He who has an ear, let him hear what the Spirit says to the churches in contrast to Rev. 13:9 "**He who has an ear, let him hear**." If the Church was still present surely John would have still included "**what the Spirit says to the churches**". But it would be logical to not include "to the churches" if the church had already been caught up and in heaven with the Lord. This fits perfectly with the view that the Church will be caught up to be with the Lord before the Tribulation begins.

The same expression "Come up here" is used in Revelation 11:12 where the Two Witnesses are raised from the dead and caught up into Heaven.

Rev. 11 The Two Witnesses

> 11 But after the three and a half days a breath of life from God entered them, and they stood on their feet, and terror struck those who saw them. 12Then they heard a loud voice from heaven saying to them, "**Come up here.**" And they went up to heaven in a cloud, while their enemies looked on.

Compare with Jesus' resurrection:

> MK 16:19 After the Lord Jesus had spoken to them, **he was taken up** into heaven and he sat at the right hand of God.

> LK 24:51 While he was blessing them, he left them and **was taken up** into heaven.

With the absence of any reference to the church after Rev. 4:1 and the similarities of all these scriptures to 1 Thessalonians 4:16-17 it makes Rev.4:1 the best possible scripture reverence to the timing of the Rapture in the book of Revelation and a good clue to where the Church is during the tribulation.

> 1TH 4: 16 For the Lord himself will come down from heaven, with a loud command, with the voice of the archangel and with the trumpet call of God, and the dead in Christ will rise first. 17 After that, we who are still alive and are left will be **caught up together** with them in the clouds to meet the Lord in the air. And so we will be with the Lord forever. 18 Therefore encourage each other with these words.

Look at other scriptures that refer to being caught or snatched up.

Rev. 12:5 refers to Jesus.

> 5 She gave birth to a son, a male child, who will rule all the nations with an iron scepter. And her child was **snatched up** to God and to his throne. -- Jesus' ascension.

Also about Jesus.

> Acts 1:9 After he said this, he was **taken up** before their very eyes, and a cloud hid him from their sight.

2 Cor. 12:2 thru 4, concerning Paul

> 2 I know a man in Christ who fourteen years ago was **caught up** to the third heaven. Whether it was in the body or out of the body I do not know--God knows. 3 And I know that this man--whether in the body or apart from the body I do not know, but God knows-- 4 **was caught up to paradise.** He heard inexpressible things, things that man is not permitted to tell.

Paul was referring to himself.

The rapture of the church is often paralleled to the "raptures" of Enoch (Genesis 5:24) and Elijah (2 Kings 2: 12). In each case, they disappeared or were caught up into-heaven

We know the two witnesses are caught up to heaven. The command to John in Rev. 4:1 would seem to be the same, a catching up although John himself was caught up and returned. While in verse 2 John said he was in the spirit doesn't mean he couldn't have been in the body also. We just saw that Paul wasn't sure if he was in the spirit only or in his body. In any event, verse one of Revelation chapter 4 appears to be where the rapture takes place in the book of Revelation.

Let me point this out again. In the first 3 chapters of Revelation we see the Church is mentioned repeatedly. But from chapter 4 verse 1 there is no more mention of the Church as to being present during the tribulation. We see an absence of the Church. With there being so many references to the Church in the first 3 chapters and no mention of the Church from Rev. 4:1 through Rev. 19, the Church is not mentioned again in the book until chapter 19 when we are seen returning with Jesus, is good evidence that the Church is not present here on earth during the 7 years of the tribulation. The church is not mentioned during the seal, trumpet, and bowl judgments because the Church is not here during the outpouring of these judgments. The true believers have been raptured, taken up to the Father's house to be with the Lord in heaven.

Revelation 19.

> 11I saw heaven standing open and there before me was a white horse, whose rider is called Faithful and True. With justice he judges and makes war. 12His eyes are like blazing fire, and on his head are many crowns. He has a name written on him that no one knows but he himself. 13He is dressed in a robe dipped in blood, and his name is the Word of God. **14The armies of heaven** were following him, riding on white horses and <u>dressed in fine linen, white and clean.</u>

> Rev. 19: 8Fine linen, bright and clean, was given her to wear." (Fine linen stands for the righteous acts of the saints.)

It should be clear this is not referring to angels. This statement shows that the rapture of the Church saints had to have happened before this point, before Jesus returns back down to the earth at his 2nd coming. We see here that the saints are returning with Jesus, not Jesus coming for the Church age saints. Add to this that we see in chapter 20 those that have been killed during the tribulation are raised to life AFTER Jesus' 2nd coming, AFTER he is here on the earth, it seems to be a good clue to where the Church is during the 7 years of the tribulation.

> REV 20:4 I saw thrones on which were seated those who had been given authority to judge. And I saw the souls of those who had been beheaded because of their testimony for Jesus and because of the word of God. They had not worshiped the beast or his image and had not received his mark on their foreheads or their hands. They came to life and reigned with Christ a thousand years.

Remember, with the Rapture the dead in Christ are raised first, then those that are alive are caught up together with them to meet the Lord in the air. I Thessalonians 4: 13 – 18.

We find another clue in verses 4 through 6.

> Rev. 4: 4 Surrounding the throne were twenty-four other thrones, and seated on them were twenty-four elders. They were dressed in white and had crowns of gold on their heads. 5From the throne came flashes of lightning, rumblings and peals of thunder. Before the throne, seven lamps were blazing. These are the seven spirits of God. 6Also before the throne there was what looked like a sea of glass, clear as crystal.

The 24 elders are said to represent the Church, we also see in verse 6 a sea of glass clear as crystal before the throne. The sea is often used to represent a multitude of people. See Rev. 17:15. We see this sea of people is before the throne of God. All this is before the opening of the first seal.

Remember what we saw in Daniel chapter 7 concerning thrones

> Dan. 7: 9 "As I looked,
> "thrones were set in place,
> and the Ancient of Days took his seat.
> His clothing was as white as snow;
> the hair of his head was white like wool.
> His throne was flaming with fire,
> and its wheels were all ablaze.

Look again at John's description of Jesus in the first chapter of Revelation.

> Rev.1: 12I turned around to see the voice that was speaking to me. And when I turned I saw seven golden lampstands, 13and among the lampstands was someone "like a son of man," dressed in a robe reaching down to his feet and with a golden

sash around his chest. 14His head and hair were white like wool, as white as snow, and his eyes were like blazing fire. 15His feet were like bronze glowing in a furnace, and his voice was like the sound of rushing waters. 16In his right hand he held seven stars, and out of his mouth came a sharp double-edged sword. His face was like the sun shining in all its brilliance.

And the thrones set in place

Rev. 4: 4Surrounding the throne were twenty-four other thrones, and seated on them were twenty-four elders. They were dressed in white and had crowns of gold on their heads.

Here at the beginning of the tribulation God and the 24 elders will sit in judgment over what is coming upon the world. These 24 thrones and elders are not mentioned anywhere in the Old Testament other than in Daniel seeing thrones (plural) set in place at the end of the age. None of the other Old Testament views of God's Throne mention these thrones. The fact that they don't appear in Old Testament accounts, but do when the End of the Age is the context implies that they have been added since the cross. It could only be a reference to the Church.

Here's another interesting point to take notice of. We see in Rev. 4 verse one that John saw a door standing open in heaven. Compare this with Rev. 3:8 I know your deeds. See, I have placed before you an open door that no one can shut, and Rev. 3:10 Since you have kept my command to endure patiently, I will also keep you from the hour of trial that is going to come upon the whole world to test those who live on the earth. This is the promised rapture to the Church. After the rapture this door will be shut. Mt. 25:10 "But while they were on their way to buy the oil, the bridegroom arrived. The virgins who were ready went in with him to the wedding banquet. And the door was shut. 11"Later the others also came. 'Sir! Sir!' they said. 'Open the door for us!' 12"But he replied, 'I tell you the truth, I don't know you.'

13"Therefore keep watch, because you do not know the day or the hour

We can find no other place in the book of Revelation that meets all the conditions that we have seen from the scriptures that could be the time of the rapture. The Church is Raptured here in Rev. 4:1.

So, from Revelation and the other scriptures we've looked at earlier concerning the Rapture you can see that if you have accepted Jesus as your Lord and Savior and he is truly in your heart and life then you have nothing to fear from reading the book of Revelation, or of what the future holds for the world. You will find yourself being taken up when Jesus returns in the air to catch up those that are in him.

Titus 2:13 while we wait for the blessed hope—the glorious appearing of our great God and Savior, Jesus Christ,

4. Why The Church is Excluded From The Tribulation.

God's purpose for the tribulation, the last 7 years before Jesus returns back down to the earth, revolves around his plan for Israel and not the Church. God's plan for Israel is unfinished at this point in time. We see this from Daniel, there are 7 years left of the 490 years. God's plan for Israel does not require the Church to be present on earth. Israel and the Church are two separate entities. When the role and mission of the Church is completed then God will call his Son's bride home to heaven. This will clear the way for the completion of Daniel's 70th week.

The Tribulation Focuses on Israel

The Bible teaches that the tribulation is a time for the restoration of Israel, to bring them to repentance and the acceptance of Jesus as the Messiah. The Old Testament calls this time the time of Jacob's trouble, a reference to Israel. The emphasis of the Tribulation primarily focuses on the Jewish people. We can see this by Old Testament Scriptures (Deut. 4: 30; Jer. 30: 7; Ezek. 20: 37; Dan. 12:1; Zech. 13:8-9), by the Olivet Discourse, Jesus' Sermon on the Mount (Matt. 24:9-26), and by the book of Revelation (Rev. 7:4-8; 12:1-2; 17, etc.). In Daniel chapter 9, we see that the angel Gabriel told Daniel it was a time for his people, Israel and the Holy City of Jerusalem.

We see in Old and New Testament Scriptures including Revelation that the tribulation deals with Jews and Gentiles, the preaching of the "gospel of the kingdom," flight on the "sabbath," the temple and the "holy place," the land of Judea, the city of Jerusalem, the twelve "tribes of the children of Israel," the covenant between the anti-Christ, the beast, and Israel, the stopping of the sacrifice and offerings, entering into the temple causing the abomination that causes desolation. All of this has to do with Israel and not the Church. None of it pertains to the Church. This clearly demonstrates that the Tribulation is mostly a time when God deals with His ancient Jewish people prior to their entrance into the promised kingdom. All the Old Testament prophesies to Israel that have yet to be fulfilled further indicate a future time when God will deal with this nation (Deut. 30:1-6; Jer. 30:8-10, etc.). God does not break his promises.

> **Deut. 30**: 1 When all these blessings and curses I have set before you come upon you and you take them to heart wherever the LORD your God disperses you among the nations, 2 and when you and your children return to the LORD your God and obey him with all your heart and with all your soul according to everything I command you today, 3 then the LORD your God will restore your fortunes and have compassion on you and gather you again from all the nations where he scattered you. 4 Even if you have been banished to the most distant land under the heavens, from there the LORD your God will gather you and bring you back. 5 He will bring you to the land that belonged to your fathers, and you will take possession of it. He will make you more prosperous and numerous than your fathers. 6 The LORD your God will circumcise your hearts and the hearts of your descendants, so that you may love him with all your heart and with all your soul, and live.

This re-gathering will be completed after Jesus returns. At that time all the Jews will be returned to Israel.

> **Jer. 30**: 7 How awful that day will be!
> None will be like it.
> It will be a time of trouble for Jacob,
> but he will be saved out of it.
>
> 10 " 'So do not fear, O Jacob my servant;
> do not be dismayed, O Israel,'
> declares the LORD.
> I will surely save you out of a distant place,
> your descendents from their land of exile.
> Jacob will again have peace and security,
> and no one will make him afraid.

11 I am with you and will save you,'
declares the LORD.
'Though I completely destroy all the nations
among which I scatter you,
I will not completely destroy you.
I will discipline you but only with justice;
I will not let you go entirely unpunished.'

None of this applies to the Church, to Christians.

It is a time to judge the nations for how they have treated Israel.

Joel 3: 1 "In those days and at that time,
when I restore the fortunes of Judah and Jerusalem,
2 I will gather all nations
and bring them down to the Valley of Jehoshaphat.
There I will enter into judgment against them
concerning my inheritance, my people Israel,
for they scattered my people among the nations
and divided up my land.

Ps. 83: 3 With cunning they conspire against your people;
they plot against those you cherish.

4 "Come," they say, "let us destroy them as a nation,
that the name of Israel be remembered no more."

Zech. 12: 8 On that day the LORD will shield those who live in Jerusalem, so that the feeblest among them will be like David, and the house of David will be like God, like the Angel of the LORD going before them. 9 On that day I will set out to destroy all the nations that attack Jerusalem.

It's also a time for judging those for their sin and for rejecting Jesus.

Rev. 9: 20The rest of mankind that were not killed by these plagues still did not repent of the work of their hands; they did not stop worshiping demons, and idols of gold, silver, bronze, stone and wood—idols that cannot see or hear or walk. 21Nor did they repent of their murders, their magic arts, their sexual immorality or their thefts.

Rev. 16: 8The fourth angel poured out his bowl on the sun, and the sun was given power to scorch people with fire. 9They were seared by the intense heat and they cursed the name of God, who had control over these plagues, but they refused to repent and glorify him.

If the bible does indeed teach a pre-trib rapture of the Church then we shouldn't see any mention of the Church as to being present during the tribulation. That's exactly what we see. All we see is Israel and the gentile nations.

The Church is excluded from the tribulation because it is a time for Judging Israel and the nations. Since the true believers have not rejected Christ and have already been tested before the tribulation, we see the Church (Christians) are being judged in the first 3 chapters of Revelation, then it does not require the Church to be present during the time of God's judgment on Israel and on those that have rejected Christ before the rapture. Thankfully there will be many that come to accept Jesus after the rapture, both Jew and Gentile.

With the Church in heaven during the tribulation, it enables God's focus to once again be on Israel. He can once again act through his chosen people. Nowhere do we see the tribulation saints given the special and peculiar promises given to the church. The nature of the church is in contrast to Israel therefore becomes an argument supporting the pre-tribulation rapture viewpoint.

God's purpose for the tribulation is to judge and restore Israel (Jer. 30:3, 10) and to judge the Gentiles (Jer. 30:11) before the establishment of his kingdom, it is clear that this purpose does not include the church since those of the Church are already going into the kingdom of God.

5. The Seven Churches – Rev. Chapters 1 through 3.

Rev. 1: 4John,

> To the seven churches in the province of Asia:

> Grace and peace to you from him who is, and who was, and who is to come, and from the seven spirits before his throne, 5and from Jesus Christ, who is the faithful witness, the firstborn from the dead, and the ruler of the kings of the earth.

> To him who loves us and has freed us from our sins by his blood, 6and has made us to be a kingdom and priests to serve his God and Father—to him be glory and power for ever and ever! Amen.

The original recipients of the Book of Revelation were seven churches in Asia Minor. But the book was obviously intended to reach much farther than to just those Christians of the first century A.D.

John greets the believers of the seven churches of Asia, over whom he had become the bishop or "overseer" after Paul's death. His greeting is similar to most of Paul's epistles in that it offers "grace and peace."

The greeting is also from Him "who is, and who was, and who is to come." This is undoubtedly a reference to God the Father. This statement shows the eternal existence of God the Father. We see in chapter 21 that after God creates a New Heaven and New Earth that God the Father will now dwell here on earth.

The Seven Spirits before His throne identifies the Holy Spirit. The number seven is used repeatedly in the Bible to indicate completeness or perfection. Thus the Seven Spirits would mean the perfect, complete Spirit, the fullness of God the Father, Son and Holy Spirit.

The greeting is also from Jesus Christ, who is the faithful witness, the firstborn from the dead, and the ruler of the kings of the earth. We see all three persons of the Holy Trinity are involved in the giving of this revelation.

The "firstborn from the dead," is an obvious reference to His Resurrection. He is "the ruler of the kings of the earth," is a preview of His glorious return mentioned in verse 7, and his reigning during the earthly Kingdom of God.

> 7Look, he is coming with the clouds,
> and every eye will see him,
> even those who pierced him;
> and all the peoples of the earth will mourn because of him. So shall it be! Amen. 8"I am the Alpha and the Omega," says the Lord God, "who is, and who was, and who is to come, the Almighty."

John here was quoting Zechariah 12 verse 10. It's also what Jesus said in Matthew chapter 24 verse 30.

> Rev. 1: 9 I, John, your brother and companion in the suffering and kingdom and patient endurance that are ours in Jesus, was on the island of Patmos because of the word of God and the testimony of Jesus. 10On the Lord's Day I was in the Spirit, and I heard behind me a loud voice like a trumpet, 11which said: "Write on a scroll what you see and send it to the seven churches: to Ephesus, Smyrna, Pergamum, Thyatira, Sardis, Philadelphia and Laodicea."

In John's day these were 7 actual Church's in Asia Minor. Scholars have wondered why this book would be sent to these Churches since they weren't even the largest or most important of their day, let alone now. Ephesus was a leading city of the time, but the Church there was small as were the others. Why wasn't the book written to the Church in Rome?

Why these 7 Church's?

One reason Jesus chose these 7 churches, is that they typify how the Church was at different stages throughout Church history. I won't go into all of the stages of the Church now but I want to point out that the Laodicean Church is the last one before Jesus returns for his bride, the true Church, those that really belong to Christ. These 7 Churches also typify the way Church denominations and non-denominational Churches are today. I believe the main reason Jesus chose these 7 churches is that not only do they describe a lot of the denominations of today, and the Church through history, but one of these characteristics of each of these churches can be seen in each individual Christian, then and all down through history.

While you can see the characteristics that Jesus commended some of the Church's for in each individual Christian, you also have the things that Jesus rebuked. Read chapters 2 and 3 for Jesus' word to the Churches.

You can find some that have forsaken their first love. You have some that hold to false teachings and committing sexual immorality. Then there are those while they may not be involved in false teachings or immorality, they tolerate it, they accept false religions and their teachings. While we should accept them as people, we shouldn't accept their false teachings as just another way to God. You have some that are asleep, dead spiritually. And you have some that have come to tolerate sin. They have become passive to it, they are neither hot nor cold, they're lukewarm. Lukewarm doesn't mean just spiritually to the things of God like not going to Church or reading your bible. Read what Jesus had to say to the Laodicean Church, it's the harshest rebuke.

Rev.3:14"To the angel of the church in Laodicea write: These are the words of the Amen, the faithful and true witness, the ruler of God's creation. 15I know your deeds, that you are neither cold nor hot. I wish you were either one or the other! 16So, because you are lukewarm—neither hot nor cold—I am about to spit you out of my mouth. 17You say, 'I am rich; I have acquired wealth and do not need a thing.' But you do not realize that you are wretched, pitiful, poor, blind and naked. 18I counsel you to buy from me gold refined in the fire, so you can become rich; and white clothes to wear, so you can cover your shameful nakedness; and salve to put on your eyes, so you can see. 19Those whom I love I rebuke and discipline. So be earnest, and repent. 20Here I am! I stand at the door and knock. If anyone hears my voice and opens the door, I will come in and eat with him, and he with me. 21To him who overcomes, I will give the right to sit with me on my throne, just as I overcame and sat down with my Father on his throne. 22He who has an ear, let him hear what the Spirit says to the churches."

Today, not only can you see these characteristics in individuals but also in different denominations. Some of the things that some Church denominations allow now is a slap in God's face. You can definitely see the apostate Laodicean Church today. Jesus didn't find anything to his liking with this Church. There are Churches condoning sin. Paul in 2 Thessalonians 2 verse 10 said of anyone who does not accept the truth, 'They perish because they refused to love the truth and so be saved.' Jesus loves everyone, even those that are living a sinful life. The bible says in 2 Peter 3 verse 9, He is patient with you, not wanting anyone to perish, but everyone to come to repentance. And don't forget John 3: 16 'For God so loved the world that He gave His only begotten Son, that whoever believes in Him should not perish but have everlasting life.' That means anyone who repents and turns to Jesus. The bible is clear; if a person is living in any kind of sinful lifestyle they are either a lukewarm Christian or not in Jesus. If they have not repented they are not in Jesus. The way the world and some Churches are accepting what the bible clearly calls sin are pushing the one true God farther and farther away. The world is becoming a world without God. In the book of Revelation we see this is exactly what happens.

There are many denominations and non-denominational pastors or teachers that don't believe what the bible teaches, don't believe in whom Jesus is and what he taught. They are not part of the true Church of Jesus Christ. They are not in Jesus. Jesus will say to them, I never knew you, away from me you evildoers. Matthew 7 21-23.

For example, there are some that are denying the Deity of Jesus, the authority of the Word, the Virgin birth, the miracles of Jesus and have taken the cross out of their Church. Many have even taken Jesus out of their sermons and teachings. There are many ministers, Pastors that have watered down their teaching and sermons. They don't teach the full gospel. There is no mention of sin and its consequences. No mention that you must repent first. There are even some that teach that there's no Satan and there's not an actual hell. I just don't understand, with so much in the bible about Satan and hell, even in the New Testament, in the gospels from the words of Jesus and from the Apostle Paul. All of Paul's letters were written after the cross and Jesus' resurrection. Oh and there are those that don't believe Jesus literally rose from the dead, they don't believe he rose physically. They have become apostate Christians, the apostate Church. Apostasy means an abandonment or desertion of principles or faith. It's obvious that there's many in the Church that don't read the bible for themselves. I could go on and on. These denominations or ministers would fall under all of the rebukes listed to the Churches. Look how the Message bible words this, Rev. 3:15-17" I know you inside and out, and find little to my liking. You're not cold, you're not hot—far better to be either cold or hot! You're stale. You're stagnant. You make me want to vomit. You brag, 'I'm rich, I've got it made, I need nothing from anyone,' oblivious that in fact you're a pitiful, blind beggar, threadbare and homeless.

Take a look at what Paul said the last days would be like. He not only describes the world now but unfortunately a lot in the Church.

1 Timothy 4: 1The Spirit clearly says that in later times some will abandon the faith and follow deceiving spirits and things taught by demons.

2 Timothy 3

1But mark this: There will be terrible times in the last days. 2People will be lovers of themselves, lovers of money, boastful, proud, abusive, disobedient to their parents, ungrateful, unholy, 3without love, unforgiving, slanderous, without self-control, brutal, not lovers of the good, 4treacherous, rash, conceited, lovers of pleasure rather than lovers of God— 5having a form of godliness but denying its power. Have nothing to do with them.

1 Corinthians 6: 9Do you not know that the wicked will not inherit the kingdom of God? Do not be deceived: Neither the sexually immoral nor idolaters nor adulterers nor male prostitutes nor homosexual offenders 10nor thieves nor the greedy nor drunkards nor slanderers nor swindlers will inherit the kingdom of God.

But he says of those who have truly repented, that have changed.

11And that is what some of you were. But you were washed, you were sanctified, you were justified in the name of the Lord Jesus Christ and by the Spirit of our God.

Read from Paul's letter to the Church at Rome.

Romans chapter 1.

God's Wrath Against Mankind

18The wrath of God is being revealed from heaven against all the godlessness and wickedness of men who suppress the truth by their wickedness, 19since what may be known about God is plain to them, because God has made it plain to them. 20For since the creation of the world God's invisible qualities—his eternal power and divine nature—have been clearly seen, being understood from what has been made, so that men are without excuse.

21For although they knew God, they neither glorified him as God nor gave thanks to him, but their thinking became futile and their foolish hearts were darkened. 22Although they claimed to be wise, they became fools 23and exchanged the glory of the immortal God for images made to look like mortal man and birds and animals and reptiles.

24Therefore God gave them over in the sinful desires of their hearts to sexual impurity for the degrading of their bodies with one another. 25They exchanged the truth of God for a lie, and worshiped and served created things rather than the Creator—who is forever praised. Amen.

26Because of this, God gave them over to shameful lusts. Even their women exchanged natural relations for unnatural ones. 27In the same way the men also abandoned natural relations with women and were inflamed with lust for one another. Men committed indecent acts with other men, and received in themselves the due penalty for their perversion.

28Furthermore, since they did not think it worthwhile to retain the knowledge of God, he gave them over to a depraved mind, to do what ought not to be done. 29They have become filled with every kind of wickedness, evil, greed and depravity. They are full of envy, murder, strife, deceit and malice. They are gossips, 30slanderers, God-haters, insolent, arrogant and boastful; they invent ways of doing evil; they disobey their parents; 31they are senseless, faithless, heartless, ruthless. 32Although they know God's righteous decree that those who do such things deserve death, they not only continue to do these very things but also approve of those who practice them.

Look at the harsh rebuke from Peter concerning false teachers.

2 Peter chapter 2.

False Teachers and Their Destruction

1But there were also false prophets among the people, just as there will be false teachers among you. They will secretly introduce destructive heresies, even denying the sovereign Lord who bought them—bringing swift destruction on themselves. 2Many will follow their shameful ways and will bring the way of truth into disrepute. 3In their greed these teachers will exploit you with stories they have made up. Their condemnation has long been hanging over them, and their destruction has not been sleeping.

4For if God did not spare angels when they sinned, but sent them to hell, putting them into gloomy dungeons to be held for judgment; 5if he did not spare the ancient world when he brought the flood on its ungodly people, but protected Noah, a preacher of righteousness, and seven others; 6if he condemned the cities of Sodom and Gomorrah by burning them to ashes, and made them an example of what is going to happen to the ungodly; 7and if he rescued Lot, a righteous man, who was distressed by the filthy lives of lawless men 8(for that righteous man, living among them day after day, was tormented in his righteous soul by the lawless deeds he saw and heard)— 9if this is so, then the Lord knows how to rescue godly men from trials and to hold the unrighteous for the day of judgment, while continuing their punishment. 10This is especially true of those who follow the corrupt desire of the sinful nature and despise authority. Bold and arrogant, these men are not afraid to slander celestial beings; 11yet even angels, although they are stronger and more powerful, do not bring slanderous accusations against such beings in the presence of the Lord. 12But these men blaspheme in matters they do not understand. They are like brute beasts, creatures of instinct, born only to be caught and destroyed, and like beasts they too will perish.

13They will be paid back with harm for the harm they have done. Their idea of pleasure is to carouse in broad daylight. They are blots and blemishes, reveling in their pleasures while they feast with you. 14With eyes full of adultery, they never stop sinning; they seduce the unstable; they are experts in greed—an accursed brood! 15They have left the straight way and wandered off to follow the way of Balaam son of Beor, who loved the wages of wickedness. 16But he was rebuked for his wrongdoing by a donkey—a beast without speech—who spoke with a man's voice and restrained the prophet's madness.

To see what Peter was referring to here, about Balaam, see Numbers chapter 22.

17These men are springs without water and mists driven by a storm. Blackest darkness is reserved for them. 18For they mouth empty, boastful words and, by appealing to the lustful desires of sinful human nature, they entice people who are just escaping from those who live in error. 19They promise them freedom, while they themselves are slaves of depravity—for a man is a slave to whatever has mastered him. 20If they have escaped the corruption of the world by knowing our Lord and Savior Jesus Christ and are again entangled in it and overcome, they are worse off at the end than they were at the beginning. 21It would have been better for them not to have known the way of righteousness, than to have known it and then to turn their backs on the sacred command that was passed on to them. 22Of them the proverbs are true: "A dog returns to its vomit," and, "A sow that is washed goes back to her wallowing in the mud."

Look at what Paul said in his letter to the Galatians.

Gal. 1: 6I am astonished that you are so quickly deserting the one who called you by the grace of Christ and are turning to a different gospel— 7which is really no gospel at all. Evidently some people are throwing you into confusion and are trying to pervert the gospel of Christ. 8But even if we or an angel from heaven should preach a gospel other than the one we preached to you, let him be eternally condemned! 9As we have already said, so now I say again: If anybody is preaching to you a gospel other than what you accepted, let him be eternally condemned!

This is not only going to be the outcome for teachers of false religions, but also for the apostate Christians and ministers that have wander away from the truth, they have wandered away from the faith. They are not preaching the gospel of Jesus Christ.

All this will be the characteristic of the new false one word religion during the tribulation. We see this religious system described in chapter 17 as a great prostitute.

These false teachers make me wonder if they were ever saved at all. Is there hope for these false teachers and preachers? Sure, if they repent and confess that they were wrong and start teaching and preaching the true word of God. By the Grace of God they will be forgiven, but if they don't.....

God's judgment,

Romans 2:

5But because of your stubbornness and your unrepentant heart, you are storing up wrath against yourself for the day of God's wrath, when his righteous judgment will be revealed. 6God "will give to each person according to what he has done." 7To those who by persistence in doing good seek glory, honor and immortality, he will give eternal life. 8But for those who are self-seeking and who reject the truth and follow evil, there will be wrath and anger. 9There will be trouble and distress for every human being who does evil: first for the Jew, then for the Gentile; 10but glory, honor and peace for everyone who does good: first for the Jew, then for the Gentile. 11For God does not show favoritism

Has God's position changed since this was written, no,

> Hebrews 13: 8Jesus Christ is the same yesterday and today and forever.

The Church has been commissioned to preach the Gospel, which includes speaking against sin, all sin regardless of what it is. The ultimate reason is that maybe some will come to realize the truth and turn away from their sin and turn to Jesus.

> Romans 6: 23For the wages of sin is death, but the gift of God is eternal life in Christ Jesus our Lord.

Now, as for these messages being prophetic concerning Church history, look at this word to the Smyrna Church. It shows you just how accurate bible prophecy is.

The Smyrna Church

> Rev. 2: 8"To the angel of the church in Smyrna write:
> These are the words of him who is the First and the Last, who died and came to life again. 9I know your afflictions and your poverty—yet you are rich! I know the slander of those who say they are Jews and are not, but are a synagogue of Satan. 10Do not be afraid of what you are about to suffer. I tell you, the devil will put some of you in prison to test you, and you will suffer persecution for ten days. Be faithful, even to the point of death, and I will give you the crown of life. 11He who has an ear, let him hear what the Spirit says to the churches. He who overcomes will not be hurt at all by the second death.

With Rev. 2:10 saying to the Smyrna Church "you will suffer persecution for ten days". Most Bible interpreters believe that the "ten days" apply prophetically to the ten eras of persecution under ten diabolical Caesars: Nero, A.D. 64-68; Domitian, who exiled John to Patmos about 90-95; Trajan, 104-117; Aurelius, 161-180; Severus, 200-211; Maximus, 235-237; Decius, 250-253; Valerian, 257-260; Aurelian, 270-275; Diocletian, 303-312.

They suffered persecution up until Rome adopted Christianity as the state religion. It was the fourth century when Constantine declared Christianity to be the official religion of the Roman Empire.

To the Church in Philadelphia

Now look at this word in chapter 3 to the Philadelphia Church and the promise they receive.

7"To the angel of the church in Philadelphia write:
These are the words of him who is holy and true, who holds the key of David. What he opens no one can shut, and what he shuts no one can open. 8I know your deeds. See, I have placed before you an open door that no one can shut. I know that you have little strength, yet you have kept my word and have not denied my name. 9I will make those who are of the synagogue of Satan, who claim to be Jews though they are not, but are liars—I will make them come and fall down at your feet and acknowledge that I have loved you. 10Since you have kept my command to endure patiently, <u>I will also keep you from the hour of trial that is going to come upon the whole world to test those who live on the earth.</u> 11I am coming soon. Hold on to what you have, so that no one will take your crown. 12Him who overcomes I will make a pillar in the temple of my God. Never again will he leave it. I will write on him the name of my God and the name of the city of my God, the new Jerusalem, which is coming down out of heaven from my God; and I will also write on him my new name. 13He who has an ear, let him hear what the Spirit says to the churches.

We see a promise is made to those that are truly part of the Church that are living in the last days just before the tribulation that they will be kept from the hour of trial that is coming upon the world.

Here Jesus said that he would keep the Church from the time of the hour of trail, remove the Church from it altogether. Remember the Strong's Greek Lexicon translation G1537 is (out of, from, by, away from). It is not keep 'through' as the post-trib view says.

The Apostle Paul said these true believers will be caught up to meet the Lord in the air to be taken back with Jesus to be in heaven during the 7 years of the tribulation. 1 Thessalonians 4:15-17.

6. The Coming One World Government and its leader:

The Beast with 7 Heads & 10 Horns

In the book of Revelation, John describes a beast with 7 heads and 10 horns. This descriptive picture symbolizes a panoramic view of kingdoms that have ruled throughout history.

Revelation 12:3 Then another sign appeared in heaven: an enormous red dragon with seven heads and ten horns and seven crowns on his heads.

This represents Satan's dominion over the 7 world empires:

1. Egypt
2. Assyria
3. Babylon
4. Medo-Persia
5. Greece
6. Rome
7. Future Revived Roman Empire. The 10 horns are placed on this Empire, based upon Daniel 7:23-25. The 10 horns are 10 kings, which arise in the future (Dan. 7:24). This is the kingdom from which the Antichrist will arise. As I've mentioned already what you've heard or read in the news about globalization; well this is it, this is where the world is headed. We see there is now a big movement to move the world to this one world global government with even certain leaders of the U.S. moving towards accepting this. The financial collapse all over the world is leading the world towards this 10 horn kingdom the bible describes. Isn't this amazing to see this happening, and that the bible foretold this. You know, I haven't heard or read this from any of the 'more popular' prophecies of Nostradamus, the I-Ching, the Mayan Calendar, Merlin or others.

We are told the dragon is Satan in verse 9 of chapter 12, the great dragon was hurled down—that ancient serpent called the devil, or

Satan, who leads the whole world astray. (He will be hurled to the earth, and his angels with him after the first 3 ½ years of the tribulation). We see this in chapter 13 along with a description of the one world government, 'the new world order'.

> Rev. 13:1 And I saw a beast coming out of the sea. He had ten horns and seven heads, with ten crowns on his horns, and on each head a blasphemous name. 2The beast I saw resembled a leopard, but had feet like those of a bear and a mouth like that of a lion. The dragon gave the beast his power and his throne and great authority. 3One of the heads of the beast seemed to have had a fatal wound, but the fatal wound had been healed.

Verse 2 describes the beast as a leopard, a bear, and a lion. These are the same beasts as described in Daniel 7:4-6, except in reverse order. Daniel was looking into the future to see these kingdoms, while the apostle John looks back on them as fulfilled in history. Throughout the book of Revelation we can see John referring back to Daniel. The kingdoms were Egypt, Assyria, Babylon (lion-Daniel 7:4), Medo-Persia (bear-Daniel 7:5), Greece (leopard-Daniel 7:6) and Rome the kingdom that was ruling at the time.

Verse 3 could be a reference to when the anti-Christ is killed and then Satan enters into him, his fatal wound being healed, for we see he receives a fatal wound by the sword. Whether this is in battle or by assassination it doesn't say. We first see this mentioned in verse 9 of chapter 12.

Notice the order of these statements

> Rev. 12: 9 The great dragon was hurled down—that ancient serpent called the devil, or Satan, who leads the whole world astray.

> Rev. 13: 3One of the heads of the beast seemed to have had a fatal wound, but the fatal wound had been healed.

We also see this in Rev. 13:14 along with reference to the false prophet in the first part of the scripture.

> Rev. 13: 14Because of the signs he was given power to do on behalf of the first beast, he deceived the inhabitants of the earth. He ordered them to set up an image in honor of the beast <u>who was wounded by the sword and yet lived</u>.

It will be at the mid-point of the tribulation that the anti-Christ will be killed and Satan actually enters into him. During the last half of the tribulation this empire will truly become a beast.

With Rome being the 6th head, verse 3 could also be referring to the Rome of John's day, receiving a fatal wound, then being revived later thus becoming the Revived Roman Empire. Rome wasn't conquered by another kingdom as was all the previous kingdoms. Rome morally decayed and fell from within. Rome had become so corrupt that it couldn't stand any longer. This is another clue that Rome will be revived.

If you do a comparison of the birth of Rome to its fall with the United States you will see amazing similarities. You can see that the condition and makeup of the U.S. is remarkably the same as Rome was when it fell. If Rome is to be any kind of example for the U.S. then if we stay on this course, then the U.S. is headed for the same outcome as Rome. Rome had mounted up a massive debt, was over taxing the people and was in moral decay. Sound familiar? If you would like to learn more of the comparison of the U.S. to Rome, go to Perry Stones web site. He has a DVD on the subject.

It is interesting how John starts off describing the world kingdoms from the past up to the last revived Roman Empire, the kingdom of the anti-Christ and connects Satan with all these kingdoms. In the last part of verse 2 John said 'The dragon gave the beast his power and his throne and great authority'. Satan has been the one controlling and giving all the world empires throughout history their power, of course only because God has allowed it.

Rev. 13: 4Men worshiped the dragon because he had given authority to the beast, and they also worshiped the beast and asked, "Who is like the beast? Who can make war against him?"

With the world now having a global government and monetary system everyone will be thinking there now will be no more war, we are all now one, no one nation could make war with this new global government. Of course the man, the anti-Christ will get credit for it so the world will worship him and think there's no way anyone would dare to come against him. But as you will see here in the book of Revelation it all will soon fall apart.

5The beast was given a mouth to utter proud words and blasphemies and to exercise his authority for forty-two months. 6He opened his mouth to blaspheme God, and to slander his name and his dwelling place and those who live in heaven.7He was given power to make war against the saints and to conquer them. And he was given authority over every tribe, people, language and nation.

We see in Rev. 13 verse 6 that the beast (the anti-Christ, Satan) will blaspheme God, slander his name and his dwelling place and those who live in heaven. Those who live in heaven are the Church age Saints that were Raptured. It says that the beast will be given power to make war against the saints and to conquer them. This cannot be the Church Saints because Jesus said the gates of hell would not prevail against his Church. Matthew 16:18. But, Satan will conquer the Jews. They will have to flee. And as we have seen, he will also conquer all those that have been saved since the rapture, all those that call on the name of Jesus. Read Revelation chapter 12 again.

The reason those that accept Jesus during the tribulation are not part of the Church is that the time during the tribulation is back under the Old Testament Covenant of Israel. This is the time of Jacobs's trouble, Israel's last 7 years allotted to them from Daniel chapter 9.

385

Apparently, people will worship Satan, the anti-Christ <u>and</u> this new one world government.

> Rev. 13: 8All inhabitants of the earth will worship the beast—all whose names have not been written in the book of life belonging to the Lamb that was slain from the creation of the world.

We see this also in chapter 17. By him saying the beast will come up out of the Abyss we see this is referring to Satan. Satan was once here on the earth. We know he was in the serpent in the Garden of Eden. For now he is not here physically. He will be here again in the anti-Christ.

> 8The beast, which you saw, once was, now is not, and will come up out of the Abyss and go to his destruction. The inhabitants of the earth whose names have not been written in the book of life from the creation of the world will be astonished when they see the beast, because he once was, now is not, and yet will come.

With verse 9 and 10 John gives a word to those that will be living during the last half of the tribulation.

> Rev. 13: 9He who has an ear, let him hear.
> 10If anyone is to go into captivity, into captivity he will go.
> If anyone is to be killed with the sword, with the sword he will be killed. This calls for patient endurance and faithfulness on the part of the saints.

With verse 14 of chapter 17 we see the outcome.

> Rev. 17: 14They will make war against the Lamb, but the Lamb will overcome them because he is Lord of lords and King of kings—and with him will be his called, chosen and faithful followers."

Daniel 2:44 also tells us "and in the days of those kings the God of heaven will set up a kingdom which will never be destroyed..." That means when Jesus returns to earth to set up His Millennial Kingdom, he will destroy the Antichrist (Satan) and the kingdom he rules.

I believe that Jesus will actually take over this 10-region world kingdom. The one world government will have already been established, Jesus will just take it over and use it to rule and govern through. He will need some way of governing the world. I'm sure he will appoint leaders or kings over each area. The bible does say he is the King of Kings.

The Seven Kings in Revelation 17

Rev. 17:9-10 tells us the 7 heads are 7 mountains and 7 kings. "Mountains" in the Bible are symbolic of kingdoms or governments. (See Ps. 30:7, Jer. 51:24-25, Dan. 2:35, 44).

9"This calls for a mind with wisdom. The seven heads are seven hills on which the woman sits. 10They are also seven kings. Five have fallen, one is, the other has not yet come; but when he does come, he must remain for a little while.

John is seeing, recording, and commenting on the past and future. This passage is providing a landscape of biblical history of the past, the present of John's time and to a future kingdom. The five that are fallen refer to the kingdoms of Egypt, Assyria, Babylon, Medes/Persia, and Greece. The sixth empire that was reigning at the time when John wrote the book of Revelation was Rome. Verse 9 is a coded verse that referred to Rome. In writing the book of Revelation John couldn't come right out and name Rome even when he was addressing a future empire of Rome. The Romans would have never let the book go out; they would have destroyed it and killed John for being an enemy of Rome, we see this also with his reference to Babylon. The city of Rome actually sits on 7 heals. This is another clue that Rome will be revived, and remember that Daniel's description said this beast was different from all the others. This last beast will be a culmination of all the past empires. This last beast will control the whole world. The seventh that is to come will be the future kingdom of the antichrist, described here in Revelation as the Beast. This is the new one world, global government.

> Revelation 17:10, says that the future leader and his empire will last for only a short time, "he must remain for a little while." And in Rev. 12:12, "he knows that his time is short". God is saying that He has decreed the time of this final empire will be shorter than the six previous.

Satan becomes the leader of the new one world government.

> Rev. 17: 8The beast, which you saw, once was, now is not, and will come up out of the Abyss and go to his destruction. The inhabitants of the earth whose names have not been written in the book of life from the creation of the world will be astonished when they see the beast, because he once was, now is not, and yet will come.

> Rev. 17: 11The beast who once was, and now is not, is an eighth king. He belongs to the seven and is going to his destruction.

Notice with verse 11 the mention of an eighth king and that he belongs to the 7. I believe that this eighth king is Satan indwelling the antichrist.

Satan is the only one that could be described as once was and will come up out of the Abyss. Verse 11 says he is an eighth king. The man, the anti-Christ would be the seventh king, then Satan in the anti-Christ will be the eighth. Some scholars don't believe the anti-Christ will actually be killed and raised up because Satan doesn't have the power to raise someone from the dead. Well, this will be a unique situation. Revelation chapter 13 verse 3 and 12 says he receives a fatal wound. In any event, whether the anti-Christ is killed or not Satan will indwell his body and at least appear to raise him from the dead. He will now truly be the little horn mentioned in Daniel. Dan. 7:19-25 describes the Antichrist as ruling this empire.

Most of Revelation is dealing with the second half of the 7 years. It's in the middle of the tribulation, after the first 3 ½ years are over that Satan enters into the antichrist. He had been a puppet of Satan up to this time.

Chapter 12 describes Satan being cast down to the earth.

> Rev. 12: 7And there was war in heaven. Michael and his angels fought against the dragon, and the dragon and his angels fought back. 8But he was not strong enough, and they lost their place in heaven. 9The great dragon was hurled down—that ancient serpent called the devil, or Satan, who leads the whole world astray. He was hurled to the earth, and his angels with him.

We see this prophesied in Isaiah chapter 14.

> 12 How you have fallen from heaven,
> O morning star, son of the dawn!
> You have been cast down to the earth,
> you who once laid low the nations!
> 13 You said in your heart,
> "I will ascend to heaven;
> I will raise my throne
> above the stars of God;
> I will sit enthroned on the mount of assembly,
> on the utmost heights of the sacred mountain.
> 14 I will ascend above the tops of the clouds;
> I will make myself like the Most High."

Read Isaiah chapter 14, you see that it is describing the tribulation, Israel being protected and brought back to their land, the anti-Christ and Satan being cast down to the grave and the pit. Revelation chapter 19 describes both the anti-Christ and the false prophet being cast into the lake of fire. Chapter 20 we see Satan bound in the Abyss. This prophesy starts in chapter 13.

You see again in chapter 13 that John tells us that it is Satan, the dragon that gives the anti-Christ and his kingdom its power.

Verse one of chapter 13 says that the beast had ten horns and seven heads, with ten crowns on his horns, and on each head a blasphemous name. This last one world government will be made up of 10 regions. We saw this first describe in Daniel chapter 2 with the statue of the feet with 10 toes.

> Dan.2: 31 You looked, O king, and there before you stood a large statue—an enormous, dazzling statue, awesome in appearance. 32 The head of the statue was made of pure gold, its chest and arms of silver, its belly and thighs of bronze, 33 its legs of iron, its feet partly of iron and partly of baked clay.
>
> 41 Just as you saw that the feet and toes were partly of baked clay and partly of iron, so this will be a divided kingdom; yet it will have some of the strength of iron in it, even as you saw iron mixed with clay. 42 As the toes were partly iron and partly clay, so this kingdom will be partly strong and partly brittle. 43 And just as you saw the iron mixed with baked clay, so the people will be a mixture and will not remain united, any more than iron mixes with clay.

The beast has seven heads with ten horns on the seventh head with 10 crowns that are ten kings. We see this described further in Revelation chapter 17.

> Rev. 17: 12"The ten horns you saw are ten kings who have not yet received a kingdom, but who for one hour will receive authority as kings along with the beast. 13They have one purpose and will give their power and authority to the beast. 14They will make war against the Lamb, but the Lamb will overcome them because he is Lord of lords and King of

kings—and with him will be his called, chosen and faithful followers."

With each head having a blasphemous name shows that each one will be opposed to Jesus. This last one world government will be anti-Christ. With Daniel's vision of the statue and here in Revelation we see that Satan has been behind all the world's kingdoms and that the last kingdom will be made up of characteristics of all the past kingdoms. We can see this now with the governments of the world including the United States.

Once Satan has entered into the anti-Christ, this 10-horn kingdom will definitely become a beast. It's during the second half of the tribulation period that Satan will make war against the Lamp, Rev. 17:14, make war against the saints, Rev.13: 7, he pursues the woman (Israel) who had given birth to the male child, Rev.12:13. I will explain this more later, this male child is Jesus. And it's when the false prophet will force everyone, small and great, rich and poor, free and slave, to receive a mark on his right hand or on his forehead, so that no one could buy or sell unless he had the mark, which is the name of the beast or the number of his name, Rev 13:16,17.

What is the difference between the 7 kings (represented by 7 heads) and the 10 kings (represented by 10 horns)?

The 7 kings (v.10) are **successive kingdoms** because they rule one after another over centuries of time. The 10 kings (v.12) are **contemporaneous kings** who rule at the same time in history. This verse tells us the 10 horns are 10 kings who "have not yet received a kingdom" at the time Revelation was written in 95 or 96 A.D. Because the 10 horns are on the 7th head, these 10 kings will come to power in the future Revived Roman Empire, the coming one world government.

We saw these 10 horns in Daniel chapter 7.

Daniel 7: 7 "After that, in my vision at night I looked, and there before me was a fourth beast—terrifying and frightening and very powerful. It had large iron teeth; it crushed and devoured its victims and trampled underfoot whatever was left. It was different from all the former beasts, and it had ten horns.

8 "While I was thinking about the horns, there before me was another horn, a little one, which came up among them; and three of the first horns were uprooted before it. This horn had eyes like the eyes of a man and a mouth that spoke boastfully.

20 I also wanted to know about the ten horns on its head and about the other horn that came up, before which three of them fell—the horn that looked more imposing than the others and that had eyes and a mouth that spoke boastfully.

23 "He gave me this explanation: 'The fourth beast is a fourth kingdom that will appear on earth. It will be different from all the other kingdoms and will devour the whole earth, trampling it down and crushing it. 24 The ten horns are ten kings who will come from this kingdom. After them another king will arise, different from the earlier ones; he will subdue three kings. 25 He will speak against the Most High and oppress his saints and try to change the set times and the laws. The saints will be handed over to him for a time, times and half a time.

Read Revelation chapters 12, 13 and 17.

Compare the 'another king' from Daniel 7 verse 24 with Revelation 17 verse 11, The beast who once was, and now is not, is an eighth king. He belongs to the seven and is going to his destruction.

Notice Revelation chapter 17 verse 12 says that they would only receive authority as kings for one hour; verse 13 tells us the purpose for these 10 kings is to give their power and authority over to the beast, the anti-Christ. These 10 kings are appointed by the anti-Christ (Satan) only to sign their authority over to him. John says they only have authority for one hour. This apparently will take place after the first 3 ½ years, after Satan has entered into the man, the anti-Christ.

These 10 regions, the one world government will already exist before the 2nd half of the tribulation, before Satan enters into the anti-Christ. We see in Daniel chapter 7 verses 8 and 24 that the little horn, Satan in the anti-Christ arises after the 10 horns.

I believe after Satan has entered the anti-Christ he's already gained enough power to appoint kings or someone to be in control of each of these regions, like president's, just to have them sign their regions over to him. Once this has happened, the anti-Christ, Satan will have control over the whole world.

The Club of Rome already has plans for the world to be divided up into 10 regions. I got this from Jack Van Impe's weekly TV program. The countries are divided up as follows:

1. America, (United States and Canada) and Mexico.
2. South America
3. Australia and New Zealand
4. Western Europe
5. Eastern Europe
6. Japan
7. South Asia
8. Central Asia
9. North Africa and the Middle East
10. The remainder of Africa

These are the 10 toes of the statue from Daniel chapter 2 and the 10 horns from Daniel chapter 7 and Revelation chapters 12, 13 and 17. The one world government will most likely be established after the rapture during the first half of the tribulation, but it could be established before the rapture. It will just become worse after the rapture and even worse during the second half of the tribulation.

There are those that believe the 10 horns will be 10 nations. There are more than 10 nations in the European Union now but they believe that there will emerge 10 prominent nations that will be in control that will have the prominent, decision making power.

With the Image in Daniel having two legs of Iron and two feet of Iron and Clay, it is believed that like in the past when Rome was divided into Western and Eastern Europe, the Revived Roman Empire will be divided also with 5 leading nations in the West and 5 in the East. I guess we will just have to wait and see. I'll be looking down from heaven. This could be the case but with the European Union already having the plan for the world to be divided up into 10 regions, I think it will be 10 regions with kings appointed over each one.

With America's forefathers migrating from Europe to Britain to here, it could be that from a bible prophecy viewpoint that America could be considered part of or an extension of the old Roman Empire, that Europe as well as America could be considered 'of the people of the Ruler who will come who destroyed the city and sanctuary' we saw in Daniel chapter 9. It could be that this last revived form of the Roman Empire that is pictured in Daniel chapter 2 with the two feet of Iron and clay is the European Continents and the American Continents.

We can see all this beginning to come about now. It's what all the leaders of the world are striving for including the United States. This has never happened in history. We see everything falling into place just like the bible reveals. With this and the way Iran, the Palestinians and all the Muslims want to destroy Israel and kill every last Jew on the planet, and the way all the other nations are against Israel we can see that we are close to the tribulation. That means we are close to Jesus returning for his Church. Here with our look at the book of Revelation you will see just what occurs during the tribulation. There will be a World War III.

There's been much speculation as to where this leader, the anti-Christ will come from. There are those that have reasons to believe he will come from Greece, others believe he will come from Rome. But the bible doesn't say the anti-Christ will have to be born Roman or Greek. The Apostle Paul was a Roman citizen but he wasn't born in Rome. But the belief has been that he will come from somewhere in Europe. But I wouldn't rule out him coming from America. If the U.S. is part of or an extension of the old Roman Empire, then an U.S. politician could become the leader of the whole world, the anti-Christ could emerge from the U.S. Daniel chapter 9 doesn't say that the man who becomes the anti-Christ is born in Rome or Europe; he just says the people of the ruler who will come will destroy the city and sanctuary. So, from a bible prophecy viewpoint if America is considered part of or an extension of the old Roman Empire, then an U.S. Political leader could become the anti-Christ. Any leader from England or Europe could become the anti-Christ. He will have to be someone that the whole world approves of, including Muslims and Jews and if the anti-Christ comes on the scene before the rapture Christians to, that is Christians that compromise, that don't stand on what the bible says. If he is from the U.S. he would first have to agree that the United States become part of the European Union, part of the new world order. This could be why the U.S. is not mentioned in bible prophecy like so many other nations. There are fascinating parallels between the old Roman Empire and the United States, from the United States and Rome's birth to what we see happening now with the economy and financial institutions. As I mentioned earlier, Perry Stone did a series on his Manafest program that was from one of his conferences. If you would like to know more you can go to his web site, PerryStone.org. He has it on CD and DVD.

Whoever he turns out to be, while there may be signs and suspicions, he won't be revealed for sure as the anti-Christ until he gets Israel and the Muslims to sign the 7 year peace agreement together with him. He won't start off evil; he will be very likeable, he will start off seeming to solve the world's problems. He won't really be a Christian even if he claims to be. A true Christian wouldn't be so influenced by Satan and definitely couldn't be indwelt by him, even after being killed. He will actually turn out to not believe in any God. Remember Daniel chapter 11 verse 37, He will show no regard for the gods of his fathers or for the one desired by women, nor will he regard any god, but will exalt himself above them all. If he is from Muslim ancestry, this could mean he doesn't regard Allah either.

We see from Daniel and Revelation that there is a one world government coming. We now see the nations of the world calling for it. Sadly, even the United States.

7. The False Prophet and Religion.

We've already covered the beast of the sea, the coming one world government and its leader in chapter 13. Now let's take a look at the beast out of the earth.

The False Prophet

We see in Revelation 13 verse 1 that the Revived Roman Empire and the anti-Christ are described as the beast coming out of the sea. With verse 11 we see another beast that is coming out of the Earth.

> Rev. 13: 11Then I saw another beast, coming out of the earth. He had two horns like a lamb, but he spoke like a dragon. 12He exercised all the authority of the first beast on his behalf, and made the earth and its inhabitants worship the first beast, whose fatal wound had been healed. 13And he performed great and miraculous signs, even causing fire to come down from heaven to earth in full view of men.

He is called the False Prophet because of the description of "He had two horns like a lamb, but he spoke like a dragon." The evidence is on "like'. Earlier in chapter 5 as well as many other scriptures in the bible we see Jesus is described as a lamb. Also this false prophet performs or at least seems to perform miracles and seems to duplicate the miracles of the prophet Elijah. So this guy will come as a prophet. He will bring all the worlds' religions together with every religion accepting the other, inclusion, tolerance and diversity at work. The belief being that there is more than one path to God and heaven. The False Prophet will be like the anti-Christ's vice president. It is the false prophet that will cause everyone to take the mark of the beast, the mark of the anti-Christ and worship him.

> Rev. 13: 14Because of the signs he was given power to do on behalf of the first beast, he deceived the inhabitants of the earth. He ordered them to set up an image in honor of the beast who was wounded by the sword and yet lived. 15He was

given power to give breath to the image of the first beast, so that it could speak and cause all who refused to worship the image to be killed.

The thought is that this image will most likely be a robot. But verse 15 says he was able to give breath to this image. Could this image be a clone?

16He also forced everyone, small and great, rich and poor, free and slave, to receive a mark on his right hand or on his forehead, 17so that no one could buy or sell unless he had the mark, which is the name of the beast or the number of his name.

18This calls for wisdom. If anyone has insight, let him calculate the number of the beast, for it is man's number. His number is 666.

There are different explanations as to just what the number 666 means. One is that with 6 being the number for man, man was created on the 6th day, then with the beast (the one world government of the anti-Christ), the anti-Christ and the false prophet you have 666, the un-holy trinity. With 7 being the number for God, you have the Father, Son and Holy Spirit, then 777 would represent God in his fullness. This 666 could represent humanity without God, a totally humanistic way of living.

Now with modern technology this mark can easily be given to each human being on the earth either with a bar code or a microchip. All a person's personal information could be stored on a microchip. Even with a barcode all a person's information will be on a super computer that could be accessed through satellite. We already have this with debit cards and credit cards. This could very well be sold to the public as a means to stop identity theft. Another really bad thing with it being a microchip is that a person's whereabouts could be tracked. You can see how for someone that has accepted Jesus, not only would they not be able to take this mark because they would have to say they are swearing allegiance to the anti-Christ and renouncing Jesus, but if they took it but was just thinking they would take it to make life easier but they didn't really mean it, the anti-Christ's government would know your every move. So the true believer in Jesus will not take this mark. With this here and throughout the book of Revelation you see a clear distinction made between the believer and non-believer. There will be no middle ground, no walking the fence. But isn't it amazing that there is now this technology and the bible foretold this 2000 years ago. They are already micro chipping pets and animals. This apparently happens after the mid-point of the tribulation, after Satan has entered the man, the anti-Christ. We see with verse 14 that the anti-Christ has already been 'wounded by the sword and yet lived'

The Prostitute and the Woman and the Beast.

You see starting with verse 1 of chapter 17 a prostitute is mentioned sitting on many waters; this is the false religion of Babylon. We are given the explanation to the 'many waters' in verse 15, we saw a similar term used in chapter 13 verse one with the beast coming up out of the sea. Verse 15, Then the angel said to me, "The waters you saw, where the prostitute sits, are peoples, multitudes, nations and languages.

> Rev. 17: 1One of the seven angels who had the seven bowls came and said to me, "Come, I will show you the punishment of the great prostitute, who sits on many waters. 2With her the kings of the earth committed adultery and the inhabitants of the earth were intoxicated with the wine of her adulteries."

> 3Then the angel carried me away in the Spirit into a desert. There I saw a woman sitting on a scarlet beast that was covered with blasphemous names and had seven heads and ten horns. 4The woman was dressed in purple and scarlet, and was glittering with gold, precious stones and pearls. She held a golden cup in her hand, filled with abominable things and the filth of her adulteries.

5This title was written on her forehead:

MYSTERY
BABYLON THE GREAT
THE MOTHER OF PROSTITUTES
AND OF THE ABOMINATIONS OF THE EARTH.

6I saw that the woman was drunk with the blood of the saints, the blood of those who bore testimony to Jesus. When I saw her, I was greatly astonished. 7Then the angel said to me: "Why are you astonished? I will explain to you the mystery of the woman and of the beast she rides, which has the seven heads and ten horns. 8The beast, which you saw, once was, now is not, and will come up out of the Abyss and go to his destruction. The inhabitants of the earth whose names have not been written in the book of life from the creation of the world will be astonished when they see the beast, because he once was, now is not, and yet will come.

We saw earlier that the beast that, "once was, now is not, and will come up out of the Abyss and go to his destruction" is Satan. We see that Satan is connected to this government and religion. Satan has been the one behind all the world's false religions. The woman represents all the false religions of the world including the future new one world government's false religious system. Remember, the beast with seven heads and ten horns the woman is riding is the coming one world government of Satan. The future new one world government will be the 7th ruling government made up of 10 regions, the 10 toes and 10 horns and the 10 kings we see here in chapter 17. In the bible a horn is often used to denote political power.

The coming false religion will be connected to this new one world government. The way this beast is described as Satan and the 10 horn government, it's like this government is Satan. It will be totally opposite to everything that is God. It's like this government and Satan are one. The prostitute on many waters is the false religious system of the world made up of all the world's religions that have now become one. The false prophet will head up and control this new religion.

The writing on the woman's head, Mystery, Babylon the Great, the mother of prostitutes is about the false one world religion that will emerge during the tribulation. It's called Babylon because it will have teachings, practices and beliefs that stem back to ancient Babylon. We can see its influence now in the world and in a lot of religions. Astrology, Witchcraft, Mysticism, black magic, demon contact, séances, sorcery, and drug use all can be traced back to the ancient religion of Babylon. This religious system was passed down from kingdom to kingdom. This all first started back with Assyria and Nimrod who built the tower of Babel. This was man's first ruling government. See Genesis chapter 10 and 11. Rome was steeped in the teachings of this ancient religion. This religious system denies the Deity of Jesus, the authority of the Word, the Virgin birth, teaches there is no sin with its consequences. It teaches that there's not an actual hell or Satan. We can see all this now. Look again at what Paul told Timothy.

> 1 Timothy 4: 1The Spirit clearly says that in later times some will abandon the faith and follow deceiving spirits and things taught by demons. 2Such teachings come through hypocritical liars, whose consciences have been seared as with a hot iron.

The Rome of Jesus' and John's day was steeped in Emperor Worship and Empire worship. From verse 8 in chapter 13 saying "All inhabitants of the earth will worship the beast—all whose names have not been written in the book of life belonging to the Lamb that was slain from the creation of the world" and here in chapter 17 verse 8 saying "The inhabitants of the earth whose names have not been written in the book of life from the creation of the world will be astonished when they see the beast", it looks like people will being worshiping this new one world government. They may think that this new global government is the answer to all the worlds' problems as well as the anti-Christ. We can see this trend now. As I believe I've said already, a one world government in itself is not a bad thing, Jesus' government during his 1000 year reign will be a one world government, it's just this government during the tribulation will be one without the one true God, without Jesus. People will be turning to the anti-Christ and this government instead of God. Because of man's sin, God allows Satan to enter into the anti-Christ and control the world. If a world without the one true God is what the world wants, that's what they are going to get.

Here's an interesting vision that Zechariah had.

Zech. 5:

The Woman in a Basket

> 5 Then the angel who was speaking to me came forward and said to me, "Look up and see what this is that is appearing."
> 6 I asked, "What is it?"
> He replied, "It is a measuring basket. " And he added, "This is the iniquity of the people throughout the land."
>
> 7 Then the cover of lead was raised, and there in the basket sat a woman! 8 He said, "This is wickedness," and he pushed her back into the basket and pushed the lead cover down over its mouth. 9 Then I looked up—and there before me were two women, with the wind in their wings! They had wings like those of a stork, and they lifted up the basket between heaven and earth. 10 "Where are they taking the basket?" I asked the angel who was speaking to me. 11 He replied, "To the country of Babylonia to build a house for it. When it is ready, the basket will be set there in its place."

Could this be the woman John was referring to?

> Rev. 17:15Then the angel said to me, "The waters you saw, where the prostitute sits, are peoples, multitudes, nations and languages. 16The beast and the ten horns you saw will hate the prostitute. They will bring her to ruin and leave her naked; they

will eat her flesh and burn her with fire. 17For God has put it into their hearts to accomplish his purpose by agreeing to give the beast their power to rule, until God's words are fulfilled. 18The woman you saw is the great city that rules over the kings of the earth."

We see that John was told the woman is the great city that rules over the kings of the earth, and in verse 5 that this is a mystery and he said it was Babylon the great. Rome was the great city that was ruling, but the Jews and the Christians referred to Rome as Babylon, like a code name because of its beliefs and practices dating back to ancient Babylon. We see that Zechariah was told when it is ready the woman in the basket will be set in its place in the country of Babylon. I believe this woman, representing wickedness, sin, false teachings will be released during the tribulation and the reference to Babylon is referring to the last one world government, not necessarily to a literal country Babylon. Just like the name Babylon referred to Rome with all its false religious practices, the one world government and religion during the tribulation will also. The place it is set could be the area where the headquarters of the new one world government will be, but Babylon, its place, could be the land of all the earth or political system as a whole.

With verse 18 John could be telling us that the headquarters of this one world government will be Rome. "The woman you saw is the great city that rules over the kings of the earth". The city that was ruling over the kings of the earth at the time of John writing the book of Revelation was Rome. Here again is another clue that Rome will be revived. With John being told this was the great city that rules over the kings of the earth is another example of how the last day kingdom will be a form of the Old Roman Empire. Also with verse 9 "This calls for a mind with wisdom. The seven heads are seven hills on which the woman sits." Rome has often been associated with the seven hills with which she sits and has often been referred to as the city on seven hills. But it could be a reference to the government as a whole.

But once Satan has entered into the man, the anti-Christ he and the government he rules will no longer have any need of the religions of the world. It looks like not only Satan will hate this religious system but also this government. Verse 16 says the beast and the 10 horns will hate the prostitute. So the new one world government will eventually hate this new religion.

Once the False prophet has caused everyone to take the mark of the beast and swear allegiance to Satan, the anti-Christ, then there will be no more need for the false religions of the world. Satan will have everyone worshiping him, that is all those whose names are not written in the Lambs book of Life. At this point we know for sure that the anti-Christ's headquarters will be moved to Jerusalem. We know this from Daniel chapter 9, Matthew chapter 24 and 2 Thessalonians chapter 2. This is what Satan has been waiting for, to enter God's temple and proclaim that he is God. He couldn't do it in heaven, so now he will do here on earth.

This continues in chapter 18.

> Rev. 18: 1After this I saw another angel coming down from heaven. He had great authority, and the earth was illuminated by his splendor. 2With a mighty voice he shouted:
> "Fallen! fallen is Babylon the Great!
> She has become a home for demons
> and a haunt for every evil spirit,
> a haunt for every unclean and detestable bird.
> 3For all the nations have drunk
> the maddening wine of her adulteries.
> The kings of the earth committed adultery with her,
> and the merchants of the earth grew rich from her excessive luxuries."

False religion is considered a spiritual departure from God and his truth, like a prostitute, and anyone that takes part in its teachings is considered committing adultery. Look at what James had to say. James 4: 4You adulterous people, don't you know that friendship with the world is hatred toward God? Anyone who chooses to be a friend of the world becomes an enemy of God. This would include an apostate Christian or Church. Remember, Apostasy means an abandonment or desertion of principles or faith.

With the angel saying in verse 2 of chapter 18 "Fallen, Fallen" could be referring to the fall of both the new one world government and the new one world religious system. Jesus destroys them both when He returns.

So, we see that the coming new world government will be like the ancient kingdom of Babylon with its religious practices. Remember from the Statue in Daniel chapter 2 that the last world government will have characteristics of all the past kingdoms.

Remember what Paul said:

2 Thessalonians 2

> 7For the secret power of lawlessness is already at work; but the one who now holds it back will continue to do so till he is taken out of the way. 8And then the lawless one will be revealed, whom the Lord Jesus will overthrow with the breath of his mouth and destroy by the splendor of his coming. 9The coming of the lawless one will be in accordance with the work of Satan displayed in all kinds of counterfeit miracles, signs and wonders, 10and in every sort of evil that deceives those who are perishing. They perish because they refused to love the truth and so be saved. 11For this reason God sends them a powerful delusion so that they will believe the lie 12and so that all will be condemned who have not believed the truth but have delighted in wickedness.

Here's something interesting to think about. As for there being a one world religion in the world, as it is now Christianity nor Islam would go along with this, but with the removal of the Church with the Rapture and defeat of Islam with the battle against Russia and the

Islamic nations, though Islam will still be here, Allah will not be the god of this religion. With these two major religions out of the way it would pave the way for the acceptance of a one world religion. By this time Christians will probably be underground. Just another point showing how all this could easily come about, just like the bible says.

8. The Woman clothed with the sun.

We've looked at the beast with 7 heads and 10 horns in verse 3 already but let's take a look at chapter 12 again to go over what we didn't cover earlier.

Revelation 12

1A great and wondrous sign appeared in heaven: a woman clothed with the sun, with the moon under her feet and a crown of twelve stars on her head. 2She was pregnant and cried out in pain as she was about to give birth. 3Then another sign appeared in heaven: an enormous red dragon with seven heads and ten horns and seven crowns on his heads. 4His tail swept a third of the stars out of the sky and flung them to the earth. The dragon stood in front of the woman who was about to give birth, so that he might devour her child the moment it was born. 5She gave birth to a son, a male child, who will rule all the nations with an iron scepter. And her child was snatched up to God and to his throne.

In verse 9 John tells us that the dragon is Satan. The woman clothed with the sun is Israel; the 12 stars are the 12 tribes of Israel. This is referring back to Joseph's dream in Genesis chapter 37. Israel gave birth to the Messiah, Jesus. You can see that verse 5 is a description of Jesus.

You see with verse 4 Satan deceived and took a 3rd of the angels with him, which became demons. We know from the gospels that Satan tried to kill Jesus from the time he was born. Herod had all the male boys up to the age of 2 killed. See Matthew chapter 2. Herod represented Rome which was the government at the time. Again with verse 3 you can see how Satan was behind the government of Rome and will be again.

Verses 1 thru 5 are of the past, and are for identifying who he is referring to. With verse 6 we go into the future, to the middle of the tribulation. The events from verse 6 thru chapter 13 will occur during the last 3 ½ years of the tribulation.

6The woman fled into the desert to a place prepared for her by God, where she might be taken care of for 1,260 days.

7And there was war in heaven. Michael and his angels fought against the dragon, and the dragon and his angels fought back. 8But he was not strong enough, and they lost their place in heaven. 9The great dragon was hurled down—that ancient serpent called the devil, or Satan, who leads the whole world astray. He was hurled to the earth, and his angels with him.

10Then I heard a loud voice in heaven say:
"Now have come the salvation and the power and the kingdom of our God,
and the authority of his Christ.
For the accuser of our brothers,
who accuses them before our God day and night,
has been hurled down.
11They overcame him
by the blood of the Lamb
and by the word of their testimony;
they did not love their lives so much
as to shrink from death.
12Therefore rejoice, you heavens
and you who dwell in them!
But woe to the earth and the sea,
because the devil has gone down to you!
He is filled with fury,
because he knows that his time is short."

13When the dragon saw that he had been hurled to the earth, he pursued the woman who had given birth to the male child. 14The woman was given the two wings of a great eagle, so that she might fly to the place prepared for her in the desert, where she would be taken care of for a time, times and half a time, out of the serpent's reach. 15Then from his mouth the serpent spewed water like a river, to overtake the woman and sweep her away with the torrent. 16But the earth helped the woman by opening its mouth and swallowing the river that the dragon had spewed out of his mouth. 17Then the dragon was enraged at the woman and went off to make war against the rest of her offspring—those who obey God's commandments and hold to the testimony of Jesus.

After the anti-Christ and his army have defeated the Islamic nations and Russia he decides to make Jerusalem his headquarters. As mentioned before it sounds like he will be killed somehow and then Satan will enter into him raising him from the dead. Now the anti-Christ will actually be Satan, of course no one will know this unless they know the bible. He will set himself up as God in the temple desecrating it, the abomination that causes desolation. This will be the mid-point of the tribulation. The Jews will flee Jerusalem and go to Petra, the place prepared for them. Rev. 12: 6The woman fled into the desert to a place prepared for her by God, where she might be taken care of for 1,260 days.

We see that the Jews will have to flee and will be protected during the last 3 ½ years of the tribulation. We saw from Matthew 24 that Jesus mentioned this and that it will happen when the abomination that causes desolation is set up, which takes place at the mid-point of the tribulation.

Some believe that the reference to Satan being cast out of heaven happened in the beginning before he tempted Adam and Eve. But the statements here tell us otherwise. Before deceiving Adam and Eve Satan lost or fell from his position of authority when he rebelled against God and deceived a third of the angels. Here, Satan is said to pursue the woman, Israel for only 3 ½ years and that he is filled with fury because he knows his time is short. After he is cast out of heaven, that is being able to go before the Father and accuse the brothers, he only has 3 ½ years, not thousands. We see this also with verse 10.

Rev. 12:10 Then I heard a loud voice in heaven say: "Now have come the salvation and the power and the kingdom of our God, and the authority of his Christ. For the accuser of our brothers, who accuses them before our God day and night, has been hurled down.

Satan and his demons are going before the Father and making accusations against each believer in Jesus now, but once he has been cast down to the earth he will no longer be able to.

The statement here in verse 10 "Now have come the salvation and the power and the kingdom of our God, and the authority of his Christ", is that there's not much time left, now there will be only 3 ½ years left until Jesus returns and sets up the kingdom of God. I believe the casting out of Satan to the earth is just after the 7th seal is opened. The 7th trumpet is toward the end of the tribulation so you can see that this is just a statement to the fact that the end is near. At this point Jesus hasn't returned so he hasn't actually begun to reign.

We see Satan falling from the sky being referred back to in Revelation chapter 9 with the 5th trumpet.

Rev. 9: 1 The fifth angel sounded his trumpet, and I saw a star that had fallen from the sky to the earth. The star was given the key to the shaft of the Abyss.

So the reference to Satan being cast out of heaven cannot be referring to an event that took place thousands of years ago or to the day that Jesus returns. We see from the words of Jesus in Matthew chapter 24, Daniel chapter 9 and here in Revelation chapter 12 that Satan will be cast out of heaven and will lose his ability to move around spiritually has he does now. We see that the other scriptures associated with his being cast down are events that will be occurring during the last half of the tribulation. Once he has been cast down he will be confined in the body of the anti-Christ. You know if you think about that for a second, that's really a scary thing for the people of the earth.

9. The Seven Seals.

Revelation 6.

Now we will begin our look at what the bible calls the judgments of God. With the seals the judgments from God begin. Everything from the first seal in chapter 6 through chapter 19 are dealing with the judgment or wrath of God which occurs during the last 7 years just before Jesus returns back down to the earth. Chapter 5 we see that it is Jesus that breaks the seals and releases the judgments.

> Rev. 5: 1Then I saw in the right hand of him who sat on the throne a scroll with writing on both sides and sealed with seven seals.

> 6Then I saw a Lamb, looking as if it had been slain, standing in the center of the throne, encircled by the four living creatures and the elders. He had seven horns and seven eyes, which are the seven spirits of God sent out into all the earth.

Critics of the book of Revelation being prophetic of yet future events argue that it all is only to be understood symbolically, not literally because of all the symbolic symbolism used, like a beast with seven horns and a women riding on the beast etc. Here with verse 6 we see symbolism being used of a Lamb looking as if it had been slain. Well, everyone agrees that this is a symbolic description of Jesus. Jesus is described in the Old as well as the New Testament as the Lamb of God. And of course he was slain when he was nailed to the cross. We see this clearly with verse 9. Well, if it's not hard to accept that John was using a symbolic description of Jesus, then why is so hard to accept that he uses symbolic descriptions of other things and events to give those through the centuries that will be reading this a way to understand or get a picture of what he was seeing.

> 7He came and took the scroll from the right hand of him who sat on the throne. 8And when he had taken it, the four living creatures and the twenty-four elders fell down before the

Lamb. Each one had a harp and they were holding golden bowls full of incense, which are the prayers of the saints. 9And they sang a new song:
"You are worthy to take the scroll
and to open its seals,
because you were slain,
and with your blood you purchased men for God
from every tribe and language and people and nation.
10You have made them to be a kingdom and priests to serve our God, and they will reign on the earth."

With the seals we come to what takes place after the Church age. Remember earlier we saw that the Church is removed in chapter 4 verse 1. Let me point out again, as of the time of this writing none of the things described from chapter 4 through the end of the book have occurred yet. The entire book after chapter 3 is prophetic. While most everyone reading this will understand this, they are those that believe the things mentioned in the book of Revelation are already occurring and have been since Jesus returned back to the Father. You can't lose sight of the fact that the book of Revelation after chapter 4 verse one through chapter 19 is dealing with the last 7 years allotted to Israel prophesied by Daniel in chapter 9.

There are different degrees of God's wrath. For with each series of judgments the wrath of God increases. The 7 Seals, 7 Trumpets, 7 Bowls. Just like we saw Jesus unfolding the scroll, the events of the tribulation will unfold, in a sequence growing greater and more intense with each series of judgments. The trumpets and bowls are all part of the 7th seal. It's like the 7th seal is a chapter or directory with the 7 trumpets and bowls subfolders, just having more detail. This is another indication that the book of Revelation is to be seen has unfolding not as some teach that the 7th seal, 7th trumpet and 7th bowl all occur at the same time. This is a scroll that Jesus is unfolding.

With the first four seals we see riders on horses. These four riders have become known as the four horseman of the Apocalypse.

The Seals

> 1I watched as the Lamb opened the **first of the seven seals**. Then I heard one of the four living creatures say in a voice like thunder, "Come!" 2I looked, and there before me was a white horse! Its rider held a bow, and he was given a crown, and he rode out as a conqueror bent on conquest.

Don't get the description here confused with the one of Jesus returning on a white horse in chapter 19. The descriptions are different. Here there is no detailed description as there is with Jesus in chapter 19. Also the rider here has a bow with no arrows and he has only one grown. In chapter 19 Jesus has many crowns. The description given in chapter 19 is clearly referring to Jesus, where here it is not. Rev. 19:11 – 16.

Verse 1 and 2 are seen as the release of the anti-Christ. With him riding on a white horse shows his deception, he is on a white horse like we see described with Jesus returning in chapter 19. The anti-Christ will claim to be the Messiah; later once Satan has entered him he will claim to be God. He has a crown, which shows him to be as a king, and he goes out as a conqueror bent on conquest. This would be the little horn mentioned in Daniel. This is the start of the tribulation when Israel signs the covenant agreement with the anti-Christ. Daniel in chapter 9 addresses the anti-Christ.

> Dan. 9: 27 He will confirm a covenant with many for one 'seven.' In the middle of the 'seven' he will put an end to sacrifice and offering. And on a wing of the temple he will set up an abomination that causes desolation, until the end that is decreed is poured out on him.

Remember the 'seven' is referring to seven years.

Remember what Paul said in 2 Thessalonians chapter 2,

The Man of Lawlessness

> 1Concerning the coming of our Lord Jesus Christ and our being gathered to him, we ask you, brothers, 2not to become easily unsettled or alarmed by some prophecy, report or letter supposed to have come from us, saying that the day of the Lord has already come. 3Don't let anyone deceive you in any way, for (that day will not come) until the rebellion occurs and the man of lawlessness is revealed, the man doomed to destruction. 4He will oppose and will exalt himself over everything that is called God or is worshiped, so that he sets himself up in God's temple, proclaiming himself to be God.

He said that the tribulation, the day of the Lord would not start until the man of lawlessness is revealed. We see that the anti-Christ is revealed here with the first seal.

> 2 Thessalonians 2: 6And now you know what is holding him back, so that he may be revealed at the proper time. 7For the secret power of lawlessness is already at work; but the one who now holds it back will continue to do so till he is taken out of the way.

Remember, this is referring to the body of Christ, the Church being taken out of the way first. This is why we don't see any mention of the Church in the book of Revelation after chapter 3.

> 8And then the lawless one will be revealed, whom the Lord Jesus will overthrow with the breath of his mouth and destroy by the splendor of his coming. 9The coming of the lawless one will be in accordance with the work of Satan displayed in all kinds of counterfeit miracles, signs and wonders, 10and in every sort of evil that deceives those who are perishing. They perish because they refused to love the truth and so be saved. 11For this reason **God sends** them a powerful delusion so that they will believe **the** lie 12and so that all will be condemned

who have not believed the truth but have delighted in wickedness.

Did you see what he said, God sends a powerful delusion, God sends the anti-Christ.

Hal Lindsey in his book on the Rapture points out that the word "come" would be better translated "Go". Therefore with Jesus opening the first four seals he is actually sending out the riders of the horses, sending these spiritual beings forth that have not been allowed to go forth until now. I guess it depends on how you're looking at it. Was the living Creature talking to John or to the Rider on the Horse? To me it makes more since that he was talking to the rider, the spiritual being, sending him forth. Remember chapter 5 tells us that it is Jesus opening the seals, releasing the judgments from Heaven. Understand that the anti-Christ is not going to be coming riding on a white horse. This is the spiritual being that represents the anti-Christ.

> EPH 6:12 For our struggle is not against flesh and blood, but against the rulers, against the authorities, against the powers of this dark world and against the spiritual forces of evil in the heavenly realms.

It appears that the first 6 seals occur during the first half of the tribulation and that the 7th seal starts the second half, which contains the 7 trumpets and 7 bowls. Remember what we saw from our study of Matthew 24. Jesus seems to be laying this out in the same order as we see here in Revelation chapter 6. It is in sequence like the seals. Matthew 24 verses 4 through 8 are during the first half of the tribulation. You can see in Matthew

1st Seal, False Peace, spiritual deception, the revealing of the anti-Christ
2nd Seal, War, Peace taken
3rd Seal, inflation
4th Seal, war, famine, plagues, death
5th Seal, divine judgment

6th Seal, Darkness, physical destruction, continuation of wars, a great earthquake

7th Seal, Catastrophic events (7 trumpets, 7 bowls) the second half of the tribulation.

The unrolling of the scroll marks the beginning of God's Judgment. Each Seal is a Judgment. Again, notice it is Jesus that is unrolling and breaking the seals of the scroll.

The second seal you see that war breaks out. With the 3rd and 4th seals you see the effects of the 2nd seal.

> 3When the Lamb opened **the second seal**, I heard the second living creature say, "Come!" 4Then another horse came out, a fiery red one. Its rider was given power to take peace from the earth and to make men slay each other. To him was given a large sword.

This could be the war of Gog and Magog of Ezekiel 38 and 39 when Russia and the Islamic nations attack Israel.

> 5When the Lamb opened **the third seal**, I heard the third living creature say, "Come!" I looked, and there before me was a black horse! Its rider was holding a pair of scales in his hand. 6Then I heard what sounded like a voice among the four living creatures, saying, "A quart of wheat for a day's wages, and three quarts of barley for a day's wages, and do not damage the oil and the wine!"

The third seal is the result of the war of the 2nd seal, massive inflation. When Russia and the Islamic nations attack Israel, the anti-Christ will come to Israel's aid and will defeat Russia and these nations. This could cause a major disruption in the Oil supply, which in turn would cause the prices of everything to sky Rocket. Today we can see the effect of the price of oil, how it is causing the price of everything to go up. You can see here that a day's wages will not buy even enough for one person to eat much less for a whole family. What are people going to do?

As you can see now, inflation doesn't affect the rich like it does everyone else, thus the statement 'do not damage the oil and the wine'. While food supplies are short in the world there will still be the finer things that only the rich will be able to afford. With this last statement there may be a wide gap between the rich and poor. There may not be a middle class. We can see the effect of today's economy on the middle class now.

> 7When the Lamb opened **the fourth seal**, I heard the voice of the fourth living creature say, "Come!" 8I looked, and there before me was a pale horse! Its rider was named Death, and Hades was following close behind him. They were given power over a fourth of the earth to kill by sword, famine and plague, and by the wild beasts of the earth.

Verse 7 you see this could be the result of the fighting that started with the 2nd seal, death, famine and plagues. This plague could be caused by nuclear, chemical and biological weapons. But it could also be a judgment all of it's on. It may be with it saying that power was given over a fourth of the earth, that if this judgment is from the results of the 2nd seal of Russia and the Islamic nations attacking Israel, then this may not be worldwide, it may be contained to the middle east, meaning it's contained to this general area, for now at least. But if this is a judgment unrelated to the 2nd seal then this could also mean that this will affect a fourth of the earth's population worldwide. Evidently, wild animals will be evolved in this somehow.

> 9When he opened the **fifth seal**, I saw under the altar the souls of those who had been slain because of the word of God and the testimony they had maintained. 10They called out in a loud voice, "How long, Sovereign Lord, holy and true, until you judge the inhabitants of the earth and avenge our blood?" 11Then each of them was given a white robe, and they were told to wait a little longer, until the number of their fellow servants and brothers who were to be killed as they had been was completed.

Since the tribulation started with the 1ˢᵗ seal this sounds like it could be referring to saints that have died since the rapture of the Church, but it could also include all those that have died throughout history since the beginning of the Church. We see in chapter 5 that the golden bowls full of incense that the 24 elders are holding are the prayers of the saints. We see in chapter 8 these saints are praying. Rev. 8: 3Another angel, who had a golden censer, came and stood at the altar. He was given much incense to offer, with the prayers of all the saints, on the golden altar before the throne. 4The smoke of the incense, together with the prayers of the saints, went up before God from the angel's hand. 5Then the angel took the censer, filled it with fire from the altar, and hurled it on the earth; and there came peals of thunder, rumblings, flashes of lightning and an earthquake.

What you see next in chapter 8 are the 7 trumpets. The judgment they are speaking of could be referring to the judgments of the trumpets and bowls, but they could also be referring to the judgment at the end of the tribulation after Jesus has returned when Jesus separates the sheep from the goats. It's during the second half of the tribulation that the judgments of God become much greater. It's after the 7ᵗʰ seal that Satan indwells the anti-Christ and that he fully becomes the little horn of Daniel. Now the Revived Roman Empire will truly become the beast that John and Daniel describes. Not only will there be saints killed by the effects of further war and nuclear attacks, but the second half of the tribulation there will be many killed by the anti-Christ for the word of God. The fifth seal could also be a prophetic statement of those killed during the second half of the tribulation by the anti-Christ. You see this in Revelation chapter 12 and 13.

12I watched as he opened **the sixth seal**. There was a great earthquake. The sun turned black like sackcloth made of goat hair, the whole moon turned blood red, 13and the stars in the sky fell to earth, as late figs drop from a fig tree when shaken by a strong wind. 14The sky receded like a scroll, rolling up, and every mountain and island was removed from its place.

15Then the kings of the earth, the princes, the generals, the rich, the mighty, and every slave and every free man hid in caves and among the rocks of the mountains. 16They called to the mountains and the rocks, "Fall on us and hide us from the face of him who sits on the throne and from the wrath of the Lamb! 17For the great day of their wrath has come, and who can stand?"

From the statement in verse 16 and 17 it sounds like what man has been dreading has finally happened, the use of nuclear weapons. With verses 12 through 14 it sounds like he is describing a nuclear explosion and its effects in the air and on the ground. With all of the fault lines in the earth you can see how with enough nuclear bombs striking the surface that it could easily cause a chain reaction with the faults causing massive earthquakes that will affect the oceans thus affecting islands and mountains. This is probably the first major nuclear exchange. There will be more.

Look at Isaiah.

Isaiah 2

10 Go into the rocks, hide in the ground from dread of the LORD and the splendor of his majesty!

11 The eyes of the arrogant man will be humbled and the pride of men brought low; the LORD alone will be exalted in that day.

12 The LORD Almighty has a day in store for all the proud and lofty, for all that is exalted (and they will be humbled),

19 Men will flee to caves in the rocks and to holes in the ground from dread of the LORD and the splendor of his majesty, when he rises to shake the earth.

20 In that day men will throw away to the rodents and bats their idols of silver and idols of gold, which they made to worship.

21 They will flee to caverns in the rocks and to the overhanging crags from dread of the LORD and the splendor of his majesty, when he rises to shake the earth.

I'm sure this will be happening up to the day Jesus returns. The Day of the Lord here is not referring to a single day but to a period of time, to a general time frame, to the time of the tribulation. The word 'day' here cannot be referring to the actual day Jesus returns. The description does not fit with the day Jesus returns. See Revelation chapter 19. Look at what Joel said concerning the day of the Lord.

Joel 1: 15 Alas for that day!
For the day of the LORD is near;
it will come like destruction from the Almighty.

Remember what Amos said.

AM 5:18 Woe to you who long
for the day of the LORD!
Why do you long for the day of the LORD?
That day will be darkness, not light.

During the tribulation the Jews and everyone that has accepted Jesus as Lord and Savior will be longing for the day He returns. The day Jesus returns will not be a day of darkness, it will be a glorious day. The word darkness sounds like it is describing the destruction occurring during the tribulation more than it does to the day Jesus returns. Those that have accepted Jesus as the Messiah and their Savior during the tribulation will be longing for his second coming and praying for this day of darkness and gloom to end.

Acts 2:19 I will show wonders in the heaven above
and signs on the earth below,

blood and fire and billows of smoke.
20The sun will be turned to darkness
and the moon to blood
before the coming of the great and **glorious** day of the Lord.
21And everyone who calls
on the name of the Lord will be saved

Notice here Peter says 'glorious day', not a day of darkness and gloom. Peter was looking forward to Jesus' return. The great and glorious day is the day Jesus returns. The signs he describes in verse 19 and 20 are before the glorious return of the Lord.

Read the Old Testament book of Joel. He is describing the day of the Lord. It is obvious the day of the Lord he is describing is longer than a single day.

As I said earlier I believe that the 6th seal is at the mid-point of the tribulation and that the 7th seal starts the mid-point when the anti-Christ is indwelt by Satan and enters the temple and desecrates it. This lines up with Matthew 24 verses 9 thru 20. With Matthew 24 verse 15 we see that Satan has now entered into the anti-Christ and has entered the Temple. We saw this foretold in Daniel chapter 9 verse 27. We see all this also in Revelation chapter 12.

The 7 trumpets are a result of the 7th seal as the 7 bowls are a result of the 7th trumpet.

Since the last 3 ½ years is much more severe, and is when Satan is here physically in the anti-Christ, Jesus in Revelation goes into more detail with the 7 trumpets and 7 bowls. From the 7th seal the book of Revelation is describing the last 3 ½ years of the tribulation until you get to chapter 20. With Matthew 24 verse 21 he is describing how the last 3 ½ years of the tribulation will be.

Matthew 24:21For then there will be great distress, unequaled from the beginning of the world until now—and never to be equaled again.

You should notice in the book of Revelation that between the ending and beginning of each series of Judgments there is a break. There seems to be a pause before the next series of judgments. You see this between the 7th seal and the first trumpet and you see this also between the 7th trumpet and the first bowl. During these pauses John gives more details of what has been happening during these judgments. We've already looked at some of these details earlier. Is this just a writing style, is John wanting to give the reader a break before continuing with the descriptions of the next judgments or will this be the way it will actually occur. Will God be giving mankind a break; giving mankind time to assess what has been happening and repent. With the seals as with the trumpets and bowls one judgment doesn't end and the next one starts. Here on earth there won't be a distinct point where one can point to and say when one ended and the next started. The first one will be continuing when the second starts and so on, they flow into the next. There just seems to be a pause between each series of judgments, at least there is in the writing.

Chapter 7 is one of those pauses where he begins with the description of the 144,000. We first see the 144,000 here in chapter 7 and that they are sealed before any harm has come to the earth so they will appear sometime after the beginning of the tribulation. They most likely come to believe in Jesus and are saved right after the rapture. Because they are called servants of God it is believed that they will be like evangelists, preaching the gospel. They will take over where the Church left off. It will now be their job to bring the Gospel to the world during Daniel's 70th Week. If the church were still here, there'd be no need for them, for the Church would still be preaching the gospel. But the Church is in Heaven, Daniel's 70th Week has begun and the Lord needs someone on Earth to be his messengers.

> Rev. 7:1After this I saw four angels standing at the four corners of the earth, holding back the four winds of the earth to prevent any wind from blowing on the land or on the sea or on any tree. 2Then I saw another angel coming up from the east, having the seal of the living God. He called out in a loud voice to the four angels who had been given power to harm the land

and the sea: 3"Do not harm the land or the sea or the trees until we put a seal on the foreheads of the servants of our God." 4Then I heard the number of those who were sealed: 144,000 from all the tribes of Israel.

With verses 5 thru 8 we see that there are 12,000 from each of the 12 tribes of Israel. We see here that they are sealed, saved if you will before any harm comes to the earth so this shows they are definitely saved before the 7th seal, before the trumpets. We don't see any mention of them again until chapter 14, which appears to be toward the end of the tribulation.

Rev. 14: 1Then I looked, and there before me was the Lamb, standing on Mount Zion, and with him 144,000 who had his name and his Father's name written on their foreheads. 2And I heard a sound from heaven like the roar of rushing waters and like a loud peal of thunder. The sound I heard was like that of harpists playing their harps. 3And they sang a new song before the throne and before the four living creatures and the elders. No one could learn the song except the 144,000 who had been redeemed from the earth. 4These are those who did not defile themselves with women, for they remained virgins. They follow the Lamb wherever he goes. They were purchased from among mankind and offered as firstfruits to God and the Lamb. 5No lie was found in their mouths; they are blameless.

As for it saying in chapter 14 these are those who did not defile themselves with women, for they are virgins, could mean that they have never had sex. They kept themselves pure. But Paul said that sex in marriage is holy and pure. It could be away of stating their Jewish purity, that they are pure Jews, that their ancestry hasn't been mixed with Gentiles, non-Jews, and that they are spiritually pure. I tend to go with the spiritually pure and to being pure Jewish rather than to the physical. This statement seems to set them apart from other Jewish men; this is why I tend to go with the spiritual purity and that they are pure Jews.

There's an interesting statement in the prophecy given by Zephaniah in chapter 3 concerning the Hebrew language of the Jewish people. He refers to it as a pure language.

> Zeph. 3: 9 "For then I will restore to the peoples a pure language, That they all may call on the name of the LORD, To serve Him with one accord. NKJV.

The Hebrew language was just about lost after the Babylonian destruction of Israel. Even during the time when Jesus was here there weren't many that spoke the ancient Hebrew language. After the destruction of the Temple and Jerusalem and the dispersion of the Jews by the Romans in 70 a.d., the language was totally lost until early in the 19th century when it began to be restored. After Israel became a nation again and greater numbers of the Jews began to return, to help unify the people it became a requirement for everyone to learn Hebrew.

Read Zeph. 3:9 from the Message bible:

> In the end I will turn things around for the people.
> I'll give them a language undistorted, unpolluted,
> Words to address God in worship

From the Amplified Bible:

> 9For then [changing their impure language] I will give to the people a clear and pure speech from pure lips, that they may all call upon the name of the Lord,

It's amazing that on May 15, 1948 Israel became a nation again and the ancient Hebrew language has been restored. Now all most all the Jews speak Hebrew. There has been no other nation that has been lost for thousands of years and then to return as a nation or a language to be lost for thousands of years to be restored. It should be obvious that we are living in the last days before the return of Jesus, and that we are in what is referred to as the end times. There are just too many bible prophecies that have been fulfilled and are being fulfilled right before our eyes. Israel becoming a nation again and the Jews returning is one major prophetic sign that had to happen before the tribulation and the return of Jesus back down to the earth. And with the ancient Hebrew language being restored it should be clear that God is not finished with Israel. He has not forgotten his promises to his ancient covenant people.

So I believe this statement, these are those who did not defile themselves with women, for they kept themselves pure, No lie was found in their mouths; they are blameless most likely refers more to their spiritual purity and to them being pure Jews.

With verses 9 through 17 we see a great multitude.

> Rev. 7: 9After this I looked and there before me was a great multitude that no one could count, from every nation, tribe, people and language, standing before the throne and in front of the Lamb. They were wearing white robes and were holding palm branches in their hands.

We see that they are wearing white robes, we saw this also with the 5th seal. This could be referring to those that have been saved right after the rapture but it also sounds like it is a prophetic reference to those that will be killed during the 2nd half of the tribulation. We see this with verses 13 through 17.

> Rev. 7: 13Then one of the elders asked me, "These in white robes—who are they, and where did they come from?" 14I answered, "Sir, you know." And he said, "These are they who have come out of the great tribulation; they have washed their robes and made them white in the blood of the Lamb. 15Therefore, "they are before the throne of God and serve him day and night in his temple; and he who sits on the throne will spread his tent over them. 16Never again will they hunger; never again will they thirst. The sun will not beat upon them, nor any scorching heat. 17For the Lamb at the center of the

throne will be their shepherd; he will lead them to springs of living water. And God will wipe away every tear from their eyes."

I'm sure for those that will be living during the tribulation and going through all this that these words will be a great comfort, some of them will have to die for their faith.

Revelation 8:

1When he opened **the seventh seal**, there was silence in heaven for about half an hour.

The second half of the tribulation is starting. Most likely Satan has now been cast out of the heavens and entered into the anti-Christ. We see this in Rev. Chapter 12. Satan being cast down to be physically here on the earth has to be seen has being wrath and a judgment from God. So it should be clear that all the trumpets are judgments and the wrath of God and it started first with the revealing of the man of sin, the anti-Christ. With Satan being cast down and with what is about to come upon the earth causes heaven to be in silence for about a half an hour. With the way it sounds there will literally be silence for about a half an hour. It's like all of heaven is taking a big gasp for air.

Again, here you can see how the 7 trumpets are part of the 7th seal. There are no judgments associated with the 7th seal. What we have next are the 7 trumpets.

10. The Seventh Seal and the Trumpets.

Revelation 8:

> 1When he opened **the seventh seal,** there was silence in heaven for about half an hour.
> 2And I saw the seven angels who stand before God, and to them were given seven trumpets.
> 3Another angel, who had a golden censer, came and stood at the altar. He was given much incense to offer, with the prayers of all the saints, on the golden altar before the throne. 4The smoke of the incense, together with the prayers of the saints, went up before God from the angel's hand. 5Then the angel took the censer, filled it with fire from the altar, and hurled it on the earth; and there came peals of thunder, rumblings, flashes of lightning and an earthquake.

The Trumpets

The trumpets are said to be judgments of thirds because they affect a third of everything.

> 6Then the seven angels who had the seven trumpets prepared to sound them.

> 7The **first angel sounded his trumpet,** and there came hail and fire mixed with blood, and it was hurled down upon the earth. A third of the earth was burned up, a third of the trees were burned up, and all the green grass was burned up.

Now this very well could be explaining the effects of the 6th Seal, the nuclear weapons that have been used in the war against Russia and the Islamic nations. This could still be limited to the Middle East, North Africa and Russia at this point, but where earlier it was covering a fourth of the area now it has spread out to a third. It will get worldwide later.

But from the way it sounds it could also be that it has now developed into WWIII. The nations of the world could now be warring against the anti-Christ. It has caused a third of everything to be burned up. This also sounds like it could be affecting a third of the whole world.

How could anyone not think this isn't also the wrath of God? As you will see from studying the book of Revelation for the most part the judgments would seem to be from manmade natural events, but this isn't unlike the Old Testament. The plaques on Egypt I'm sure looked just like natural things happening. I've seen documentaries explaining how all the plaques on Egypt could have happened, even the river turning to blood. But the bible says they were judgments. Because something could be seen as being from natural causes doesn't mean there not from God. You see in the Old Testament at times the judgments against Israel were by the armies from other nations, they were the instruments by which God was pouring out his judgment. It will be the same during the tribulation.

The natural effects from enough nuclear blasts would cause a lot of debris and smoke in the sky thus darkening the sun and the moon. Once the atmosphere starts clearing it will be different. The Ozone layer will have been destroyed more. Scientist already say that the earth's temperatures will become increasingly higher, extremely hotter. Saying that a third of the grass and trees were burned up doesn't necessarily mean by fire. The intense heat and lack of rain would cause the grass and trees to dry up thus looking like they were burned, and of course as we see happening so often in California and in the west, fires could start from such dry conditions. From such dry conditions one strike of lighting or a single match or cigarette can cause major fires, so it shouldn't be hard to imagine the grass and trees being burned up from nuclear weapons.

8The **second angel sounded his trumpet,** and something like a huge mountain, all ablaze, was thrown into the sea. A third of the sea turned into blood, 9a third of the living creatures in the sea died, and a third of the ships were destroyed.

Now this could be the result from a nuclear missile and fallout or it could be something falling from outer space into one of the Oceans. John said it was like a huge mountain all ablaze. It probably is a Meteor or Asteroid.

> 10The **third angel sounded his trumpet**, and a great star, blazing like a torch, fell from the sky on a third of the rivers and on the springs of water— 11the name of the star is Wormwood. A third of the waters turned bitter, and many people died from the waters that had become bitter.

Now this also could still be the result of a nuclear missile and fallout but there are those that believe this could also be a Meteor or Asteroid. From the description it does sound more like a Meteor or Asteroid. Whatever it is, it looked different from that of the 2nd trumpet for it looked like a star and is blazing like a torch. So this is bigger and brighter than the 2nd trumpet judgment. You see that it affects a third of the water. Wormwood means bitterness.

> 12The **fourth angel sounded his trumpet**, and a third of the sun was struck, a third of the moon, and a third of the stars, so that a third of them turned dark. A third of the day was without light, and also a third of the night.

Again, this will probably be from the result of all the fallout and debris filling the atmosphere from nuclear explosions as well as conventional bombs and/or from Meteors or Asteroids, and of course from volcanic eruptions caused by earthquakes. It sounds like that a third of the world's light from the sun, moon and stars is affected.

Just stop and think about the timing of all this. If the 2nd and 3rd trumpets are indeed Meteors and/or Asteroids, it should be obvious that it's not just a coincidence that this is happening during the 7 years of the tribulation. It should be clear that this is the time of God's wrath and judgment on the world.

Now just look at what is said before the next trumpet and notice there is a change with the next three trumpets.

13As I watched, I heard an eagle that was flying in midair call out in a loud voice: "Woe! Woe! Woe to the inhabitants of the earth, because of the trumpet blasts about to be sounded by the other three angels!"

These three Woe's, do they not sound like they are judgments, wrath. They are important enough that they are enounced with a woe. And notice it's the next three trumpets, not only the 7th. If the woe of the 7th trumpet is the wrath of God then the woes of the 5th and 6th trumpets are also, thus showing that the wrath of God starts before the 7th trumpet. So the belief that the wrath of God only starts with the 7 trumpet doesn't hold up. With the next three trumpets things are going to get worse.

Rev 9: 1The **fifth angel sounded his trumpet**, and I saw a star that had fallen from the sky to the earth. The star was given the key to the shaft of the Abyss. 2When he opened the Abyss, smoke rose from it like the smoke from a gigantic furnace. The sun and sky were darkened by the smoke from the Abyss.

Again, this could be a Meteor or Asteroid striking the earth, as if all the nuclear explosions haven't been enough. Jesus did say there would be signs in the heavens. This could cause a massive volcanic eruption. Notice what happens when it strikes the earth. It must be pretty major for it opens up a deep hole in the earth. Notice this also cause's the sun and sky to be darkened. But could this be referring to something other than a Meteor or Asteroid. Look at what happens next.

Rev. 9: 3And out of the smoke locusts came down upon the earth and were given power like that of scorpions of the earth. 4They were told not to harm the grass of the earth or any plant or tree, but only those people who did not have the seal of God on their foreheads. 5They were not given power to kill them, but only to torture them for five months. And the agony they suffered was like that of the sting of a scorpion when it strikes a man. 6During those days men will seek death, but will not find it; they will long to die, but death will elude them.

Now this could be a Meteor or Asteroid or even a Comet. But it could just as well be a reference to a fallen angel, demon or even to Satan. In the first chapter of Revelation we see that stars are used to refer to angels of the Churches.

Rev. 1: 20The mystery of the seven stars that you saw in my right hand and of the seven golden lampstands is this: The seven stars are the angels of the seven churches, and the seven lampstands are the seven churches.

Could this be referring back to Satan being cast out of the heavens? Remember, Satan is cast out with the 7th seal. We saw Satan being cast out and bringing his demons with him in chapter 12. Notice that he said he saw a star that 'had' fallen from the sky. Some believe this is referring to either a fallen angel or to Satan because verse 2 says it is given the key to the shaft of the Abyss and opens the Abyss. Verse 2 says, "When **he** opened the Abyss". I don't think that John would have phrased it like this if it were an object like and Meteor or Asteroid. Satan could use a Meteor or Asteroid to open up this hole to the Abyss, but look at verse 2 again, John didn't say something struck the earth to open this hole, he just said the star that had fallen to the earth opened the Abyss, again 'had' meaning it has already fallen, not he just saw it fall or that it was falling with the sounding of this trumpet. The star falling is not a result of the fifth trumpet but verses 2 thru 6 are. The last part of verse 1 says the star was given the key to the Shaft of the Abyss. Look at the description of these locusts.

Rev. 9: 7The locusts looked like horses prepared for battle. On their heads they wore something like crowns of gold, and their faces resembled human faces. 8Their hair was like women's hair, and their teeth were like lions' teeth. 9They had breastplates like breastplates of iron, and the sound of their wings was like the thundering of many horses and chariots rushing into battle. 10They had tails and stings like scorpions, and in their tails they had power to torment people for five months.

Some believe the descriptions given in verses 9 thru 10 could be of modern weaponry like an attack Helicopter. John said their shapes were like locusts and they looked like horses prepared for battle. The reflection of the sun off the pilot's helmets could have looked like crowns of gold. He saw the pilot's faces through the front window. The propellers could have looked like a woman's hair blowing in the wind. The front looked like lions teeth. Of course the Helicopters are made of iron and he described their sound as like the thundering of many horses and chariots rushing into battle.

But they could be some kind of massive bug or insect that we haven't seen before. Now I don't know exactly what these locusts are, but could these actually be deformed looking demons? Some believe they are actually demons. Notice that there told not to harm the grass, plants or trees but only those people who did not have the seal of God which would be those that have not accepted Jesus. They also were not given power to kill them but only to torture them for five months. ONLY God could control this. The pain inflicted by this judgment is so severe that men who are afflicted would rather die than suffer this torment, but they are not allowed to take the easy way out of death. As in the whole book of Revelation, God's Sovereignty is seen. This length of time may be allowed by God to give men the possibility to repent, though it appears from the last verses of this chapter that none of them do so, Revelation 9:19-20. Once the Abyss, or bottomless pit is opened, if these are indeed demons, its demonic inhabitants are set loose for the purpose of torturing people. Like locusts, they are numerous and destructive. Like scorpions, they inflict pain. But they are not allowed to kill. Each description is symbolic of some aspect of their power and activity. They are like horses prepared for battle, a description of strength. They seem to have crowns of gold, standing for power and authority, limited by God that they may not kill their victims. A human face implies intelligence. Lion's teeth picture ferocity, breastplates of iron show that they are invincible. Like normal locusts, they have wings. Wings symbolize mobility and speed. Their sound in flight is loud and terrifying like horses and chariots in battle.

So it sounds like this star could very well be referring back to Satan when he was cast down to the earth. This star wasn't ablaze like the star with the 3rd trumpet. Perhaps the most terrifying aspect of this fifth trumpet judgment is that these locusts could actually be the demons which have been imprisoned in the Abyss, or bottomless pit. Jude 1: 6And the angels who did not keep their positions of authority but abandoned their own home—these he has kept in darkness, bound with everlasting chains for judgment on the great Day.

Notice verse 11, They had as king over them the angel of the Abyss, whose name in Hebrew is Abaddon, and in Greek, Apollyon. Abaddon and Apollyon mean Destroyer. These are Hebrew and Greek words which are used in connection with hell, and normally refer to it as the place of destruction.

What do you think, does this sound like it's a judgment from God, and that it's the wrath of God. Again, it's not just a coincidence that this is occurring during the 7 years of the tribulation. This is a judgment from God, part of his wrath against the Christ rejecting world. This judgment could continue into the time of the bowls. But it could be that this one judgment will last 5 months, that the 6th trumpet will not occur until 5 months later.

12The first woe is past; two other woes are yet to come.

13The **sixth angel sounded his trumpet**, and I heard a voice coming from the horns of the golden altar that is before God. 14It said to the sixth angel who had the trumpet, "Release the four angels who are bound at the great river Euphrates."

The 6th trumpet is the second woe. John doesn't tell us that the second woe has passed until chapter 11 with verse 14. The 6th trumpet will release the 4 angels who will prepare the way for the armies of China to come into the Middle East for the battle of Armageddon. When we look at the bowls you will see that the 6th bowl is connected to the 6th trumpet, a result of the releasing of the four angels. So here again you can see that the trumpets have to also be the wrath of God for the 6th bowl started with the 6th trumpet, with the 6th bowl it gets much worse. It looks like the fighting starts here with the 6th trumpet and finds its climax with the 7th bowl at the battle of Armageddon. The 6th bowl is preparing for the 7th bowl, the last battle of Armageddon. The 6th trumpet only affects a third of mankind, the 6th and 7th bowls appear to be worldwide. Each series of judgments doesn't stop with the next judgment. The effects of the first trumpet judgment which started with the 7th seal can still be occurring during the bowl judgments.

> 15And the four angels who had been kept ready for this very hour and day and month and year were released to kill a third of mankind. 16The number of the mounted troops was two hundred million. I heard their number.
>
> 17The horses and riders I saw in my vision looked like this: Their breastplates were fiery red, dark blue, and yellow as sulfur. The heads of the horses resembled the heads of lions, and out of their mouths came fire, smoke and sulfur. 18A third of mankind was killed by the three plagues of fire, smoke and sulfur that came out of their mouths. 19The power of the horses was in their mouths and in their tails; for their tails were like snakes, having heads with which they inflict injury.

Now WWIII is well underway and China is now coming into it. Because of China's ties with Russia, Russia and China are already allies now; China is now coming against the anti-Christ's army and government. Only China can come up with an army of two hundred million. Most likely North Korea, India and Vietnam will be in this with China. The Euphrates River is what separates the east from the west. Remember the drying up of the Euphrates River can be done easily now by closing the Atatuak Dam in Turkey. An interesting fact about this verse is that during the time John was witnessing all this and writing it down, there wasn't 200 million people in the whole known world. John said he heard their number. Apparently the very hour and day and month and year for this are already predetermined. Everything will happen according to God's plan and word.

Notice the description in verses 17 through 19. It sounds like he saw nuclear missiles being fired and traveling thru the air and then exploding. Verse 19, "The power of the horses was in their mouths and in their tails; for their tails were like snakes, having heads with which they inflict injury". The description of a snake tail is a good description of the smoke trail behind a nuclear missile. Of course the front of a missile is what has the nuclear war head on it. Fiery red, dark blue, smoke and sulfur are good descriptions of the effects of nuclear explosions. We see with verse 18 that all this will kill a third of mankind. Could this now be global, no longer contained to just the Middle East and Europe? Read a description given by Zechariah. It sounds just like the effects of a thermal nuclear blast. We see in chapter 16 that this battle ends in the valley of Megiddo which is just outside of Jerusalem.

> Zech. 14: 12 This is the plague with which the LORD will strike all the nations that fought against Jerusalem: Their flesh will rot while they are still standing on their feet, their eyes will rot in their sockets, and their tongues will rot in their mouths. 15 A similar plague will strike the horses and mules, the camels and donkeys, and all the animals in those camps.

Now notice verse 20.

> 20The rest of mankind that were not killed by these plagues still did not repent of the work of their hands; they did not stop worshiping demons, and idols of gold, silver, bronze, stone and wood—idols that cannot see or hear or walk. 21Nor did they repent of their murders, their magic arts, their sexual immorality or their thefts.

With verses 20 and 21 you can see the purpose of all the judgments, God is trying to get people to repent and accept Jesus, but because of the hardness of their hearts they don't. Fortunately there will be some that will turn to God and accept Jesus.

With chapters 10 thru 15 we have a pause before the bowl judgments. We will see the blowing of the 7th trumpet in chapter 11 but we do not see the bowls until chapter 16.

We see in chapter 10 before the 7th trumpet and the 7 bowls that there is to be a further witness, warning or preaching if you will for God says "You must prophesy again' to the world. This is after the 6th trumpet, after the 2nd woe but before the 3rd woe and the mention of the 7th trumpet. It appears that this will be occurring between the 6th and 7th trumpet.

With the sounding of the 7th trumpet everyone has decided who he or she is going to follow, Jesus or the anti-Christ (Satan). By this time those that have rejected Jesus have taken the mark of the beast, they can no longer be saved. The fulfillment of the words of the prophets is about to be completed. So in chapter 10, before the sounding of the 7th trumpet and the pouring out of the bowl judgments we see one more warning, one more attempt by God to turn those that have not taken the mark of the beast yet to turn to his son Jesus. Here we are close to the end of the tribulation, just how close we don't know. We don't know the length of time it will take for the bowls.

The last statement in chapter 10 concerning the little scroll was "You must prophesy again about many peoples, nations, languages and kings." The preachers we see from the book of Revelation are the two witnesses and the 144,000, but I believe the 144,000 will have to go into hiding once Satan has entered into the anti-Christ.

The Two Witnesses.

The next description you have with chapter 11 verses 1 thru 14 is of the two witnesses. They will prophesy and preach the gospel for 1260 days, 3 ½ years, warning the world about the deception of the anti-Christ.

Some commentators believe that the two witnesses will be preaching during the first half of the tribulation and it's in the middle of the tribulation that the two witnesses are killed and then raised and taken up to heaven. They will be killed after Satan has entered into the man the anti-Christ. Then there are others that believe the two witnesses will be preaching during the second half of the tribulation, then are killed towards the end of the tribulation, then raised and taken up to heaven. The fact that Satan has now entered into the anti-Christ and the 144,000 Jewish servants have to go into hiding along with everyone that calls on the name of Jesus tends to support this for now there would be a need for supernatural witnesses from heaven that Satan will not be allowed to harm until their ministry is completed, so there would be a need for these supernatural witnesses. Whether they testify during the first or second half of the tribulation, they are not allowed to be killed until after their ministry is complete just to be a further witness and testimony when they are raised from the dead for the entire world to see. There are convincing arguments for both views. Those that will be here after the rapture will find out for sure.

It is Jerusalem that is being referred to by the statement, "the great city, which is figuratively called Sodom and Egypt, where also their Lord was crucified". Jesus was crucified in Jerusalem. Being figuratively called Sodom and Egypt is a way of describing their sinfulness and their turning away from God.

Could the time of year that this takes place be Christmas? John said they celebrated by sending each other gifts. Or will this be the new holiday. Christmas is already being changed to Holiday season.

Some believe that these two witnesses could actually be Elijah and Moses. The judgments from the two witnesses are like those of Elijah and Moses. Fire comes from their mouths and devours their enemies. These men have power to shut up the sky so that it will not rain during the time they are prophesying. This sounds like what we see from Elijah. And they have power to turn the waters into blood and to strike the earth with every kind of plague as often as they want. This sounds a lot like the judgments God poured out on Egypt through Moses. It was also Moses and Elijah that appeared with Jesus on the Mount when he was transfigured. (Mt. 17, Mark 9). Moses and Elijah represent the Law and the Prophets.

There are also those that believe the two witnesses will be Enoch and Elijah because both of them didn't die, God took them up to heaven. See Genesis chapter 5 and 2 Kings Chapter 2. They are the first reference to anyone being raptured. There are good arguments for both Moses and Enoch. It really doesn't matter who they actually are, they are both still servants of God. The people living during the tribulation may not know who they actually are and they may not either. They may just seem like two ordinary men. The point is that God is pouring out judgments through these two witnesses. They are testifying against the anti-Christ. They are preaching the return of Jesus and the coming kingdom. All the judgments through Moses just seemed like natural disasters and pestilence to the Egyptians. It wasn't until after the first-born died that pharaoh believed they were from God and agreed to let the Israelites go. It will most likely be the same during the tribulation.

How everyone will look upon the two witnesses' dead bodies.

We see in chapter 11 after Satan has entered the anti-Christ he kills the two witnesses. He leaves their bodies in a street in Jerusalem and they will be gazed upon all over the world. Then after 3 ½ days Jesus raises them up and takes them up to heaven.

We can now understand how everyone in the whole world will look upon their dead bodies and witness their resurrection. Satellite TV,

Dish, Cable TV. Before Satellite TV no one could understand how this could happen. There were those that wanted to throw out the book of Revelation entirely and those that spiritualized or allegorized revelation because they couldn't understand how everyone in the whole world could be looking on their dead bodies and they couldn't understand other things that we can now see are the results of nuclear, chemical and biological warfare, so since they couldn't see how it all could possibly happen, they dismissed the book of revelation being meant literally. The majority of the plagues of the Trumpet and bowl judgments appear to be from nuclear, biological and chemical weapons. We can see and understand all of this now. It was also really hard to understand the book of Revelation before Israel became a nation again. That is how post-millennialism and amillennialism and then preterism got started. How a lot of interpreters started allegorizing the book of Revelation.

It appears in chapter 14 there will be 3 angels also warning the world about the anti-Christ. God is really trying to convince the world to turn to him. We are told what their message is; this could also be a reference to what the two witnesses will be preaching also. The first angel will be telling everyone to worship God and that this is the time of his judgment. The second angel will be prophesying about the fall of the anti-Christ's one world government. The third angel will telling everyone not to believe and worship the anti-Christ, Satan, and whoever receives his mark will suffer the wrath of God. After telling how the two witnesses are killed and then raised and taken up to heaven by Jesus, John then mentions the 7th trumpet. We see that the 2nd woe has passed. After mentioning the 7th trumpet but before John goes into the 7 bowls of the 7th trumpet he pauses again with Chapters 12 through 15, another interlude to describe in more detail the events that have been taking place with the 6 trumpets. All this is before the 7 bowls. We don't see the bowls mentioned until chapters 15 and 16. Chapter 15 is the preparing of the pouring out of the bowls. Chapters 12 thru 14 John gives a panoramic view describing the events that will be occurring during the last 3 ½ years of the tribulation. The last thing we see in chapter 14 and before the pouring out of the bowl judgments is a harvest of the earth. We see there is a clear distinction now between those that have accepted Jesus and those that have accepted the anti-Christ. We see it will only be those that have accepted the anti-Christ that go to fight in the valley of Megiddo at the last battle of Armageddon. We see here also that no one else can be saved after the blowing of the 7th trumpet.

The Temple in Revelation 11

While we are at chapter 11 let me show you some interesting things we find in the first 2 verses. Verse one and two in chapter 11 tells us that John was told to go and measure the Temple of God and the altar, and count the worshipers there. He's told to exclude the outer court; do not measure it, because it has been given to the Gentiles.

It should be apparent now from what we have already covered from the book of Revelation that John is obviously transported into the future in order to view the events that occur during the tribulation as they unfold. This is why the word "saw" is used 49 times in 46 verses in Revelation because John is witnessing future events. This is the case also here in chapter 11.

When John received the revelation he was on the isle of Patmos in the year 95 or 96 A.D. at which time there was no Temple in Jerusalem. The Romans had destroyed the Temple and Jerusalem in 70 A.D. and all the Jews had been scattered. Preterist, for their view to work they have to date the book of Revelation before 70 A.D. so they use the fact that John was told to go and measure the temple as proof that the book was written before the temple's destruction. Actually it does not matter at all if the temple is not still standing in Jerusalem at the time John receives this revelation, since that would not have any bearing upon a vision or to the fact that John was sent into the future. John is told by the angel accompanying him to "measure the temple" (Rev. 11:1). Measure what temple? The Temple that is in the future. Even if there were a temple still standing in Jerusalem, John was on the Island of Patmos and would not have been allowed to go and measure that Temple. So John was not being told to physically go and measure an existing temple. In fact, Ezekiel, during a similar vision (Ezek. 40—48)

440

was told to measure the temple. When Ezekiel was told to go and measure the temple, there was not a Temple standing in Jerusalem. Thus, there is no compulsion whatsoever that just because a temple is referenced in Revelation 11 that it implies that there had to be a physical temple standing in Jerusalem at the time. So John and Ezekiel saw a yet future Temple.

There will have to be another Temple built for the scriptures tell us that the anti-Christ will enter the temple and desecrate it. It will be Israel's third Temple. This will probably be the most significant sign for the end times and of the return of Jesus. It probably will be rebuilt after the anti-Christ and Israel sign the covenant with the Islamic nations. But boy, wouldn't it be exciting to see Israel start rebuilding the temple before then, before the rapture.

Here's something interesting I got from Perry Stone from his Manafest program. It was either him or a friend of his that had talked to a prominent Jewish Rabbi about the rebuilding of the temple. He was asked how long he thought it would take for it to be rebuilt. The Rabbi said today it wouldn't take long at all, but what was interesting is that he said once it was built, because of the cycle of the Jewish feasts they would have to go through for its purification, this cycle would take 3 ½ years. The first half of the tribulation is 3 ½ years. Could it be that once it is built and the purification process is complete, Satan has now entered the anti-Christ and will actually stop the daily sacrifice before it is even able to get started? See Matthew 24, 2 Thes. 2:4 and Daniel 12 again.

Let me show you something else that is amazing. I first read this from a couple of Hal Lindsey's books. Since then I've seen Grant Jeffrey and others on TV talking about this also.

> Rev.11: 1I was given a reed like a measuring rod and was told, "Go and measure the temple of God and the altar, and count the worshipers there. 2But exclude the outer court; do not measure it, because it has been given to the Gentiles. They will trample on the holy city for 42 months.

It has been thought that the Jews could not rebuild their temple because of the Muslim Dome of the rock. Well back in the early 80's an archaeologist discovered an old alter of Moses among other things. From ancient documents describing the temple placed the Eastern gate exactly on the east/west centerline of the temple itself. A little domed cupola on the north/west corner of the present temple platform called the "Dome of the Tablets" and also the "Dome of the Spirits" covers one of the only two exposed protrusions of bedrock in the ancient Temple area. This little piece of bedrock is exactly on the east/west centerline of the ancient Eastern gate. This, and many other reasons, has led scholars to believe that this is the actual place within the ancient Holy of Holies where the Ark of the Covenant rested. They have laid out the exact Temple foundation location using other discoveries (such as a cornerstone of the inner court wall and an ancient subterranean water cistern). They all fit exactly with the present archeological discoveries and ancient descriptions of the Temple. By measurements taken from these locations they have discovered where the temple was actually built. John was told to measure the temple and the altar, and count the worshipers there but to exclude the outer court; do not measure it, because it has been given to the Gentiles. Where do you think the Muslim Dome of the rock is? In the outer court. Now isn't that something....

The Bible is the Word of God. Jesus is Lord, the only begotten Son of God the Father.

11. The Seventh Trumpet and the Bowls.

Here we continue with the Judgments. Remember, with chapters 10 thru 15 John pauses before he goes into the bowl judgments. Notice again like we saw with the 7th seal, there is no judgment associated with the 7th trumpet like they were with the 6 previous. It's because the 7 bowls are the judgments of the 7th trumpet.

The 7th trumpet is the third woe. The 5th trumpet was the first woe; the 6th trumpet was the second. John doesn't mention that the third woe has passed like the first two, I guess because there is no need to.

Since the 7 bowls are the result of the blowing of the 7th trumpet, I will start back in chapter 11 with the blowing of the 7th trumpet.

The Seventh Trumpet

Rev. 11:15 The seventh angel sounded his trumpet, and there were loud voices in heaven, which said:
"The kingdom of the world has become the kingdom of our Lord and of his Christ, and he will reign for ever and ever."
16And the twenty-four elders, who were seated on their thrones before God, fell on their faces and worshiped God,
17saying: "We give thanks to you, Lord God Almighty, the One who is and who was, because you have taken your great power and have begun to reign.
18The nations were angry; and your wrath has come.
The time has come for judging the dead, and for rewarding your servants the prophets and your saints and those who reverence your name, both small and great— and for destroying those who destroy the earth."
19Then God's temple in heaven was opened, and within his temple was seen the ark of his covenant. And there came flashes of lightning, rumblings, peals of thunder, an earthquake and a great hailstorm.

The 7th trumpet and the 7 bowls occur very close to the end of the 7 years of the tribulation. We see that those that are in heaven are proclaiming the coming of the kingdom of God here on earth.

Now we will jump to the bowls in chapter 15 since they are a continuation of the judgments and the 7th trumpet. Actually, the dragon, the beast out of the sea (the anti-Christ) and the beast out of the earth (the false prophet) that we see in chapters 12 and 13 are judgments also, they're just not associated with any particular trumpet, they are occurring during the trumpets and bowls. This is the case also with the descriptions we see with chapters 17 and 18.

Revelation 15

Seven Angels with Seven Plagues

> 1I saw in heaven another great and marvelous sign: seven angels with the seven last plagues—last, because with them God's wrath is completed.

The pre-wrath and post-trib folks say that only the bowls are the wrath of God. I'm not going to go into all the arguments that can be made against only the bowls being the wrath of God, what John said in verse one should be enough. Notice he said **last**, not the first. It says **God's wrath is completed** not beginning thus implying that there has already been God's wrath before this and so, God's wrath is not just starting. So the time before the 1st bowl is also God's wrath. So from this verse alone the argument that it's only the 7 bowls that are God's wrath doesn't hold up.

The pre-wrath and post-trib advocates in saying that this is when the wrath of God starts focus on it saying in verse 7 "the wrath of God." Because the bowls are the only place in Revelation that it uses the phrase wrath of God they say only the bowls are God's wrath. John was just saying that this is "seven" "bowls" filled with the wrath of God. It doesn't say that the bowls are only the wrath of God and that the seals and trumpets were not also. John had just said in verse 1 with the bowls the wrath of God is completed and that they were the last of God's wrath. So God's wrath has to be occurring before the bowls of wrath. With John referring to the bowls as the wrath of God and saying that the bowls are the last of his wrath and with these his wrath is completed implies that what came before was also the wrath of God. Nowhere does this imply that the seven seals or the seven trumpets were not also the wrath of God. He's just describing this phase of the wrath of God. **Rev. 14:10** describes this part of the wrath of God as **the wine** of God's fury, which has been poured **full strength** into the **cup of his wrath.** Look at **Rev. 14:19**, it refers to this part as the great **winepress of God's wrath.** Now in **Rev. 15** verse 7 **Rev. 16** verse 1 its **bowls** filled with God's wrath. John gives descriptions to the wrath of the 7th trumpet for it is indeed the most severe. The fact that the judgments of the bowls are 'poured out' indicates they are more severe than the previous judgments and would occur in a much shorter time frame and with much more intensity. Verses 9 and 10 of Rev. 14 says that those that worship and takes the mark of the beast will drink of the wine of God's fury, which has been **poured full strength into the cup of his wrath.**

The last 7 bowls are the final, full strength, wine of God's wrath. In the 7th trumpet is the climax of WWIII, the battle of Armageddon. There will be one massive worldwide nuclear exchange, destroying just about everything.

We see in chapter 6 that the people are saying that the great day of God's wrath has come, and in chapter 11 that his wrath has come. So the people living during the tribulation see the judgments of the seals and trumpets as the wrath of God.

I mentioned this in the beginning of this book. Another problem with the wrath of God being only the 7 bowls is that if the rapture happened just before the 7th trumpet whether it is a few months before Jesus' return or especially if it occurred on the same day as his return then there wouldn't be anyone left on earth that are saved to go into the kingdom of God.

If the rapture happens with or after the 7th trumpet there would not be any mortals to go into the 1000-year kingdom of God. All the righteous would have been raptured. Remember, the bowls of wrath happen after the earth was harvested, after those who worship the beast and his image have received his mark on the forehead or on the hand. No one can be saved by the time of the 1st bowl is poured out. Here in Revelation chapter 15 verse 8 says no one could enter the temple in Heaven until the seven plagues of the seven angels were completed. "8And the temple was filled with smoke from the glory of God and from his power, and no one could enter the temple until the seven plagues of the seven angels were completed." This is a way of saying no one else can be saved, that by this time everyone has sealed their fate. They have either accepted Jesus or accepted Satan by taking the mark of the beast. If anyone takes the mark of the beast they have denied Jesus and accepted the anti-Christ. See Revelation chapter 13. We know that the anti-Christ and the false prophet by this time have already forced everyone to take the mark of the beast by verse 2 here in chapter 15.

> 2And I saw what looked like a sea of glass mixed with fire and, standing beside the sea, those who had been victorious over the beast and his image and over the number of his name.

Read verses 9 and 10 of chapter 14 again,

> Rev. 14: 9A third angel followed them and said in a loud voice: "If anyone worships the beast and his image and receives his mark on the forehead or on the hand, 10 he, too, will drink of the wine of God's fury, which has been poured full strength into the cup of his wrath. He will be tormented with burning sulfur in the presence of the holy angels and of the Lamb.

If anyone receives this mark they cannot be saved. So there's no way you can say they got saved after the 7th trumpet is blown, after the pre-wrath rapture or on the day Jesus returns as with the post-trib view. Remember, the rapture has to occur before God's wrath.

So the rapture has to occur before the 7th trumpet. Again, the 7 bowls are the results of the 7th trumpet.

The pre-wrath view along with the post-trib view can't answer who would populate the 1000 years, for as we have just seen by the time the 7 bowls are being poured out no one else can be saved. By this time everyone has decided if they were going to take the mark of the beast or not. Everyone that was going to be saved has been saved. If the rapture happened at this point with the 7th trumpet then all those left would not be saved thus those that are in the valley of Megiddo would be slain at Jesus' 2nd coming, the rest would be separated by the angels after Jesus has returned with the separation of the sheep and the goats. All the righteous would have been raptured with no righteous people left on the earth. There would be no mortals to go into the 1000 years. Only those that survived the tribulation that are found righteous, those that are saved that have accepted Jesus as their Savior will go into the kingdom of God. So you can't say that the rapture occurs with the 7th trumpet for the 7 bowls are the results of the 7th trumpet. The rapture has to occur before the 7th trumpet.

The post-tribulation rapture view has the 7th trumpet with all seven bowls occurring on the actual day Jesus returns taking us up into the air and then immediately returning to the earth, like a big u-turn. I'll say this again, the rapture has to occur before the 7th trumpet. Everyone would have had to be saved before the 7th trumpet, during the 7 seals and 6 trumpets. The day Jesus returns is the end. The only thing that is left is Jesus sitting on the judgment seat. This is why we don't see any reference to the rapture in chapter 19 with Jesus' return. We see the resurrection of those that have died during the tribulation in chapter 20 after Jesus has returned and is here on earth. If the rapture was to occur just before Jesus returns or on the day of his returned then there would not be anyone to be raised after he has returned, everyone that is saved would have already been raised. One more time, the rapture has to occur before the 7th trumpet. As I pointed out earlier in our look at Revelation, this is why Rev. 4:1 is the best place in the book of Revelation for the timing of the rapture. While John doesn't come right out and say it, he does imply it with him being taken up, and from the fact we don't see the Church mentioned as being here throughout the seals, trumpets or bowls.

One argument I read from the post-trib view is that there will be little children that will be left to go into the kingdom. I'm sorry but this just doesn't make since. For one, if they were considered worthy to go into the kingdom then they would be worthy to go up in the rapture.

The kingdom of God starts out with only those that are saved, those that are righteous that have lived through the tribulation. By the time of the 7th trumpet, if the rapture was to occur now, then if someone is worthy of going into the kingdom then they would have been found worthy of going up in the rapture. Again, there would be no one here on earth as mortals to go into the 1000 years.

For those reading this that don't understand what I'm referring to about mortals and the 1000 years, there has to be people living during the 1000 year reign of Christ like we are now, mortals. Those that have been raised to life or raptured will be immortal. Our bodies will be like Jesus' is now.

Verse 2 and 3 of chapter 15 are referring to those that have been killed during the tribulation that are now in heaven. We see that they have been martyred for not taking the mark and swearing allegiance to the anti-Christ. Notice that he said they were victorious for dying for the Lord. Even those that die in the Lord, those that are killed for the word of God are considered victorious over Satan.

> 2And I saw what looked like a sea of glass mixed with fire and, standing beside the sea, those who had been victorious over the beast and his image and over the number of his name. They held harps given them by God 3and sang the song of Moses the servant of God and the song of the Lamb:
> "Great and marvelous are your deeds,
> Lord God Almighty.
> Just and true are your ways,
> King of the ages.

4Who will not fear you, O Lord,
and bring glory to your name?
For you alone are holy.
All nations will come
and worship before you,
for your righteous acts have been revealed."

They are praising God for what is about to come, they are proclaiming what will take place during the kingdom of God here on earth after Jesus has returned.

5After this I looked and in heaven the temple, that is, the tabernacle of the Testimony, was opened. 6Out of the temple came the seven angels with the seven plagues. They were dressed in clean, shining linen and wore golden sashes around their chests. 7Then one of the four living creatures gave to the seven angels seven golden bowls filled with the wrath of God, who lives for ever and ever. 8And the temple was filled with smoke from the glory of God and from his power, and **no one could enter the temple until the seven plagues of the seven angels were completed.**

Revelation 16, The Bowl Judgments.

Now let's read Chapter 16. Remember, these are the judgments of the 7th trumpet.

REV 16:1 Then I heard a loud voice from the temple saying to the seven angels, "Go, pour out the seven bowls of God's wrath on the earth."

The first 5 Bowls of God's Wrath could very well be the result of radiation fallout and poisoning from the nuclear and chemical weapons from the previous trumpets. From the descriptions you can see that this is worldwide. Remember, those that have not taken the mark of the beast are in hiding.

2The **first angel went and poured out his bowl** on the land, and ugly and painful sores broke out on the people who had the mark of the beast and worshiped his image.

3The **second angel poured out his bowl** on the sea, and it turned into blood like that of a dead man, and every living thing in the sea died.

4The **third angel poured out his bowl** on the rivers and springs of water, and they became blood. 5Then I heard the angel in charge of the waters say:
"You are just in these judgments,
you who are and who were, the Holy One,
because you have so judged;
6for they have shed the blood of your saints and prophets,
and you have given them blood to drink as they deserve."
7And I heard the altar respond:
"Yes, Lord God Almighty,
true and just are your judgments."

8The **fourth angel poured out his bowl** on the sun, and the sun was given power to scorch people with fire. 9They were seared by the intense heat and they cursed the name of God, who had control over these plagues, but they refused to repent and glorify him.

This could be from the nuclear weapons or from sun bursts.

10The **fifth angel poured out his bowl** on the throne of the beast, and his kingdom was plunged into darkness. Men gnawed their tongues in agony 11and cursed the God of heaven because of their pains and their sores, but they refused to repent of what they had done.

With the fifth bowl, you see the fulfillment of what the second angel in Revelation chapter 14 was proclaiming in verse 8 "A second angel followed and said, "Fallen! Fallen is Babylon the Great, which made all the nations drink the maddening wine of her adulteries." This will be the collapse of not only his government but also the false religion, the Mystery Babylon of Revelation chapter 17. This could be why the angel said "fallen, fallen".

The nations of the world have now rebelled against the anti-Christ and are now fighting against each other. WWIII is well underway. The revived Roman Empire, the one world government, the 10-region empire of the anti-Christ is falling apart. These bowls are a continuation of what started with the trumpets.

All this sounds like the first five bowls are the results from massive nuclear exchanges all over the world that occurred during the trumpets. The radiation fallout will cause ugly and painful sores; will pollute the water and eat the ozone layer away causing the heat from the sun to be much greater. You can also see that this is occurring over an extended period of time, not on a single day. Don't forget what we see described here with the 7 bowls are all part of the 7th trumpet. So the 7th trumpet takes longer than one day to occur. From verses 8 thru 14 it sounds like they would have to take at least several months. We see this with the 6th trumpet.

Compare again what we've read so far with Zech. 14:12 thru 15.

Zech. 14:12 This is the plague with which the LORD will strike all the nations that fought against Jerusalem: Their flesh will rot while they are still standing on their feet, their eyes will rot in their sockets, and their tongues will rot in their mouths. 13 On that day men will be stricken by the LORD with great panic. Each man will seize the hand of another, and they will attack each other. 15 A similar plague will strike the horses and mules, the camels and donkeys, and all the animals in those camps.

John we know was taken up to heaven and then sent into the future to actually see all these things. Zechariah and the other prophets whether they were sent into to the future or just saw a vision, they were still seeing, witnessing these same future events. Verse 12, 'Their flesh will rot while they are still standing on their feet, their eyes will rot in their sockets, and their tongues will rot in their mouths'. This definitely sounds like what happens if you're close to a nuclear explosion. You're melted from within. Notice a similar plague striking the animals.

Read all of **Joel Chapters 1, 2 and 3** but for now notice these verses.

JOEL 1: 2 Hear this, you elders; listen, all who live in the land. Has anything like this ever happened in your days or in the days of your forefathers?

JOEL1:10 The fields are ruined, the ground is dried up; the grain is destroyed, the new wine is dried up, the oil fails.

JOEL 1:15 Alas for that day!
For the day of the LORD is near;
 it will come like destruction from the Almighty.

JOEL 1:19 To you, O LORD, I call, for fire has devoured the open pastures and flames have burned up all the trees of the field.

JOEL 1:20 Even the wild animals pant for you; the streams of water have dried up and fire has devoured the open pastures.

JOEL 2:1 Blow the trumpet in Zion; sound the alarm on my holy hill. Let all who live in the land tremble, for the day of the LORD is coming. It is close at hand--

JOEL 2:2 a day of darkness and gloom, a day of clouds and blackness. Like dawn spreading across the mountains a large and mighty army comes, such as never was of old nor ever will be in ages to come. 3 Before them fire devours, behind them a flame blazes. Before them the land is like the garden of Eden, behind them, a desert waste-- nothing escapes them.

JOEL 2:10 Before them the earth shakes, the sky trembles, the sun and moon are darkened, and the stars no longer shine.

JOEL 2:11 The LORD thunders at the head of his army; his forces are beyond number, and mighty are those who obey his command. The day of the LORD is great; it is dreadful. Who can endure it?

JOEL 2:30 I will show wonders in the heavens and on the earth, blood and fire and billows of smoke. 31 The sun will be turned to darkness and the moon to blood before the coming of the great and dreadful day of the LORD.

Look at this from Isaiah.

ISA 13:9 See, the day of the LORD is coming --a cruel day, with wrath and fierce anger-- to make the land desolate and destroy the sinners within it. 10 The stars of heaven and their constellations will not show their light. The rising sun will be darkened and the moon will not give its light.

ISA. 34: 4 All the stars of the heavens will be dissolved
and the sky rolled up like a scroll;
all the starry host will fall like withered leaves from the vine,
like shriveled figs from the fig tree

In 2 Peter chapter 3 with the 7th and 10th verses he said "the present heavens and earth are reserved for fire, being kept for the day of judgment and destruction of ungodly men" and "The heavens will disappear with a roar; the elements will be destroyed by fire, and the earth and everything in it will be laid bare".

All this is referring to the tribulation, not to Jesus' 2nd coming. When Jesus returns he is not going to destroy the land, sea or water. He's only going to destroy those that have assembled in the valley of Megiddo against him. He's not going to destroy those across the world that have rejected him and accepted Satan at his 2nd coming. They will be judged later after he sits on his throne in judgment. Remember the separation of the sheep and the goats.

With the sixth bowl we come to the last battle of Armageddon.

> **Rev. 16**: 12The **sixth angel poured out his bowl** on the great river Euphrates, and its water was dried up to prepare the way for the kings from the East. 13Then I saw three evil spirits that looked like frogs; they came out of the mouth of the dragon, out of the mouth of the beast and out of the mouth of the false prophet. 14They are spirits of demons performing miraculous signs, and they go out to the kings of the whole world, to gather them for the battle on the great day of God Almighty.

This is when the anti-Christ (Satan) will convince all the nations of the world that were not part of the conflict with Russia's and the Islamic nations invasion of Israel to unite with him to meet the threat of China and the other Asian nations.

China and the Asian countries with them will decide that the time is ripe to come against the ant-Christ and his army and come into the Middle East. The Euphrates River is dried up to make a way for them. This second phase lead by China will most likely be because the anti-Christ came to Israel's aid against Russia and the Islamic nations. It could also be because once Satan is in the man, the anti-Christ that he is such a ruthless dictator that the nations with China will not fallow him any longer.

If China defeats the anti-Christ then China will have control over the whole earth. After the anti-Christ, the Revived Roman Empire has defeated Russia and the Islamic nations then the anti-Christ will have control over the oil supply. So you can see how the anti-Christ will be able to convince all the nations that are still part of his one world government to come and help him against this threat from China. This will culminate into the battle of Armageddon where all the countries of the world will meet in one last attempt to take control of the world. When you read Revelation and Ezekiel you see that nuclear weapons have already been used in the battle of the anti-Christ against Russia and the Islamic nations. We see that Russia will be defeated and later Moscow will be totally destroyed. You would think that the nations would have learned something from all this already. But, not only will they fight each other in the valley of Megiddo but as we have and will see, they release a massive nuclear attack on each other all over the world causing all the faults under the surface of the earth to shift causing worldwide earthquakes, for we see that all the cities of the world collapse.

It doesn't appear that Russia was totally destroyed earlier so they will be in this with China. This is totally global now. Back with the 6th trumpet before this massive accumulation of armies arrives in this valley they kill a third of the world's population. You can see how the bowls are a continuation of the trumpets.

> Rev. 9: 13The sixth angel sounded his trumpet, and I heard a voice coming from the horns of the golden altar that is before God. 14It said to the sixth angel who had the trumpet, "Release the four angels who are bound at the great river Euphrates." 15And the four angels who had been kept ready for this very hour and day and month and year were released to kill a third of mankind. 16The number of the mounted troops was two hundred million. I heard their number.

What began with the 6th trumpet has now escalated into what will be the last battle of WWIII, the battle of Armageddon.

This battle here is not when Jesus returns, this is when all the nations of the world, China and Russia and the other eastern nations come into the valley of Megiddo to come against the armies of the anti-Christ, which is actually Satan now, and the armies of the nations that are still part of the revived Roman Empire of the anti-Christ. The anti-Christ, Satan has already made Jerusalem his headquarters so all the armies from the east are marching to Jerusalem; the anti-Christ will come to the valley of Megiddo to meet them. Here with this battle they just about destroy everything.

It's after this battle that Satan gets what is left of the armies of the world to unite with him. They gather together to try to stop Jesus and his armies of heaven.

> REV 16:15 "Behold, I come like a thief! Blessed is he who stays awake and keeps his clothes with him, so that he may not go naked and be shamefully exposed."

Verse 15 is like John was taking a breath, with the magnitude of what he was writing he was pausing reminding those that would be reading this before the tribulation started to be sure to keep watch and be ready for the Lord's return, be ready and watching for the rapture, reminding us that Jesus said he will come back for us like a thief, before the day of the Lord. Don't forget that the book of Revelation was first sent as letters to 7 churches to be read.

Jesus to the Church,

> Rev.3:3 Remember, therefore, what you have received and heard; obey it, and repent. But if you do not wake up, I will come like a thief, and you will not know at what time I will come to you.

Remember what Jesus said in Matthew 24 and Paul in 1 Thessalonians chapter 5 and 2 Thessalonians chapter 2. While the rapture, Jesus coming for his bride will occur like a thief, the day of the Lord will also, the day of the Lord is the tribulation. The rapture will usher in the day of the Lord.

Paul wrote:

> 1TH 5:1 Now, brothers, about times and dates we do not need to write to you, 2 for you know very well that the day of the Lord will come like a thief in the night. 3While people are saying, "Peace and safety," destruction will come on them suddenly, as labor pains on a pregnant woman, and they will not escape. 4 But you, brothers, are not in darkness so that this day should surprise you like a thief.

While people are saying there's peace and safety. As you can see from all we have read here in the book of Revelation and from the Old Testament prophets, at Jesus' second coming there is no peace and safety.

Remember, his second coming will not be like a thief, but the day of the Lord, the Tribulation will. The rapture is what starts the day of the Lord. The 7 year count down just doesn't start until the anti-Christ, Israel and the Islamic nations sign the covenant peace agreement together.

This was written to Christians, to the Church, first to 7 Churches. It is a message to the Church. It's ultimately a message of victory. This is part of the Gospel also. Although most of the book of Revelation is a prophecy of the 7 years just before Jesus returns back to earth, it has a message of victory through Jesus, that no matter what kind of trials and tribulations you might be going through, if you stand firm with Jesus through this life you will stand with him in heaven and the kingdom of God. This message could be applied to everyone throughout the whole Church age. It will also be a message to all those that will be living during the tribulation. It shows that Jesus will triumph and Satan will be defeated. Those in Jesus will triumph. Remember what we read in the first chapter.

> Rev. 1:The revelation of Jesus Christ, which God gave him to show his servants what must soon take place. He made it known by sending his angel to his servant John, 2who testifies to everything he saw—that is, the word of God and the testimony of Jesus Christ. 3Blessed is the one who reads the words of this prophecy, and blessed are those who hear it and take to heart what is written in it, because the time is near. 4John, To the seven churches in the province of Asia:

I'm sure that those left after the Rapture will be reading it like crazy. You may ask if the Church is not going to be present during all of this then why did he give this message to the Church; my answer would be because the Church is to keep the words of this prophecy alive and intact. It tells us to be watching and waiting for the Lords return for his Church. As we have seen from the words of Jesus and the Apostle Paul, all Christians since Jesus ascended back to heaven are to live in a constant expectancy of his return, we're to be watching. This is to be a motivation for our Christian living. Also, as we can see now with world events lining up and occurring, with the way nations are allying themselves together, we can see that the prophecies in the bible are true. We can see that the requirements and technology are here now for what we see described here in the book of Revelation.

This is a warning that if you reject Jesus, if you are alive at the time of Jesus' coming for his Church you will go through all this. For those that will be living during the tribulation it is a warning to not be deceived by Satan. For those alive before the tribulation as well as for those that will be living during it, these prophecies shows that the God of the bible is the one and only true God. That Jesus is the only begotten Son of God the Father. Jesus is Lord.

12. The Seventh Bowl and the Battle of Armageddon.

Let's continue with chapter 16.

> 16Then they gathered the kings together to the place that in Hebrew is called Armageddon.

The seventh bowl is completed right before Jesus returns. It's the battle of Armageddon. Rev. 16:17-21. It appears that there will be a massive nuclear exchange causing massive earthquakes. Did you know that they now have bombs that they call 'earthquake bombs'?

> 17The **seventh angel poured out his bowl** into the air, and out of the temple came a loud voice from the throne, saying, "It is done!" 18Then there came flashes of lightning, rumblings, peals of thunder and a severe earthquake. No earthquake like it has ever occurred since man has been on earth, so tremendous was the quake. 19The great city split into three parts, and the cities of the nations collapsed. God remembered Babylon the Great and gave her the cup filled with the wine of the fury of his wrath. 20Every island fled away and the mountains could not be found. 21From the sky huge hailstones of about a hundred pounds each fell upon men. And they cursed God on account of the plague of hail, because the plague was so terrible.

The 7th bowl is the final battle of Armageddon. It is describing one massive nuclear exchange apparently all over the world. As I've mentioned earlier, this is the climax of WWIII. All the armies of the world are now in the valley of Megiddo. This is the final battle when all the nations of the world fight against one another. Man has finally done it. They probably will be releasing just about all the nuclear missiles they have. They have released massive nuclear exchanges on all the major cities of the world. You can look at the descriptions of the trumpets and bowls and see how they are from the natural effects of nuclear explosions and radiation fallout and most likely from the effects of chemical weapons also.

Remember this from Zechariah.

> Zech. 14:12 This is the plague with which the LORD will strike all the nations that fought against Jerusalem: Their flesh will rot while they are still standing on their feet, their eyes will rot in their sockets, and their tongues will rot in their mouths. 13 On that day men will be stricken by the LORD with great panic. Each man will seize the hand of another, and they will attack each other.

It says that the great city split into three parts. It sounds like there will be a massive nuclear explosion in Jerusalem. His description of flashes of lightning, rumblings, peals of thunder is how nuclear explosions looked and sounded to John. Look at a description from Zechariah. He starts off describing the battle of Armageddon.

> Zech. 14:3 Then the LORD will go out and fight against those nations, as he fights in the day of battle. 4 On that day his feet will stand on the Mount of Olives, east of Jerusalem, and the Mount of Olives will be split in two from east to west, forming a great valley, with half of the mountain moving north and half moving south. 5 You will flee by my mountain valley, for it will extend to Azel. You will flee as you fled from the earthquake in the days of Uzziah king of Judah. <u>Then the LORD my God will come, and all the holy ones with him.</u>

Look at this description of the day that Jesus returns.

> Zech. 14:6 On that day there will be no light, no cold or frost. 7 It will be a unique day, without daytime or nighttime--a day known to the LORD. When evening comes, there will be light.

From the way it sounds with them marching into the valley of Megiddo, the nation's probably first try to fight this out without using anymore nuclear weapons, but the battle must not go so good for any one of the armies so now all the nations have just gone crazy sending nuclear bombs all over the world. Verse 18 says that a severe earthquake occurs. That no earthquake like it has ever occurred since man has been on earth. Verse 20 says every island fled away and the mountains collapse. With so many nuclear bombs striking the earth it causes major earthquakes and tidal waves. The continents will be changed. With all the craters and fault lines under the earth you can see how massive nuclear blasts could cause a chain reaction that would affect every city and island all over the world. You see the cities of the world collapse, Islands disappear from the massive tidal waves, and from the earthquakes, mountains grumble, Volcano's erupt. Verse 21 mentions huge hailstones of about a hundred pounds. Scientists call this a nuclear winter. This is what will happen in the atmosphere after a major thermal nuclear blast. Amazing.

Only those that have rejected Jesus will take part in this last battle of Armageddon. The Jews have fled Jerusalem and are in hiding and I'm sure any one that has not taken the mark of the beast has had to go into hiding by this time from the anti-Christ. For we saw back in chapter 12 verse 17 that the anti-Christ was enraged at Israel and went off to make war against the rest of her offspring—those who obey God's commandments and hold to the testimony of Jesus. And notice, he said the rest of Israel's offspring, not the Church. While those that are Israel's offspring and hold to the testimony of Jesus are now Christians, they are not part of the Church, the Church has already been taken to the Father's house. I would think here for sure if the Church was here during this time John would have described them as the Church, not as Israel's offspring.

This battle will happen; the bible describes it here in Revelation and in the Old Testament. All of this describes WWIII. Isn't it interesting how the number 3 is a significant number we see used throughout the bible and that we have had two actual world wars already and we see a third one described in the Old Testament and especially in Revelation. Something interesting about the first two world wars is that after WWI the Jews were allowed to start returning to Israel, after WWII Israel became a nation again. After the next world war, WWIII, the Jews will finally receive what they have longed for, the Messiah and the kingdom of God here on earth. World War III will bring the return of Jesus back to the earth to establish the earthly kingdom of God.

We can see from the trumpets and the bowls that this is a continuing war that just continues to escalate to the point we see here in Rev. 16. In Revelation chapter 6 with the 4th seal you see a 4th part of the earth was affected. Then in chapter 9 with the 6th trumpet you see a 3rd of mankind is killed. You can see how each series of judgments increase. We can see that this, WWIII is a judgment from God and the instrument in which he pours out his wrath for it effects the whole world. This war started back with the 2nd seal. This will be the battle of or at Armageddon. This valley is also called Armageddon.

Preterist say there is no valley of Armageddon and there will be no battle there. The bible says there is. The valley of Jehoshaphat and the plain of Megiddo are both the same as the valley of Armageddon as well as the valley of decision. This valley exists today. It's in northern Israel. You can go and look out over it. Megiddo was an ancient city that's in ruins today that's on a plateau on the eastern side of Mount Carmel facing the valley. It was made into a fortress by King Solomon. In 1800 Napoleon, after being defeated in Egypt, while passing through this valley on his way back to France said that all the armies of the world could assemble their forces and fight in this valley. There have been many battles throughout history that have been fought in this valley. There will be one more battle that all the nations of the earth will fight against each other.

But this is not then end yet. This isn't when Jesus returns, he returns after this battle. We see Jesus returning in chapter 19. We don't know how much time there will be after this battle, though there may be a clue in Daniel chapter 12, but after this last battle of Armageddon the anti-Christ somehow convinces what is left of the people of the world to unite with him against Jesus' return. Like I've said before, it would appear that they know he his returning.

Here it's the nations fighting one another, in chapter 19 you see what's left of the armies of the world gathered together to fight against Jesus returning. Compare the description here in chapter 16 of the 7th bowl with that in Revelation 19. In chapter 16 you see the bowls are nuclear explosions and their effects, and with the 7th bowl apparently one massive nuclear exchange, in chapter 19 its description is not like the one in chapter 16, there's no nuclear weapons, no fighting, Jesus doesn't cause the cities of the world to collapse or the mountains to crumble, we're told in chapter 19 they are destroyed by the word of God out of the mouth of Jesus.

> Rev. 19: 11I saw heaven standing open and there before me was a white horse, whose rider is called Faithful and True. With justice he judges and makes war. 12His eyes are like blazing fire, and on his head are many crowns. He has a name written on him that no one knows but he himself. 13He is dressed in a robe dipped in blood, and his name is the Word of God. 14The armies of heaven were following him, riding on white horses and dressed in fine linen, white and clean. 15Out of his mouth comes a sharp sword with which to strike down the nations. "He will rule them with an iron scepter." He treads the winepress of the fury of the wrath of God Almighty.

Once the armies of the nations have just about destroyed themselves and the earth, then they gather together to make war against Jesus, the rider on the white horse and his army we see described in Revelation chapter 19. This is just astonishing. The nations have just about destroyed and wiped out themselves and everything on the earth and now they will unite together to try to stop Jesus. I'm sure the same three evil spirits we saw with the 6th bowl that looked like frogs; that came out of the mouth of the dragon, out of the mouth of the beast and out of the mouth of the false prophet will deceive the nations again into joining forces against Jesus returning.

Because of all the destruction caused by the battle of Armageddon, the fighting and releasing of nuclear weapons the light of the sun and stars will not be able to get through all the smoke and debris in the air.

The Rapture and End Time Prophecies for Beginners

Remember what Jesus said in Matthew 24.

> Mt. 24: 29"Immediately after the distress of those days
> "'the sun will be darkened,
> and the moon will not give its light;
> the stars will fall from the sky,
> and the heavenly bodies will be shaken.

After all the fighting has stopped, Satan sees that Jesus and his army are coming. Could it be because Jesus and those with him, the Church, will be in physical immortal bodies, they pick us up on radar coming through space. At some point in space we will just appear, but how far out from the earth. And don't forget, Satan will be able to calculate the timing of Jesus' return. Satan most likely convinces them that all this has been Jesus' fought and they must stop him from returning or deceives them in thinking that we are aliens from outer space. Rev. 19 11 - 21. He may have told the world that it was aliens that took us up in the rapture.

We saw in Ezekiel 38 and 39 he gave us the details of Russia, the king from the far north, Gog and Magog and the other Northern European countries along with the Islamic countries coming against Israel. In Daniel chapter 11 he also gives the details of the King of the North, the anti-Christ, and the King of the South, Egypt and the Northern African Islamic countries coming against the anti-Christ when he comes against them on Israel's behalf. We see that this starts with the 2nd seal in Revelation.

Then Daniel gives the details of Russia, the king from the far north in Ezekiel, and China, the kings of the East coming against the anti-Christ, which we just saw here in Revelation happens in the valley of Armageddon. And you also have in Isaiah, Zachariah, Job and many other Old Testament books the description of the war of the Tribulation.

When you put all this together you're able to get a good idea of WWIII and the last battle of Armageddon in the valley of Megiddo. We just saw here in Revelation that the number of the troops that will be coming with just China will be two hundred million. Add the number from all the other countries of the world that will be assembled in this valley and there could be over 3 or 4 hundred million or more that take part in the last battle of Armageddon. No wonder after Jesus has returned it will take Israel 7 months to cleanse the land of all the dead.

You cannot find any time in history that any of this occurred. The destruction of Israel in 70 a.d. will not fit with all of this. Since this has not happened in the past, AND because the bible says it will happen, this has to be for a yet future time. God, through his prophets said it would come, so you can count on it happening.

Concerning the battle of Armageddon, you can read or hear some prophecy teachers refer to the day Jesus returns as the battle of Armageddon because the armies of the world will be assembled there in the valley of Megiddo. As we just saw they are already there when Jesus returns. This can get confusing. I guess the battle of Armageddon could refer to both the battle where the nations of the world fight against each other and to when Jesus returns. As we just saw there will be a battle in the valley of Megiddo where the nations fight each other. It sounds more like that the bible with the 6th and 7th bowls is referring to the last battle of Armageddon when all the nations of the world are assembled in the valley of Megiddo to fight against each other, not to fight against Jesus. Jesus is not part of the battle where the nations are fighting each other. The descriptions of the 7th bowl given in verses 17 thru 21 do not occur with the return of Jesus. There are no nuclear weapons used on the day Jesus returns. In Revelation chapter 19 when we see Jesus returning there isn't any battle at all. You see another clue that this is not the return of Jesus with verse 21, from the sky huge hailstones of about a hundred pounds each fell upon men. And they cursed God on account of the plague of hail, because the plague was so terrible. We see them cursing God for all these plagues. There has to be some time after this battle for them to be cursing God. Once Jesus has returned everyone will know the truth, that he is the Son of the Living God. They won't be cursing God then.

Keep this in mind. The 7 bowls are a result of the 7th trumpet. We don't know just how long it takes for the 7 bowls to be completed and we are not told how long it will be after this last battle of WWIII until Jesus' return. You can see that after this, in Rev.19, the armies of the world come together to make war against Jesus returning from heaven. We don't know just how long it will take the anti-Christ, Satan to accomplish this, but it doesn't appear it will take long.

You can look at all of WWIII as Armageddon with its climax in the valley of Megiddo or Armageddon. The battle of Armageddon will be the last campaign of WWIII. The tribulation could be referred to as Armageddon. Armageddon has become a term to describe the end of the world. Today you see Armageddon used to describe mass destruction of any type. In movies today, the term Armageddon is used to describe the end, whether it is from tornados, hurricanes, volcanoes, earthquakes or nuclear weapons. The movie Armageddon is a good example. From all the destruction that will be caused by nuclear weapons and possibly comets, meteors and asteroids it will certainly look like the end of everything. Remember, the world is not going to end. Jesus returns before man and everything has died.

Remember what Jesus said in Matthew 24; 22If those days had not been cut short, no one would survive, but for the sake of the elect those days will be shortened. It all occurs on his time table. This last battle at Armageddon will be what brings Jesus back. Remember the 6th trumpet in chapter 9 verse 15 "the four angels who had been kept ready for this very hour and day and month and year were released to kill a third of mankind". This last battle has its time determined also. In the 17th verse with the 7th bowl he said 'It is done'. Man's rebellion and the evil of his heart has reached its full. From all the destruction that has been caused and now with the 7th bowl if Jesus doesn't return to stop it and restore everything no life could survive. As I already mentioned, from all the smoke that will be in the sky from the nuclear blasts, fires, volcanos, Meteors, Asteroids there won't be any light from the sun, moon or stars. Just think of all the pollution in the air and water. Nothing could survive. But as I will show you later Jesus does indeed cleanse and restore the earth.

Read what the Old Testament Prophets Isaiah and Jeremiah had to say about this time. These are only a few of the scriptures. Isaiah and Jeremiah as well as other Old Testament prophets are full of prophecies of the tribulation. These last 7 years that we saw from Daniel chapter 9 allotted to Israel are probably the most prophesied about in the whole bible.

Isaiah 24

The LORD's Devastation of the Earth

1 See, the LORD is going to lay waste the earth
and devastate it;
he will ruin its face
and scatter its inhabitants-

2 it will be the same
for priest as for people,
for master as for servant,
for mistress as for maid,
for seller as for buyer,
for borrower as for lender,
for debtor as for creditor.

3 The earth will be completely laid waste
and totally plundered.

4 The earth dries up and withers,
the world languishes and withers,
the exalted of the earth languish.

5 The earth is defiled by its people;
they have disobeyed the laws,
violated the statutes
and broken the everlasting covenant.

6 Therefore a curse consumes the earth;
its people must bear their guilt.
Therefore earth's inhabitants are burned up,
and very few are left.

13 So will it be on the earth
and among the nations,
 as when an olive tree is beaten,
or as when gleanings are left after the grape harvest.

17 Terror and pit and snare await you,
O people of the earth.

18 Whoever flees at the sound of terror
will fall into a pit;
whoever climbs out of the pit
will be caught in a snare.
The floodgates of the heavens are opened,
the foundations of the earth shake.

19 The earth is broken up,
the earth is split asunder,
the earth is thoroughly shaken.

20 The earth reels like a drunkard,
it sways like a hut in the wind;
so heavy upon it is the guilt of its rebellion
that it falls—never to rise again.

As we have seen, all the nuclear explosions all over the world will bring this about. Scientists say that the earth's axis could change, tilt. Interesting. All that Isaiah just described we don't see happening in chapter 19 where we see Jesus returning but we do see it occurring throughout the tribulation.

21 In that day the LORD will punish
the powers in the heavens above
and the kings on the earth below.

22 They will be herded together
like prisoners bound in a dungeon;
they will be shut up in prison
and be punished after many days.

23 The moon will be abashed, the sun ashamed;
for the LORD Almighty will reign
on Mount Zion and in Jerusalem,
and before its elders, gloriously.

Isaiah 34

1 Come near, you nations, and listen;
pay attention, you peoples!
Let the earth hear, and all that is in it,
the world, and all that comes out of it!

2 The LORD is angry with all nations;
his wrath is upon all their armies.
He will totally destroy them,
he will give them over to slaughter.

3 Their slain will be thrown out,
their dead bodies will send up a stench;
the mountains will be soaked with their blood.

Isaiah 65

11 "But as for you who forsake the LORD
and forget my holy mountain,
who spread a table for Fortune
and fill bowls of mixed wine for Destiny,

12 I will destine you for the sword,
and you will all bend down for the slaughter;
for I called but you did not answer,
I spoke but you did not listen.
You did evil in my sight
and chose what displeases me."

You see here that the judgments of the tribulation are because the people of the world have forsaken the Lord Jesus and have forgotten that Jerusalem is his holy mountain. We see that he has called to them but they did not answer. We see this in Revelation also.

Jeremiah 23:

19 See, the storm of the LORD
will burst out in wrath,
a whirlwind swirling down
on the heads of the wicked.

20 The anger of the LORD will not turn back
until he fully accomplishes
the purposes of his heart.
In days to come you will understand it clearly.

Jeremiah 25:

29 See, I am beginning to bring disaster on the city that bears my Name, and will you indeed go unpunished? You will not go unpunished, for I <u>am calling down a sword upon all who live on the earth</u>, declares the LORD Almighty.'

30 "Now prophesy all these words against them and say to them:

"'The LORD will roar from on high;
he will thunder from his holy dwelling
and roar mightily against his land.
He will shout like those who tread the grapes,
shout against all who live on the earth.
31 The tumult will resound to the ends of the earth,
for the LORD will bring charges against the nations;
he will bring judgment on all mankind
and put the wicked to the sword,' "
declares the LORD.

32 This is what the LORD Almighty says:
"Look! Disaster is spreading
from nation to nation;
a mighty storm is rising from the ends of the earth."

33 At that time those slain by the LORD will be everywhere—
from one end of the earth to the other. They will not be
mourned or gathered up or buried, but will be like refuse lying
on the ground.

Compare this with Joel chapter 3.

JOEL 3

2 I will gather all nations and bring them down to the Valley of
Jehoshaphat. There I will enter into judgment against them
concerning my inheritance, my people Israel, for they scattered
my people among the nations and divided up my land.

Divide up the land of Israel and Jerusalem. The Jews already don't
possess all of what once belonged to Israel and the Muslims want
more. Actually they want it all. I mentioned this earlier; this is what
they want to do now. This is what the world is calling for, now even
the United States.

All these judgments of the tribulation are a result of Israel and Jerusalem being divided up, along with the fact that the Jews are going to rely on a man and a peace agreement instead of God and because of the world's acceptance of the man the bible calls the anti-Christ. The world's disbelief and rejection of Jesus, the one true God is setting the stage for all that has been prophesied. We already see the whole world calling for a one world government and currency. They are even calling for one man to be the leader of this new one world order. The judgments and the wrath of God start with the first seal. We see in 2 Thessalonians chapter 2 that Paul said all this will not start until the anti-Christ is revealed and he isn't revealed until the restrainer has been removed. With the removal of the Church God is taking his restraining hand off and letting man do as he pleases. Everything we have seen here in the book of Revelation is a result of man's on sin and wickedness. Man brings all this on himself. It's a result of a world without Jesus.

We see there is a pause again after the 7th bowl with chapters 17, 18 and the first half of chapter 19 before we see Jesus returning.

With chapters 17 and 18 John pauses with the flow of the judgments that have been taking place and goes back over things that will be the result of the bowls. It appears that with the trumpets and bowls he is describing the warfare and its effects and with the pauses he describes other things that will be taking place along with these judgments. Chapters 17 and 18 are describing the destruction of the false religion of Babylon and the destruction of the Revived Roman Empire, the anti-Christ's one world government. Chapter 19 starts off with great praise in heaven then we see Jesus returning.

13. Jesus returns to put a stop to it all.

Before telling of the return of Jesus, chapter 19 starts off with great praise in heaven, every angel and every person that is in heaven are praising God. The mystery of God has been accomplished. It is done. Next you see the anti-Christ and the armies of the nations gathered together to make war against Jesus and his army coming from heaven. Jesus returns and destroys them, putting a stop to all the destruction and sets up his kingdom here on earth.

Here I will start at the return of Jesus.

Revelation 19.

> 11I saw heaven standing open and there before me was a white horse, whose rider is called Faithful and True. With justice he judges and makes war. 12His eyes are like blazing fire, and on his head are many crowns. He has a name written on him that no one knows but he himself. 13He is dressed in a robe dipped in blood, and his name is the Word of God. **14The armies of heaven** were following him, riding on white horses and <u>dressed in fine linen, white and clean.</u>

> Rev. 19: 8Fine linen, bright and clean,
>   was given her to wear." (Fine linen stands for the righteous acts of the saints.)

Remember this statement, it shows that the rapture of the Church saints had to have happened before this point, before Jesus returns back down to the earth at his 2nd coming. The fine linen was given to the saints in heaven. We see here that the saints are returning with Jesus, not Jesus coming for the Church age saints. Notice he said 'given to her'. This is the bride of Christ.

> 15Out of his mouth comes a sharp sword with which to strike down <u>the nations</u>. "He will rule them with an iron scepter. "He treads the winepress of the fury of the wrath of God Almighty.

Psalm 110 is a prophesy of this

> 8 Ask of me, and I will make the nations your inheritance,
>   the ends of the earth your possession.
> 9 You will rule them with an iron scepter;
>   you will dash them to pieces like pottery."

> Rev. 19:16On his robe and on his thigh he has this name written:
> KING OF KINGS AND LORD OF LORDS.

> Rev. 19:17And I saw an angel standing in the sun, who cried in a loud voice to all the birds flying in midair, "Come, gather together for the great supper of God, 18so that you may eat the flesh of kings, generals, and mighty men, of horses and their riders, and the flesh of all people, free and slave, small and great."

Remember Ezekiel.

> Ez. 39: 17"Son of man, this is what the Sovereign LORD says: Call out to every kind of bird and all the wild animals: 'Assemble and come together from all around to the sacrifice I am preparing for you, the great sacrifice on the mountains of Israel. There you will eat flesh and drink blood. 18 You will eat the flesh of mighty men and drink the blood of the princes of the earth as if they were rams and lambs, goats and bulls—all of them fattened animals from Bashan. 19 At the sacrifice I am preparing for you, you will eat fat till you are glutted and drink blood till you are drunk. 20 At my table you will eat your fill of horses and riders, mighty men and soldiers of every kind,' declares the Sovereign LORD.

Just imagine all the bodies in this valley. There could be over a billion from the last battle of Armageddon. We saw that China alone has two hundred million. Add to it what will be left of those that gather together to try to fight against Jesus when he returns, as I've said before, it's no wonder it takes 7 months to bury all the dead and cleanse the earth of all the bodies.

Remember what Ezekiel said.

> Ez. 39:12 "'For seven months the house of Israel will be burying them in order to cleanse the land. 13 All the people of the land will bury them, and the day I am glorified will be a memorable day for them, declares the Sovereign LORD.

> **Rev. 19:19Then I saw the beast and the kings of the earth and their armies gathered together to make war against the rider on the horse and his army.**

Look at Psalm 2

> 1 Why do the nations conspire and the peoples plot in vain?

> 2 The kings of the earth take their stand and the rulers gather together against the LORD and against his Anointed One.

> Rev. 19:20But the beast was captured, and with him the false prophet who had performed the miraculous signs on his behalf. With these signs he had deluded those who had received the mark of the beast and worshiped his image. The two of them were thrown alive into the fiery lake of burning sulfur. 21The rest of them were killed with the sword that came out of the mouth of the rider on the horse, and all the birds gorged themselves on their flesh.

Look at Isaiah 11,

> 4 but with righteousness he will judge the needy,
> with justice he will give decisions for the poor of the earth.
> He will strike the earth with the rod of his mouth;
> with the breath of his lips he will slay the wicked.

Look also at Psalm 110,

> 5 The Lord is at your right hand;
> he will crush kings on the day of his wrath.
>
> 6 He will judge the nations, heaping up the dead
> and crushing the rulers of the whole earth.

Compare all this again with Matthew.

> Matthew 24: 27For as lightning that comes from the east is visible even in the west, so will be the coming of the Son of Man. 28Wherever there is a carcass, there the vultures will gather.
>
> 30"At that time the sign of the Son of Man will appear in the sky, and all the nations of the earth will mourn. They will see the Son of Man coming on the clouds of the sky, with power and great glory.

Chapter 20 starts off telling us what Jesus does first after he has returned.

Revelation 20.

The Thousand Years

> 1And I saw an angel coming down out of heaven, having the key to the Abyss and holding in his hand a great chain. 2He seized the dragon, that ancient serpent, who is the devil, or Satan, and bound him for a thousand years. 3He threw him into the Abyss, and locked and sealed it over him, to keep him from deceiving the nations anymore until the thousand years were ended. After that, he must be set free for a short time.
>
> 4I saw thrones on which were seated those who had been given authority to judge. And I saw the souls of those who had been

beheaded because of their testimony for Jesus and because of the word of God. They had not worshiped the beast or his image and had not received his mark on their foreheads or their hands. They came to life and reigned with Christ a thousand years.

As I have pointed out already, these that died during the tribulation are raised after Jesus has returned, if the rapture occurred just before or with Jesus' return then these would have already been raised.

Isaiah in chapter 62 describes Jesus' return.

11 The LORD has made proclamation
to the ends of the earth:
"Say to the Daughter of Zion,
'See, your Savior comes!
See, his reward is with him,
and his recompense accompanies him.' "

After Jesus has bound Satan he will judge the nations. Let's read Matthew again.

Matthew 25: 31"When the Son of Man comes in his glory, and all the angels with him, he will sit on his throne in heavenly glory. 32All the nations will be gathered before him, and he will separate the people one from another as a shepherd separates the sheep from the goats. 33He will put the sheep on his right and the goats on his left. 34"Then the King will say to those on his right, 'Come, you who are blessed by my Father; take your inheritance, the kingdom prepared for you since the creation of the world. 41"Then he will say to those on his left, 'Depart from me, you who are cursed, into the eternal fire prepared for the devil and his angels.

Read all of Matthew 13 but for now notice these verses,

> Matthew 13: 36Then he left the crowd and went into the house. His disciples came to him and said, "Explain to us the parable of the weeds in the field." 37He answered, "The one who sowed the good seed is the Son of Man. 38The field is the world, and the good seed stands for the sons of the kingdom. The weeds are the sons of the evil one, 39and the enemy who sows them is the devil. <u>The harvest is the end of the age, and the harvesters are angels.</u>
>
> 40"As the weeds are pulled up and burned in the fire, so it will be at the end of the age. 41The Son of Man will send out his angels, and <u>they will weed out of his kingdom everything that causes sin and all who do evil.</u> 42They will throw them into the fiery furnace, where there will be weeping and gnashing of teeth. 43Then the righteous will shine like the sun in the kingdom of their Father. He who has ears, let him hear.

This is the answer to the purpose of the tribulation. Not only is God judging Israel but also the nations. Only the righteous, those that have accepted Jesus will go into Christ's earthly Kingdom. The whole purpose of all the judgments we see in Revelation is to try to get people to repent and accept him as the Son of God before he returns. The time for Jesus to return and set up the kingdom of God has come, so with all the judgments of the tribulation God is trying to get the people living to realize all that the bible has said about Jesus is true. Everything has been to testify and to be a witness to the truth. Jesus will not judge anyone without first doing everything he can to get a person to turn to him. But you see in Rev. Chapter 9 John says they 'still did not repent' and in chapter 16 'they refused to repent'.

Jude in the 14th and the 15th verse said, "See, the Lord is coming with thousands upon thousands of his holy ones to judge everyone, and to convict all the ungodly of all the ungodly acts they have done in the ungodly way, and of all the harsh words ungodly sinners have spoken against him."

Matthew 13: 47"Once again, the kingdom of heaven is like a net that was let down into the lake and caught all kinds of fish. 48When it was full, the fishermen pulled it up on the shore. Then they sat down and collected the good fish in baskets, but threw the bad away. 49This is how it will be at the end of the age. The angels will come and separate the wicked from the righteous 50and throw them into the fiery furnace, where there will be weeping and gnashing of teeth.

We see the mention of two separate resurrections.

Rev. 20: 5(The rest of the dead did not come to life until the thousand years were ended.) This is the first resurrection. 6Blessed and holy are those who have part in the first resurrection. The second death has no power over them, but they will be priests of God and of Christ and will reign with him for a thousand years.

The first resurrection has two stages. First with the rapture and then the second with the resurrection we see here after Jesus has returned. All the Old Testament saints are raised here also. We covered this also with chapter 12 of Daniel.

Anyone who's names that have not been written in the Lambs book of Life will be raised with the second resurrection and will stand before the Great White Throne judgment and will go through death once more, the second death, for they have already died once.

Rev. 20: 11Then I saw a great white throne and him who was seated on it. Earth and sky fled from his presence, and there was no place for them. 12And I saw the dead, great and small, standing before the throne, and books were opened. Another book was opened, which is the book of life. The dead were judged according to what they had done as recorded in the books. 13The sea gave up the dead that were in it, and death and Hades gave up the dead that were in them, and each person was judged according to what he had done. 14Then death and Hades were thrown into the lake of fire. The lake of fire is the second death. 15If anyone's name was not found written in the book of life, he was thrown into the lake of fire.

As we saw earlier, the 7 bowls are part of the 7th trumpet and the 7 trumpets are part of the 7th seal. We saw in chapters 5 and 6 that Jesus is the only one found to be worthy to judge the world and to open the seals of the scroll. The scroll is describing the judgments of God, which occur during the last 7 years allotted to Israel we saw in Daniel chapter 9.

There's really no reason anyone should find themselves here during the tribulation. All one has to do is believe on the Lord Jesus, repent and accept his sacrifice on the cross and live for him, have him in your life and you will find yourself in heaven with him during the time of the tribulation. Repent and call on the name of the Lord Jesus. It's just that simple.

> Romans 10: 9That if you confess with your mouth, "Jesus is Lord," and believe in your heart that God raised him from the dead, you will be saved. 10For it is with your heart that you believe and are justified, and it is with your mouth that you confess and are saved. 11As the Scripture says, "Anyone who trusts in him will never be put to shame."

A word from the Lord.

> Luke 21: 34"Be careful, or your hearts will be weighed down with dissipation, drunkenness and the anxieties of life, and that day will close on you unexpectedly like a trap. 35For it will come upon all those who live on the face of the whole earth. 36Be always on the watch, and pray that you may be able to escape all that is about to happen, and that you may be able to stand before the Son of Man."

Don't get to depressed with all this doom and gloom, all the destruction that is described for the future, it is not the end of Man or the Earth. When Jesus returns he restores all things. The earth will enjoy a 1000-years of peace and rest. It will be a time of the government of God, a time when Jesus will rule and reign. Then after these 1000 years are completed we will have eternity.

Next we will look at some scriptures that describe the kingdom of God here on earth.

14. The Glorious Kingdom of God.

Here are a few Old Testament scriptures that describe the glorious kingdom of God here on earth that commences after the 7 years of the tribulation.

Verses 1 thru 5 of Isaiah 11 are about Jesus during the 1000 years of the kingdom of God. Jesse was David's Father of whom Jesus through his mother Mary as well as Joseph was a descendant.

1 A shoot will come up from the stump of Jesse;
from his roots a Branch will bear fruit.

2 The Spirit of the LORD will rest on him—
the Spirit of wisdom and of understanding,
the Spirit of counsel and of power,
the Spirit of knowledge and of the fear of the LORD -

3 and he will delight in the fear of the LORD.
He will not judge by what he sees with his eyes,
 or decide by what he hears with his ears;

4 but with righteousness he will judge the needy,
with justice he will give decisions for the poor of the earth.
He will strike the earth with the rod of his mouth;
with the breath of his lips he will slay the wicked.

5 Righteousness will be his belt
 and faithfulness the sash around his waist.

This is how it will be during the 1000 year Kingdom of God here on Earth.

6 The wolf will live with the lamb,
the leopard will lie down with the goat,
the calf and the lion and the yearling together;
and a little child will lead them.

7 The cow will feed with the bear,
their young will lie down together,
and the lion will eat straw like the ox.

8 The infant will play near the hole of the cobra,
and the young child put his hand into the viper's nest.

9 They will neither harm nor destroy
on all my holy mountain,
for the earth will be full of the knowledge of the LORD
as the waters cover the sea.

Holy Mountain refers to his Holy Kingdom.

10 In that day the Root of Jesse will stand as a banner for the peoples; the nations will rally to him, and his place of rest will be glorious. 11 In that day the Lord will reach out his hand a second time to reclaim the remnant that is left of his people from Assyria, from Lower Egypt, from Upper Egypt, from Cush, from Elam, from Babylonia, from Hamath and from the islands of the sea.

12 He will raise a banner for the nations
and gather the exiles of Israel; he will assemble the scattered people of Judah from the four quarters of the earth.

Jeremiah 31

This also is describing the Kingdom of God here on earth.

31 "The time is coming," declares the LORD,
"when I will make a new covenant with the house of Israel
and with the house of Judah.
32 It will not be like the covenant I made with their forefathers
when I took them by the hand to lead them out of Egypt,
because they broke my covenant, though I was a husband to them," declares the LORD.

33 "This is the covenant I will make with the house of Israel
after that time," declares the LORD.
"I will put my law in their minds
and write it on their hearts.
I will be their God,
and they will be my people.
34 No longer will a man teach his neighbor,
 or a man his brother, saying, 'Know the LORD,'
because they will all know me,
from the least of them to the greatest,"
declares the LORD.
"For I will forgive their wickedness
and will remember their sins no more."
35 This is what the LORD says,
he who appoints the sun
to shine by day,
who decrees the moon and stars
to shine by night,
who stirs up the sea
so that its waves roar—
the LORD Almighty is his name:
36 "Only if these decrees vanish from my sight,"
declares the LORD,
"will the descendants of Israel ever cease
to be a nation before me."

Verse 36 and 37 blows the teaching that the Church has replaced Israel
out of the water. They also show that the promises of the kingdom of
God are thru Isaac to Israel.

37 This is what the LORD says:
"Only if the heavens above can be measured
and the foundations of the earth below be searched out
will I reject all the descendants of Israel
because of all they have done,"
declares the LORD.

38 "The days are coming," declares the LORD, "when this city will be rebuilt for me from the Tower of Hananel to the Corner Gate. 39 The measuring line will stretch from there straight to the hill of Gareb and then turn to Goah. 40 The whole valley where dead bodies and ashes are thrown, and all the terraces out to the Kidron Valley on the east as far as the corner of the Horse Gate, will be holy to the LORD. The city will never again be uprooted or demolished."

Isaiah 66

18 "And I, because of their actions and their imaginations, am about to come and gather all nations and tongues, and they will come and see my glory.

19 "I will set a sign among them, and I will send some of those who survive to the nations—to Tarshish, to the Libyans and Lydians (famous as archers), to Tubal and Greece, and to the distant islands that have not heard of my fame or seen my glory. They will proclaim my glory among the nations. 20 And they will bring all your brothers, from all the nations, to my holy mountain in Jerusalem as an offering to the LORD -on horses, in chariots and wagons, and on mules and camels," says the LORD. "They will bring them, as the Israelites bring their grain offerings, to the temple of the LORD in ceremonially clean vessels. 21 And I will select some of them also to be priests and Levites," says the LORD.

22 "As the new heavens and the new earth that I make will endure before me," declares the LORD, "so will your name and descendants endure. 23 From one New Moon to another and from one Sabbath to another, all mankind will come and bow down before me," says the LORD. 24 "And they will go out and look upon the dead bodies of those who rebelled against me; their worm will not die, nor will their fire be quenched, and they will be loathsome to all mankind."

Are you remembering the other scriptures from Ezekiel, Daniel and Revelation that used the same statements?

Isaiah again describes the Kingdom of God here on earth. It's going to be pretty amazing.

Isaiah 65

> 19 I will rejoice over Jerusalem
> and take delight in my people;
> the sound of weeping and of crying
> will be heard in it no more.
>
> 20 "Never again will there be in it
> an infant who lives but a few days,
> or an old man who does not live out his years;
> he who dies at a hundred
> will be thought a mere youth;
> he who fails to reach a hundred
> will be considered accursed.
>
> 21 They will build houses and dwell in them;
> they will plant vineyards and eat their fruit.
>
> 22 No longer will they build houses and others live in them,
> or plant and others eat.
> For as the days of a tree,
> so will be the days of my people;
> my chosen ones will long enjoy
> the works of their hands.
>
> 23 They will not toil in vain
> or bear children doomed to misfortune;
> for they will be a people blessed by the LORD,
> they and their descendants with them.

24 Before they call I will answer;
while they are still speaking I will hear.

25 The wolf and the lamb will feed together,
and the lion will eat straw like the ox,
but dust will be the serpent's food.
They will neither harm nor destroy
on all my holy mountain,"
says the LORD.

After the 1000 years God will create a New Heavens and a New Earth. We see this in Revelation chapter 21 and 22 as well as in Isaiah chapter 60 and 65. But first in chapter 20 after the 1000 years are over we see Satan's doom and the Great White Throne judgment.

With verse 6 of chapter 22 the prophecy of the book of Revelation ends. Chapter 22 ends with some words from John and Jesus.

6The angel said to me, "These words are trustworthy and true. The Lord, the God of the spirits of the prophets, sent his angel to show his servants the things that must soon take place."

7"Behold, I am coming soon! Blessed is he who keeps the words of the prophecy in this book."

Just like with verse 15 of chapter 16, John is telling us Jesus Is Coming. He is reminding all those that would be reading this before the tribulation started to be sure to keep watch and be ready for the Lord's return, be ready and watching for the rapture, reminding us of our blessed hope. Jesus said he will come back for us like a thief, before the day of the Lord. The rapture is truly a blessing. Like I said before the book of Revelation was first sent as letters to 7 churches to be read. Jesus repeats it again that he is coming soon in verse 12.

We see starting with verse 6 that there is a shift from the prophetic to him speaking to, warning the Church to keep watch. We see that the words of this prophecy are not to be sealed up because the time is near. Boy, if it was considered near then, how much nearer is it now. We are told that it is Jesus that sends this message to the Church. Again John tells us that he actually heard and saw all these things. John was literally transported into the future. This was not just a vision.

8I, John, am the one who heard and saw these things. And when I had heard and seen them, I fell down to worship at the feet of the angel who had been showing them to me. 9But he said to me, "Do not do it! I am a fellow servant with you and with your brothers the prophets and of all who keep the words of this book. Worship God!"

10Then he told me, "Do not seal up the words of the prophecy of this book, because the time is near. 11Let him who does wrong continue to do wrong; let him who is vile continue to be vile; let him who does right continue to do right; and let him who is holy continue to be holy."

Where Daniel in chapter 12 was told to seal up the words of his prophecy, John is told not to.

Now final words from Jesus.

12"Behold, I am coming soon! My reward is with me, and I will give to everyone according to what he has done. 13I am the Alpha and the Omega, the First and the Last, the Beginning and the End. 14"Blessed are those who wash their robes, that they may have the right to the tree of life and may go through the gates into the city. 15Outside are the dogs, those who practice magic arts, the sexually immoral, the murderers, the idolaters and everyone who loves and practices falsehood. 16"I, Jesus, have sent my angel to give you this testimony for the churches. I am the Root and the Offspring of David, and the bright Morning Star."

17The Spirit and the bride say, "Come!" And let him who hears say, "Come!" Whoever is thirsty, let him come; and whoever wishes, let him take the free gift of the water of life. 18I warn everyone who hears the words of the prophecy of this book: If anyone adds anything to them, God will add to him the plagues described in this book. 19And if anyone takes words away from this book of prophecy, God will take away from him his share in the tree of life and in the holy city, which are described in this book.

Unlike in Islam, Christians are not told in the Bible to do anything to bring all this about as some accuse us of, but just the opposite. We are to warn the world of what will come if they continue to reject Jesus, continue to mock him, continue in their sin. All this could possibly be delayed if enough people repent and turn to Jesus, if there was a major revival in the world. Just like with Lot, if there had been 10 righteous in Sodom God would not have destroyed it. But from the scriptures and from the way the morals and character of people in the world is decaying and especially the way the world is towards Israel and now against Christians too, it doesn't look like this will happen. People that hate Christians actually hate Jesus. Jesus said in Matthew 15 verse 18 that the world hates Christians because they hated him first.

You can't do anything about anyone else, but if you haven't already, repent and turn to Jesus. Take the words of this prophecy to heart. Don't let it be wasted on you.

> 20He who testifies to these things says, "Yes, I am coming soon."

Amen. Come, Lord Jesus.

21The grace of the Lord Jesus be with God's people. Amen

Chapter Nine

Who does the Bible say Jesus is?

Who does the Bible say Jesus Is?

If after reading this you have come to see and believe that the bible has accurately foretold the future, if you have come to believe the bible is the word of God then you should believe what it says about who Jesus is. You should be able to by the accuracy of all these prophecies we have looked at.

Before I leave you I would like to show you just what the bible has to say concerning Jesus, who the bible says Jesus is. There are many that think that Jesus was just a good and wise man, others who think he was just an angel that God sent to the earth. You will see that he is more than just a man or an angel. You may have already accepted the bible and Jesus as the truth but don't know who Jesus actually is. So I would like to leave you with these verses.

Proverbs 30:

4Who has gone up to heaven and come down?
Who has gathered up the wind in the hollow of his hands?
Who has wrapped up the waters in his cloak?
Who has established all the ends of the earth?
What is his name, and the name of his son?
Tell me if you know!

Here are some scriptures that reveal who Jesus is.

Matthew 16

Peter's Confession of Christ

13When Jesus came to the region of Caesarea Philippi, he asked his disciples, "Who do people say the Son of Man is?"
14They replied, "Some say John the Baptist; others say Elijah; and still others, Jeremiah or one of the prophets."
15"But what about you?" he asked. "Who do you say I am?"

16Simon Peter answered, "You are the Christ, the Son of the living God."

John 1

The Word Became Flesh

1In the beginning was the Word, and the Word was with God, and <u>the Word was God. 2He was with God in the beginning.</u> <u>3Through him</u> all things were made; without him nothing was made that has been made. 4In him was life, and that life was the light of men. 5The light shines in the darkness, but the darkness has not understood it.

6There came a man who was sent from God; his name was John. 7He came as a witness to testify concerning that light, so that through him all men might believe. 8He himself was not the light; he came only as a witness to the light. 9The true light that gives light to every man was coming into the world.

10He was in the world, and though <u>the world was made through him</u>, the world did not recognize him.

11He came to that which was his own, but his own did not receive him. 12Yet to all who received him, to those who believed in his name, he gave the right to become children of God— 13children born not of natural descent, nor of human decision or a husband's will, but born of God.

<u>14The Word became flesh</u> and made his dwelling among us. We have seen his glory, the glory of the One and Only, who came from the Father, full of grace and truth.

15John testifies concerning him. He cries out, saying, "This was he of whom I said, 'He who comes after me has surpassed me because <u>he was before me.</u>'"

John said that Jesus was before him yet John was born first. Remember verse one, Jesus was with the Father in the beginning.

> 16From the fullness of his grace we have all received one blessing after another. 17For the law was given through Moses; grace and truth came through Jesus Christ. 18No one has ever seen God, but God the One and Only, who is at the Father's side, has made him known.

Now if it wasn't clear to you let me point out that the word is Jesus. Let's exchange 'word' with 'Jesus' and for God where it is referring to God the Father I will exchange God with God the Father.

> 1In the beginning was Jesus, and Jesus was with God the Father, and Jesus was God. 2He was with (God the Father) in the beginning._3Through (Jesus) all things were made; without (Jesus) nothing was made that has been made. 4In (Jesus) was life, and that life was the light of men.

> 10(Jesus) was in the world, and though the world was made through him, the world did not recognize him.

> 14 Jesus became flesh and made his dwelling among us. We have seen his glory, the glory of the One and Only, who came from the Father, full of grace and truth.

> 17For the law was given through Moses; grace and truth came through Jesus Christ.

> 18No one has ever seen (God the Father), but God (the Son, Jesus) the One and Only, who is at the Father's side, has made him known.

Paul gives us a clear explanation. It will help make what we just read from John become clearer.

Who Does the Bible Say Jesus Is?

Colossians 1

The Supremacy of Christ

15He is the image of the invisible God, the firstborn over all creation. 16For by him all things were created: things in heaven and on earth, visible and invisible, whether thrones or powers or rulers or authorities; all things were created by him and for him. 17He is before all things, and in him all things hold together. 18And he is the head of the body, the church; he is the beginning and the firstborn from among the dead, so that in everything he might have the supremacy. 19For God was pleased to have all his fullness dwell in him, 20and through him to reconcile to himself all things, whether things on earth or things in heaven, by making peace through his blood, shed on the cross.

All the scriptures from the Old as well as from the New Testament say that Jesus created everything, heaven as well. You see that God the Father created everything through Jesus. Jesus created it all. You see here in Colossians 1 verse 15 that Paul said that Jesus was the first born of all creation, not the first created. Jesus was born out of God the Father in the beginning. Jesus was born from the center of the being of God the Father. Jesus was not created like the angels, he actually created the angels. He was born out of the Father. He is before all creation. Paul, by using two separate words, born and created, shows that there are two separate and distinct acts of God the Father, Jesus was born while the angels and everything else were created. With Jesus creating everything this is why he is God. Remember Matthew chapter one verse 23, "The virgin will be with child and will give birth to a son, and they will call him Immanuel" —which means, **"God with us."**

Let's do the same with using his name here with Colossians 1: 15 thru 20.

15(Jesus) is the image of the invisible God, the firstborn over all creation. 16For by (Jesus) all things were created: things in heaven and on earth, visible and invisible, whether thrones or powers or rulers or authorities; all things were created by (Jesus) and for (Jesus). 17(Jesus) is before all things, and in (Jesus) all things hold together. 18And (Jesus) is the head of the body, the church; (Jesus) is the beginning and the firstborn from among the dead, so that in everything he might have the supremacy. 19For God (the Father) was pleased to have all his fullness dwell in him, 20and through (Jesus) to reconcile to himself all things, whether things on earth or things in heaven, by making peace through his blood, shed on the cross.

Here are some scriptures that refer to Jesus as God.

Romans 9: 4the people of Israel. Theirs is the adoption as sons; theirs the divine glory, the covenants, the receiving of the law, the temple worship and the promises. 5Theirs are the patriarchs, and from them is traced the human ancestry of Christ, **who is God over all**, forever praised! Amen.

Titus 2:13 while we wait for the blessed hope--the glorious appearing of **our great God and Savior, Jesus Christ,**

The blessed hope, the Apostle Paul is referring to the rapture

1 John 5: 20We know also that the Son of God has come and has given us understanding, so that we may know him who is true. And we are in him who is true—**even in his Son Jesus Christ. He is the true God and eternal life.**

Hebrews 1

The Son Superior to Angels

1In the past God spoke to our forefathers through the prophets at many times and in various ways, 2but in these last

days he has spoken to us by his Son, whom he appointed heir of all things, and **through whom he made the universe.**
3<u>The Son is the radiance of God's glory and the exact representation of his being,</u> sustaining all things by his powerful word. After he had provided purification for sins, he sat down at the right hand of the Majesty in heaven. 4So he became as much superior to the angels as the name he has inherited is superior to theirs.

5For to which of the angels did God ever say,
"You are my Son;
today I have become your Father"? Or again,
"I will be his Father,
and he will be my Son"? 6And again, <u>when God brings his firstborn into the world</u>, he says,
"Let all God's angels worship him." 7In speaking of the angels he says,
"He makes his angels winds,
his servants flames of fire." 8But about the Son he says,
Your throne, <u>O God</u>, will last for ever and ever,
and righteousness will be the scepter of your kingdom.
 9You have loved righteousness and hated wickedness;
therefore God, your God, has set you above your companions by anointing you with the oil of joy." 10He also says,
"<u>In the beginning, O Lord, you laid the foundations of the earth, and the heavens are the work of your hands.</u>
11They will perish, but you remain;
they will all wear out like a garment.
12You will roll them up like a robe;
like a garment they will be changed.
But you remain the same,
and your years will never end." 13To which of the angels did God ever say, Sit at my right hand until I make your enemies a footstool for your feet?
14Are not all angels ministering spirits sent to serve those who will inherit salvation?

Notice that Jesus is not or was not an angel. He created the angels. Let's look at some Old Testament scriptures.

Isaiah 40

21 Do you not know?
Have you not heard?
Has it not been told you from the beginning?
Have you not understood since the earth was founded?
22 He sits enthroned above the circle of the earth,
 and its people are like grasshoppers.
He stretches out the heavens like a canopy,
and spreads them out like a tent to live in.
28 Do you not know?
Have you not heard?
The LORD is the everlasting God,
the Creator of the ends of the earth.

Did you notice that verse 22 said the earth was a circle, I think this was about 2000 years before it was discovered that the world was round and people stopped believing the earth was flat. We see here that it was revealed to Isaiah by the Holy Spirit. Look at what Peter tells us about prophesy.

2 Peter 1,

19And we have the word of the prophets made more certain, and you will do well to pay attention to it, as to a light shining in a dark place, until the day dawns and the morning star rises in your hearts. 20Above all, you must understand that no prophecy of Scripture came about by the prophet's own interpretation. 21For prophecy never had its origin in the will of man, but men spoke from God as they were carried along by the Holy Spirit.

Isaiah 43

10 "You are my witnesses," declares the LORD,
  "and my servant whom I have chosen,
so that you may know and believe me
  and understand that I am he.
Before me no god was formed,
  nor will there be one after me.

11 I, even I, am the LORD,
  and **apart from me there is no savior.**
12 I have revealed and saved and proclaimed—
I, and not some foreign god among you.
You are my witnesses," declares the LORD, "that I am God.
13 Yes, and <u>from ancient days I am he</u>.
No one can deliver out of my hand.
When I act, who can reverse it?"

Isaiah 54

5 For your Maker is your husband—
the LORD Almighty is his name—
the Holy One of Israel is your Redeemer;
he is called the God of all the earth.

Notice the use of LORD and Lord. He's saying the Father says to my Lord (Jesus). These are actually two different Hebrew words.

Psalm 110

1 The LORD says to my Lord:
"Sit at my right hand
until I make your enemies
a footstool for your feet."

2 The LORD will extend your mighty scepter from Zion;
you will rule in the midst of your enemies.

3 Your troops will be willing
on your day of battle.
Arrayed in holy majesty,
from the womb of the dawn
you will receive the dew of your youth.
4 The LORD has sworn
and will not change his mind:
"You are a priest forever,
in the order of Melchizedek."
5 The Lord is at your right hand;
he will crush kings on the day of his wrath.

6 He will judge the nations, heaping up the dead
and crushing the rulers of the whole earth.

Jesus testifies concerning himself and salvation, and Martha, Lazarus' sister believes and confesses. This is a hint to the Rapture.

John 11

25Jesus said to her, "I am the resurrection and the life. He who believes in me will live, even though he dies; 26and whoever lives and believes in me will never die. Do you believe this?"
27"Yes, Lord," she told him, "I believe that you are the Christ, the Son of God, who was to come into the world."

Paul and Peter testify and explain the way of salvation.

Ephesians 1

7In him we have redemption through his blood, the forgiveness of sins, in accordance with the riches of God's grace 9And he made known to us the mystery of his will according to his good pleasure, which he purposed in Christ, 10to be put into effect when the times will have reached their fulfillment—to bring all things in heaven and on earth together under one head, even Christ.

18I pray also that the eyes of your heart may be enlightened in order that you may know the hope to which he has called you, the riches of his glorious inheritance in the saints, 19and his incomparably great power for us who believe. That power is like the working of his mighty strength, 20which he exerted in Christ when he raised him from the dead and seated him at his right hand in the heavenly realms, 21far above all rule and authority, power and dominion, and every title that can be given, not only in the present age but also in the one to come.

1 Corinthians 15

1Now, brothers, I want to remind you of the gospel I preached to you, which you received and on which you have taken your stand. 2By this gospel you are saved, if you hold firmly to the word I preached to you. Otherwise, you have believed in vain.

3For what I received I passed on to you as of first importance: that Christ died for our sins according to the Scriptures, 4that he was buried, that he was raised on the third day according to the Scriptures,

5and that he appeared to Peter, and then to the Twelve. 6After that, he appeared to more than five hundred of the brothers at the same time, most of whom are still living, though some have fallen asleep. 7Then he appeared to James, then to all the apostles, 8and last of all he appeared to me also, as to one abnormally born.

Here we see the requirements for being saved. You must believe that Christ died for our sins according to the Scriptures, that he was buried, that he was raised on the third day according to the Scriptures. You must believe the scriptures; you must believe the entire bible. If you don't believe anyone of these requirements then you are not saved, born again. You are not going to get into heaven.

John 14: 6, Jesus answered, "I am the way and the truth and the life. No one comes to the Father except through me.

Acts 4: 12, Salvation is found in no one else, for there is no other name under heaven given to men by which we must be saved."

2 Peter 1

13I think it is right to refresh your memory as long as I live in the tent of this body, 14because I know that I will soon put it aside, as our Lord Jesus Christ has made clear to me. 15And I will make every effort to see that after my departure you will always be able to remember these things.

16We did not follow cleverly invented stories when we told you about the power and coming of our Lord Jesus Christ, but we were eyewitnesses of his majesty. 17For he received honor and glory from God the Father when the voice came to him from the Majestic Glory, saying, "This is my Son, whom I love; with him I am well pleased." 18We ourselves heard this voice that came from heaven when we were with him on the sacred mountain.

Here Peter is referring back to when they were on the Mount when Jesus was transfigured before them. Matt. 17:5; Mark 9:7; Luke 9:35

Peter is in jail for preaching the gospel and is about to be taken and crucified; yet he is still saying that he personally witnessed and saw all that Jesus did. This is like his death bed confession, the most important thing he wants to leave with them. If he and the other disciples didn't know for sure that Jesus rose from the dead, if they weren't sure in who he was, if they knew it wasn't true then I don't think they would have been willing to die for him or the gospel.

There are so many more scriptures I could give. We see that Jesus is not or was not an angel.

Who Does the Bible Say Jesus Is?

So it should be clear that there wouldn't be anyone else to come as the Messiah or a prophet from God since Jesus was here, since Jesus is not only the Son of God, he is our God. Since the creator of the universe himself came to earth, becoming God in a human body, his word would be the final word; there would be no need for another.

Philippians 2: 5-11

5 In your relationships with one another, have the same mindset as Christ Jesus:

6 Who, being in very nature God,
did not consider equality with God something to be used to his own advantage;
7 rather, he made himself nothing
by taking the very nature of a servant,
being made in human likeness.
8 And being found in appearance as a man,
he humbled himself
by becoming obedient to death—
even death on a cross!

9 Therefore God exalted him to the highest place
and gave him the name that is above every name,
10 that at the name of Jesus every knee should bow,
in heaven and on earth and under the earth,
11 and every tongue acknowledge that Jesus Christ is Lord,
to the glory of God the Father.

Jesus himself said:

John 6: 47I tell you the truth, he who believes has everlasting life.

John 8: 24I told you that you would die in your sins; if you do not believe that I am the one I claim to be, you will indeed die in your sins."

John 10: 9I am the gate; whoever enters through me will be saved.

The Apostle John tells us why he writes his letters,

1 John 5: 13I write these things to you who believe in the name of the Son of God so that you may know that you have eternal life.

1 John 5: 20We know also that the Son of God has come and has given us understanding, so that we may know him who is true. And we are in him who is true—even in his Son Jesus Christ. He is the true God and eternal life.

John also tells us,

2 John 9Anyone who runs ahead and does not continue in the teaching of Christ does not have God; whoever continues in the teaching has both the Father and the Son.

Jesus is Lord. Jesus is the God of all creation, the spiritual as well as the physical. With this being the case, doesn't it make since that there would be only one truth, only one way to God. There wouldn't be many ways to God.

Read the four gospels and then find the Old Testament scriptures that foretold the things that Jesus fulfilled, or Google 'prophecies fulfilled by Jesus'. You will be amazed at how many prophecies Jesus fulfilled that he had no 'earthly' control over. The odds of one man fulfilling just a few of these prophecies are astronomical.

John 14: 6Jesus answered, "I am the way and the truth and the life. No one comes to the Father except through me.

.

Chapter Ten

Final Remarks

1. Final Remarks.

There's certainly more that could be said about end time prophecies and the Rapture. I'm learning more all the time. This should be enough to give you a good understanding and insight about end time prophecies. You should now have a good idea of just what the bible says about the future of mankind. There are some terrible times ahead, but the end is not one of doom and gloom but a glorious one. I encourage you to continue to research and study. There is just so much that can be learned from studying bible prophecy. You should now have a good foundation to start with. You should now be able to read the Bible and recognize other scriptures that are dealing with the end times, those that are referring to the tribulation.

It just dumfounds me, with everything we can see lining up with bible prophecy how so many just can't believe the bible is the Word of God and that it could be speaking of events that would occur 2000 or more years later.

People seem to be willing to accept the predictions of Nostradamus, the I-Ching, the Mayan Calendar etc. but they don't want to accept what the bible says or even consider it. With the bible being the only source that's been a 100% accurate, and the most precise, it should be obvious; The Bible is the Word of God.

Read the book of Revelation and tell me where in history all the things described happened. When did one man rule the whole world? When was the whole world made up of one government? When was the two witnesses killed and then raised from the dead and everyone on earth see it? When was the Euphrates River dried up that made way for a 200 million-man army from China? When did hail stones the size of a 100 pounds fall on men? As we can tell now, the book refers to nuclear war. I could go on and on. The plain truth is that the bible does speak of things that will happen in our future, possibly soon.

Final Remarks

Promises made to Israel.

We see that all the things in the book of Revelation as well as in the Old Testament are over the Land of Israel and Jerusalem. The truth is the land of Israel was given to the Jews as an inheritance by God. The Land of Israel was promised to the Jews forever.

Gen. 13: 14 The LORD said to Abram after Lot had parted from him, "Lift up your eyes from where you are and look north and south, east and west. 15 All the land that you see I will give to you and your offspring forever.

While Ishmael was a son of Abraham also, the promise was to Isaac, not Ishmael

Gen. 17: 15 God also said to Abraham, "As for Sarai your wife, you are no longer to call her Sarai; her name will be Sarah. 16 I will bless her and will surely give you a son by her. I will bless her so that she will be the mother of nations; kings of peoples will come from her."

17 Abraham fell facedown; he laughed and said to himself, "Will a son be born to a man a hundred years old? Will Sarah bear a child at the age of ninety?" 18 And Abraham said to God, "If only Ishmael might live under your blessing!"

Gen. 17: 19 Then God said, "Yes, but your wife Sarah will bear you a son, and you will call him Isaac. I will establish my covenant with him as an everlasting covenant for his descendants after him. 20 And as for Ishmael, I have heard you: I will surely bless him; I will make him fruitful and will greatly increase his numbers. He will be the father of twelve rulers, and I will make him into a great nation.

21 **But my covenant I will establish with Isaac**, whom Sarah will bear to you by this time next year."

Gen. 21: 8 The child grew and was weaned, and on the day Isaac was weaned Abraham held a great feast. 9 But Sarah saw that the son whom Hagar the Egyptian had borne to Abraham was mocking, 10 and she said to Abraham, "Get rid of that slave woman and her son, for that slave woman's son will never share in the inheritance with my son Isaac."

11 The matter distressed Abraham greatly because it concerned his son. 12 But God said to him, "Do not be so distressed about the boy and your maidservant. Listen to whatever Sarah tells you, because <u>it is through Isaac that your offspring will be reckoned</u>. 13 I will make the son of the maidservant into a nation also, because he is your offspring."

The promised covenant is reconfirmed through Jacob.

Gen. 28: 1 So Isaac called for Jacob and blessed him and commanded him: "Do not marry a Canaanite woman. 2 Go at once to Paddan Aram, to the house of your mother's father Bethuel. Take a wife for yourself there, from among the daughters of Laban, your mother's brother. 3 May God Almighty bless you and make you fruitful and increase your numbers until you become a community of peoples. 4 May he give you and your descendants the blessing given to Abraham, so that you may take possession of the land where you now live as an alien, the land God gave to Abraham." 5 Then Isaac sent Jacob on his way, and he went to Paddan Aram, to Laban son of Bethuel the Aramean, the brother of Rebekah, who was the mother of Jacob and Esau.

10 Jacob left Beersheba and set out for Haran. 11 When he reached a certain place, he stopped for the night because the sun had set. Taking one of the stones there, he put it under his head and lay down to sleep. 12 He had a dream in which he saw a stairway resting on the earth, with its top reaching to heaven, and the angels of God were ascending and descending on it. 13 There above it stood the LORD, and he said: "I am the LORD,

the God of your father Abraham and the God of Isaac. I will give you and your descendants the land on which you are lying. 14 Your descendants will be like the dust of the earth, and you will spread out to the west and to the east, to the north and to the south. All peoples on earth will be blessed through you and your offspring.

The place where Jacob was lying and saw the stairway with angels ascending and descending was the place that later became known as Jerusalem. This is also the place where Abraham took Isaac to offer him as a sacrifice to God. See Genesis 22. The blessing God was talking about is Jesus.

Hebrews 11: 8 By faith Abraham, when called to go to a place he would later receive as his inheritance, obeyed and went, even though he did not know where he was going. 9 By faith he made his home in the promised land like a stranger in a foreign country; he lived in tents, as did Isaac and Jacob, who were heirs with him of the same promise.

If we believe that all God's promises are kept then we should believe the promises to Israel will be kept also. Some say well Israel rebelled, turned their back on God, they rejected God when they rejected Jesus so the promises are no longer valid. They say that all the promises to Israel have been given over to the Church. Well, haven't we all in one way or another rebelled, turned are backs on Jesus, not followed his word, haven't kept his commandments. We believe his promises to us that he will never leave us or forsake us. That he will always be with us. We believe his promise that if we ask forgiveness that he is just to forgive us. If we believe that all his promises to us are going to be kept then why shouldn't we believe that all the promises to Israel are going to be kept also.

Jeremiah 31: 36 "Only if these decrees vanish from my sight," declares the LORD,
"will the descendants of Israel ever cease
to be a nation before me."

509

We see in Israel's history that when they returned to God he healed and restored them. That's the purpose of the Tribulation, to turn Israel as a nation back to God, for them to accept Jesus as their Messiah before He sets up his earthly Kingdom. See Romans 9, 10 and especially 11. He promised Israel a Kingdom here on earth ruled by the Messiah. The 7 years of the tribulation are a time when God is trying to get all on the face of the earth to recognize Jesus as the only begotten son of God, the true Messiah before he returns to set up his kingdom here on earth, for he is going to weed out all unrighteousness from the earth before and after he returns.

In the first chapter of Acts right before he ascended after telling them to wait for the promised Holy Spirit the disciples asked him was he going to restore the kingdom to Israel at this time. His answer was that it's not for them to know the times or dates the Father has set. You see he acknowledged the restoring of the kingdom to Israel. The Father has the time set. He said he will return to the earth to set up a kingdom that he will rule and reign over the whole earth. His throne will be in Jerusalem. He promised it. You can count on it.

Need I say more?

Let me mention one last thing. In T.V. specials they keep referring to the end of the World, the end of all things. As I've shown, the bible never says that the earth will be totally destroyed, that it will end. Jesus comes back at the end of the tribulation and restores all the damage that man has done to the earth. Nothing would be able to survive all the destruction and fallout from all the nuclear weapons. That's why Jesus returns when he does, if he didn't man would have totally destroy himself as well as the earth.

We see that the end will be a glorious one, the glorious return of Jesus and then the Kingdom of God here on earth, just like Jesus prayed, thy kingdom come, thy will be done, on earth as it is in heaven. At the end of the 1000 years of Jesus' reign, God is going to make all things new. The earth will go on forever.

Final Remarks

For all those that are truly Christians that are living at the time all this is about to begin, we have nothing to fear, we have the blessed hope of Jesus coming to take us out before all this comes upon the world.

> Titus 2: 13while we wait for the blessed hope—the glorious appearing of our great God and Savior, Jesus Christ,

For as we have seen, he promised that we would not suffer his wrath, but will be taken out, spared all this just like Noah and his family and Lot and his family. Just like a true loving Father would do for his children or a true loving husband would do for his bride.

I hope that, if you haven't already, that from all of the prophecies that we have looked at that have already come true and with all the current events that we can see lining up with bible prophecy, that are unfolding right before our very eyes, and with the immoral condition the world is in just like the bible says it would be, I hope you see that Bible prophesy is true and is meant to be interpreted literally, and that the Bible is the infallible Word of God.

The scriptures are clear; there will be a time of war and mass destruction on the earth before Jesus returns. Hey, even all the so called non-biblical prophecies like Nostradamus' are saying this also, so it shouldn't be that hard to believe the bible, especially with the bible proving to be so accurate. With modern technology and the way things are in the world and especially concerning Israel and Jerusalem, with all we can see in the world that is lining up with bible prophecy, we may not be that far from the beginning of all these things. That means Jesus' coming for his Church could be even nearer. We don't know exactly just how near all this is, but we could be close, very close. It appears that the stage is being set.

Jesus is Lord. His word is true. He could be coming soon. Are you watching and waiting for him? Are you ready?

Come Lord Jesus.

2. What's your decision?

Someday each of us will meet Jesus Christ face to face: "It is appointed for men to die once, but after this the judgment" (Heb. 9:27). God declares that "all have sinned and fall short of the glory of God" (Rom. 3:23). It is impossible for a Holy God to allow an unrepentant sinner into a sinless heaven.

"For the wages of sin is death, but the gift of God is eternal life in Christ Jesus our Lord" (Rom. 6:23). God the Father loves us so much that He sent His Son Jesus to suffer the punishment for our sins, for everyone who would confess his sin and ask forgiveness there is forgiveness and eternal life. Jesus loves us so much that he came to suffer the pain of dying on the cross so that we could have eternal life. The Father and Son are in agreement.

You may say I'm a nice person; I don't do anything that hurts anyone. Well, have you had sex while not married? Have you ever lusted? Jesus said in Matthew 5: 28 But I tell you that anyone who looks at a woman lustfully has already committed adultery with her in his heart. This would go for a woman looking at a man lustfully also. Have you ever stolen anything no matter how small? Have you ever told a lie? Have you ever been dishonest? Have you ever used the Lords name in vain? Have you ever used bad language? If you can answer yes to any of these then you have fallen short, you too are a sinner and need to repent and accept Jesus as your Lord and Savior. The fact is that everyone has sinned in the eyes of God.

Isaiah 45:

> 22 "Turn to me and be saved, all you ends of the earth;
> for I am God, and there is no other.

2 Corinthians 5:

> 21God made him who had no sin to be sin for us, so that in him
> we might become the righteousness of God.

512

Final Remarks

Ephesians 2:1As for you, you were dead in your transgressions and sins, 2in which you used to live when you followed the ways of this world and of the ruler of the kingdom of the air, the spirit who is now at work in those who are disobedient. 3All of us also lived among them at one time, gratifying the cravings of our sinful nature and following its desires and thoughts. Like the rest, we were by nature objects of wrath. 4But because of his great love for us, God, who is rich in mercy, 5made us alive with Christ even when we were dead in transgressions—it is by grace you have been saved.

8For it is by grace you have been saved, through faith—and this not from yourselves, it is the gift of God— 9not by works, so that no one can boast.

Titus 3:3 At one time we too were foolish, disobedient, deceived and enslaved by all kinds of passions and pleasures. We lived in malice and envy, being hated and hating one another. 4 But when the kindness and love of God our Savior appeared, 5 he saved us, not because of righteous things we had done, but because of his mercy. He saved us through the washing of rebirth and renewal by the Holy Spirit, 6 whom he poured out on us generously through Jesus Christ our Savior, 7 so that, having been justified by his grace, we might become heirs having the hope of eternal life. 8 This is a trustworthy saying. And I want you to stress these things, so that those who have trusted in God may be careful to devote themselves to doing what is good. These things are excellent and profitable for everyone.

You can see that there is nothing we can do to earn our way into heaven. The fact that Jesus had to become a human and go to such an extreme as to dying such an agonizing and violent death on the cross for us to have eternal life shows that there is nothing we could do on our own, if there was then Jesus' death was in vain. We all have sinned and fallen short. None of us could become righteous enough to enter into God the Father's presence.

But thanks to Jesus we can have his righteousness. Jesus' sacrifice washes all our sins away.

In the third chapter of John Jesus sums it all up.

John 3

> 1Now there was a man of the Pharisees named Nicodemus, a member of the Jewish ruling council. 2He came to Jesus at night and said, "Rabbi, we know you are a teacher who has come from God. For no one could perform the miraculous signs you are doing if God were not with him."
>
> 3In reply Jesus declared, "I tell you the truth, no one can see the kingdom of God unless he is born again."
>
> 4"How can a man be born when he is old?" Nicodemus asked. "Surely he cannot enter a second time into his mother's womb to be born!"
>
> 5Jesus answered, "I tell you the truth, no one can enter the kingdom of God unless he is born of water and the Spirit. 6Flesh gives birth to flesh, but the Spirit gives birth to spirit. 7You should not be surprised at my saying, 'You must be born again.' 8The wind blows wherever it pleases. You hear its sound, but you cannot tell where it comes from or where it is going. So it is with everyone born of the Spirit."

We are born physically into this world but because of Adam and Eve's sin everyone is born spiritually dead. Jesus said we must be born again, born of the Spirit. The only way to be born spiritually is to believe that God the Father sent his son Jesus; you must believe that Jesus is who he and the other scriptures of the bible say he is. You must recognize that you are a sinner and repent and accept Jesus' sacrifice on the cross; then you will receive the free gift of eternal life.

Final Remarks

9"How can this be?" Nicodemus asked.

10"You are Israel's teacher," said Jesus, "and do you not understand these things? 11I tell you the truth, we speak of what we know, and we testify to what we have seen, but still you people do not accept our testimony. 12I have spoken to you of earthly things and you do not believe; how then will you believe if I speak of heavenly things?

13No one has ever gone into heaven except the one who came from heaven—the Son of Man. 14Just as Moses lifted up the snake in the desert, so the Son of Man must be lifted up, 15that everyone who believes in him may have eternal life.

While the Israelites were having to wonder in the desert they began to sin against the Lord so he sent snakes amongst them, whoever was bitten would die so the people asked Moses to pray to God, so God told Moses to make a snake and put it on a tall pole so that if anyone was bitten, if they would look at that snake he would live. See Numbers chapter 21 verses 6 thru 9. The snake represented sin. This goes back to the Garden of Eden. This was a foreshadowing of Jesus being lifted up on the cross.

The next verse, John 3:16 is probably the most known verse in the bible, but Jesus' statement doesn't stop there.

16"For God so loved the world that he gave his one and only Son, that whoever believes in him shall not perish but have eternal life.

17For God did not send his Son into the world to condemn the world, but to save the world through him.

18Whoever believes in him is not condemned, but whoever does not believe stands condemned already because he has not believed in the name of God's one and only Son.

19This is the verdict: Light has come into the world, but men loved darkness instead of light because their deeds were evil. 20Everyone who does evil hates the light, and will not come into the light for fear that his deeds will be exposed. 21But whoever lives by the truth comes into the light, so that it may be seen plainly that what he has done has been done through God."

Verses 19 and 20 explain why so many don't want to accept the bible and Jesus. If a person did then they would have to accept the fact that they are a sinner and are not living the way God wants. You would have to accept that you are not worthy of going to heaven. Most people don't want to give up their sinful living.

At the end of chapter 3 we see John the Baptist testifies about Jesus.

JN 3:31 "The one who comes from above is above all; the one who is from the earth belongs to the earth, and speaks as one from the earth. The one who comes from heaven is above all. 32 He testifies to what he has seen and heard, but no one accepts his testimony. 33 The man who has accepted it has certified that God is truthful. 34 For the one whom God has sent speaks the words of God, for God gives the Spirit without limit. 35 The Father loves the Son and has placed everything in his hands. 36 Whoever believes in the Son has eternal life, but whoever rejects the Son will not see life, for God's wrath remains on him."

1 John 5: Faith in the Son of God

1Everyone who believes that Jesus is the Christ is born of God, and everyone who loves the father loves his child as well. 2This is how we know that we love the children of God: by loving God and carrying out his commands. 3This is love for God: to obey his commands. And his commands are not burdensome, 4for everyone born of God overcomes the world. This is the victory that has overcome the world, even our faith. 5Who is it that overcomes the world? Only he who believes that Jesus is the Son of God.

6This is the one who came by water and blood—Jesus Christ. He did not come by water only, but by water and blood. And it is the Spirit who testifies, because the Spirit is the truth. 7For there are three that testify: 8the Spirit, the water and the blood; and the three are in agreement. 9We accept man's testimony, but God's testimony is greater because it is the testimony of God, which he has given about his Son. 10Anyone who believes in the Son of God has this testimony in his heart. Anyone who does not believe God has made him out to be a liar, because he has not believed the testimony God has given about his Son. 11And this is the testimony: God has given us eternal life, and this life is in his Son.

12He who has the Son has life; he who does not have the Son of God does not have life.

13I write these things to you who believe in the name of the Son of God so that you may know that you have eternal life.

John Chapter 14

6 Jesus answered, "I am the way and the truth and the life. No one comes to the Father except through me.

1 John Chapter 2

23No one who denies the Son has the Father; whoever acknowledges the Son has the Father also.

The Roman Road to salvation:

Romans 3: 22This righteousness from God comes through faith in Jesus Christ to all who believe. There is no difference, 23for all have sinned and fall short of the glory of God, 24and are justified freely by his grace through the redemption that came by Christ Jesus. 25God presented him as a sacrifice of atonement, through faith in his blood. He did this to demonstrate his justice, because in his forbearance he had left the sins committed beforehand unpunished — 26he did it to demonstrate his justice at the present time, so as to be just and the one who justifies those who have faith in Jesus.

Romans 5: 6You see, at just the right time, when we were still powerless, Christ died for the ungodly. 7Very rarely will anyone die for a righteous man, though for a good man someone might possibly dare to die. 8But God demonstrates his own love for us in this: While we were still sinners, Christ died for us.

9Since we have now been justified by his blood, how much more shall we be saved from God's wrath through him! 10For if, when we were God's enemies, we were reconciled to him through the death of his Son, how much more, having been reconciled, shall we be saved through his life! 11Not only is this so, but we also rejoice in God through our Lord Jesus Christ, through whom we have now received reconciliation.

Romans 6: 23For the wages of sin is death, but the gift of God is eternal life in Christ Jesus our Lord.

Romans 10:9That if you confess with your mouth, "Jesus is Lord," and believe in your heart that God raised him from the dead, you will be saved. 10For it is with your heart that you believe and are justified, and it is with your mouth that you confess and are saved.

A final word to all.

Concerning the Rapture, Jesus' coming for his own, don't let that it's been 2000 years since he left here and went back to the Father and that every generation since has been looking for his return, saying he could be coming back soon cause you to not believe. We are told to be watching.

Paul and Peter told us that in the last days, the days close to his coming there would be scoffers, those that deny there will be a Rapture of the Church.

> Acts 13: 40 Take care that what the prophets have said does not happen to you: 41 "'Look, you scoffers, wonder and perish, for I am going to do something in your days that you would never believe, even if someone told you.

> 2 Peter 3: 3Above all, you must understand that in the last days scoffers will come, scoffing and following their own evil desires. 4They will say, "Where is this 'coming' he promised? Ever since our ancestors died, everything goes on as it has since the beginning of creation."

The truth is that there will be a generation that does see his return. How do you know that you're not living in the generation that will be alive when he returns.

> Hebrews 4: 1Therefore, since the promise of entering his rest still stands, let us be careful that none of you be found to have fallen short of it. 2For we also have had the gospel preached to us, just as they did; but the message they heard was of no value to them, because those who heard did not combine it with faith.

The Holy Scriptures declare that the choice regarding eternal salvation is very clear. Who will be the God of your life? Jesus Christ or you?

It is your choice. Ultimately, you must choose.

If you choose to commit your life to Jesus Christ you will be assured that you will meet Him as your Savoir. If you reject His offer to be the Lord of your life, you will have chosen to meet Him as your final judge at the end of your life. The apostle Paul quoted Isaiah when he said, "Every knee shall bow to me, and every tongue shall confess to God" By myself I have sworn, my mouth has uttered in all integrity a word that will not be revoked: Before me every knee will bow; by me every tongue will swear. They will say of me, 'In the LORD alone are righteousness and strength.' "All who have raged against him will come to him and be put to shame. (Isa. 45:23, 24).

So then, each of us will give an account of himself to God. (Rom. 14:11, 12).

I have two kids. They both are such a blessing to me. If you are a born again Christian, are you a blessing to the Father, are you a blessing to the Lord Jesus. Are you pleasing to the Lord? Do you do what he asks, commands. Do you obey his word? Is your life an example and a witness for the Lord? Are you honoring him?

This doesn't mean if you're considered successful by the world's standards, if you make a lot of money, if you have a lot of material things. You can be the poorest of the poor. You could be living on the street under a bridge and you can still be pleasing to the Lord. He could consider you a blessing. Your life can still be an example and witness to others.

It's your life, the person you are, your attitude, your character, your love for others that makes you a blessing to Jesus. It's obeying his word.

- I John 2:

> 3We know that we have come to know him if we keep his commands. 4Whoever says, "I know him," but does not do what he commands is a liar, and the truth is not in that person.5 But if anyone obeys his word, love for God is truly made complete in them. This is how we know we are in him: 6Whoever claims to live in him must live as Jesus did.

520

Final Remarks

I John 3:

> 4 Everyone who sins breaks the law; in fact, sin is lawlessness. 5 But you know that he appeared so that he might take away our sins. And in him is no sin. 6 No one who lives in him keeps on sinning. No one who continues to sin has either seen him or known him.

> 7 Dear children, do not let anyone lead you astray. The one who does what is right is righteous, just as he is righteous. 8 The one who does what is sinful is of the devil, because the devil has been sinning from the beginning. The reason the Son of God appeared was to destroy the devil's work. 9 No one who is born of God will continue to sin, because God's seed remains in them; they cannot go on sinning, because they have been born of God. 10 This is how we know who the children of God are and who the children of the devil are: Anyone who does not do what is right is not God's child, nor is anyone who does not love their brother and sister.

Are you living in a sinful life style, are you in a life of sin? Are you living a life influenced by the devil? If so, just repent. Truly from your heart just ask Jesus for forgiveness and turn away from the sin in your life. If you truly mean it, he will forgive you.

1 John 1:

> 9 If we confess our sins, he is faithful and just and will forgive us our sins and purify us from all unrighteousness.

1 John 2:

> 1 My dear children, I write this to you so that you will not sin. But if anybody does sin, we have an advocate with the Father—Jesus Christ, the Righteous One. 2 He is the atoning sacrifice for our sins,

1 John 5:

> 13 I write these things to you who believe in the name of the Son of God so that you may know that you have eternal life. 14 This is the confidence we have in approaching God: that if we ask anything according to his will, he hears us.

No one thinks about their Treasure and Reward in heaven. You don't even hear much preached about it. It's more important than anything here on earth, for it's for eternity.

Matthew 6:

> 19 "Do not store up for yourselves treasures on earth, where moths and vermin destroy, and where thieves break in and steal. 20 But store up for yourselves treasures in heaven, where moths and vermin do not destroy, and where thieves do not break in and steal. 21 For where your treasure is, there your heart will be also.

Psalm 62:

> 12 and with you, Lord, is unfailing love"; and, "You reward everyone according to what they have done."

Jeremiah 17:

> 10 "I the LORD search the heart and examine the mind,
> to reward each person according to their conduct,
> according to what their deeds deserve."

Jeremiah 32:

> 19 great are your purposes and mighty are your deeds. Your eyes are open to the ways of all mankind; you reward each person according to their conduct and as their deeds deserve.

Final Remarks

2 Corinthians 5:9So we make it our goal to please him, whether we are at home in the body or away from it. 10For we must all appear before the judgment seat of Christ, that each one may receive what is due him for the things done while in the body, whether good or bad.

Did you know you can lose your reward in heaven.

Matthew 13:

> 12 Whoever has will be given more, and they will have an abundance. Whoever does not have, even what they have will be taken from them.

Luke 8:

> 17 For there is nothing hidden that will not be disclosed, and nothing concealed that will not be known or brought out into the open. 18 Therefore consider carefully how you listen. Whoever has will be given more; whoever does not have, even what they think they have will be taken from them."

If you continue in your sin, you can lose your reward in heaven. You probably won't be earning any reward, even if you do things that would deserve a reward. You will still have his salvation, just won't have much treasure and reward throughout eternity.

If you were to die tonight, how will it be when you stand before Jesus?

> 2 Corinthians 6:2 For God says,
> "At just the right time, I heard you.
> On the day of salvation, I helped you."
> Indeed, the "right time" is now.
> Today is the day of salvation. (NLT)

Jesus is Lord, Come Lord Jesus.

CPSIA information can be obtained at www.ICGtesting.com
Printed in the USA
BVOW05s2030060815

411954BV00009B/136/P